A MILITARY HISTORY OF INDIA
AND SOUTH ASIA

A MILITARY HISTORY OF INDIA AND SOUTH ASIA

From the East India Company to the Nuclear Era

Edited by Daniel P. Marston and Chandar S. Sundaram
Foreword by Stephen P. Cohen

INDIANA UNIVERSITY PRESS
Bloomington and Indianapolis

This book is a publication of

Indiana University Press
601 North Morton Street
Bloomington, IN 47404-3797 USA

http://iupress.indiana.edu

Telephone orders   800-842-6796
Fax orders   812-855-7931
Orders by e-mail   iuporder@indiana.edu

The paper used in this publication meets the minimum requirements of
American National Standard for Information Sciences—Permanence of Paper for
Printed Library Materials, ANSI Z39.48-1984.

Manufactured in the United States of America

Cataloging information is available from the Library of Congress.

ISBN 978-0-253-21999-2 (pbk.)

1 2 3 4 5 13 12 11 10 09 08

Contents

Foreword

Not only is this volume a breakthrough in the study of Indian military history, it bears witness to the argument made by the editors that this field has been grossly neglected by the South Asian studies community and by military historians. I would add that the changing international order makes the study of the military history of approximately one-fifth of the world's people especially relevant to our times.

This is the first edited scholarly book to deal with the study of India's military history (India being broadly defined to cover all of South Asia). Many volumes have been recently released covering specific episodes (the books on the 1999 India-Pakistan Kargil war fill one shelf in my library), but this volume ranges back in time and moves to the present as well.

Touching upon a few key themes, it is not a comprehensive overview—the field still awaits the grand synthesis. However, of special value is the contribution of a number of younger scholars, or scholars new to the field. This is important because the "New" military history is already at least 40 years old, and the influx of new scholars to the field is important to keep interpretations fresh. Some of the chapters distill work done by well-known scholars, and this book now makes them accessible to a wider audience. Some chapters are based upon new and original research, and the authors have wisely decided to move beyond the colonial period and include substantive chapters on Indian-Pakistani military relations, on the nuclear problem, and on the region's most intractable insurgency, that in Sri Lanka.

As the editors note, the study of India's military history (let alone that of Pakistan, Bangladesh, and Sri Lanka) has been neglected badly by contemporary scholars, both in the region itself, and in the well-funded academic enclaves of the West. With a few exceptions, such subjects as military organization, the role of caste, defense economics, and the issue of civil-military relations are bypassed in favor of interesting and even important, but often trendy subjects. At best, there is some interest in Indian military history by students of the expansion and modernization of the European military systems, but that interest is fleeting and often not based upon an intimate knowledge of historical India's cultural, geographical, and technical peculiarities, all essential for solid work.

Finally, it is clear that greater interdependence (often called globalization), triggered by the end of the Cold War and the working out of at least three technological revolutions has changed the way in which states, and their armies, function. Ideological warfare continues (communism having been supplanted by nationalism, ethnic separatism, and radical Islamism), but those who oppose the state, and states themselves, have to cope with revolutions in the way in which people, goods, and ideas are now moved around the world. The wide-bodied jet moves people, the container ship moves goods, and ideas flow freely through an electronic world from the village to the center and beyond.

This has contributed to the growth of what is called "asymmetric" war: a conflict in which a supposedly weaker insurrectionary or separatist movement can indefinitely hold at bay a modern army. Such wars now rage in Afghanistan, India, Iraq, the Middle East, Sri Lanka, and (until recently) Nepal. Meanwhile, at least six or seven states prepare to fight a nuclear war at the ultimate level of destructiveness. Thus, around the world, defense budgets and violence have increased; although the risk of a major war in Europe has lessened, the prospects for one in South Asia, the Middle East, and Northeast Asia remain high.

A good military history tells us something about how a culture and a government approached the problem of war in the past, a subject that is increasingly relevant to the present world order. Because South Asia is a region where many kinds of wars can take place (asymmetrical guerilla, conventional, and nuclear), this book, which offers an overview of India's military history, is especially welcome.

Stephen P. Cohen
The Brookings Institution
Washington, DC, July 2006

Acknowledgments

Daniel P. Marston:

I would like to thank Chandar Sundaram for agreeing to serve as coeditor of this book; his efforts were key to the book's timely and successful completion. I would also like to thank our editor, Heather Staines, for first proposing the project and for flexibility of mind throughout the process. Thanks are also due to the contributors for taking part and for their excellent work. The librarians of Royal Military Academy Sandhurst, Oriental and India Office Collection, the British Library, the National Army Museum, and the Imperial War Museum provided valuable assistance in completing the necessary archival research. Last but not least, I would like to thank Alan Jeffreys and my wife, Nancy Owens, for their helpful comments on my own chapters.

Chandar S. Sundaram:

I would like to thank Daniel Marston for initially suggesting coeditorship. I would also like to thank the following people for "being there": Roger Buckley, DeWitt Ellinwood, Susan Sinkinson, Samir Kant Acharya, Lydia Chan, Jim Rice, David Lloyd Smith, and friends—mostly from the English Department of Lingnan University—who inhabited lunchtimes at the Lingnan University Club. I would also like to thank the contributors for writing such excellent chapters. Last, but certainly not least, I would like to thank my parents, Bhavani and "Sandy" Sundaram, for their abiding love and unstinting support of my endeavors.

Why This Book?

The British Army in India[1] was one of the main institutions of the Raj. It was primarily responsible for the spread and consolidation of Britain's Indian Empire. It is important to remember that Tipu Sultan, the Marathas, the Sikhs, and the sepoy rebels at Delhi, Meerut, and Lucknow were defeated not by trade and diplomatic skulduggery, but, in the final analysis, by armed force. Early on, armed force was a handmaid to "effective"—that is, advantageous for British—trade. In the aftermath of military victories at Arcot (1751), Plassey (1757), and Buxar (1764), Company officials and their *Gumastahs* (Indian commercial middlemen) regularly employed sepoy detachments to coerce up-country Indian producers who held out for higher prices,[2] thus setting up a basis for the military fiscalism that undergirded the Raj.[3] Indeed, the notion that an effective armed force was the most important component in the rise and maintenance of British expansion in India soon became a central plank of Anglo-Indian ideology and remained remarkably constant in both the Company and Crown phases of British rule.[4] The centrality of armed force to the British colonial "enterprise" in South Asia is further underlined by the fact that, in 1930, a mere 17 years before independence, military expenditures accounted for a little over 60 percent of the Government of India's revenues.[5] Finally, the emergence of the Indian National Army (INA)—a force formed from the roughly 45,000 Indian soldiers captured by the Japanese during World War II, whose stated purpose was to wrest India militarily from British rule—signalled to the British that their reliance on armed force to maintain their hold on India was on shaky ground. This was a crucially important factor in hastening their exit from India in 1947.[6]

Largely in the past decade, scholars have begun to focus attention on the army in India. Mostly, they have adopted the methodologies of the "new military history." The new military history, or the history of war and society, first emerged in European historiography about 40 years ago, with the work of Corvisier, Roberts, and Ropp.[7] Whereas the old military history focused on the course of military operations, tactics, strategies, weapons, and generalship in a didactic, lessons-oriented way, the newer form of the subject analyzes war as the military activities of societies. On the macro level, the new military history conceives of armed forces as social institutions, which cannot be considered in isolation, divorced from their parent societies. On the micro level, new insights have been generated about the ordinary soldiers, such as: their origins, in terms of both geography and social class; their motives for enlistment and reasons for staying on; and the formation of their military culture, through features such as welfare mechanisms, corporate identity, and the experience of combat.[8]

Though, as stated above, the burgeoning of writing on the colonial Indian Army from a new military history perspective only really occurred in the last decade, the earlier work of Barat, Cohen, Callahan, Longer, and Ellinwood pointed the way.[9] We now have studies of the political economy of the East India Company (EIC) armies (the precursor of the Indian Army), the EIC's relationship with its *sepoys,* Anglo-Indian military culture and ideology, the social construction of recruitment, the later Indian Army's welfare mechanisms toward *sepoys,* their links with Indian society, and aspirations and frustrations of Indian soldiers as India drew close to independence.[10] Historians have also begun to shed new light on the nettlesome question of why the armies of indigenous states —the Mysoreans, the Marathas, the Gurkhas, and the Sikhs —were ultimately defeated by the Company's armies.[11] Aspects of the old military history, such as frontier and jungle warfare, have also been reassessed from a war-and-society perspective.[12]

Despite this output, the recent writing on the colonial Indian Army has made but little impact upon the narratives that dominate South Asian historiography. Examples of the the neglect of war and society in recent Indian historiography include: Burton Stein, *A History of India;* B. Metcalf and T. Metcalf, *A Concise History of India*; and B. Chandra et al., *India After Independence, 1947–2000.* Thomas Metcalf's otherwise excellent *Ideologies of the Raj* pays scant attention to the martial races theory, which was a central plank of the Anglo-Indian world view.

But this book does not cover only colonial India. A significant part of it covers the military history of independent India, with chapters on such subjects as India's nuclear policy, India's conflicts with Pakistan over the thorny question of Kashmir, and India's involvement in the Sri Lankan civil war. We, the editors, feel that these chapters are as equally important as the earlier chapters on colonial warfare, because they demonstrate how a former colony—albeit one of the biggest and most important ones in the British Empire—has struggled to become a mature state in terms of military power and capability. Perhaps these later chapters will serve as a template to other developing states wishing to do the same.

The purpose of this book, then, is to present the military history of India and South Asia in a way that will be accessible to academics, students, and general readers alike. We hope that the book will come to form an integral part of undergraduate and graduate reading lists.

Daniel P. Marston
Chandar S. Sundaram

CHAPTER 1

The Armed Expansion of the English East India Company: 1740s-1849

Kaushik Roy

The eighteenth century in South Asia was characterized by two major transformations. While on one hand, the Mughal Empire gave way to several regional states, on the other hand the small European enclaves along the coast started expanding towards the core of the subcontinent. The end of the century witnessed successful transformation of the British East India Company (henceforth EIC) from a peripheral actor to a major power broker. This chapter will focus on the great sieges undertaken and decisive battles fought by the EIC, which established a pan-Indian British Empire.[1] The pacification campaigns that resulted in consolidation of British rule do not fall within the purview of this essay. The British expansion in India was part of a larger process of European expansion in the extra-European world. Unlike in South America and Siberia, the numerically superior number of white settlers did not swamp the inhabitants of South Asia. In 1700, India had 180 million people, which comprised about 20 percent of the world's population. India's economic power was also impressive. In the beginning of the eighteenth century, India remained the world's centre of artisan production and accounted for a huge amount of the world trade. However, economic potential and demographic resources did not necessarily generate great military power. In order to understand combat superiority of the EIC, we must focus not only on the administrative and fiscal fabric of the Company state, but also on the military organizations and state apparatus of its indigenous opponents.

The East India Company's Hybrid Military Machine

Early modern Europe witnessed the rise of drilled and disciplined infantry, equipped with firearms and supported by mobile field artillery. From the sixteenth century, European forces acquired an edge in keeping cohesion and control in battle far longer than their adversaries, which permitted more sophisticated tactics in deploying and moving units on the battlefield and effective fire discipline. However,

British organizational, technical, and fiscal superiority was not overwhelming in the subcontinent. So, the EIC had to absorb certain features of the Indian military system.

Technology played a vital role in continuous British victories. In most of the encounters, British field and siege artillery along with small arms carried the day. Use of indigenous raw materials generated firepower superiority for the EIC's troops. The EIC acquired saltpeter (potassium nitrate) from Orissa. Sulphur for the manufacture of gunpowder was procured from the Indian *bazars*. By 1822, Fort William had a huge stock of sulphur, and it supplied the demands of the other two presidencies. The EIC set up several ordnance factories from the late seventeenth century for manufacturing cannons, mortars, and howitzers. Some sorts of research and development activities were also undertaken. The Military Board was in charge of introducing innovations connected with carriages and improvements of artillery. In 1830, for the artillery personnel, a laboratory was opened at the powder magazine of Dinapore.[2]

Besides technology, another vital factor behind British superiority in warfare remained the management and education of the officer corps. In Britain, the Royal Military Academy at Woolwich was founded in 1741, and the Royal Military College at Sandhurst was set up in 1799. In 1809, for training the officers, the EIC opened a military seminary at Addiscombe, near Croydon, Surrey. The syllabus of the two years' course at Addiscombe closely followed the syllabus of the Royal Military Academy at Woolwich. Between 1809 and 1811, the EIC also ran a military college at Barasat, near Calcutta. At the training academy of Barasat, the cadets were taught drill, tactics, and Hindustani language. Knowledge of Hindustani was required for commanding *Purbiya* sepoys.[3] The Indian powers had no such comparable institutions for training their officer corps. From the standpoint of military professionalism, the British officers of the EIC's white army were much better than the officers of the British infantry and cavalry regiments. This was because, while the career graphs of the EIC's white officers depended on merit, the officers of the British Army were often promoted on the basis of political connections and wealth. The EIC's British officers were generally of lower social background compared to those joining the British regiments. Some British officers of the EIC were pastors' and merchants' sons, while a few were younger sons of poor Irish and Scottish landed families. The white officers of the EIC developed initiative much earlier than the officers of the British Army because the EIC officers were given commands of detachments operating in the outlying parts of the British-Indian Empire. In the last decade of the eighteenth century, the EIC's white officers gained *furlough,* passage money, and pensions. By betterment of service conditions, the EIC was able to induce a sense of professionalism among its white officer corps. An aspect of military professionalism was that the EIC's European officers initiated several tactical innovations. For instance, due to their numerical inferiority in India's battlefields, the Company's European officers started massing artillery in an antipersonnel role.[4]

The engineering branch of the British Army was formed in 1717. It should be noted that the British officers of the Royal Artillery and the Royal Engineers came from the educated middle class families. The officers in these two branches were promoted on the basis of merit. In contrast, the officers of the cavalry and infantry regiments of the British Army were mostly scions of the landed families who bought their commissions until the 1870s and who spent most of their time hunting and playing polo. So, the British officers of the artillery and engineering branches were much more technically skillful compared to their counterparts in the infantry and cavalry units. The engineers studied mathematics and fortifications and were skilled in drawings. Many officers were trained as military draftsmen. They recorded the critical features of India's landscape for the military commanders who campaigned across the hitherto uncharted terrain. The engineering branch, with its sappers and pioneers, were vital in conducting siege operations. The sappers, with their picks, shovels, and gabions, constructed zigzag trenches around the enemy forts and prepared emplacements for the siege batteries. The EIC, like the Mughals, built roads to improve its logistical infrastructure. The sappers and the miners were in the forefront of road making.

During emergencies, the EIC received assistance from the British units. In 1783, around 6,000 soldiers of the British Army were deployed in India. In 1797, about 13,125 British soldiers were serving in India. In 1797, one British dragoon regiment (460 horsemen) deployed in India cost 2,970 sterling pounds per month. A British infantry regiment (950 men) in Madras cost 2,200 sterling pounds every month. In 1805, the London government demanded 1,553,600 sterling pounds from the EIC for the operation of British troops deployed in India between 1793 and 1803.[5] The EIC could afford to pay the British troops operating in the subcontinent out of the revenues extracted from India.

Money was the sinew of warfare. One of the principal factors behind British supremacy was the ability of the EIC to keep its troops in the field without bankrupting itself. For conducting the four Mysore Wars and the First Maratha War, the EIC took a loan of six million sterling pounds. In 1805, the Court of Directors calculated that due to continuous warfare in India, the EIC's debt exceeded 20 million sterling pounds. The economic resources of India enabled the EIC to finance its warfare. Every year during the 1780s and the 1790s, exports costing more than one million sterling pounds were dispatched to London on EIC ships. In 1801, annual exports from Bengal were valued at 2.5 million sterling pounds. The EIC's exports from India included spices, pepper, sugar, coffee, raw silk, and cotton-piece goods.[6]

Besides income from trade, the EIC became dependent on revenues derived from the acquisition of new territories and booties from defeated Indian princes. In a way, war paid for further war. In 1792, after the Third Mysore War, the victorious EIC extracted three million sterling pounds from Tipu Sultan. In 1793, revenues from the area under the EIC amounted to 6,963,625 sterling pounds. In 1807, the revenues rose to 14,535,739 sterling pounds. The EIC also increased pressure on its client states for extracting more money. Between 1793 and 1807, annual receipt from Awadh *Nawabi* rose from 530,000 to 1,742,534 pounds sterling. The Nepal War (1814–15) cost the EIC Rs 6.5 million. To finance this war, the EIC took a loan from Awadh, which was never repaid. The cost of the

Table 1.1   Military Manpower Establishment of the East India Company: 1813–30

Date	King's Troops	EIC's Troops (including white and brown soldiers)	Total	Relative Proportion
1813	21,490	179,632	201,122	1:8.3
1814	20,049	175,423	195,472	1:8.7
1815	19,828	208,257	228,085	1:10.5
1816	20,432	211,275	231,707	1:10.3
1817	18,709	208,281	226,990	1:11.1
1818	20,110	223,954	244,064	1:11.1
1819	17,680	228,459	246,139	1:12.8
1820	16,743	241,266	258,009	1:12.6
1821	16,290	241,547	257,837	1:14.8
1822	15,876	230,261	246,137	1:14.5
1823	16,652	222,022	238,674	1:13.3
1824	16,395	227,934	244,329	1:13.9
1825	16,683	260,856	277,539	1:15.6
1826	16,832	275,330	292,162	1:16.2
1827	18,249	256,394	274,643	1:14.04
1828	19,612	240,454	260,066	1:12.2
1829	20,132	224,390	244,522	1:11.1
1830	20,292	204,152	224,444	1:10

Source: Number of Troops of the King's & Company's Service employed in India from 1813–1830, British *Parliamentary Papers*, Colonies East India 11 Session, East India Company Affairs, 1831–32 (Shannon: Irish University Press, 1970), Para 98, 31.

First Sikh War (1845–46) came to about 17,029,825 rupees. In 1846, the money extracted from the defeated *Khalsa* Kingdom amounted to about Rs 1,250,000,000 or 12,500,000 sterling pounds.[7]

The EIC maintained its own private white army. In 1781, the EIC opened a recruiting depot in England. Most of the European recruits who joined either the Company's army or the army of the French East India Company were of tender age. The dregs of British society joined the British Army. Some of them were criminals and the recruiters tricked the urban unemployed into joining the military service. The rank and file of the EIC's white army were a bit better than the privates of the British Army. Those who joined the EIC's white army were miners, clerks, and artisans, and in general were literate. Most of the white recruits came in a slow trickle and fell prey to scurvy and malnutrition during the voyage to India. Since the regiments on foreign stations faced problems in getting recruits, the commanding officers were not willing to discharge worn-out men. So, the personnel of the regiments on overseas service began to age and their efficiency declined. During the eighteenth century, due to low training and unfit personnel, the white regiments deployed overseas were capable only of modest exertion. The British mess culture in colonial India encouraged excessive drinking, which sent many of them to their graves quite early. Tropical disease further ravaged white military strength. In 1794, illness prevented 17.5 percent of the EIC's white soldiers from reporting to duty. In 1797, casualties among British troops deployed in India from all causes came to about 53 per 1,000 every month. Between 1770 and 1799, out of every 1,000 British soldiers, about 55 died. In 1804 (during the Second Maratha War), the average mortality rate was 134 out of 1,000. Between 1800 and 1829, the average mortality figure was 85 British soldiers out of 1,000. Between 1830 and 1856, the mortality rate remained 58 out of 1,000.[8]

The Indian troops were in general healthier and cheaper than the white troops. The EIC's victories would have been impossible without utilization of Indian military manpower. Initially, the Indian warlords with their infantry contingents were hired by the EIC. Gradually, the EIC moved towards a more systematic technique for mobilizing and disciplining military manpower. Even before the EIC, the latter's rival, the French *Compagnie des Indes,* started raising sepoys from the Indian military laborers. The word "sepoy" is derived from the Persian word *sipahi* (soldier). Joseph François Dupleix's predecessor, Monsieur Dumas, raised, trained, and equipped the sepoys (Indian infantry drilled and disciplined in Western fashion) like the white line infantry. And the EIC imitated this technique. The EIC got rid of the jobber commanders of the precolonial era. All the regiments recruited separately, with the aid of British regimental officers. In 1757, each Indian infantry regiment had three British officers and 890 Indians. In 1796, there were five British officers and 585 Indians. The British resorted to gradual Westernization. In 1804, jackets and pantaloons were issued for the sepoys. Initially the men were armed with flintlock muskets. In 1844, percussion firelocks were issued. After 1805, artillery manned by Indians was raised because European gunners were very costly.[9]

Cavalry remained important for conducting warfare in India. Until the end of the eighteenth century, inadequate cavalry prevented the EIC from completing the victory obtained in the field by the firepower of heavy infantry. Initially, both the British and French utilized mercenary Indian cavalry. In 1760, just before the Battle of Wandiwash, Comte de Tollendal Lally's army hired 3,000 Maratha horsemen. Eyre Coote also wanted to hire the Marathas, but since he could not offer them ready cash like the French, the Marathas refused to change sides. After the Battle of Buxar (1764), Najaf Khan, a Mughal warlord, was hired by the EIC at the cost of Rs. 200,000 annually. In May 1765, he fought on the EIC's side against the Maratha chieftain Malhar Rao Holkar. The British commanders also depended on the cavalry contingents supplied by their Indian allies. Towards the end of the eighteenth century, British policy laid down that the *Nawab* of Awadh should maintain cavalry that would accompany the infantry brigades of the EIC during campaigns. The EIC started raising Indian cavalry. Between 1793 and 1809, the Bengal Cavalry grew from 500 to 5,000 horses. The Indian cavalry regiments just could not operate without the aid of Indian officers such as Dufadars, Risaldars, and others. Each sowar was armed with a sword and a smoothbore pistol.[10]

The EIC's military establishment required noncombat laborers and animals for logistical purposes. The EIC's Indian cavalry regiments recruited Indian doctors, syces, grass cutters, puckallies, lascars, tindals, and sweepers. Not only was a graded pay structure introduced, but these laborers were also paid in cash systematically each month. For carrying the sick and the wounded, each sepoy regiment during the 1830s possessed eight doolies. After Tipu was defeated, the Madras Army took over the public cattle establishment of Mysore. In 1803, during the Second Maratha War, the Karnatak cattle pulled the heavy equipment of the Madras Army commanded by General James Stuart. The Mughal Army used elephants as beasts of burden. During the Third Maratha War (1817–18), while operating in the Western Ghats, the EIC's army used elephants for dragging mortars and howitzers, which then were used to blast the *peshwa's* (hereditary prime minister of the Maratha Confederacy) forts.[11]

During the Third Mysore War (1790–92), Tipu introduced rockets in large numbers. The Mughals used rockets. Tipu systematized the production of rockets. Some of the rockets could travel 1,000 yards, and a few were designed to burst. They functioned as antipersonnel weapons. Another type of rocket was designed to set fire on enemy objects. Each rocket weighed about 2 kgs, with a 1-kg propellant. It consisted of an iron tube about a foot long and an inch in diameter, fitted to a bamboo rod about 10–12 feet in length. The tube was filled with combustible materials and was then set on fire and directed by hand. After the Fourth Mysore War in 1799, the EIC's troops captured 700 rockets at the Turkananhalli Ordnance Factory near Seringapatnam. The British were impressed with Tipu's wonder weapon. After Tipu's death, rockets were introduced in the Bengal Army and Colonel Congreve was ordered to conduct further experiment. In 1814, he wrote a detailed treatise on the rocket for the benefit of the British officers.[12]

The EIC started expanding in India from three points: Calcutta, Madras, and Bombay. The enclaves around these three power centers gradually expanded into Bengal, Madras, and Bombay presidencies respectively. Since these three presidencies formulated their policies in a semiautonomous manner, each presidency maintained its own separate sepoy army, and all three were known as Bengal, Madras, and Bombay armies. While the Bengal Army recruited *Purbiyas* from Awadh and south Bihar, the Madras Army recruited the Tamils and Telingas from Tamil Nadu, Karnatak, and Andhra Pradesh. The Bombay Army depended mostly on the men from Konkan and Malabar regions. Since the three Sepoy armies recruited Indian personnel from different regions, the EIC's officials believed that maintenance of three separate armies would prevent any pan-Indian revolt among the Indian military laborers. In accordance with the strategic requirements, the British units stationed in India, as well as the EIC's private white units, were brigaded with the different sepoy armies.

The EIC faced opposition from both indigenous and foreign powers. The EIC's military establishment (which included the Indian soldiers and the white troops of the Madras, Bombay and Bengal presidencies plus the King's troops serving in India) does not appear to be very big when compared with the militaries maintained by the other big powers in the world. In 1808, the EIC had 24,500 Europeans and 130,000 Indian soldiers. By comparison, in 1774, Russia possessed about 55,000 cavalry, and in 1805, the Russian Army numbered 300,000 troops.[13] Nevertheless, the EIC's military apparatus was adequate to overcome the rapidly modernizing indigenous polities. The greatest challenge came from Mysore, the Maratha Confederacy, and the Sikh *Khalsa* Kingdom. The EIC's tussle with these polities was partly an extension of the British-French rivalry in India. For instance the Seven Years War in Europe (1757–63) also spilled into the subcontinent. Moreover, infighting among the various indigenous powers blended with rivalry with the Europeans.

The East India Company against Mysore

Under Haidar Ali and his son Tipu, Mysore fought four wars with the EIC. While he was an excellent cavalry general, Haidar realized the rising importance of firepower in the new form of warfare introduced by the *feranghis* in India. Therefore, Haidar hired some German officers in order to integrate firepower with his cavalry. The cavalry was organized in *risalas* (regiments), each with two four- or six-pounders and two eight-pounders, along with two munition wagons and one cart to transport the cannonballs. Until 1799, most of the Mysore Army's gunners were Portuguese. While conducting sieges, Haidar had to depend on the French officers. Through Mahe, Haidar received military stores from the French. In March 1779, the EIC, in order to severe the connection between Haidar and the French, occupied Mahe within the Mysore kingdom. This prompted Haidar to turn against the EIC, and the Second Mysore War started.[14]

In 1780, with 20,000 Westernized infantry and 20,000 cavalry, Haidar cooperated with the French commanders in India. Haidar's light cavalry acted as eyes and ears of Marquis Bussy. Moreover, Bussy received bullocks from Haidar, which were necessary for military transportation. At Kanjiveram, Haidar's force clashed with 3,000 sepoys and 600 Europeans of the EIC under Colonel William Baillie. Lally with 2,000 infantry and 100 cavalry cooperated with Haidar. In September 1780, Baillie surrendered to Haidar. However, Haidar's army was not yet a match as regards firepower and discipline with the EIC's infantry in a set piece battle. At the Battle of Porto Novo, fought on July 1, 1781, Haidar retreated after losing 3,000 men. In contrast, the EIC lost only 500 soldiers. On December 7, 1782, Haidar died and Tipu was crowned *sultan*. The Franco-British struggle in India was part of a global struggle between Britain and France which extended from America in the west to India in the east. France provided aid both to the Americans and to Mysore. In 1782, Britain sued for peace and the American War of Independence came to an end. Once the news about the Treaty of Paris of January 20, 1783, which recognized American independence, became known in India, the French, though allied with Tipu, unilaterally made peace with the EIC.[15] Meanwhile, the Marathas had also made peace with the EIC and the First Maratha War came to an end. The EIC was not in a position to destroy Tipu completely because Mysore's light cavalry ravaged Karnatak, which supplied revenue and provision to the Madras presidency. The Second Mysore War was brought to a close by the Treaty of Mangalore signed in March 1784.

Tipu realized that British ascendancy in India was due mostly to their technological superiority. He thus tried to procure European artisans for making cannons and muskets and for training his army. In 1788, Tipu sent an embassy to Louis XVI of France to enlist the services of French craftsmen and cannon makers. Tipu understood that if he desired to prosecute war with the British successfully, he had to create an indigenous industrial base. Mysore was able to produce wrought iron. Most of the guns manufactured by Tipu were smoothbore cannons. In 1785, the muskets manufactured at Seringapatnam were at par with those manufactured in Europe.[16]

During the Third Mysore War, which started in 1790, Tipu's field force failed to check the advancing EIC's army. So, Tipu resorted to positional warfare. Tipu's defense was based on a string of forts. However, the forts fell before the firepower generated by the 12-pound iron guns of the EIC's besieging army. Tipu escaped total extirpation because the British by that time had failed to evolve proper anticavalry techniques against the harassing tactics of Mysore's light cavalry. The EIC's force under Lord Cornwallis (who had surrendered at Yorktown on October 19, 1781, to the "rebel" American force) invaded Mysore but failed to capture Seringapatnam due to the "scorched-earth policy" followed by Tipu's light cavalry. An Indian military officer of the mid-nineteenth century wrote:

> Tipu Sultan's troops had so well obeyed his orders for the destruction of every kind of forage in the neighbourhood of the British camp, that scarce a blade of grass was to be found. The cavalry was half dismounted, and the cattle of Lord Cornwallis were daily dying by hundreds. His [Tipu] guards on the roads were also so diligent, that not a bullock load of grain could reach the camp; and all communication with the allies was so completely cut off, that no intelligence respecting the Maratha armies, under the command of Parasuram Bhao and Harripunt, who long before this period ought to have arrived at Seringapatnam, could be obtained. Thus situated, Lord Cornwallis was compelled to destroy his battering train of artillery, throw his shot into the river, burns his carts and tumbrils, and on the 26th of May, commence his retreat towards Bangalore.[17]

Due to the cooperation of 32,000 Maratha cavalry, in 1792 Cornwallis was able to annex Malabar, Coorg, Dindigul, and Baramahal districts of Mysore.

The news that the governor of Mauritius had promised to send Tipu a large force precipitated the EIC's final attack on Mysore, which resulted in the Fourth Mysore War in 1799. The governor-general, Richard Wellesley, feared that Pierre Cuillier Perron, the French commander of the Westernized contingents in Sindia's army, would support Tipu. The governor-general probably overplayed to the British government the threat posed by Tipu and his connection with the French. The EIC mobilized 57,000 soldiers and was supported by Nizam and the Marathas, who had territorial claims on Mysore. Colonel Arthur Wellesley, along with Mir Alum, commanded the Company-Hyderabad *Nawabi's* coalition forces of 21,000 men. The whole affair was quite small compared to the high-intensity warfare that Europe experienced at that time. By the summer of 1794, the French Army numbered 750,000 men.

Tipu attempted a last stand at his capital Seringapatnam, which was an island on the river Cauvery. Through the French officers, *trace Italienne* had finally reached Mysore. On the northwest angle of the Seringapatnam fort, a new bastion with faces and flanks were added. The old fort had a mud wall. Tipu converted it into a second rampart and dug a ditch in front of it. The fort had a continuous bastioned curtain wall, with a natural wet ditch in the shape of the river Cauvery and a number of outworks. On April 5, 1799, the Madras Army's 20,071 soldiers, supported by 18-pounders and 8-inch and 5.5-inch howitzers under Lieutenant-General George Harris, took position on the west side of the fort. On April 16, the Bombay Army's 6,430 men was encamped on the northern bank of Cauvery. The British set up breaching batteries at a distance of 300 yards from the main wall. On the evening of May 3, the British guns were able to demolish the walls. Then the infantry assault started, and Tipu was shot dead by an unnamed British private. On May 4, the scene around the fort was horrid. The day was sultry and the wounded moaned for water. At the cost of a mere 1,342 casualties, the EIC captured Seringapatnam.[18]

The EIC versus the Maratha Confederacy

After the collapse of Mysore, the Marathas remained the EIC's principal threat. The Maratha Confederacy was a loose agglomeration of five chiefs. The *peshwa* ruled Maharashtra, Gaekwad was in charge of Gujarat, Bhonsle ruled Orissa, and Holkar eastern Malwa. The Sindia clan's power spilled over western Malwa, eastern Rajasthan, and the western part of north India. The First Maratha War lasted from 1774 to 1783. The *peshwa's* political economy was in shambles. On paper, the annual revenue of the confederacy was about 14 crores of rupees. But, in practice, incessant fighting among the semiautonomous chieftains prevented the steady flow of cash into the Poona treasury. As a result, neither the *peshwa* could pay his *gardis* (Westernized infantry under mercenary French officers) nor the *sirdars* loyal to him could raise an adequate number of sowars for fighting the EIC.[19]

Besides fiscal superiority, the EIC enjoyed a technological edge over the Marathas. The iron working in western Deccan was backward. The Marathas imported broadsword blades from Germany, Italy, and Spain. The Maratha cannons were not mobile due to their heavy weight, and they were not adjustable to a particular angle or a particular range. The *peshwa* faced opposition in purchasing cannons and munitions from the Portuguese and British officials in India. So, in 1765, he established a cannonball factory at Ambegavan. However, this factory failed to produce state-of-the-art products.[20]

The Maratha attitude towards warfare was to an extent shaped by the traditional Hindu culture of warfare as expounded by Kautilya in *Arthashastra*. Kautilya's philosophy accepts that internal divisiveness and external aggression are inevitable and interrelated. Troubles in the core might encourage the external powers to threaten the periphery of the state. To tackle them, the trump card in Kautilya's arsenal is diplomacy. Kautilyan military culture, unlike Clausewitzian military culture, did not accept the dictum of clear division between war and peace. While conducting war, the Marathas continued diplomatic negotiations. In February 1776, the *peshwa* informed the British envoy that the confederacy would cede Salsette if the EIC agreed to withhold support to Raghoba, alias Raghunath Rao, a Maratha chieftain who had allied with the British.[21] The British did not agree to this proposal.

Due to the 24-pounders and a battery of 20 mortars constructed at a distance of 500 yards from the fort, General Thomas Goddard captured Bassein on December 11, 1780, after losing only 13 men. With 6,152 men (including 346 Europeans), Goddard advanced into Maharashtra. Then the Marathas waged *ganimi kava.* The Maratha light cavalry followed a scorched-earth policy by burning and ravaging their own territories to prevent Goddard from drawing any supplies from the countryside. The Maratha mode of warfare emphasized rapidity. Even firearms were integrated within the overall ambit of mobile warfare. The Marathas used mounted infantry by putting two men on a camel. While one drove the camel, the other was armed with a firelock capable of throwing a three-ounce ball. About 30,000 cavalry plus 4,000 irregular infantry (foot soldiers armed with matchlocks and not disciplined in Western fashion) continued to attack Goddard day and night and cut his communication with Bombay. Goddard could not march due to lack of cattle. As Goddard started to retreat, the terrain favored the Maratha irregular infantry. From the cover of the rocks, bushes, and ravines they shot at the EIC's column. During September 1781, the EIC troops' supplies were continually intercepted by Mahadji Sindia's troops stationed at Sipri Kolaras region. Sporadic attacks continued on the British caravans bound for Kalyan. In January 1782, Haidar proposed to the Poona *durbar* that the Marathas must send a force to ravage Orissa, and he would pay for the expedition. That same month, the Poona government planned to send 40,000 troops to occupy Benaras.[22]

Ganimi kava partly succeeded because the Marathas achieved overwhelming numerical superiority over the EIC, especially with regard to cavalry. This was possible because all the principal chiefs of the confederacy were united, and because Mysore fought on the side of the Marathas. During the next conflict between the EIC and the Marathas, these conditions did not recur. First, the EIC expanded its army, especially the cavalry. Secondly, the confederacy became fragmented. And thirdly, before the Second Maratha War, the EIC destroyed Mysore. Therefore, the First Maratha War was the swan song of the traditional form of Maratha warfare. The Poona government's policy was that no treaty should be signed with the EIC unless it had the approval of Haidar. But, the fragmentary nature of the Maratha polity aided British diplomatic victory. At Mahadji's insistence in 1782, the Maratha Confederacy signed the Treaty of Salbai with Warren Hastings. In early 1783, Mahadji advised Tipu to make peace with the EIC.[23]

Mahadji was the principal figure within the confederacy to realize the impotence of the Maratha light cavalry in pitched encounters against the EIC's infantry. To Europeanize his army, Mahadji hired 260 European officers, the most famous of whom was the Savoyard Benoit De Boigne, who was commissioned to raise several *campoos* (brigades). Each *campoo* had 10 infantry battalions with integral artillery and cavalry.[24] Each recruit was drilled for six months before being inducted into a battalion. In the first 28 days, the recruits were taught to handle muskets. Another 40 days were reserved for gunnery practice. And for three months military maneuvers were taught. With the aid of French officers, Sindia manufactured latest-style French guns with elevating screws at Agra and Gwalior. In total, the Westernized forces of Sindia included 58 infantry battalions with 400 guns.

In 1803, when the Second Maratha War broke out, Major-General Arthur Wellesley (the future Duke of Wellington) commanded the EIC force in Deccan, and Gerard Lake was in charge of the EIC forces in north India. The *peshwa* and the Gaekwad supported the EIC. And Jaswant Rao Holkar remained neutral due to his rivalry with Daulat Rao Sindia (the nephew and successor of Mahadji). In Deccan, Raghuji Bhonsle of Nagpur supported Daulat Rao. The Marathas were suffering from doctrinal confusion. While the *campoos* desired a set-piece battle with the EIC, the Maratha light cavalry preferred to conduct *ganimi kava* all over India. Just before the onset of hostilities, Lieutenant-Colonel John Collins warned Arthur in the following words: "I tell you General, as to their cavalry, you may ride over them, wherever you meet them; but their infantry and guns will astonish you."[25]

Arthur advanced towards the Marathas with 5,000 allied cavalry (2,000 of *Nizam* and 3,000 belonging to the *peshwa*), 1,900 cavalry (the 19th Light Dragoons plus three Indian cavalry regiments) and 4,000 infantry (two British and five Indian regiments), plus 34 guns. On September 24, 1803, the Maratha and EIC forces clashed at Assaye. Arthur crossed Kaitna and deployed his infantry in two lines. When the EIC's infantry was 400 yards from the village of Assaye, the Maratha guns opened up and caused great carnage. However, lack of cooperation between the Maratha light cavalry and Sindia's *campoos* allowed Arthur to overrun the Maratha position. In north India, Lake's troops were able to overwhelm Sindia's *campoos* at the battles of Delhi and Laswari. The continuous failure of the *campoos* against the EIC's troops was due to the absence of an institutionalized officer cadre in the *campoos*. The Marathas lacked a general staff for planning and coordinating warfare at the theater level. Most of the European officers of the *campoos* deserted to the EIC. Their desertion adversely affected the morale of the infantry, and those officers who remained with the troops were not trusted.

Jaswant entered the fray after Daulat Rao was humbled by the EIC. Nature continued to function as a brake on the pace of Western warfare introduced by the EIC in the subcontinent. Arthur Wellesley realized that he would not be able to take the army into Malwa to fight Jaswant because of the famine in central India. Lake sent Colonel William Monson with the directive of crossing river Chambal. Monson could not effect a junction with the army sent from Bombay. Monson recrossed the Chambal harassed by Holkar's cavalry. The Maratha cavalry laid the country waste and prevented any supplies from reaching Monson. Gradually, Monson's troops became demoralized. Small detachments were cut off; guns were stuck in the heavy mud and captured. And due to rainfall, the rivers became impassable. The retreat became a rout when the column neared Agra. It was possible for Jaswant to crush Monson's contingent because John Murray's force, sent from Gujarat, failed to cooperate with Monson. A certain parallel existed between the fate of Monson and Goddard's detachments. It proves that though light cavalry by itself cannot win a battle, even drilled infantry equipped with firearms is helpless without cavalry. Finally, Lake mobilized the main army against Jaswant. In 1805, Lake caught up with Jaswant near the borders of Punjab and the latter was forced to submit.[26]

Both *Peshwa* Baji Rao II and Raghuji Bhonsle's successor Mudhoji had signed a subsidiary treaty with the EIC. In accordance with this treaty, both princes had to pay a certain sum to the EIC. In return the EIC maintained a British-officered force for the princes' protection. Very soon both princes were irritated due to continuous curbing of their autonomy by the EIC. In 1817, they finally decided to throw in the towel. If the Marathas attacked the EIC when it was engaged in the Nepal War (1814–15), then fate might have favored the former. By 1815, EIC deployed 48,000 troops against Nepal. However, the Marathas started the war two years after the EIC's Nepal ordeal. The *peshwa* and Raghuji's armies constituted a conglomeration of contingents (light cavalry and irregular infantry) raised by various chiefs. Lieutenant-Colonel Valentine Blacker, a contemporary British observer, noted that the Marathas were very backward as far as firing and maintenance of mortars were concerned.[27] The severance of the flow of European mercenaries after 1805 increased the technological deficiency of the Marathas. The Maratha position further worsened because Holkar and Daulat Rao remained neutral.

On November 1817, the *peshwa's* commander Moro Dixit, with 18,000 light cavalry, 8,000 irregular infantry, and 14 guns, attacked the EIC's 2,000 sepoys and 800 Europeans at Kirkee. A chance grape shot killed Moro Dixit. Lacking a clear-cut, hierarchical chain of command, the *peshwa's* army retreated after the death of Dixit. In September 1818, Brigadier-General Lionel Smith commanding the EIC's troops clashed with the *Peshwa's* forces at the village of Ashti. About 3,000 soldiers of the *peshwa* took a position behind a *nala*. Smith charged at the enemy with three British cavalry regiments. The Maratha cavalry was soon routed by the heavier horses of the 22nd Dragoons and the firepower generated by horse artillery. The British lost one killed and 19 wounded.[28] Mudhoji had about 15,766 cavalry, 17,826 infantry, and 85 obsolete guns. Both at the battles of Sitabaldi and Nagpur, superior tactics and firepower discipline of the EIC's troops enabled the latter to emerge victorious.

Compared to the other wars against Indian powers, the EIC mobilized the largest army during the Third Maratha War. About 120,000 men including 81,000 infantry were set in motion in the three presidencies. In contrast, during the Second Maratha War, the EIC mobilized only 55,000 infantry. The size of the EIC's army deployed against the Marathas needs to be compared with the size of another field army deployed by a big European power against a non-European power. In 1828, Russia attacked the European portions of the Ottoman Empire with 100,000 men. The EIC's army launched a pincer movement against the Marathas. The northern part of the pincer was the Army of Hindustan with 29,000 infantry, 14,000 cavalry and 140 guns and the Army of Deccan comprised the southern pincer with 52,000 infantry, 18,000 cavalry and 62 guns. Surrounded on all sides by the EIC's field armies, the *Peshwa* retired to his forts along the Western *Ghats*. But, these forts lacked good guns. And *trace Italienne* did not reach Maharashtra. A participant in this campaign, John Macleod, had written about a fort near Satara, which was captured by the EIC's army: 'We found nearly thirty pieces of ordnance altogether in the fort, but none, that could be called serviceable.'[29] Once the forts started to fall due to the superior siege techniques of the EIC, the *peshwa* surrendered in May 1818 and Mudhoji fled to Punjab. The Maratha Confederacy finally passed into history.

Dal Khalsa against the EIC

In 1805 Jaswant Rao, retreating before Lake's troops, arrived in Punjab. Ranjit Singh, the ruler of Punjab, heard with astonishment about the combat effectiveness of the EIC's military machine. Beginning in 1807, Ranjit built up Westernized infantry battalions from the deserters and demobilized soldiers of the *campoos* and the EIC. Ranjit, like Haidar, Tipu, and Sindia, depended on the European instructors for Westernizing his army. In total there were over 100 European officers, some of whom were from the *Grande Armee*. Most of the European officers were French, and the rest were Italians and Germans. Ranjit knew about the treachery of the European officers in the *campoos*. But, the *maharaja* was forced to depend on the European instructors due to their technical skill, though he never trusted them. And once employed, Ranjit was loath to allow them to leave his service. In addition, the officers were forced to take an oath that if required, they would fight their mother country. The requirement of paying the Westernized infantry in cash resulted in the monetization of Punjab's economy. The mint at Amritsar produced Nanak Shahi rupees.[30] Banking facilities were available through the system of *hundis*. Some of the European officers were employed to set up gunpowder factories. Saltpeter for manufacturing gunpowder was found around Lahore.

The Sikh martial culture posed problems for Ranjit's Westernizing program. Infantry fighting was against the Sikh warriors' masculine identity. In the Sikh cultural paradigm, a true warrior was a mounted soldier. The system of marching in step seemed silly to the Sikhs. The *sirdars* sneered at it and called it as *ruqsi-i-lulooan,* or "bloody fool's ballet." So, the first battalions were raised from the Hindustanis, Gurkhas, and Dogras. The *Khalsa* military establishment, like the Marathas, failed to develop disciplined heavy cavalry. The Sikh horsemen opposed the imposition of uniforms and European discipline. The proponents of light cavalry argued that until 1822, Ranjit Singh's army consisted mostly of such horsemen. And in that period, Ranjit gained most of his kingdom. This anti-European lobby questioned the utility of employing European officers and reorganization of the army, its equipment, and its doctrine. Since the horsemen — i.e., the landed class — constituted the most powerful social group in the *Khalsa* kingdom, Ranjit could not overcome their cultural blockage.[31] And due to the absence of an adequate number of disciplined heavy cavalry in the battles against the EIC, the British heavy cavalry repeatedly drove away the light cavalry of the Sikhs and turned the flanks of the Sikh Westernized infantry.

After the death of Ranjit Singh in 1839, the anti-European lobby rose to prominence in the *durbar*. This led to the outflow of the European instructors from Punjab. Those European officers who remained in the *Dal Khalsa* (Sikh army) lost all hold over the soldiers. The latter elected *panches* (body of five). Each company elected five members and those elected representatives from various companies elected five among them for each battalion. And the *panches* controlled the soldiery.[32]

When the First Sikh War broke out in 1845, the EIC deployed 32,479 men and 68 guns. The Sikh artillery enjoyed quantitative and qualitative superiority over the EIC's artillery. Both the EIC's infantry and the Sikh Westernized infantry were armed with Brown Bess. On December 18, 1845, Lal Singh with 12,000 Sikhs and 22 guns arrived at the village of Mudki. Mudki was a chance encounter which started at about 4:00 in the afternoon. As the Sikhs withdrew, dust and darkness prevented any pursuit by the EIC's troops. The next confrontation occurred on December 21, at Ferozeshah, 10 miles from Mudki. At Ferozeshah, the Sikhs constructed a for- tified camp that formed a sort of parallelogram about a mile in length and half a mile in breadth, defended by 35,000 infantry and supported by 100 artillery pieces. The Sikh strategy was to wear out the EIC's forces by encouraging the latter to attack the entrenched camp. Hugh Gough, the commander of the EIC's force, opted to soften up the Sikh defense with an artillery bombardment and then to storm the Sikh camp with a bayonet charge by the infantry. At the end of the day, the EIC's troops were able to penetrate into the Sikh camp. Early morning the next day, December 22, a Sikh relief army appeared under Tej Singh. The EIC's troops had run out of ammunition and Governor-General Viscount Hardinge, who had accompanied Gough, was on the verge of being captured. Thanks to treachery, the Sikh relief army withdrew without a fight. On February 10, 1846, at Sobraon, 30,000 *Khalsa* troops with 70 cannon opposed the EIC's soldiers. The *sirdars* were so eager to destroy the power of the disobedient army that on the eve of the encounter, through his agent Shams-ud-din, Lal Singh sent a report to Gough on the nature of Sikh entrenchment and deployment of the guns within it. The *durbar* surrendered after being defeated in the four successive battles — Mudki, Ferozeshah, Aliwal, and Sobraon. On the EIC's side, the total casualties came to 6,332[33] which was almost double the EIC's total casualties during the Third Maratha War.

In 1846, the *durbar* signed the Treaty of Lahore with the EIC. Under the terms of the treaty, the *Dal Khalsa* surrendered its artillery to the EIC, and its strength was reduced to 20,000 infantry and 12,000 cavalry. The disbanded Sikh soldiers forced *Diwan* Mulraj at Multan to become their leader. They appealed to the Sikh chieftains to join them in expelling the *feranghis*. Thus started the Second Sikh War. Just before the Battle of Chillianwala, Gough possessed 12,000 infantry and 3,000 cavalry. Sher Singh commanded a force comprising roughly 25,000 men. Gough had 60 guns against 62 artillery pieces of the Sikhs. On January 13, 1849, Gough's troops started advancing towards the village of Chillianwala, which the Sikhs had heavily fortified. For an hour, the Sikh artillery was able to hold the EIC's infantry formations at bay. Then the Sikh fire slackened, and slowly but steadily, the EIC's infantry regiments advanced and spiked the Sikh guns. At Chillianwala, about 5 percent of the EIC's force deployed for battle died, and the proportion of wounded amounted to 12 percent of the force. On January 20, 1849, Governor-General Lord Dalhousie in a private letter expressed his feelings about Chillianwala: "The result is that we have only 12 guns captured and lost 3 of our own, and we have suffered a horrible carnage of 2,375 killed and wounded — about 650 killed.... We have gained a victory for we have routed the enemy, committed great slaughter on him...and remained masters of the field; but I repeat, 'another such would ruin us.'"[34]

On January 16, 1849, Chattar Singh, father of Sher Singh, joined the latter with 6,000 soldiers. Meanwhile tension developed between the governor-general and his commander-in-chief. Dalhousie repeatedly pressured Gough to destroy Sher Singh's army as quickly as possible. However, remembering the drubbing at the hands of Sikh artillery during earlier battles, Gough decided to wait for reinforcements. On January 26, due to deployment of heavy siege guns by the EIC's troops, the fort of Multan surrendered and reinforcement was on its way to meet Gough. Sher Singh decided to try his luck at Gujerat on the bank of the river Chenab. On February 21, Gough bought 20,000 soldiers in the field.[35] Superior artillery gave victory to the British.

Conclusion

In comparison with the contemporary European battles, the battles that the EIC's army fought in India were quite small both in terms of the number of soldiers engaged and the casualties suffered. In the Indian context, British utilization of indigenous manpower, animal, and economic resources proved crucial in establishing their military supremacy within the subcontinent. The absence of a military revolution was most prominent in the sphere of logistics. The net result was the genesis of a composite military organization under the EIC. To a great extent, EIC's superiority in South Asia was due to the British success in exploiting the conflicts and divisions within indigenous societies and in harnessing indigenous aid. This was possible because the EIC's Indian opponents failed to construct strong centralized states backed up by impersonal institutions. The Indian polities adopted Western military technology at a rapid pace. While they succeeded in military modernization, they failed miserably in the sphere of political upgradation. Even then, British victory was not a foregone conclusion. If the Marathas did not cooperate with the EIC during the Fourth Mysore War, if the confederacy functioned unitedly during the Second Maratha War, and if the Sikh *sirdars* cooperated during the First Sikh War, then history of India in general and the British Empire in particular might have taken an alternate course.

CHAPTER 2

The Great Sepoy Mutiny

Raymond Callahan

Allahabad, June 1857

Allahabad stands at the confluence of the Ganges and Jumna at the eastern end of the Doab, the fertile, densely populated area between those rivers that was the heart of the East India Company's North-Western Provinces. In 1857 the city's military importance was considerable—it straddled not only river communications but the Grand Trunk Road, the strategically vital artery that linked Calcutta with the recently annexed Punjab, and it contained the second-largest arsenal in India. Despite its crucial role as both a communications and logistics center, however, there were no European troops there. Sixty "pensioners" from the Company's artillery and a few ordnance and commissary sergeants were a slender, and unimpressive, European presence in its fort. There were also some 400 Sikhs, one of the new units raised after the annexation of the Punjab a decade earlier. The 6th Bengal Native Infantry (BNI), a regular Bengal army unit, was quartered several miles from the city.

By early June, the mutinies in the Bengal army were several weeks old, Delhi had fallen into the mutineers' hands, and units as far away as the Punjab and as close as Benares (70 miles to the east) had risen in revolt. All seemed secure at Allahabad, however. When news of the first mutinies reached the 6th BNI, its men had volunteered for service against their compatriots at Delhi. The regiment was assembled for evening parade on June 6 to hear read out to them the thanks of the Governor General, Lord Canning, for their loyalty. The men cheered and proclaimed again their undying fidelity to the Company.

A few hours later 6th BNI, frightened by a rumor that European troops were on the way to disarm them, rose in mutiny. Five British officers were shot down on the parade ground; seven young ensigns, in transit to other units, were also murdered. Allahabad fort was saved only because the Sikhs remained loyal to their commander, Lieutenant Jeremiah Brayser, and disarmed the company of the 6th BNI stationed there. Having mutinied, the 6th immediately disintegrated, scattering in all directions. The city rose, however. Isolated European civilians were killed, and the fort, held by Brayser's Sikhs and the pensioners, was besieged—not very effectively—until a small force of European infantry arrived by river steamer a few days later.

Allahabad is a perfect miniature of the "Great Sepoy Mutiny." A regiment whose officers were certain of the loyalty of "their" sepoys; soldiers who acted—and perhaps were—fervently loyal until the minute that, swept by fear the British were about to betray them, they turned on those officers; the incredibly scanty British presence even in strategically crucial locales; and the vital role of newly raised troops from the only recently conquered Punjab, whose sometimes precarious loyalty to the British was in part based on hostility to the Hindus who made up the regular Bengal army. Finally, there was the fortunate fact that both the mutineers and the civilian population of the city were devoid of any real plan or effective leadership.

Why the Mutiny Matters

The 1857 Mutiny left a great scar across the face of the British Raj. The most written-about episode in nineteenth-century imperial history, it permanently changed the way the British governed, defended, and thought about their Indian empire.[1] Even in the twilight of the Raj, memories of 1857 exerted a powerful influence over British behavior. As Indian independence loomed in August 1947, Lieutenant General Sir Francis Tuker, an Indian Army officer who was GOC (General Officer Commanding), Eastern Command, ordered a party of British army sappers to Lucknow, where the defense of the British residency by a heavily outnumbered garrison had been one of the iconic episodes of the Mutiny. Since then, the Union Jack had flown day and night over the carefully preserved ruins of the residency building. Fearing that this revered imperial memorial might become the focus of triumphal nationalist demonstrations, Tuker had decided on preemptive action. After dark on August 13, 1947, the flag was lowered in his presence. Then the sappers demolished the flagpole and its base. Tuker sent the flag to Field Marshal Sir Claude J.E. Auchinleck, the last Commander-in-Chief of the old Indian Army. From him it went to the last King-Emperor, George VI, to be preserved at Windsor Castle among the relics of a rapidly shrinking empire.

Not surprisingly, the historiography of the Mutiny reflected the strong emotions it aroused and the equally powerful memories it left behind. John William Kaye, who began his career as an officer in the Company's Bengal army and ended it in the Company's London office, was a prolific historian who began but did not live to complete a study of the Mutiny. Kaye understood that it was a very complex event whose roots reached deeply into Indian society. Later Victorian writers, especially Colonel G.B. Malleson, who completed Kaye's work on the Mutiny, saw it more simplistically as a rising of disaffected soldiers supported by many of the turbulent elements in Indian society, previously held in check by British power. Malleson, followed by a number of writers down to the present, also believed there had been a conspiracy that had knit together and provided leadership for the soldiers and the "criminal classes" who rose with them. The conspirators, the theory went, were dispossessed Indian princes, landowners yearning to escape British supervision, and Muslim preachers. This interpretation had the great advantage of bypassing the considerable degree of popular support, which Kaye recognized that the Bengal army mutiny had evoked. It was precisely this widespread popular support that led an Indian nationalist writer, V.D. Savarkar, to entitle his account (published anonymously in London in 1909 and long banned by the authorities in British India) *The Indian War of Independence of 1857*. The argument over the nature of the events of 1857 easily survived the end of the British Raj, with both British and Indian historians coming gradually to a ragged consensus: 1857 was more than simply a mutiny of disaffected soldiers, supported by restive groups happy to profit from chaos; there was widespread popular unrest, especially in the North-Western Provinces (later renamed the United Provinces, now Uttar Pradesh), and in the adjacent and recently annexed client Kingdom of Oudh (Awadh). It was not, however, a "nationalist" uprising but rather a confused reaction to the changes that the British, sometimes unwittingly, had set in motion. The Victorian belief in a conspiracy, a "guiding hand," is not sustained, historians have generally agreed, by any evidence that has yet to come to light.[2]

In the welter of historical argument on the Mutiny, one point has always been uncontroversial. The crucial event in 1857 was the revolt of a large part of the East India Company's Bengal Army. If Indian soldiers had not mutinied in very large numbers, alienation from the Company's Raj, widespread as it may have been, would nonetheless have remained just that—unhappiness, resentment and anger, simmering under the surface and perhaps occasionally breaking out into local revolt, but unlikely to have ever produced the widespread upheaval that the collapse of the Bengal Army triggered. If 1857 was a central event in the history of the British Raj, it was also a crucial chapter in the history of the Indian Army. Any consideration of 1857 from this point of view immediately raises three questions: Why did it happen? How did the British, a small, surprised minority ruling a vast and populous land, survive it? What were the long-term consequences for the Indian Army that had to remain the bedrock of British rule after, as before, the Mutiny?

How the Mutiny Came

The Company's armies were perhaps the most unusual British creation during their long overseas adventure. It is worth recalling certain salient points about those armies that made 1857 not inevitable, certainly, but possible and perhaps even likely. In the first place, the Company maintained not a single unitary army, but three separate armies in India. Based on the Company's three presidencies, the Bengal, Bombay, and Madras armies had all developed their own jealously guarded customs, traditions and patterns of recruitment. Although nominally linked together by common subordination to the Commander-in-Chief in India, since the late eighteenth century, the Bombay and Madras armies retained considerable autonomy, aided by the fact that the Commander-in-Chief was also Commander-in-Chief of the Bengal Army and the governor-general's principal military advisor and therefore spent most of his time in the northern presidency. By 1857 that presidency was enormous, stretching from coastal Burma to the Khyber Pass. As it had grown by conquest and annexation, so had the Bengal army; and as it grew, its peculiarities hardened into unbreachable traditions. The crux was the pattern of recruitment. The Bengal army was able, at an early point, to tap into the large military manpower

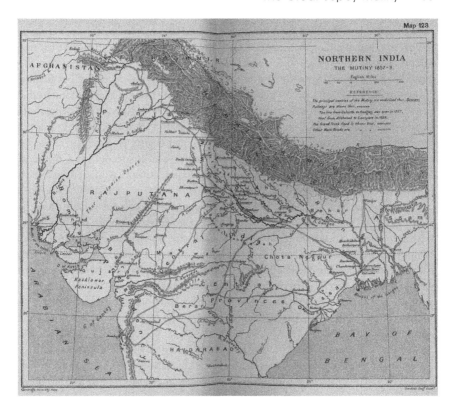

Map 123

Northern India, 1857–1859 (Courtesy of the University of Texas Libraries, The University of Texas at Austin)

pool that existed in north India. The client kingdom of Oudh and the North-Western Provinces stretching from Oudh to Delhi were its favored—and, soon enough, its exclusive—recruiting grounds. It may have helped that the men recruited there—taller, fairer—conformed more to European ideas of what a soldier should look like than the smaller, slighter, darker soldiers recruited by the Madras army. Without plunging into the complexities of rural India's social structure, it is clear that the Bengal army's recruitment biases guaranteed that the overwhelming majority of the 140,000 Indian soldiers on its rolls in 1857 were knit tightly together by ties of clan, caste, and village origin. Anything that aroused concern—either in the villages or the cantonments—would rapidly diffuse armywide. (By contrast, most of the Madras army's troops were raised in south India. The Bombay army originally had virtually no recruiting territory of its own and got accustomed to taking whomever it could get. In both presidency armies the few disturbances suffered in 1857 were largely the work of recruits from the north.)

The Company's soldiers were commanded by a body of officers who had elected Indian service as a career. During the second half of the eighteenth century, the formative years of the Company's military service, officers' death rate was very high, less from combat than from climate and disease allied to a lifestyle that featured oceans of alcohol. Men gambled their lives against the rather slight chance that they would survive to retire to Britain with a "competency"—necessary because the Company initially provided no pensions. Not very surprisingly, they structured their service to provide a network (ultimately, mind-bogglingly vast) of official and unofficial perquisites that would aid them in amassing that competency. Promotion by strict seniority gave everyone a theoretically equal chance to reach the few senior ranks and the rich rewards that came with them—and protected the Company's officers against the forces of wealth and family connection that made possible the rapid advancement of so many British army officers. An attempt by London to overhaul this system in the 1790s foundered on the adamant opposition of the officers of the Bengal army, who threatened the governor-general, Sir John Shore, with a mutiny—in which, they assured him, the sepoys would support them. London backed down (and saved face by sacking Shore). Thereafter, no one seriously disturbed the Bengal army's cherished seniority promotion system. It was extended as well to Indian "officers"—in reality more like warrant officers in a Western army— with the result that in 1857, not only were many British officers elderly and unfit, so were many of the long-serving Indian officers who were their indispensable link with the troops.

The Company aggravated the situation by holding down the number of officers per unit in order to contain costs. An Indian battalion was much more lightly officered than a comparable British unit. This fact, and seniority promotion, meant that officers could languish for a decade and more as subalterns. By the time they finally became lieutenant colonels, they could have passed a quarter-century in India. This led to an exodus of officers who got themselves "seconded" away from their units. They might serve in the civil administration, especially as "Politicals" managing relations with the Company's numerous client states. Or they might serve with newly raised "irregular" formations in recently acquired territories, answering not to army headquarters but to the local civil authorities. Such appointments brought excitement, adventure, and enhanced responsibilities as well as higher (if temporary) rank and pay. Very capable officers were drained away from regular units in this way, some for years, some forever. Those who soldiered on with their units were often men of less ability and drive. Although the defects of the system were obvious, the Bengal army did not welcome criticism from outsiders. Even governors-general seldom meddled with the Company's officers, and that not too effectively.[3]

The clannishness and parochialism of the Bengal officers was reinforced by another peculiarity of Indian service—the anomalous situation of officers who held their commissions from a company of merchants that became apparent in the mid-eighteenth century, when units of the regular British army arrived. The most junior officer holding a royal commission outranked every Company's officer of the same grade. The Company's officers bent their considerable energies to rectifying this situation. When they turned London's attempt at reorganizing them in the 1790s into a test of strength, which they won, one of the concessions that they extracted was "local" royal commissions. They henceforward received a commission from the Crown that ran concurrently with their Company commission—a Company's captain, for example, was also a royal captain. These commissions, however, were valid in India only; and they did nothing to protect a Company's officer from the fact that the seniority promotion system might keep him a captain for a decade or more, while a regular British officer could purchase his way up much more rapidly. Moreover local royal commissions still marked Company officers as professionally and socially inferior to their regular British counterparts. (Between 1822–1922, for example, there were 22 commanders in chief in India, but only seven were from the Company's service, or, as it became after 1858, the Indian Army.) This situation made the Company's officers even more insular, defensive and resistant to criticism.[4]

But at least the fundamental loyalty of the officers was not in question. One of the principal concerns of the Company's civil and military authorities in India and their distant masters in London was that British rule rested on the continued loyalty of a quarter-million Indian soldiers. How firm was that loyalty? How could its continuance be assured?

One answer was the presence of European troops. At an early stage, the Company had established European regiments in each of the presidency armies. These were supposed to guarantee the loyalty of the "native black troops." This was mostly fantasy. Expensive to maintain and subject to high rates of wastage due to climate, disease, and alcohol, the Company's European units (numbering in 1857 about 8,500 divided between the three presidency armies) were the symptom of an abiding concern rather than an effective response to it. In addition to the Company's Europeans, however, units of the regular British Army were a continuous presence in India from the end of the eighteenth century, serving tours that could be a decade or more in length. Their presence testified to the vastly enhanced significance of India to British policymakers—and to the fact that, paid for by the Company, they were off the War Office vote and effectively free to the British taxpayer (as, of course, were the Company's armies). In 1857, there were about 30,000 regular British soldiers in India, most of them concentrated in the newly acquired Punjab.[5] Forty thousand Europeans were simply not enough to either hold India or guarantee the loyalty of the sepoys. That loyalty was in fact the product of multiple interacting factors, some only dimly understood by the British and all, by 1857, under severe stress in the Bengal army.

British soldiers and officers came from a country with a strongly developed sense of national identity and an equally strong sense of their nation's claims upon them. Nationalism, Europe's most explosive export, had not yet spread among the Indians who soldiered for the Company. Their loyalties were very different—clan, caste, faith, and locale. The men who made up the regular regiments of the Bengal army had taken up an occupation that supported their status and whose fruits, financial and intangible, were what made the Company's military service attractive to them. The Company's history of continued success at war buttressed their loyalty. So did strong regimental ties. Certainly the sepoys were aware of the European troops and their role as watchdogs, but there were too many of them and too few Europeans for their loyalty to the Company to rest solely on fear of their white brethren. In any case, great armies do not fight well simply because they fear their employers' praetorians—and the Company had, however inadvertently, created a very formidable army. The sepoys' loyalty started with the attractions of victory and a web of valued payments and perquisites—in that sense, the Company's armies somewhat resembled other premodern mercenary forces, such as Spain's great Army of Flanders in the sixteenth century. There was however something else, unique to India. An unspoken but supremely important covenant with their foreign rulers was: we will fight and die for you, and deliver victory and dominion, but you must not only pay us but honor our own loyalties. After about 1830, invariable military success was no longer routine, and a systematizing and rationalizing government began to trim valued perquisites and impose alarming changes. Above all, the sepoys began to question whether the covenant was being honored—or, indeed, whether it was even still understood—by British officers and officials.

The Bengal army was no stranger to mutiny; its history had been spattered with incidents going back to its infancy in the 1760s. The best known of the pre-1857 mutinies, however, was not in the Bengal army but at Vellore in the Madras presidency in 1806. Caused by the unimaginative imposition of new standards intended to make the sepoys look more European, it might well have been a cautionary lesson for Bengal officers in the explosive possibilities of changes that seemed to breach the covenant (but it took place in the Madras army, which they viewed with condescension).[6] There had also been mutinies among the Company's European infantry as well as among its officers, and the Bengal officers had walked right up to the brink of revolt against the authorities in Calcutta and London in 1795–96. These disturbances—Vellore apart—had been largely over pay and perquisites and had usually been settled by concessions on the part of the Company. Beginning in the 1830s, however, the nature of the outbreaks, especially in the Bengal army, began to change.

The Company's aura of invincibility was seriously dented by the disasters of the wretchedly mismanaged Afghan War (1839–42) and the bloody battles of the two Sikh wars (1845–46; 1848), in which an Indian army fought the Company's forces nearly to a standstill. Then the "bean counter" mentality common to all financial administrators throughout history began trimming the extra allowances given soldiers for service outside the Company's domains on the grounds that territories newly annexed as a result of war were no longer outside the Company's rule. The result was a ripple of mutinies. John Jacob, a brilliant and innovative Bombay army officer, in published criticisms of the Bengal army, remarked that, to Bombay army eyes, the Bengal army's normal state looked like mutiny.[7] But defeat, or victory barely distinguishable from it, and dwindling financial perquisites were far from the only causes of unease. As the Company's domains spread outside India proper, and as policy makers in London came to think of the forces in India as the Empire's strategic reserve in the East, the use of Indian troops overseas became a steadily more important issue. They had already gone to Manila in 1762, to Egypt in 1799–1800, and to Java in 1811–14, but most of the sepoys involved were not from the Bengal army. The commander of the Egyptian expedition, Major General Sir David Baird, had remarked that getting Indian soldiers to serve overseas, which involved assuaging their concerns over possible loss of caste, required great care. The Bengal army then proved that without such care, serious trouble would arise. In 1824, a unit ordered to Burma (by overland march, to be sure) was badly mishandled and mutiny, bloodily suppressed, was the result. The Commander-in-Chief, General Sir Edward Paget, was (like the Madras Commander-in-Chief at the time of Vellore) a British regular with neither experience of, nor much sympathy for, the Company's service, an example of the high cost paid for the jealousy and condescension that kept Company officers out of the most senior military positions in India.

The repeated tremors of unrest in the company's Bengal army peaked in the 1850s. New annexations drained more officers from the regular units, and the new "irregular" units raised in the Punjab led the Bengal sepoys to wonder whether the Company was planning to replace them. The cumulative impact of changes introduced since the 1830s—"reforms" to British eyes, assaults on custom, caste and faith to many Indians—spread interlocking ripples of unease, unsettling if not alienating many groups in Indian society outside the already agitated Bengal army. The most disturbing of the concerns aroused by the actions of both the Company's government and some individual officers was that the British were planning to undermine the sepoys' caste and then make Christians of them, the more freely to use them outside India in pursuit of the Company's aggrandizement. After all, a deeply disillusioned native officer told a horrified Company's general on the eve of the Mutiny, the sepoys knew they were cheaper to maintain than Europeans, so why wouldn't the Company want to make maximum use of them?[8]

In the villages from which the Bengal sepoys came, British land revenue assessments bore heavily on the peasantry, some of whom were clinging precariously to their status by serving in the Company's army to supplement the meager proceeds of their holdings (lands that status issues forbade them to cultivate with their own hands). The client state of Oudh, home to so many Bengal sepoys, was annexed by the Company in 1856, adversely impacting many of them who suddenly lost their special, favored positions there. Another rationalizing change, the General Enlistment Act of 1856, added to the unease by making all Indian soldiers liable to service anywhere—Burma, Persia or farther afield—with all the implications for caste such service carried in the eyes of Bengal army sepoys. Moreover, by stoking such concerns, it also called into question their ability to send their sons into an army that they had come to regard not only as their personal preserve but as an essential prop of their status. All in all, by the mid-1850s there were abundant causes of unrest in the Company's India and particularly in the Bengal Army and its recruitment areas. In his study of the Indian Army, Philip Mason acutely observed "on every occasion when there was trouble in the Indian Army,...there have been present in some degree the three classical factors—ineffective officers, a general political unease or some general grievance in the villages, and a direct military grievance as the immediate spark."[9] The absence of many able officers and the incapacity of some who remained provided the first, the preceding 30 years the second, and the famous "greased cartridges" the third, igniting element.

The transition during the 20 years preceding the Mutiny in both the Company's service and the regular British army, from the smoothbore, flintlock musket to the rifled musket and then to the Enfield rifle, was part of the continuous process of technical upgrade in weaponry that the Industrial Revolution was making both possible and necessary. To load the rifled musket and the Enfield, it was necessary to ease the bullet's way down the grooved barrel with a lubricant. In the case of the Enfield, that lubricant was the grease on the paper cartridge that contained both powder and projectile. The soldier was supposed to bite the cartridge open with his teeth, pour the powder down the barrel, and then use the ramrod to push home the bullet wrapped in the greased cartridge paper. The rifled musket had similarly required a greased "patch" to facilitate loading. This had caused no trouble —the grease used was supposed to be, and probably was, a compound of vegetable oil and beeswax. The Enfield cartridge differed in several important ways. The loading drill called for it to be placed in the mouth—and it was introduced in an atmosphere rife with the Bengal sepoys' suspicion of both their officers and the Company. It also seems very likely that, as originally compounded, the tallow used did contain beef and pork fat, the former anathema to Hindus and the latter to Muslims. At the beginning of January 1857, no greased cartridges had in fact yet been issued, but in that month something far more deadly came out of the Company's principal arsenal at Dum Dum near Calcutta. A low-caste worker told a high-caste sepoy that his caste pride would soon be humbled—he and his fellows would soon be compelled to bite cartridges whose grease would defile them. Europeans had long marveled at the speed with which news and rumor had disseminated in India. In the volatile mood of the Bengal army, this story spread like wildfire—and was believed, if not universally, certainly very widely. No conspiracy in needed to explain what happened next.

As the rumors about the cartridges spread, experienced Company officers saw immediately that they had a potentially very serious problem on their hands. Major General Sir John Hearsey (a member of a distinguished Indian service family, some of whose members had married Indian women) commanded the large station at Barrackpore near Calcutta. As a colonel in 1844, Hearsey had faced down a mutiny over the cutting of allowances. He now insisted that he needed immediate authorization to tell his men that they would be issued Enfield cartridges ungreased and allowed to select their own lubricant. He got it within weeks of the original incident at Dum Dum—lightning speed for the Company's administration. Even so, however, it came too late.

In late February at Berhampore, 100 miles north of Barrackpore, the 19th BNI mutinied over the cartridges (which had not yet been issued). It was talked back to duty by its colonel, but its disbandment was deemed essential as a signal to the army. The 19th was then marched to Barrackpore, to be disbanded in the presence of Hearsey's brigade and a British battalion hastily summoned back from Rangoon. On March 29, two days before the disbandment parade, Mangal Pande, a sepoy of the 34th BNI (one of Hearsey's units, and one apparently deeply disaffected), while drunk, attacked the battalion's European sergeant major and the adjutant, calling on his comrades to join him in defense of caste and faith. No sepoy did so, but neither did any come to the Europeans' aid while some struck at them. Finally, one Muslim sepoy intervened to allow them to escape. At this juncture Hearsey arrived. Pande then attempted suicide. Hearsey's prompt action was decisive, and a precarious order was restored in the 34th. The disbandment of the 19th on March 31 was, by contrast, a very tame affair. The men were sent home at government expense, with full pay, wearing their uniforms; they cheered Hearsey as they departed.[10] Pande, once recovered, was tried and hung (bequeathing a version of his name— "pandy"—to British slang during the Mutiny as a generic label for mutineers).

Several points about this episode are instructive. Hearsey was a Company's officer of immense experience, with a fluent command of his men's language and clear sympathy for their concerns. He had taken the lead in January in forcing a reconsideration of army policy on handling the new cartridges and had several times addressed his brigade to reassure them that neither the army nor the Company had designs on either their caste or their faith. Yet that now weighed less with many sepoys than their passionately held conviction that the British planned to degrade them preparatory to making Christians of them. Another fear surfaced as well. Mangal Pande was convinced—and tried to convince his fellow soldiers—that the final proof of the Company's plot against them was the arrival of British troops at Barrackpore. These surely had been summoned, he screamed, to enforce the acceptance of the cartridges and the destruction of caste. This belief in a British plot and fear that the arrival of European troops signaled its commencement would reappear repeatedly, and no assurances, even from deeply respected officers like Hearsey, would do more than keep the lid on temporarily.

For the moment, however, an uneasy calm settled over the Bengal army. On April 8, Mangal Pande was hanged. On April 13, army headquarters reiterated that Enfield cartridges would be issued ungreased and the sepoys could apply lubricants of their choice; moreover, the drill for loading the new rifle would be altered to allow the cartridge to be torn with the fingers, rather than bitten open with the teeth. On May 3, the 34th BNI was disbanded. Doubtless both the army hierarchy and the Company's government hoped these steps would put an end to unrest in the Bengal army. Matters had reached a point, however, in which one misstep, by an officer less well attuned to his men than Hearsey, would touch off the final explosion. That came not in Bengal proper but in the North-Western Provinces, at the great military station at Meerut, near Delhi, in May.

The first of Mason's trinity of causes—ineffective officers—was present in abundance at Meerut. The station commander, Major General W.H. Hewett, was an apt symbol of the Bengal army's rigid seniority system. Seventy years old and a veteran of an unbroken half-century in India, he was well past his best, physically and mentally. Brigadier Archdale Wilson, the second-ranking officer, was slow and cautious. Left to themselves, neither Hewett nor Wilson were likely to have precipitated a crisis. The problem was Lieutenant Colonel Carmichael-Smyth of the 3rd Light Cavalry, a Bengal army unit that had, for the cavalry, an unusually high proportion of Hindus. On April 24, Carmichael-Smyth paraded the "skirmishers" of his regiment, 15 picked men from each of its six squadrons. The purpose was to explain the new drill that required troops to tear, not bite, their cartridges in order to open them. The 3rd, of course, had neither Enfields nor the new cartridges, only the unrifled carbines and cartridges they had used for years. Nonetheless, 85 of the 90 refused to accept cartridges that day. They were remanded for court-martial, where the verdict could only be guilty. Clearly the state of suspicion among the rank and file had become so great that even cartridges that they had routinely used were now objects of revulsion. Many were now sure that the cartridge paper itself was contaminated, and concessions by the army authorities served merely as proof that there had been a plot, which the Company was now trying to cover up. Like the "Great Fear" that swept the peasantry on the eve of the French Revolution, these deep anxieties, however irrational in British eyes, were so intense as now to be almost beyond assuaging. Having forced the issue, Carmichael-Smyth made matters even worse by holding a punishment parade on Saturday, May 9, at which the 85 troopers were stripped of their uniforms and manacled before the assembled garrison. The process, under a blazing sun, was interminable, and the manacled troopers had abundant time to berate their brethren loudly for failing to support the stand they had made for caste and faith. Carmichael-Smyth intended the punishment parade to make an impact on his men's minds. He succeeded. The next day, Sunday, May 10, the assembly of the British infantry battalion at Meerut (the 60th Rifles) for evening church parade, a normal garrison routine, was taken by the Indian troops as the signal that they were about to be attacked. The 3rd Light Cavalry and the two Bengal infantry regiments at the station rose. Some officers (and British families) were killed, much of the station fired, and the 85 imprisoned troops liberated while Hewitt, Wilson, and Carmichael-Smyth failed to organize any response at all. Carmichael-Smyth stayed well away from his regiment, while the 60th were marched aimlessly hither and yon. By morning much of the station was in ashes and the sepoys were on their way to Delhi, 40 miles away. Upon their arrival, they would rally the three Bengal infantry regiments garrisoned there, more British officers and civilians would die, and the aged Mughal emperor, Bahadur Shah, long a pensioner of the Company, would be turned into the figurehead of a revolt against British rule. The "Great Sepoy Mutiny" had begun.[11]

How the Raj Survived

The final embers of the Mutiny that exploded at Meerut in May 1857 would not die until 1859. Its crucial phase, however, after which British success was assured, fell between May and September 1857, when Delhi was retaken. Much hard fighting remained, but it was essentially a protracted, bloody mop-up operation. It is beyond the scope of this essay to cover all the detail; but fortunately, recent extensive accounts are available.[12] The focus here will be on the crucial four months and the "lessons learned" that shaped the future of the Indian Army.

At first glance, the British in May 1857 were in a perilous situation. The largest of the Company's armies had defected, and with its collapse, the security of the most important presidency seemed about to disintegrate. The 40,000 European troops available in India was a mere drop in what suddenly seemed a hostile ocean of millions. The sepoys who seized Delhi, proclaiming the end of white rule, and the peasants who rose, turning military mutiny into widespread revolt in the North-West Provinces, had every reason in the euphoria of the moment to feel that they had won. This was particularly the case as mutiny spread from station to station throughout the North-West Provinces, as well as among Bengal army units stationed in the Punjab and Oudh during the remainder of May and into June. Despite appearances, however, the British still had considerable assets that, once the initial shock had passed, they quickly mobilized to mount an effective defense and then a successful counterattack.

Perhaps the most important of those assets was the fact that the sepoys had no long-range plan and no effective centralized direction—only a panicky dread of what their white masters might be plotting and a fixed determination to escape it. Their seizure of Delhi was followed by no further initiatives, inaction of immense value to the British. (Nor did the angry peasants have any plans—only fears and hopes.) The Company still had an intact and functioning chain of command. The Commander-in-Chief, Sir George Anson (known mostly as an accomplished whist player), died within weeks of the Mutiny's outbreak, quickly followed by two successors. There were, however, numbers of able, energetic, and ruthless officers in the Company's service (as well as in the regular British units) suddenly empowered by the emergency and the collapse of so many of their elderly, unfit seniors. In Lord Canning, the British had a governor-general who did not panic and was not intimidated by his own lack of military experience, and he began systematically marshaling British assets to contain and suppress the mutiny. Above all, the British remained masters of militarily crucial communications. The best proof that there was no conspiracy behind the Mutiny is that the vital and vulnerable telegraph system, although occasionally interrupted, continued functioning to give the British the central nervous system crucial to effective command. The railway network, still in its infancy, remained under British control and functional, as did the Grand Trunk Road. A splendid, if fleeting, opportunity to disrupt the latter presented itself to the mutinous sepoys and their civilian supporters at Allahabad in early June; but, as noted, in the absence of effective leadership, it was not grasped.

The question of the quality of Indian leadership during the Mutiny is important. That no one individual or group coordinated the actions of the military and civilian components of the revolt is clear enough. The sepoys, the backbone of that revolt, suffered from command problems that stemmed from the structure of the Company's armies. Time and again, sepoy units, facing British and Indian (or Gurkha) forces that they outnumbered, were nevertheless defeated. The problem was not of course lack of courage or skill with weapons (sepoy gunners proved to be all too capable, from the British point of view), but the absence of the tactical skills that had been supplied by British field grade officers. Indians had never filled these roles in the Company's service—and would not in the Indian Army until the latter stages of World War II.[13] Courage and a willingness to die, even when allied to superior numbers, are not guarantors of victory, absent tactical skill. This problem would haunt the sepoy mutineers throughout.

There were, of course, other Indian leaders who emerged during the fraught summer of 1857. The most colorful by far was the Rani of Jhansi, whose gender and death in battle made her an object of fascination to the British at the time and popular novelists since (as well as an icon to later nationalists). Whatever may be made of her motivations and abilities, she was a figure of regional rather than wider appeal. The person known to the British as "Tatya Tope" (Ramchandra Pandurahga) certainly demonstrated leadership skills and a flair for irregular warfare but, like the Rani, had a regional rather than wider impact. Had the revolt produced a leader with widespread popular appeal, the story might well have ended differently (as it did when such a leader appeared 75 years later to lead a very different sort of revolt). As it was, however, the British retained the advantage they had long had—the best civil and military command structure in India.

An effective command structure and functioning communications enabled forces to be marshaled to attack the heart of the revolt—Delhi, the North-West Provinces and Oudh—from two directions. European units were summoned from Madras, Bombay, and Mauritius, and an expeditionary force on its way to China was diverted to Calcutta. This gathering of European reinforcements was made possible not only by the telegraph (and undersea cable) but equally by the fact that the Madras and Bombay armies remained loyal—not a single regular formation of the former mutinied, and only two battalions of the latter. Madras and Bombay sepoys in fact provided the bulk of the troops used to contain and eradicate the spillover of the Mutiny into central India in 1857–58. (It needs to be remembered that mutiny was not universal even in the Bengal army—a loyal residue fought for the Company throughout.) Reinforcements flowing through Calcutta could be pushed upcountry to secure the Grand Trunk Road, contain any further spread of the Mutiny (and civilian revolt) and prepare to relieve Lucknow, the capital of recently annexed Oudh, where mutinous sepoys, discharged and unemployed Oudh soldiery, and armed civilians were besieging the British Residency. However symbolically important the relief of Lucknow was to the British, the crucial position, both strategically and psychologically, was Delhi. Containment and counterattack here could only be organized from the Punjab.

Conquered in two hard-fought and clumsy wars that helped damage the prestige of the Company's army, the Punjab was very heavily garrisoned. Fourteen of the 19 European regiments in the Bengal presidency were stationed there—as were 32 Bengal Native Infantry and cavalry regiments. In addition to the concentration of European troops, two other factors worked in favor of the British. The Punjab administration was headed by John Lawrence, a member of a distinguished family of Company soldiers and administrators and destined to become viceroy after the Mutiny. As befitted what at that point was an occupation administration in a recently conquered province, the Punjab government was less bureaucratic and more disposed to direct action than administrations in Bengal's older "regulation provinces." Then there was the success of the Punjab administration in sopping up many of the unemployed soldiery of the disbanded and very formidable Sikh army by embodying them in the Punjab Irregular Force. Although officered by "seconded" Company regulars, the force answered to the Punjab administration rather than to the army chain of command. More units were easily raised in the Punjab, where hostility to the "purbiyas" (the Hindu soldiery from Bengal) ran deep among the Sikh and Muslim peasantry. The British did not create this animosity but certainly benefitted from it—and, in using it, probably deepened it as well. The significance of the Sikh units has been seen in the case of Allahabad, where Brayser's "Ferozepore Sikhs" played a crucial role. ("Brayser's Sikhs," later the 1/11th Sikh Regiment, would remain on the army list, a reminder of the luck and skill with which the British turned recent enemies into defenders of the Raj.) The Punjab, its administration, and the new units raised there would be crucial in retaking Delhi.[14]

First, however, the Punjab administration had to guarantee the security of its own territory. John Lawrence and his deputy, Robert Montgomery (grandfather of the future field marshal), were clear in their minds that this meant disarming regular units of the Bengal army. About half the Bengal units in the Punjab in fact did mutiny. Most of the others were disarmed and disbanded preemptively at Peshawar, Lahore, and elsewhere. The story of the 21st BNI at Peshawar, however, indicates that Lawrence and Montgomery may have missed an opportunity to rally some of the regular Bengal units. The 21st was spared disbandment because it had given no indication of disloyalty. Perhaps buoyed by this show of confidence, it soldiered on through the Mutiny and into the reconstructed Bengal army afterwards. Similarly Skinner's Horse, a cavalry regiment, raised in 1803 by the Eurasian James Skinner (son of a Company officer and an Indian woman) and commanded in 1857 by Captain Neville Chamberlain, remained loyal after Chamberlain ostentatiously demonstrated his trust in his men, a tactic also used by Brayser at Allahabad. How many more units might have been rallied by young, energetic commanders remains forever unknowable; in any case, such commanding officers were far from plentiful in the Bengal army in 1857.

The Punjab secure, a column of troops followed by further reinforcements and a siege train, was pushed south to Delhi where, joining the remnants of the Meerut garrison, they laid siege to the great walled city.[15] It was one of history's most curious sieges. The "British" besieging force, never less than half Indian, numbered at its maximum about 9,000 men. The besieged were initially about 35,000–40,000 strong, supported by numerous armed civilians. The British settled into positions on a ridge–later famous as "The Ridge"–northwest of the city in June and clung to their position throughout the ensuing brutal summer, enduring a series of assaults that were never quite well-coordinated or strong enough to succeed. During those interminable, fly-plagued weeks, there began to take shape one of the military legends that would endure as long as the British Raj and, indeed, outlive it to flourish to this day: the Gurkhas. The Company had faced these tough hillmen from Nepal in a hard-fought war (1814–16). Once beaten, they were recruited, as the Sikhs would later be (and as the Scottish Highlanders had been a century earlier). However, the quality of the Gurkha infantryman first grabbed British attention during the

Mutiny. Among the units that marched from the Punjab to Delhi was the "Sirmoor Battalion" of Gurkhas. Throughout the siege, it held one of the most exposed positions on The Ridge, a ruined structure known as "Hindu Rao's House," under the command of Major (later Major General Sir) Charles Reid. Beating off some 16 major attacks, they lost 327 men, killed and wounded, out of 490 and then went on to join the final assault—and eventually to become the 2nd King Edward's Own Gurkha Rifles, the regiment to which, much later, Tuker belonged. (The ruler of Nepal, Jang Bahadur, shrewdly assessing the likely winner after the eventual fall of Delhi, joined the British with some 9,000 Gurkhas early in 1858, thus further showcasing these redoubtable soldiers.)

At length, in mid-September, the British were ready. On September 14, four columns, totaling 6,800 (two-thirds Indian or Gurkha) assaulted the walls. The mutineers' numbers had dwindled through casualties and departures to some 10,000–12,000 with an indeterminate number of armed civilians. After a hard fight that left nearly a sixth of the assaulting force as casualties, the British got into the city. Once inside and facing brutal urban combat, the morale of the much-tried British infantry began to falter. Fortunately, the morale of the defenders collapsed even faster, and by September 20 the city was in British hands. The price had been high. A third of the European infantry had become casualties, as had half of the British officers.

The high officer casualties not only indicate how expensive street fighting is—and how officers tried to overcome "stickiness" among their troops by leading from the front—but point to another significant fact about the Mutiny. As elderly and unfit senior officers fell by the wayside—or had the sense to stand aside, like the brigadier at Multan, a veteran of the 34 years in India, who deferred to Neville Chamberlain, a mere captain—the talented and aggressive mid levels of the Company's service came into their own. The most famous of these are Fred Roberts, later a field marshal; John Nicolson, who had escaped the seniority system by service in the Punjab, and who died in the assault; and William Hodson, a formidable leader of irregular cavalry who executed Bahadur Shah's heirs after the fall of Delhi and was killed during the final assault on Lucknow. But there were many others, not only at Delhi but scattered across the Bengal presidency. The seniority promotion system did not by itself cause the Mutiny, but it weakened the Bengal army, slowing the army's response to the mounting unrest in the spring of 1857 and then contributing to many of the initial fumbles in handling the outbreak. Certainly its effective collapse helped the British to make the best of their assets in the summer of 1857.

The fall of Delhi was not the end of the Mutiny, but it was the decisive moment in its suppression. The other two great symbols of the Mutiny—the siege, surrender, and subsequent massacre of the defenders of Cawnpore, and the long siege and multiple reliefs of Lucknow (June–November)—were by comparison less militarily than emotionally significant. The besieged defenders of Lucknow (nearly half loyal Bengal regulars and Sikhs), led until his death by John Lawrence's brother Henry, became a magnet for British effort, compelling the deployment of relief forces all out of proportion to Lucknow's real military significance. The ruined Residency, with its defiant Union Jack, became the best-known symbol to the British of their courage in adversity and ultimate triumph. But Cawnpore added a savage edge to British behavior as they stamped out the Mutiny. The station was commanded by Major General Sir Hugh Wheeler, another of the Bengal Army's septuagenarians, but in this case one still reasonably fit and vigorous. When the three regiments of sepoys at Cawnpore mutinied on June 5, Wheeler had about 300 Europeans to defend a hastily scratched out entrenchment. They did so successfully for three weeks and then surrendered on terms that would allow the garrison, with its women and children, to leave by boat. Whether there was ever any intention to honor these terms is doubtful. As the garrison began to embark, fire was suddenly opened and the men were killed. A large number of women (73) and children (124) survived, only to be massacred a few weeks later as a relief force pushed upriver from Allahabad. "Cawnpore" became the most emotionally charged word in the vocabulary of the British in India. The slaughter of the women and children, and especially the belief that British women had been raped, set the stage for counter atrocities, mostly inflicted upon the innocent. (The British fervently believed that rapes had occurred at Cawnpore and elsewhere, but subsequent investigations found the accusations impossible to substantiate.) There is no doubt that even without Cawnpore, the British—frightened, shaken, and determined to reestablish their authority—would not have been very concerned about the niceties of justice as they put down the Mutiny. The massacre, however, provided a justification in the minds of many British soldiers and officials for wholesale, indiscriminate retribution. It did not help that many of the officers, like Brigadier James Neill of the Company's Madras Fusiliers, who relieved Allahabad and then retook Cawnpore, believed in a fierce Old Testament god who demanded vengeance. The prominence of Sikhs and Punjabi Muslims in the British forces further complicated issues—they had no reason to restrain their animosity toward not only the "purbiya" sepoys but also the largely Hindu countryside. And certainly their British officers made little attempt to rein them in.

The only brake on the whole process of bloody revenge was applied by Lord Canning, who was conscious that after victory the British would still have to rule India with the cooperation and support of Indian soldiers, policemen, officials, and taxpayers. His instructions of July 31, 1857—the famous "Clemency Resolution"—was in fact simply an attempt to mandate some form of investigation and due process before imprisonment or execution. Widely derided and attacked in both India and Britain, it was in fact an intelligent and farsighted attempt to retain as much Indian support as possible. The governor-general's clear statement—"I will not govern in anger"—was not simply an avowal of personal belief, but common sense and good politics. Canning's action did not stop indiscriminate reprisals, of course, but it damped down the instinct for retribution and prevented the suppression of the Mutiny from doing even greater long-term damage.[16]

While it is possible to give a precise start time for the Mutiny, there is no neat terminal date. It gradually sputtered out in 1858–59. Long before that time, however, British attention had turned to restructuring the Government of India and applying the "lessons learned" from the Mutiny to rebuilding the armies the Company had created. In mid-1858 Canning had set up an inquiry. At the same time in London, a Royal Commission was sitting on the future of the Indian Army. From these two studies came recommendations that shaped the new army.

Although the Crown assumed direct responsibility for India, complete amalgamation of the Company's armies with the British army was neither feasible nor acceptable to the Company's officers. The Indian Army therefore remained a separate service under its existing officer corps. Future entrants would come from Sandhurst and be on the same footing, at least with regard to the source of their commissions, as regular British army officers (though tension between the two services would last until 1947). The Company's European regiments became part of the British army, after what amounted to a strike, known as the "White Mutiny," over the terms of the transfer.[17] The three presidency armies remained separate institutions. But if there was some continuity, there was also striking change. The seniority promotion system for officers was swept away. The Mutiny underscored the importance of European troops, and the new arrangement stipulated a one-to-two ratio. This remained the theoretical norm for the duration of the Raj. (It would finally break down during World War II, causing Winston Churchill some pungently expressed anxiety.) The most dramatic changes, however, were not those that affected officers or the number of European soldiers available, but the nature of the Indian units.

For years, critics of the Bengal army had pointed not only to the seniority system and the army bureaucracy that deprived commanding officers of much effectual authority over their men, but to the feebleness of the Indian officers, due to seniority promotion and lack of authority. The solution, these critics argued, was the "irregular" structure used in the new Punjab units and some Bombay army formations. These had a smaller number of British officers, carefully selected and actually present with their units, and real authority and responsibility for the Indian officers. Brigadier John Jacob of the Bombay army was a tireless advocate of this approach before the Mutiny, and that event settled the argument. The Bengal army was reconstructed on an "irregular" pattern; British officers were selected for duty with units, not automatically promoted to command; seniority was tempered by merit and competence in selecting Indian officers; and commanders reclaimed much disciplinary authority—which, however, they henceforth exercised cautiously. The old uniforms, intended to give units a European appearance, gave way to styles more Indian in appearance, including turbans. All these changes were important, but none perhaps as important as the changes in recruitment.

The homogeneity of the Bengal army's regiments had been, from the British perspective, one of its greatest weaknesses. Henceforth there would be few such "single-class" units, and mixture of castes and faiths became the norm. Furthermore, who was recruited changed dramatically. The decades after the Mutiny saw the "Punjabization" of the Bengal army, a trend that continued after the separate presidency armies were folded into a single Indian Army in 1895. On the eve of World War II, the Punjab supplied about half the Indian Army. Sikhs were strongly overrepresented in the army's ranks. The Gurkha units increased in number as well.

It is not too fanciful to see the Gurkha Rifles as, ultimately, the Indian Army's equivalent of the Brigade of Guards—the gold standard of Indian soldiering.[18] All this reflected, of course, who had stood with the British during the Mutiny, and it was buttressed by that interesting construct of imperial anthropology, the "martial races" theory. The military significance of the Punjab after the Mutiny would strongly affect many aspects of British policy in India until 1947.[19]

Perhaps the greatest of the lessons taken forward from the Mutiny was the importance of the ties of loyalty and trust between British officers and the Indians and Gurkhas they commanded. Brayser's Sikhs, Chamberlain's troopers of Skinner's Horse, and numerous other units had remained with the British because of such links. Through all the changes that followed the Mutiny, the army cultivated and cherished them. As archaic and paternalistic as those bonds may now look, they were what gave the Indian Army its strength and resilience. As that army neared its end, it produced officers like Claude Auchinleck, "Bill" Slim, and hundreds of others, many by then Indians who, from the largest voluntarily enlisted force in history, forged the splendid 14th Army that turned in one of the great battlefield performances of the twentieth century. Sometimes institutions do learn.

CHAPTER 3

The Martial Races and the Indian Army in the Victorian Era

Douglas M. Peers

It is one of the essential differences between the East and the West, that in the East, with certain exceptions, only certain clans and classes can bear arms; the others have not the physical courage necessary for the warrior.[1]

These words exemplify a distinctive feature of the colonial army in India; namely, the ethnographic imperatives that shaped its composition by deliberately excluding a large swath of Indian society from its ranks while simultaneously targeting a few select communities of "natural warriors." Such soldiers conformed to certain stereotypes: they tended to be rural; were hardened by harsher climates and often inhabited marginal agricultural lands; and they were relatively uneducated and thought to be "clannish." The label also assumed an aptitude, even a longing, for fighting and for the glory that came with it. These were men of honor, and they could be counted upon to be reliable on and off the battlefield. This depiction also served as a welcome antidote to the corrosive effects of modern industrial society, an image that not surprisingly played well to an officer class whose collective identity drew on an aristocratic and nostalgic reading of society.[2] The weight of such views, and the need to find a supply of dependable soldiers, stemmed from the central role played by the army in the political and cultural life of the Raj, for most British officials accepted that India was not only won by the sword but would be retained by the sword, an axiom sounded even more incessantly in the aftermath of the Rebellion of 1857–58.[3] The end result was that by the beginning of the twentieth century, the composition of the Indian Army bore little resemblance to the wider society from which it was drawn: instead, particular groups, Muslims and Sikhs from the Punjab and Gurkhas from Nepal, predominated.

Orientalism and Martial Races

While the idea that some people were inherently more warlike than others and hence better suited to military service drew upon earlier British experiences in India, was informed by precolonial military cultures and idioms, and was not confined either to India or the British—for they can also be identified elsewhere in the British as well as other colonial empires—martial race as a popular and pervasive idea reached its apogee in the last quarter of the nineteenth century.[4] At that time it was systematically integrated into military planning by Lord Roberts, Commander-in-Chief of the Indian Army (1885–93), who was determined to forge an army capable of withstanding an attack from without. It was also manifested in a series of handbooks designed to familiarize British officers with the characteristics of the sepoys under their command. And it was widely disseminated by the writings of Lieutenant-General Sir George MacMunn, who dashed off a number of popular accounts of India that were all framed by a crude taxonomy of India's peoples. While MacMunn is perhaps best known today for his writings on the army, in which the theme of martial race was ever present, he also wrote many other books on aspects of history and society. What is striking about them is his obsession with caste, race, and what for him were the often perverse gradations in society. His works epitomize the systemic preoccupations with what made India different from, and inferior to, Western society, which scholars have identified as the key characteristic to orientalist writings on Asia. Yet while MacMunn certainly played an important role in popularizing the idea of martial race, his credibility as an expert on India was at times questioned by his contemporaries. His obituary in the *Times,* in assessing his scholarly impact, concluded that "His unconventional style and his trust in an imaginative memory made him an unreliable guide..."[5] It is worth noting that MacMunn was a founding member of the Kipling Society, established to honor Rudyard Kipling, that other great imperial romantic and propagandist whose poem "Bobs" in turn helped bolster Lord Roberts' stature as an imperial icon.

Collectively, the actions and writings of Roberts, MacMunn, Kipling, and others identified the most suitable recruits as coming from the conquered communities on the northwestern and northern peripheries of British India. Such people were thought to be economically and socially less advanced, and because of the more hostile environment in which they lived, it was assumed that they had an aptitude for war.[6] Moreover, such communities were believed to be relatively unencumbered by caste traditions, which contemporaries held accountable for the mutinies in the Bengal Army in 1857. Those who failed to meet these standards were systematically barred from military service. By 1880, British recruiters favored the Punjab, a province described in one Parliamentary Enquiry as "the home of the most martial races of India, and the nursery of our best soldiers."[7] And in the case of those groups declared lacking in martial fiber, their presence in the army was steadily cut back over the second half of the nineteenth century. The Madras Army, singled out as particularly bereft of martial races, witnessed a regular culling: eight battalions of the 40 on its strength in 1882, and a further seven by the end of the century. Into this vacuum poured increasing numbers of recruits from the northwest, especially the Punjab, as well as Gurkhas from Nepal.

Much of the impetus towards classification along martial lines came in the aftermath of the Rebellion. Security preoccupations meant that particular groups were identified as having the physical, moral, and mental facilities to become good soldiers, just as others were labeled as inherently given to a life of crime (the so-called "criminal tribes"), while still more were characterized as best suited to commercial or agricultural employment. Army officers played a critical role in the collection, analysis, and organization of this ethnographic and cultural information. They were not simply consumers of colonial knowledge, but were producers as well and were positioned to do so not only by the obvious need for military intelligence but also by their proximity to society.[8] Martial races are therefore an excellent example of what Nicholas Dirks has declared as a defining characteristic of the "ethnographic state," namely one in which "Colonialism was made possible, and then sustained and strengthened, as much by cultural technologies of rule as it was by the more obvious and brutal modes of conquest that first established power on foreign shores."[9] Key to these ethnographic calculations was the emphasis on establishing stable and "authentic" definitions that would help not only to delineate differences between various communities, but also serve to identify individuals who properly fell within the category from those who lay outside. What constituted a Gurkha or a Sikh was largely the product of these efforts at identification and classification, and the end result was a series of categories that were as much the product of imperial imaginations as they were the result of indigenous development.[10] In fact, the British obsession with authenticating real Sikhs or real Gurkhas encouraged many of the practices that we have to come to associate with them.

Hence, on one level, the popularity of martial race theory confirms the influence of ethnographic imperialism and the power of the colonial state to impose rigid taxonomies based on caste and race upon society. The practice of pigeonholing people into discreet categories accelerated in the nineteenth century as colonial officials struggled to make sense of the diversity before them. Yet it would be a mistake to assume that this happened smoothly or suddenly, or that it was completely imposed by the British. While the presence of "orientalist" readings of society is undeniable, and that the often crude stereotypes contained within them encouraged representations of society that invented nonexistent social relations while freezing others that had historically been more fluid, discussions about "martial races" expose the often contested and ambivalent discussions about Indian society that undermined the totalizing power of colonial authority that some have claimed. The very idea of martial races, and whether the army should limit itself to these groups, was a topic of continuous and often torturous debate.

A close study of the chronological development of martial race theory confirms that this theory was as much a consequence of narrowing the recruiting pool as it was a catalyst in creating a constrained pool. Necessity was at least in part the mother of invention: the disintegration of the old Bengal Army in 1857–58 forced the British to grab what troops they could, leading to an influx of solders from nearby Punjab. As the Governor-General, Lord Canning, noted at the time, "The difference, therefore, between our position in 1858 and our position in 1857, is that there is a larger native force, and that the bulk of it, instead of being drawn from Oude, is drawn from the Punjab."[11] According to Canning, the total number of regular and irregular troops in the Bengal Army in 1858 was around 130,000, of which 75,000 were from the Punjab; and of that number, he believed 23,000 were Sikhs. Martial race theory emerged as a rationalization of what was in part a pragmatic response to an emergency, though its success as a rationalization depended greatly on the extent to which it dovetailed with ethnographic mappings of India. It was also self-fulfilling in important respects, for those units deemed more martial received better officers and more field experience, thus ensuring that their military efficiency maintained a higher standard. Finally, we must note that "not only did the British select their recruits, the recruits selected the British":[12] the resilience of martial race theory ultimately depended on the willingness of groups so identified to respond to the opportunities afforded to them, and in a manner consistent with the theory.

That martial race theory emerged fitfully, and in response to earlier developments, suggests that it was not quite the totalizing discourse that has sometimes been assumed. It tended to draw upon precolonial customs and traditions, for many of the communities the British declared to be martial did in fact have long histories of engagement in warfare. Furthermore, some of the typecasting in which the British engaged, such as declaring Bengalis to be unwarlike, echoed Mughal prejudices. The identification of select groups as more martial than others was not necessarily based on negative traits, for definitions of what constituted a "martial race" called on idealizations that were analogous to those characteristics, albeit of a stereotypical nature, within which the British themselves liked to bask. The Scottish Highlander provided a prototype for the martial race, and many of the so-called martial races of India were explicitly compared to them. Thus, martial races in India often epitomized the best traits of British soldiers, though these were redolent of class prejudices. MacMunn noted of the Sikh that "as a fighting man, his slow wit and dogged courage give him many of the characteristics of the British soldier at his best."[13] In other words, an appreciation of the relationship between martial races, recruiting, and the social and cultural characteristics of the Indian Army requires that we look not only at what the British believed and did, and the reference points they used, but also the initiatives and responses of those communities from which the recruits were drawn.

The word race is in fact somewhat misleading, in that color or other obvious "racial" markers familiar to us today were not necessarily integral to the definition. Caste, class, and race were often used interchangeably.[14] We must remember that in the eighteenth and early nineteenth centuries, race was a more flexible term, often signifying people who shared a common heritage that could be marked by various combinations of linguistic, cultural, and religious affinities, but not necessarily grounded in biology. By the later nineteenth century, the impact of scientific thinking and efforts to produce more systematic taxonomies pointed to a more restricted sense of the term. Race became much more deterministic and suggested inheritable characteristics that could be scientifically identified and subject to classification. And while race came to occupy a more pronounced place in British military thinking, it never fully displaced caste and class as descriptors as these continue to appear in military documents. Such ambiguities, while demonstrating on a theoretical level the inconsistencies within colonial discourse, also bolstered its practical impact, for therein lay this discourse's authority. The many meanings that could be assigned to martial race enabled it not only to be deployed more readily to different situations, but also to be recalibrated as time progressed and the context changed.

The Company's Armies and the Origins of Martial Race Theories

Writing retrospectively in 1909, the Government of India, in assessing the impact of the 50 years of Crown rule that had followed the abolition of the East India Company in the aftermath of the Indian Rebellion of 1857–58, boasted that "The proportion of soldiers drawn from unwarlike races has been greatly reduced, while the proportion of Goorkha regiments and of soldiers from the martial races of northern India has been increased."[15] The narrowing of the recruiting pool not only to select communities but also to a particular region of India was such an obvious feature of the post-mutiny army that its very visibility can blind us to the fact that well before the formal articulation and popularization of a theory of martial races (however ambiguous and contested it was in practice), the British in India had already shown a marked preference for particular segments of Indian society. Such prejudices and their legacies informed later Victorian sentiments. So too did ongoing disagreements between British officers as to the manner in which the armies of India should be organized. These disputes can largely be accounted for by the different contexts and historical experiences of the three "native" armies of India: the Bengal Army, the Madras Army and the Bombay Army (which correspond to the three presidencies under which Company rule in India was organized), and which at the close of the century would be combined into a single Indian Army. In broad terms, the Bengal Army, the largest and most prestigious by the early nineteenth century, practiced the most exclusive recruiting strategies, while the armies of Madras and Bombay were not only less preoccupied with caste but also more willing to jumble recruits from different communities together. With the outbreak of mutiny within most units of the Bengal Army (and its relative absence in the Bombay and Madras armies), the exclusiveness of the Bengal Army came under intense scrutiny. But exclusiveness per se was not necessarily identified as the problem, though there were critics who argued that the army should recruit indiscriminately from all who met the basic standards. Instead, the thrust of most criticisms was that the Bengal Army had allowed itself to become the virtual prisoner of the highest castes, rendering military discipline subordinate to the customs and traditions of its recruits, and leading, in the words of one officer, to "an immense quasi-masonic brotherhood from Peshawar to Calcutta, and from the Himalaya to the Nerbudda."[16]

The definition of what constituted the ideal recruit differed between the three presidencies. These discrepancies were mainly the result of historical accidents and the unique characteristics of their local labor pool. Bengal had more stringent requirements as far as caste and physical appearance were concerned. This preference became codified into terms that dictated which north communities were "natural" soldiers, but it did not originate in a clearly articulated policy of selective recruitment. The exclusiveness of the Bengal Army, which eventually would be ideologically defended in terms of the sepoys' innate traits, was the result of the British tapping into the preexisting military labor market. Moreover, while the Madras and Bombay armies were much more polyglot in their composition, officers in their corps were also determined to exclude certain peoples.

When the Bengal Army was in its formative stages, the British took what soldiers they found around them, whose homelands lay in north central India. The Company's service drew from those classes that had traditionally taken up arms, thus making recruiting self-perpetuating and self-regulating. One British officer claimed that "there are, in all parts of India, thousands and tens of thousands who have lived by the sword, or who wish to live by the sword, but cannot find employment suited to their tastes."[17] The family and village ties of sepoys already in the service were then exploited to gather more recruits. Direct recruitment was used only as a last resort, when military necessity required a sudden and drastic expansion. The British deliberately targeted the higher castes, from Awadh and neighboring areas, partly to conciliate rural elites and partly because of their conviction that such men were not only more warlike but were also men of better character on account of their social ranking. Despite problems in identifying exactly what constituted a caste—contemporary muster rolls reveal a confusing range of criteria including occupation, region and ritual ranking—the Rajputs and Brahmins of Awadh were declared to be more martial and hence provided a prototype for the theory of martial races. The higher castes had the added advantage of possessing characteristics dear to the hearts of army officers; for example, the higher castes' observations of ritual purity satisfied "the great military virtue of cleanliness."[18] The lower castes, no matter from where they came, were deliberately excluded. So too were Christians and, after 1793, persons of mixed ancestry, ostensibly because it was believed that higher castes would not agree to serve alongside them, but just as importantly because such individuals were deemed to be socially inferior by British officers. Muslims were recruited though never in great numbers. Some officers were concerned that Muslims, having only recently been dislodged from their positions of command and influence in North India, were more reluctant to submit to British rule. Religion also played a role; the historical tendency to view Muslims as more fanatical was frequently put forth in the early nineteenth century as an objection to relying upon them for military service, and this concern would occasionally resurface in the later nineteenth century.

Once Bengal officers had accepted the principle of recruiting only from the higher castes, they quickly conceded rights and privileges to these sepoys, a move intended to ensure that they could maintain their ritual status. Religious rites and observations were not only confirmed but encouraged, and in what is arguably one of the most compelling indicators of their status, the lash was rarely used on Bengal sepoys. British officers were convinced that the character of their high-caste recruits would be broken if corporal punishment was used too frequently—a sensitivity noticeably lacking in their treatment of Madras and Bombay sepoys, not to mention the British rank and file.[19] The British preoccupation with caste in the Bengal Army, and their willingness to sanction rituals and traditions, provided opportunities for recruits in the Bengal Army to turn this British obsession to their own advantage. Caste, in fact, was being reworked such that these recruits were able to claim enhanced status on account of the British assumption that caste practices were not only timeless but central to the social and religious life of North India. Critics of the Bengal Army certainly believed that this was the case, and spoke harshly of just how completely the army had been seduced by high-caste rituals. Brigadier John Jacob, in one of his more scathing denunciations of the Bengal Army, complained that "In the Bengal army there is a constant studying of men's castes, which the Europeans appear to think as much of, and to esteem as highly, as do the natives themselves; and the sepoys, instead of looking on the European officers as superior beings, are compelled to consider them as bad Hindoos!"[20]

The situation in the Madras and Bombay armies was quite different, though they too initially depended on precolonial military practices and formations for recruits. There was not the same slavish devotion to restrictive recruitment in Madras, though caste had been used in the eighteenth century to identify the best recruits but with less consistency than had been the case in Bengal. The constant warfare in which the Madras Army found itself required a constant supply of manpower that could be obtained only by relaxing recruiting standards. Moreover, the Madras Army operated in a region in which linguistic and religious differences appeared to be more significant than caste, and into which many soldiers from the north had migrated in search of employment. The few surviving lists and reports on recruiting tend to categorize on the basis of "country" rather than caste. Yet the Madras Army never completely opened itself up to all prospective recruits. The British initially showed a marked preference for recruits of Turkish and Arabian descent.[21] This bias was due in part to the tendency of such recruits to be taller than average; a similar emphasis on physical characteristics helps account for the Bengal Army's favoring of Brahmins and Rajputs from Awadh, and would later figure in the idealization of Punjabis. Efforts were made in the late eighteenth century to prohibit the employment of Telugu-speakers from the Circars, a community then thought to be insufficiently warlike. This attempt failed and Telugus formed a large part of the army. Their reputation as nonmartial died out at least for the first half of the nineteenth century. But the lowest castes were discouraged from joining the army—following the Vellore mutiny of 1806, orders were issued prohibiting the recruitment of untouchables.[22] Officers in the Madras establishment may not have had the opportunity to develop the same prejudices as their counterparts in Bengal, but they were just as committed to keeping the army free from the lowest castes.

The Bombay Army was not only the most diverse of the three armies, but also the most tolerant of lower-caste recruits. It had little choice; historically it had proven difficult to raise troops from its heartland, aside from the Konkan, and it therefore had to make its regiments out of whoever could be recruited from their own territories and from further afield. Eventually the Bombay Army would incorporate into its ranks a very diverse range of peoples, including Africans, Bene Jews, and Arabs. A significant proportion of its recruits in the early nineteenth century were drawn from the Mahars, a very numerous low-caste community in Maharashtra who had traditionally served a variety of menial roles within local villages. But in the 1600s, considerable numbers of Mahars, despite their lowly status, found service in Sivaji's army, and future generations looked to the military for employment and as a means of securing upward mobility. They would by the early nineteenth century comprise upwards of a quarter of the Bombay Army, and were quite likely the largest single group of low-caste recruits.[23] Only the most depressed castes, such as scavengers, sweepers, and hangmen, were excluded.

British fascination with military ethnography became even more evident in the 1830s when articles began to appear in the military press detailing the various communities in India and their suitability for military service. This curiosity can be seen in the training received by officers destined for India. The first issue of a magazine established at the East India Company's military seminary at Addiscombe contained a number of articles on different peoples—including, rather oddly, one on the "esquimaux" [eskimo].[24] In India, a similar fascination with India's cultural composition was apparent in the magazines and newspapers intended for officers serving there. One article, originally written in or about 1809, insisted that in the eighteenth century, the population of Bengal was much more warlike and hence made better soldiers, and that by the 1780s, one-third to one-half of the Bengal Army consisted of the sons of landlords or zamindars. But the same author also noted the malleability of caste identities, claiming that "For instance, a Bramin subadar whose original name was Jei-gopaul, on enlisting took the name of Gopaul Singh, enrolling himself as a Rajhpoot; this is universally practised all over the native army."[25] Another article reiterated the importance of using caste as the basis for recruiting, identifying Rajputs and some Brahmins as being the most appropriate Hindu castes for military service, while "Moguls" and "Pathans" are to be preferred amongst the Muslims. But readers are cautioned that "in entertaining Mussulman recruits, the chief attention is to be directed to their being of decent respectable families, and that they have not been employed in any menial or degrading occupation."[26] Hence, character, whether grounded in caste or class, was of great concern. So too was the need to ensure that recruits had an appropriate pedigree. A similar theme emerged in another article, which registered a warning that many Muslim sepoys are either "the descendants of foreign adventurers or the offspring of low caste Hindoo prostitutes." The author was clearly alarmed that because no new noble Central Asian blood was being introduced, Muslims were seen as degenerating, whereas the Hindus, because of their division into closed-off castes, were able to preserve their qualities.[27]

A key argument underpinning explanations as to why some recruits were better than others lay in the widespread conviction that environment shapes social formation. The eighteenth-century chronicler of the British conquest of India, Robert Orme, noted in his *Historical Fragments* that environment determined who were more or less martial. In particular, he argued that recruits from areas of wheat production made better soldiers than those from rice-producing zones because they were better built. For Orme, caste was a structure that had emerged to vouchsafe differences produced by climate.[28] Climatological arguments insisted that conditions in the north produced hardier soldiers: such convictions would later be extended as part of the justification for the emphasis on the Punjab as a principle source for military recruits. It was widely believed that the effeminacy of males, and particularly Bengalis, was due to climatic and environmental conditions. The land was too luxuriant and fertile, and hence there was no need to struggle. General Sir O'Moore Creagh, Commander-in-Chief in the years immediately before the First World War, stated the climatological position very starkly, "In the hot, flat regions, of which by far the greater part of India consists...are found races, timid both by religion and habit, servile to their superiors, but tyrannical to their inferiors, and quite unwarlike."[29]

This emphasis on climate and environment frequently overlapped with a conviction that the best soldiers could also claim Aryan roots.[30] Eighteenth-century philologists had identified linguistic links between Sanskrit and European languages, which suggested to them a common, though very distant, Aryan origin. The utility of the Aryan theory for British commentators is that it not only helped to justify the alleged military superiority of the peoples of northern India over the non-Aryan peoples of the south, but it could also be turned around to explain the northerner's inferiority to the British, for while they shared a distant Aryan heritage, climate and intermarriage over the centuries had diluted the Aryan bloodlines in India.

Officers in the Bengal Army took great pride in the fact that their recruits were gathered from the "Brahmin and Rajpoot Yeomanry of the Upper Provinces," a class of individuals ranked as the "middle order of the agricultural classes."[31] The description of these sepoys as north India's yeomanry clearly indicates British biases for these sepoys were presented in romanticized terms strikingly similar to those used on Scottish Highlanders, another popularly identified martial race. Both groups were depicted as sturdy independent farmers, physically and morally well equipped to deal with the privations of military service. Bengal officers took great pride in what they saw as the more respectable character of their recruits. The more enthusiastic of them dismissed the idea that the Bengal sepoy was "a common mercenary," arguing instead that he was usually "a small landholder, who has an interest in good order and in the permanency of a government."[32] By imposing upon these communities British conceptions of martial qualities and rural society, the British also strengthened their own dominant position, for their officers had to be sufficiently strong in character to command the respect of these subjects. Such idealizations confirm the tendency of the British to frame India in medieval/quasi-feudal terms. Nowhere was this more evident than in contemporary treatments of the Rajputs as attested to by the writings of Colonel Tod.[33] The feudal-martial qualities of these communities were played up; loyalty was the product of a vassalage system, but it was also undercut by the persistence of feuds that necessitated the British presence to keep order. Medieval-feudal motifs informed ideas of loyalty by stressing personal fealty and obligation. It is then no wonder that MacMunn idealized martial races as "the yeoman peasant, the grazier, and the landowner," or that an earlier commentator declared that "Infantry best succeeds among a people with robust bodies and obstinate minds; whereas the Mahrattas are the most subtle of nations, and the most delicately formed."[34]

A further reason for this fixation on sturdy and independent farmers, as hinted at in the last quote, was that such individuals were thought to be less quick-witted, and therefore less likely to question their place in society. Stereotypes abound of the limited imagination and mental dullness of the typical recruit from the martial races. Contemporary British assessments of their mental facilities were characteristically blunt and derogatory; one officer declared that "the Jat [while physically the best in India] is a stupid credulous fellow."[35] Provided that such individuals were protected from wily intrigues, they were viewed as a critical bulwark against the emerging middle class, whose educational attainments and political aspirations underpinned the nationalist movement of the late nineteenth and early twentieth centuries. This can be correlated with the generally lower levels of education in those regions from whence recruits were drawn: literacy rates, as far as can be deduced from nineteenth-century data, were lower in the Punjab and the northern hills than in India as a whole.

The enthusiasm with which officers viewed their high-caste recruits notwithstanding, there were dissenting voices, mostly outside the Bengal Army but some within as well, who not only questioned its obsession with caste, but feared that its perpetuation meant that the army had in effect become the prisoner of its high-caste sepoys. The Bengal Army's regulations in force in 1855 tacitly acknowledged these concerns, concluding that "It is not considered desirable to have too large a proportion of Brahmins in any regiment, but in other respects commanding officers, when enlisting Hindoos of the respectable classes, are not to be biased in favour of any particular religion or caste," but then went on to qualify these recommendations, by advising that "special care, however, must be taken to reject all men of the inferior castes," and to list a number of examples of those groups who should be rejected.[36] Whatever unease was felt regarding the monopoly of the higher castes in the Bengal Army was ultimately tempered by a long-standing belief that these individuals most closely approximated the ideal recruit on account of their manliness, sense of honor, and codes of conduct. Such beliefs would be blown apart by the outbreak of the Rebellion in 1857.

Martial Race Theories in the Aftermath of the Rebellion of 1857–58

Historians have quite rightly fastened on to the Rebellion of 1857–58 as forming a watershed in British attitudes towards India. This was particularly apparent in the reconfiguration of racial attitudes, for it is not too much of an exaggeration to claim that the rebellion took on many of the attributes of a race war. The existing composition of the Bengal Army was not only found wanting, but there was an urgent need to rebuild British forces in northern India to forestall any further outbreaks. A royal commission, often labeled the Peel Commission as it was chaired by Lieutenant-General Jonathon Peel, the Secretary of State for war in 1858, was struck to provide recommendations as to the future organization and composition of the Bengal Army.[37] The challenge it faced, however, was that while most commentators were quick to find fault with the recruiting policies of the Bengal Army, and in particular its dependence on high-caste recruits, there was little consensus as to the solution, either among officers in general or those interviewed by the Peel Commission.

Broadly speaking, the evidence collected by this commission and reflected in their report points to the existence of three schools of thought. The first eschewed racial or caste taxonomies, preferring instead to take whoever wished to join provided they had the ability. It took a particularly dim view of the high-caste prejudices of the Bengal Army, which had landed the British in this mess. But it was not willing to discount entirely the communities from which recruits had previously been drawn—instead, these critics objected to the monopoly enjoyed by such recruits as well as their officers' willingness to concede to them too much autonomy and independence as far as caste requirements were concerned. Their position rested upon two different principles—the first was that, ultimately, the quality of the soldier relied upon the quality of his officer. The second, which would continue to resonate for years to come, was that the internal security needs of the British in India were best guaranteed by balancing different communities against each other. In other words, divide-and-rule was the best strategy, and this could best be achieved by having different communities, and ultimately different armies, serve as counterweights to each other. Another group of officers' opinions can be grouped together on the basis of their identifying specific communities who should be excluded from military service; though they did not always agree precisely on whom, they generally concurred that the traditional high-caste recruits from Awadh ought to be avoided in the future. There remained, however, a lingering opposition to taking soldiers from the lowest castes. The third camp contained those officers with decided opinions as to who should be recruited, in some cases going so far as to advocate the use of recruits from outside India (Africa, Southeast Asia, or even further afield). Their views come closest to those that would later become associated with the theory of martial races, for they were less concerned with divide-and-rule, and they believed that martial qualities were not so much the product of discipline and good officers but were inherent to certain "races" (however ill-defined race was in practice).

Samples of the evidence collected by the Peel Commission reveal just how divided contemporary opinions were. Colin Campbell, the Commander-in-Chief during and after the Rebellion, in his written submission to the commission, advised against selective recruitment and urged the commission to support as broadly based a recruiting strategy as possible.[38] George Clerk, onetime lieutenant-governor of the Northwest Provinces and later governor of Bombay, believed that the British should not turn their back completely on recruits from Awadh. When asked whether more Sikhs and Gurkhas should be introduced, he was decidedly opposed to the suggestion. When approached by a subsequent Committee of Enquiry, he maintained this same position and stressed the importance of recruiting from the more martial of local communities, as it was an important means of livelihood for so many of them.

The Marquis of Tweeddale, on the other hand, reminded the commission that "We commenced the conquest of India with low-caste men; and our experience of the Madras and Bombay armies has proved them to be faithful soldiers to the British Government." Other officers, such as James Outram, recommended rebuilding the Bengal Army exclusively around irregular regiments, and leaving the only regular sepoy regiments in Madras and Bombay as a reward for their loyalty. The Bombay Army was more problematic; while it did not flare up into open rebellion, there were ominous signs of insurrection, attributed to the practice in that presidency of relying upon recruits from northern India. The fact that the Bombay Army had difficulties in reducing the inflow of recruits from northern India even after the Rebellion would later fuel the arguments of those who wished to merge all the presidency armies into one. There was even talk of bringing in foreign mercenaries.

The Peel Commission trimmed and tacked and came down precisely in the middle. It concluded that "the Native Army should be composed of different nationalities and castes, and as a general rule, mixed promiscuously through each regiment."[39] It did not spell out precisely who should or should not be brought into the Indian Army, emphasizing instead that in order to protect against a repeat of 1857, the British needed to ensure that they could play different communities against each other. In the aftermath of the Indian Rebellion, the means to do so were at hand. The Madras and Bombay armies were largely intact, and together they counterbalanced the Bengal Army, which had become more diverse on account of the numbers of Sikhs and Punjabi Muslims that had been taken up in 1857–58. Some units of the old Bengal Army had not broken into revolt, and these in turn would be a counterweight to sepoys from the Punjab. The higher castes no longer had a monopoly, but the idea of an army based exclusively on discrete martial races had not yet arrived. But racial thinking was clearly influencing decision making. As evidence of this, the Adjutant General of the army forcefully argued against admitting Eurasians into the army, for "as a class or rather a race, neither their habits nor their physique are suited to service in our army."[40]

Within the context of these guidelines, discussions came to focus on where the mixing should occur. In other words, should recruits from different backgrounds be mixed together in the same regiment, or should regiments be relatively homogenous but offset by regiments drawn from other communities? The former model became known as the class company system and reflected preoccupations with loyalty and discipline; for in its purest form, the class company model advocated that each regiment comprise three companies, each of which would be drawn from a different community. Critics of the model, however, warned that bringing different communities too close together ran the risk that "class feeling and esprit de corps would become stronger than natural race antagonism."[41] In the end, many of the regiments of the Bengal Army tended to be more internally homogenous than was recommended by champions of the class company system.

As discussions continued as to the right mix of recruits, the numbers of sepoys taken from the Punjab grew. But as the research of Tan Tai Yong has convincingly shown, Punjabis were drawn in "not so much to replace but to balance the Hindustanis."[42] Not all officers at this point were convinced that the Punjab ought to be the principal recruiting ground; some officers worried that the British were merely replacing one dependency for another, which could prove to be just as dangerous. Officers such as Herbert Edwardes, while quick to praise the contribution of Sikhs to the suppression of the rebellion, warned against remilitarizing the Punjab, should the British focus too much of their effort on the province: "It is quite sufficient to draw on the Sikhs, the border Pathans, and other martial races of the Punjab, for as many soldiers as we actually require to keep up the balance of races in our new native army in India, without turning whole races once more into soldiers by profession."[43] Even as late as 1875, Punjabis of all denominations formed just over a quarter of the Bengal Army.

It is apparent from the tone and language of many of these discussions that a critical element in Victorian thinking about martial races was that of masculinity— whether commentators discussed the physical qualities of prospective recruits, or whether the recruits' moral character had come under scrutiny. Tellingly, the novelist and essayist, Nirad Chaudhuri, would describe the martial races as "an insulated body of manhood in the midst of a thoroughly disarmed and emasculated population."[44] While masculinity was never absent from colonial discourse, it took on a more urgent tone in the aftermath of the Indian Rebellion. The rebellion came to be understood within sharp dichotomous terms, with gender being one of the more critical framing devices. The rebels, by virtue of their attacks on women and children (whether real or imagined), were depicted as brutal, vicious and sneaky—attributes that were distinctly at odds with the idealized manly virtues exhibited by the British soldiers sent to restore order, and that through association were extended to those Indian troops who remained loyal, particularly the Sikhs and Gurkhas, whose outward appearances so easily fired domestic imaginations. As a recent scholar has noted, "Virility was a metaphor for political power and sociomoral strength; a metaphor that mixed together elements of masculine psychology and colonial ideology."[45] According to MacMunn, nonmartial races could be characterized as those whose virility had been sapped by "early marriage, premature brides, and juvenile eroticism."[46] The growing influence of social Darwinism, with its emphasis on moral and national fitness, clearly had an impact. Captain H. W. L. Hime, the gold medalist of the Royal United Service Institution in 1875, argued in his winning essay, "Natural Selection in War," that the "law of Natural Selection is the law of victory."[47]

Imperial Strategy and the Crystallization of Martial Race Theory

The catalyst that ensured that this growing propensity to tie more closely together military efficiency and colonial ethnography came in the 1880s with a shifting set of strategic priorities. Beforehand, the discipline and organization of the Indian Army had largely been conditioned by concerns for the internal security of colonial India. This preoccupation underpins the divide-and-rule practices that had resulted in the decision to maintain three distinct armies and to ensure that within each of these armies no single group predominated. Developments in Asia, more particularly apprehensions that Russia posed a serious threat to British interests in the region, persuaded policy makers that external security urgently needed to be addressed. Commanders in chief of the Indian Army, like Roberts and Kitchener, looked beyond India's frontiers as likely theaters of action and wanted to transform the Indian Army from a colonial gendarmerie into a more easily deployable force, sufficient to defend Britain's investments throughout the region. They and others insisted that recruitment could no longer be determined primarily by internal security concerns, but that the British should instead recruit only the best soldiers; otherwise, the Indian Army would be unable to contend with an army as powerful as that of Russia. Roberts pressed this argument vigorously, writing in his autobiography that "Great Britain now occupies in Asia the position of a Continental Power, and that her interests in that part of the globe must be protected by Continental means of defence."[48] Once that became the operating principle, the idea that somehow certain groups in India were more martial, which had long been bubbling away, broke through to the surface and received official imprimatur. Not only was it argued that recruiting had to become more selective, and more focused on those communities that had proven their warlike mettle, but the case was also made that military efficiency was being hamstrung by the continued existence of the Madras and Bombay armies, for the efficiency of their regiments had deteriorated. While both of these armies were not without their defenders, the fact that neither had seen much action, and that both had become backwaters that ambitious officers avoided, meant that their protests did not make much of an impact.

Advocates of an army based more exclusively on the martial races of northwest India, to which they added the Gurkhas, bolstered their case with references to the report of a Parliamentary Commission of 1879, which had concluded that while the system of having separate presidential armies had served the British well by creating a series of watertight compartments, this had been achieved only at the cost of military efficiency. To render the army more efficient and hence more useful to wider imperial objectives, in particular the threats seen to be building along the northwest frontier, the least warlike elements within the army had to be replaced by more virile warriors. To improve the efficiency of the army, Roberts insisted that "the first step to be taken towards this end was, it seemed to me, to substitute men of the more warlike and hardy races for the Hindustani sepoys of Bengal, the Tamils and Telugus of Madras, and the so-called Mahrattas of Bombay." Of the Madras Army, and the sepoys which comprised it, Roberts speculated that "long years of peace, and the security and prosperity attending it, had evidently had upon them, as they always seem to have on Asiatics, a softening and deteriorating effect; and I was forced to the conclusion that the ancient military spirit had died in them, as it had died in the ordinary Hindustani of Bengal and the Mahratta of Bombay, and that they could no longer with safety be pitted against warlike races, or employed outside the limits of southern India."[49]

While the government did not go so far as to recommend that recruits from southern and western India be done away with completely, which Roberts had advocated, their numbers would be reduced and recruiting would be confined to a select number of communities. Eventually, however, in 1892, the Government of India successfully persuaded the Secretary of State for India to give permission to do away with the last vestiges of the presidential system and merge the three armies into one. In making the case for this change, the Government of India urged that henceforth the army should have a preponderance of recruits from northern India, in particular "Pathans, Baluchis, Sikhs and Punjabi Mahomedans, with a certain number of Gurkhas."[50] These troops were to form the "fighting edge" of the army; the rest would serve to garrison southern, western and eastern India. But their argument that only martial races should serve in the Indian Army failed to carry the government completely. In his reply to the Government of India, the Secretary of State revived the old divide-and-rule arguments. He reminded the Government of India that "it is scarcely less important that the reserve, and the troops which will remain in garrison, should be a loyal and contented body, efficient and capable of maintaining internal order, and repressing the various elements of discord and sedition, which, in the event of a war beyond the frontier, might be fomented in our own territories."[51] This led Roberts to lament that he "found it difficult to get my views accepted, because of the theory which prevailed that it was necessary to maintain an equilibrium between the armies of the three Presidencies, and because of the ignorance that was only too universal with respect to the characteristics of the different races, which encouraged the erroneous belief that one Native was as good as another for the purposes of war."[52] Yet the pressure on the India Office to concede to the demands for a single Indian Army, based on a narrowly defined range of martial races, continued, and by 1900 over half the recruits for the entire Indian Army came from the Punjab, up from about one-quarter in 1875. And 60 percent of the nearly 700,000 recruits who joined the Indian Army in World War I came from the Punjab.

In reaching his conclusions as to the relative merits of various Indian communities, Roberts was clearly influenced, at least in part, by his concerns for military efficiency, and by his experience as onetime Commander-in-Chief of the Madras Army, an army that he quickly came to disparage. But Roberts's opinions cannot be reduced simply to empirical evidence and experience; racial attitudes as well as his own ambitions came into play.[53] His logic did not allow him to conceive of Indian troops as ever being the equal of British troops, for "I have known many Natives whose gallantry and devotion could not be surpassed, but I have never known one who would not have looked to the youngest British officer for support in times of difficulty and danger."[54] Nor was Roberts the detached professional that his champions portrayed him to be. Intensely ambitious and extremely political, he played the media in order to advance his own interests, which depended on raising the profile of the Indian Army and impressing decision makers in Britain with the efficiency and effectiveness of the army under his command. This he pursued by placing himself at the head of an army whose warlike qualities reflected favorably on those officers strong enough to earn its respect.

Martial Races and the Punjab

If the route from an army of high-caste sepoys to one built around martial races was neither as smooth or as predetermined as some of the rhetoric might suggest, by the end of the nineteenth century the Indian Army had become undeniably associated with the Punjab, and that region of India was most affected by the idea of a martial race. Concerns that the British were only exchanging one dependency for another had become much more muted, and the virtues of the mainly Sikh and Muslim sepoys of the Punjab had become widely accepted. In explaining this fixation on the Punjab, much has been made of their willingness to serve alongside the British in the suppression of the Indian Rebellion. Physical characteristics were also important: these recruits tended to be taller and larger framed than males elsewhere in India. But of equal importance was the fact that many of the communities singled out in the Punjab by British recruiters had long-standing military traditions that could be exploited. The militarization of Punjabi society is largely explained by its strategic location. Prone to frequent invasion, this region epitomized many of the characteristics of a frontier zone, lying between the states of Central Asia and precolonial empires anchored in Delhi. Rural society was constantly pressured, and it developed a militarized ethos that not only was intended to protect the struggling polities in the region, but also came to be associated with the defense of the Sikh faith against Mughal attacks. The welding together of many of these polities under the rule of Maharaja Ranjit Singh at the beginning of the nineteenth century established many of the region's social and political characteristics, which made the province such a powerful foe to the British (two wars were fought in the 1840s, culminating in the annexation of the region in 1849) but also created the conditions that made it such a useful military labor market. Ranjit Singh raised well-trained armies, disciplined and equipped in European fashion; and owing to their historic rivalry with soldiers from the Gangetic heartland, the remnants of his armies were less likely to identify with them.

Yet as already noted, annexation did not immediately lead to the area becoming a favored recruiting ground; instead, British officials initially leaned towards demilitarization. They looked to the economic potential of the region, not to its role as a recruiting pool. Major-General Mansfield, chief of staff of the Army in India, was wary of the Sikhs, arguing that while the British could momentarily gain by tapping into the "esprit de corps of the old Khalsa Army," their willingness to serve was motivated more by a desire for revenge over the Hindustani troops that had conquered the region than by any good feeling towards the British.[55] Officers in the Bengal Army doubted whether the Sikhs would make loyal soldiers, and were apprehensive that their religious beliefs coupled with the resentment over their recent defeat rendered them suspect. Lord Dalhousie, Governor-General before the 1857–58 Rebellion, and John Lawrence, viceroy after the rebellion, were both very reluctant to draw too heavily upon them. So too was Charles Wood, the Secretary of State for India in 1862, who opined,

> Heretofore you have held the Sikhs in subjection by the aid of the sepoys, and the sepoys by means of the Sikhs. But so what is happening now—the Sikh soldiers are quartered all over India. They are fraternizing with the natives of the south—adopting their customs and even their faiths. Half the soldiers in a regiment lately stationed at Benares were converted to Hindooism before they left that holy place. Beware, or you will shortly have to cope in India with a hostile combination more formidable than any of those which you have encountered before.[56]

Even the urgent need for manpower in the suppression of the Indian Rebellion of 1857–58 only produced what many contemporaries thought and in some cases hoped would be at most a temporary draw on the region.

Such reservations were eclipsed by the rising chorus of officers who were convinced that the Punjab was the most fertile area from which soldiers could be drawn. But upon closer scrutiny, it was not the Punjab per se which was favored: instead, particular communities and districts were singled out. Sikhs sui generis were not targeted as much as Sikhs from a particular area around Amritsar and Lahore, while Muslims were sought from the western Punjab and avoided elsewhere.[57] Recruiting depots were set up with such groups in mind. In 1891, they were established at Peshawar for Pathans, Rawalpindi for Punjabi Muslims, and Amritsar for Sikhs, while Jullunder and Delhi served as centers for Dogra and Jat recruits respectively. Dogras and Jats were agricultural castes designated as sufficiently manly for recruitment, and many Sikh pedigrees could be traced back to these groups. There were two reasons for this localization of recruitment: they helped to create self-reinforcing characteristics, as officers tried to encourage customary and cultural commonalities among their soldiers; and focused recruiting allowed local authority and status to become replicated in the regiments. Localization also met the lingering political purposes of divide-and-rule, though in a more restricted setting, for it helped to perpetuate the social and ethnic divisions that prevailed in the Punjab, thereby discouraging the growth of a wider pan-Punjabi identity.

Noticeably absent from this list of prospective recruits were urban dwellers and the most menial castes. Somewhat of an exception was made in the case of the Mazhbis, originally low-caste sweepers or Chamars (also leatherworkers), who had converted to Sikhism and had been recruited by both Ranjit Singh and the British. However, the history of their military service shows considerable ambivalence over their rights to military service, thereby demonstrating that the linkage between martial qualities and the Sikh faith was itself heavily qualified by notions of status. In the half-century before the British conquest of the Punjab, they featured in Ranjit Singh's army, though they were collected together into separate units as higher-caste Sikhs had refused to serve alongside them. The need for troops during the Rebellion of 1857–58 led the British to raise three regiments of Sikh Pioneer regiments, and for these they turned to the Mazhbis. But the Mazhbis could not overcome the extent to which caste and class impinged on definitions of martial race, and while they were never marginalized as completely as other lower castes who could point to a tradition of military service, such as the Mahars, their numbers did fall, only rising during times of intense demand such as that of the First World War.

The agrarian foundations of these peasant soldiers were ensured by government actions intended to prevent a capitalist transformation of the Punjab economy. Legislation was passed designed to protect the agricultural holdings of those communities from whom they recruited from passing into the hands of moneylenders and outsiders. The 1900 Land Alienation Act declared that land could not be transferred to nonagricultural classes, a decision fundamentally rooted in the fear that these communities needed a buffer from the kinds of destabilizing influences that could accrue should non-Punjabi merchants and moneylenders gain a foothold. Other examples of government intervention were introduced so as to retain the tacit loyalty of these communities. Investment in irrigation was much more widespread in the Punjab than elsewhere, and long-service sepoys were entitled to land grants intended to reward them for their loyalty. Interestingly, one of the reasons advanced by the Government of India not to declare the use of opium illegal in British India was the "deep root the habit has taken amongst the more martial races of the community of the north of India."[58] In seeking to perpetuate a rural way of life deemed to be integral to these martial communities, the colonial state, despite its oft-quoted commitment to social reform, went so far as to force Jat widows, against their will, into remarriages with their brothers-in-law so as to keep family landholdings intact.[59] And finally, under the terms of the Government of India Act of 1919, political authority in the Punjab was placed primarily in the hands of those the British could most trust. All soldiers, for example, were given the vote.

The increasing monopoly over military service by a select few groups was not only criticized by some British officers, but it was also resented by those communities who were excluded from military service. Their desire to serve was due partly to the same economic incentives that attracted Sikhs and Punjabi Muslims, and this desire was particularly felt by those communities working marginal lands for whom incomes remitted by soldiers would have greatly aided their extended family networks. But it was not simply material needs that prospective recruits sought; military service also carried with it the possibility of enhanced status and prestige. Being declared a martial race denoted masculinity qualities, honor and respectability, which were particularly sought by low-caste groups eager to rise up the social and economic ladder. It is therefore not surprising that many groups petitioned the government to be reclassified as martial races and therefore entitled to join the Indian Army. Some went even further and took to the courts to secure those rights. An interesting example of the politics of martial identities is offered by the Mahars who, as noted earlier, were well-represented in the Bombay Army despite their low-caste origins. But after 1857 they were declared to be a nonmartial community, and their numbers began to dwindle, with recruitment ending in 1893. This caused considerable resentment as many Mahars had secured upward mobility through military service, gaining status and education as well as income. Their efforts to have this decision rescinded were unsuccessful, and while there was a brief relaxation of the rules in World War I because of the pressing demand for manpower, the Mahars were never able to regain the status they once enjoyed under the British. They even pitched their case in terms familiar to the British; that is, they defended their claims to a place in the army not on the basis of precedence, but rather by insisting that they were actually of Kshatriya origins (the second-highest, or warrior caste).[60] Jotirao Phule, who led a low-caste protest in Maharashtra, argued that Brahmins had infiltrated southern and western India, stripping the cultivators of their historic rights and status, and by labeling them low-caste had denied to them the possibility of military service that they had previously enjoyed.[61] This struggle by the Mahars to assert their claims to the status of a martial race would be taken up by Dr. B.R. Ambedkar, the famed leader of the untouchables in their struggles against both the British and the Indian National Congress.

Conclusion

The idea that the population of India could be separated into martial and non-martial races was a defining characteristic of the Victorian Empire. While it was never as complete or stable as some have suggested, it nevertheless played a powerful role in identifying who should serve in the Indian Army and why, and in terms legible within the cultural characteristics of the Raj. A correspondent of the *Times* reminded his readers that the Indian Army was much more than simply a military tool to be used to defend the empire: it is "one of the most valuable links between the ruling and the subject races" and provides as proof of this that "it has been our good fortune to win over successively to our service all the finest and most martial races of India."[62]

Martial race theory not only characterized the popular image of the army of the Raj, but it would in turn inform the postindependence military cultures of India and Pakistan, where so-called martial races continue to populate the ranks of their armies, leaving a colonial legacy that, in the case of Pakistan, has frustrated the development of a stable and durable civil society. In Pakistan, statistics collected from the 1980s show that three-quarters of the army was recruited from three districts in the Punjab and two from the Northwest Frontier province, districts that between them amount only to approximately 9 percent of the population.[63] Today, there are more Sikhs in the Indian Army than Muslims, though Sikhs make up less than 4 percent of the Indian population while Muslims in India are at nearly 12 percent.[64] This overrepresentation of Sikhs caused considerable alarm in the 1980s when movements for an independent Sikh state, or Khalistan, threatened to unsettle the foundations of military discipline. Ultimately, martial race theory provides one of the best proofs of just how resilient colonial structures and ideologies can be.

"The Greatest Training Ground in the World": The Army in India and the North-West Frontier, 1901–1947

Tim Moreman

Between 1901 and 1947, the independent Pathan inhabitants of the mountainous "No Man's Land" located between the administered areas of the North-West Frontier Province (NWFP) and Afghanistan posed an insistent threat to British India's security.[1] In many respects this local and immediate problem of tribal control overshadowed the far more remote and waxing and waning threat of war with Afghanistan or Imperial Russia/the USSR, on this the most sensitive strategic frontier of the British Empire. It tied down large numbers of British and Indian troops in a long series of inconclusive skirmishes and major campaigns. To generations of soldiers, what was known as alternatively hill warfare, tribal warfare, mountain warfare, and most commonly as frontier warfare was the most prevalent form of actual war fighting they encountered during normal "peacetime" service.[2] Indeed, it was not an unwelcome experience for many, providing a refreshing break from humdrum life in downcountry Indian cantonments, an opportunity to win promotion and gain practical experience of "real soldiering" under active service conditions "in the greatest training ground in the world" with comparatively small risk to life and limb. This chapter briefly charts the changing characteristics and lessons learned about frontier operations, caused by improving tribal military effectiveness and changes in the organization, equipment and training of imperial troops. In particular, it demonstrates how the lessons learned by the Army in India during these operations were passed on to successive generations of officers and men in the form of official specialized training manuals and systems of instruction.

The Army in India and the North-West Frontier

Following the annexation of the Punjab in 1849, the new British administration was first brought into direct contact with the heavily armed trans-border Pathan tribes, who repeatedly raided lowland areas and attacked trading caravans. A localized armed force was quickly raised specifically to protect the trans-Indus areas—the Punjab Irregular Force (PIF)—that quickly learned, during a long series of "butcher and bolt" punitive military expeditions, that fighting in mountainous terrain against tribal *lashkars* (war parties) posed difficulties very different from those encountered in conventional warfare. When operating in tribal territory, Indian troops were tied to protecting long, vulnerable, and cumbersome columns of pack transport, carrying food, water, and ammunition on which they depended in the barren hills. Freedom of movement was restricted to the valley floors, while lightly equipped opposing tribesmen operated with comparative freedom on the hillsides. A lack of reliable intelligence and maps made it difficult to select suitable objectives, while the difficult climate and endemic local diseases often inflicted heavier casualties than the enemy. On the other hand, Pathan tribesmen were well acquainted with the intrinsic difficulties of fighting in their native mountains, matching their relative strengths of mobility, flexibility, and superior marksmanship in elusive guerrilla warfare against cumbrous Indian columns.

By trial and error, the PIF evolved a series of specialized principles and minor tactics tailored to local conditions in tribal territory. To meet the tribesmen on equal terms, its infantry regiments deliberately emphasized light infantry skills—skirmishing, skill-at-arms, marksmanship, self-reliance, and fieldcraft—modeled on those of their opponents during training. Mountain artillery batteries were also raised, equipped with light ordnance capable of being transported into the hills on muleback. When operating in tribal territory, the heart of the tactical problem for the British and Indian troops lay in successfully bringing the tribesmen to battle and preventing their harassment of the cumbrous self-contained main body of imperial

March through tribal territory (Tim Moreman Collection)

columns. Offensive tactics were emphasized at all stages of a campaign to bring the enemy to battle and to demoralize tribal opposition. Since this often proved impossible, recourse was made to the destruction of villages, orchards, and crops as a means of exacting collective punishment. It was quickly discovered that the key to success lay in controlling the flanking high ground and dominating the surrounding terrain by fire. Outlying piquets, detachments normally of platoon strength, shielded vulnerable British columns as they moved by "crowning the heights" on either side of the route of march, withdrawing to rejoin the main body only when it had passed by. Initially, the short range of Pathan firearms (300 yards) meant that piquets were seldom overlooked by other positions within effective range and were secure except from direct assault. The evacuation of a piquet was often, however, the point of greatest danger when tribesmen normally seized the vacant position and attacked its retreating garrison. To prevent successful attacks, the posting and withdrawal of piquets involved considerable skill and led to the development of elaborate codes and drills by the PIF. At night, encampments located on the valley floors would be surrounded in a similar manner by piquets intended to keep the tribesmen at arms' length. Elaborate field defenses, consisting of a perimeter wall constructed from rocks, stores, or bales of fodder, encompassed each camp to stop rushes by swordsmen, provide cover from sniping and shelter for sleeping troops, and prevent infiltration by rifle thieves. The withdrawal of the British and Indian columns represented the biggest tactical difficulty for any expedition. During this phase, tribal attacks on rearguards normally intensified, making their extraction under fire the greatest problem for commanders and necessitating the development of further tactical drills. The brutal treatment frequently meted out to British or Hindu dead and wounded by tribesmen exerted a powerful influence on hill warfare, necessitating immediate

Entrenched camp in tribal territory (Tim Moreman Collection)

rapid counterattacks to recover them as they could not be allowed to fall into enemy hands.

Those principles and minor tactics developed by the PIF—renamed the Punjab Frontier Force (PFF) in 1865—were a comparatively simple and pragmatic response to combat against an irregular tribal opponent. A combination of repeated practical experience and specialized training directed solely toward hill warfare made its units highly effective as guardians of the administrative border of the Punjab (later the NWFP), which they monopolized. Yet as the PFF was a localized force retained under the control of the Punjab Government rather than the military authorities until 1886, these methods were not passed on to the regular army in a coherent manner. Until regular troops were deployed in the Punjab for the first time in large numbers during the 1880s and 1890s, mountain warfare remained the prerogative of the frontier regiments and batteries. Following the 1897–98 Tirah campaign, in which British and Indian regulars suffered comparatively heavy casualties at tribal hands, a range of official specialized manuals for frontier warfare were produced, and appropriate training introduced, during the early 1900s. This was of particular importance when the PFF was finally delocalized in 1903 (greatly simplifying organizational problems caused by maintaining a specialized force) and made liable for service throughout India.

In 1908 this new approach to training for colonial warfare on the frontiers of India was thoroughly vindicated during the Zakka Khel and Mohmand punitive expeditions, when small, lightly equipped, and highly trained columns of regular troops inflicted heavy casualties on the opposing tribesmen. Nevertheless, in 1909 the specialized manuals promulgated following the 1897–98 campaigns were abandoned by the Indian military authorities when, in accordance with a decision made at the Imperial Defence Conference, the manual *Field Service Regulations* (*FSR*) was adopted as the basis of training for all the imperial armies. Henceforth British and Indian troops relied for guidance in frontier fighting on the general principles of war and six condensed paragraphs that provided only a bare outline of the specialized tactics required in tribal territory.[3] This important change in providing guidance, however, had no significant impact on the efficiency of the Army in India, which by 1914 contained large numbers of officers and men who had considerable experience and a long tradition of frontier fighting.

The Impact of the First World War and the 1919 Waziristan Campaign

The First World War quickly exposed the shortcomings of this approach to written doctrine and training for frontier fighting, when nearly all highly experienced prewar regulars were sent overseas. Their underofficered and poorly equipped replacements were far below the same standard of training in mountain warfare, causing serious concern to the military authorities as unrest spread in the hills. When British Territorial Army (TA) regiments were deployed in the NWFP, whose officers lacked any real military knowledge or training, the inherent limitations of relying solely on the principles of war and limited information contained in *FSR* to govern training were exposed. As a stopgap measure, a Mountain Warfare School opened in May 1916, using innovative teaching methods specifically to train cadres of TA officers and NCOs in frontier fighting, who in turn would instruct their own men. Despite this important development, a serious lack of uniformity was evident in applying the principles and minor tactics of mountain warfare during operations conducted by 1st (Peshawar) and 2nd (Rawalpindi) divisions in November 1916. A series of disastrous skirmishes in Waziristan during the spring further underlined the need for specialized training. On May 2, 1917, the GOC Northern Command warned that "If we employ troops inexperienced in hill warfare, it appears to me that incidents in the Gomal are likely to be repeated...To frontier warfare the second reserve is quite untrained."[4] Despite further efforts by the Mountain Warfare School during 1917–1918 to improve training, by the end of the First World War the efficiency of the border garrisons had plummeted far below prewar standards.

The short-lived Afghan invasion in May 1919, carried out by regular troops and tribesmen, forcibly reminded the Army in India that disturbances on and along the North-West Frontier still posed a serious threat to security. Although Afghan regulars were quickly repulsed the ensuing tribal rising in Waziristan (where various militias raised to police tribal territory had mutinied) was a far more difficult proposition (see map).[5] Heavy casualties were inflicted on the raw, ill-trained, and increasingly demoralized Indian troops comprising the Derajat Column when punitive operations were finally carried out. As imperial troops advanced into tribal territory every pass and hill feature was bitterly contested by Mahsud tribesmen, who inflicted an unprecedented number of casualties. Indeed, in the heaviest fighting ever witnessed in tribal territory imperial troops were nearly defeated at Palosina between December 19–21, 1919, by well-armed and trained Mahsud and Wazir *lashkars,* whose ranks included a significant number of ex-servicemen. Fire and movement was skilfully employed with deadly effect by tribesmen, who, whenever an opportunity offered, unhesitatingly engaged in desperate hand-to-hand combat. Writing on January 13, 1920, Major General Skipton Climo, GOC Waziristan Field Force, observed:

> It is, perhaps, to be expected that those who do not know India and the frontier, and even some who have fought on the frontier in pre-war days, but lack the knowledge and imagination to realise that conditions have altered with the great improvement of the armament of the tribesmen, cannot understand or believe the standard of training that is required for the Infantry in the conditions that now prevail on the Frontier to-day. To such, the belief is natural that the mere frontier tribes cannot be formidable opponents to modern troops nor can they believe that the standard of training or method of tactics that succeeded in the great war can, in former cases, be insufficient for and, in the latter cases, be inapplicable to a Frontier campaign.[6]

Large numbers of modern .303 Lee Enfield service rifles in tribal hands, with greater range, accuracy, and rate of fire than earlier small arms, transformed the fighting effectiveness of Pathan *lashkars.* It altered the characteristics of frontier warfare by slowing down every phase of operations and dramatically increased imperial casualties. In response a slow, deliberate and heavily contested advance, only 2–4 miles a day, was adopted as the Derajat Column advanced deeper into Waziristan. This sustained heavy fighting taught British officers that existing methods had to be adapted and new tactics developed to ensure victory. The latter included the widespread use of permanent piquets on all commanding positions within effective rifles range (1,000–1,500 yards) of a column, a fixed line of communications to service spiralling logistical requirements and the widespread use of night operations to nullify the effect of tribal riflemen. Despite deploying large numbers of men and support from modern aircraft, 3.7" pack howitzers and Lewis light machine guns, Waziristan Force had lost 366 dead, 1,683 wounded, and 237 men missing by the end of hostilities. This unprecedented "butchers bill" indicated that a new era had begun in frontier warfare. Henceforth all operations in tribal territory clearly had to be deliberate, governed by a fixed line of communication and carried out by large numbers of troops except where very light opposition was encountered.

The near disasters in Waziristan, and the fact that large numbers of regular troops were permanently deployed on the frontier following the Third Afghan War as part of the newly designated Covering Troops, convinced the Indian General Staff that it had to act quickly to restore the combat effectiveness of imperial troops. On February 1, 1920, the Mountain Warfare School reopened at Abbottabad to provide sufficient qualified trained instructors for imperial units. Under the command of Colonel William Villiers-Stuart, the school ran a series of courses during the spring, summer, and autumn of 1920. Each course began with an explanation of the basic principles of war—a deliberate attempt to avoid overspecialization—before introducing the modifications required in their application to "trans-border" warfare. Members of the Directing Staff emphasized the importance of individual skills—skill-at-arms, self-reliance, vigilance, and personal judgement—to overcome "transborder loneliness." Particular attention was directed toward the various tactical modifications and the lessons learned regarding the employment of modern equipment in mountain warfare during the recent fighting.[7] Although the Mountain Warfare School proved highly successful, the Army in India did not retain it as a permanent training establishment. At the end of the year, unit COs were made responsible for training under the direction of the staff of the higher formations to which they belonged. To assist them in training, the provision of an authoritative source of written guidance became pressing once again. It was clear that something more was needed than *FSR*, as the 1920 provisional edition still referred to "savage warfare" solely in terms of fighting against opponents reliant on shock tactics, and its small section on mountain warfare lacked the detail inexperienced junior officers and NCOs required. A small pamphlet was hurriedly prepared to fill this gap for units garrisoned in the NWFP and Baluchistan. Published in January 1921, with 15,000 copies issued, the pamphlet laid down general rules to conduct "uncivilized" warfare, as well as the general principles governing military operations against the transborder Pathan tribes for all three arms of service. It covered piqueting, protection on the march, protection of the lines of communication, camps and bivouacs, and

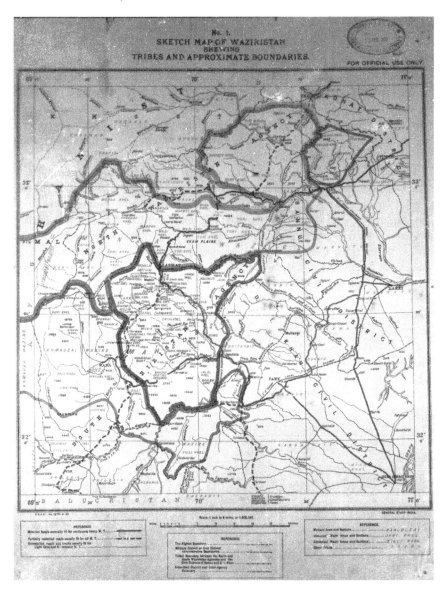

Tribal area of Waziristan (Tim Moreman Collection)

night operations. Moreover, it provided tentative guidance regarding the use of new equipment such as Lewis guns.[8] For units in action in Waziristan, the Wazirforce headquarters produced and distributed its own tactical notes tailored to conditions in that area.[9] Several unofficial textbooks discussing frontier fighting also appeared during the early 1920s, written by experienced Indian Army officers and complementing official sources.[10]

The low-intensity fighting that dragged on in Waziristan between 1920 and 1924, as a new Modified Forward Policy of road building and peaceful penetration of tribal territory was implemented, ensured many British and Indian units gained practical experience of mountain warfare. This, when combined with specialized instruction, meant that by 1924 most had reached a semblance of prewar standards. It also supplied further valuable practical experience about the capabilities and limitations of new equipment previously utilized only in small quantities on the North-West Frontier (aircraft, machine guns, motor transport, and modern mountain artillery). Many officers eagerly sought to use military technology originally developed on the Western Front. Employing poison gas was carefully investigated in 1919–20, for example, and tanks were tested in tribal territory with mixed success during the early 1920s. Due to the terrain, however, most heavy weapons and equipment could not be employed except on or near the growing network of roads built in Waziristan and the NWFP. Other factors worked against the use of more destructive types of military equipment. As Colonel Frederick Keen reminded readers of the *Journal of the United Service Institution of India* (*JUSII*) in 1923: "We should realise, as we have perhaps not done in the past, that in fighting the Pathans we are engaging in civil war and that it is to our advantage that enemies of to-day should be turned into our friends of to-morrow...In a word, our coercive measures should always be directed with a view to eventual pacification and control."[11] A combination of drastic cutbacks in the military budget and shortages of skilled Indian technical personnel effectively decided the issue by preventing the acquisition of large quantities of new arms and equipment. The RAF, moreover, turned to independent operations rather than cooperation with the army. As a result, the infantryman and pack mule still reigned supreme in frontier warfare.

Gurkha heliograph team (Tim Moreman Collection)

The need for authoritative up-to-date guidance in frontier fighting for imperial troops deployed in the NWFP remained pressing. Although the revised 1924 edition of *FSR* incorporated a chapter that addressed warfare in "undeveloped" and "semi-civilized countries," it was widely accepted that just relying on the general principles of war and a brief section on mountain warfare was an insufficient basis for training. Earlier pamphlets, moreover, needed far greater elaboration. In response, the lessons learned in Waziristan since 1919 were compiled at AHQ that year and incorporated in a new manual intended to complement *FSR* and the training manuals for the various arms of service.[12] The *Manual of Operations on the North-West Frontier of India*, published in 1925, reflected the important changes that had occurred in frontier warfare since the First World War. No fewer than 35,000 copies were printed, and by October 1925 it had been issued to units serving throughout India. Its pages reflected the Indian Army's extensive experience of frontier operations and updated the existing doctrine and system of training caused by improved tribal tactics, leadership, and equipment as well as changes in the organization, training, and equipment of imperial troops. It represented a significant improvement over sole reliance on *FSR* as the basis of all training, although it still discussed the conduct of mountain warfare with close reference to the principles of war. This manual included chapters describing the trans-border Pathans and tribal territory; fighting troops and their characteristics; protection on the march and when halted; the organization and protection of the lines of communication; the conduct of the attack and withdrawal for all three arms; and foraging and demolitions as well as administrative routine in camp and on the line of march. It emphasized the importance of appropriate training for all three arms of service, especially with regard to the development of individual skills of self-reliance, vigilance, and initiative to overcome the peculiar difficulties encountered when fighting in tribal territory. It discussed the use of the RAF in co-operation with columns, and it even covered the employment of tanks in hill warfare, although they were still unavailable in India.[13]

The Search for Mobility

The Army in India quickly settled down into the normal routine of peacetime service. Throughout the remainder of the interwar period, Indian regiments served a two-year tour out of every six in the Covering Troops' districts, allowing them to steadily accumulate a cadre of trained and experienced officers and men. By comparison, British infantry battalions served only an infrequent one-year tour of duty. While stationed in the border cantonments, all units trained intensively in mountain warfare based on the *Manual of Operations on the North-West Frontier of India,* supervised by the staff and senior officers of the formations to which they belonged. Standing Orders periodically issued by the formations permanently stationed in the NWFP provided a further source of guidance for both peacetime training and active service, amplifying points laid down in the official manual and taking into account local conditions at each station.[14] Those British and Indian units serving in the Field Army concentrated on conventional "open" warfare against a "second class enemy" during individual and collective training, into which each year was divided. The priority attached by the Army in India to training in mountain and open warfare, however, was a subject of considerable professional controversy between officers, whose attention focused on a likely conventional conflict, and those concerned with the day-to-day requirements of Indian defense. Many British service officers were highly critical of the specialized doctrine for "savage warfare" employed on the frontier, believing that the lesser was by default contained in the greater. Most Indian Army officers for whom frontier service formed such a large part of normal military experience, however, more readily appreciated its importance, given that the mountains of Afghanistan was the most likely theater of war in which it would fight and that so many troops were permanently deployed in the NWFP.

The criticism leveled at the methods employed by British and Indian units on the North-West Frontier redoubled during the summer of 1930, when civil disturbances in the NWFP sparked widespread unrest in tribal territory. During the ensuing operations it appeared to many outside observers that army units had grown ponderous and overcautious and their tactics had become too stereotyped, especially after large Afridi *lashkars* raided Peshawar District and then escaped largely unscathed. In comparison, the high mobility of the lightly equipped Scouts and Frontier Constabulary (elements of the Civil Armed Forces) enabled them to deal successfully with elusive tribal raiders, prompting accusations that the military was incapable of performing its allotted role in the watch and ward of tribal territory.[15] The very fact that the garrison in Peshawar District had to be reinforced with irregulars appeared to indicate that its effectiveness had declined, prompting several suggestions in the press for the reestablishment of a localized force organized, trained, and equipped exclusively for operations against the trans-border Pathans.

Most of the lessons the Indian Army learned from the 1930 operations were mixed and contradictory. The mobility conferred by the road network in Waziristan and within the NWFP, together with the provision of armored cars and motor transport, had clearly altered the strategic, tactical, and administrative conduct of frontier warfare, enabling reinforcements to be rushed to threatened points along the border. The speed of MT convoys also eased piqueting and lightened the task of the road protection troops in areas where light opposition was encountered. Perhaps more significantly, MT greatly simplified the logistical and administrative problems encountered by troops operating in tribal territory. Indian columns utilizing MT were tied to advancing along predictable routes, enabling hostile tribesmen to anticipate their lines of approach, to concentrate and prepare defences.

The off-road mobility and tactical effectiveness of British columns deployed in Waziristan, however, had undoubtedly sharply declined due to the large numbers of troops deployed and changes in their organization, equipment, and training. As a result, the pace of an advance and the distance a column could march in a single day were lower than 50 years earlier as the number of mules on which they depended had dramatically increased due to the higher scales of arms, equipment, supplies, and maintenance services now required in the field. This growing "tail" of pack animals compounded the administrative and tactical problem faced by Indian commanders and acted as a brake on mobility; it reduced the circuit of action of columns and slowed down every stage of operations, lengthening the line of march and exacerbating the already difficult problem of ensuring all-around protection. To complicate matters, a company of Vickers MMGs formed in each British and Indian infantry battalion in 1929 (in accordance with a new establishment adopted throughout the Empire) meant additional mules were now needed to carry these heavy weapons. This considerably reduced the rifle strength of Indian battalions despite restrictions being initially placed on the number of weapons to maintain mobility in the hills. An infantry battalion could no longer provide the same number of piquets as before, lowering the distance it could protect from three miles to two, which in turn effectively limited the distance a column could march in a single day.[16] The extra firepower conferred by the additional machine guns dramatically increased the expenditure of ammunition, making *lashkars* wary of engaging Indian columns or following up rearguards, thereby limiting opportunities to inflict heavy casualties. Further problems were caused by an obsession with security that overrode other operational requirements, slowed movement to a crawl, and tied Indian columns to cautious and unimaginative advances along the valley floors. It now took longer to piquet a route as periodic halts were necessary while covering machine gun and artillery fire was carefully arranged to support the placement and withdrawal of piquets. Fear of casualties, the recovery of dead and wounded, and efforts to prevent the theft of arms and ammunition also stultified efforts to bring hostile *lashkars* to battle or to achieve surprise. An inability to differentiate between the tactical requirements of conventional warfare and those on the frontier compounded the problem. On many occasions, deliberate set-piece attacks were mounted backed with a full panoply of supporting arms, despite the fact that the *lashkars* seldom awaited the results.

During the spring of 1931 the Army in India's performance on the North-West Frontier was carefully examined by members of the Tribal Control and Defence Committee. Its final report echoed earlier press criticisms and suggested that the military authorities should consider various measures to lighten the arms and equipment of regular units and the merits of forming a new PFF.[17] The latter view was dismissed out of hand by the General Staff in India, however, given the inherent organizational difficulties involved and the fact it ignored the other important roles the Covering Troops performed. Instead, senior officers argued that an organization, equipment and training designed to fight Afghanistan, supported by foreign troops and the frontier tribes, was by default automatically suited to fighting the tribesmen alone. Moreover, as long as the North-West Frontier remained the most likely theater of operations of the Indian Army, it strongly believed that all imperial troops required experience of the terrain and tactics similar to those required in Afghanistan.[18] This view was also supported in the service press. Writing in response to calls for radical changes in the army's current organization, training, and equipment to make it more effective in operations in tribal territory, one anonymous officer observed in 1932:

> Any tendency for specialization for mountain warfare operations on the North-West Frontier must be resisted...The thinking soldier, if he is to be any value to his profession, must avoid parochialism. The "khaki" of the Frontier is undoubtedly fascinating, but it is not the only topic of thought for the British officer.[19]

Rather than fundamentally changing current organization, the General Staff directed particular thought towards increasing the circuit of action of mechanised Indian columns and the cross-country mobility of India soldiers in the hills.

The strategic mobility and circuit of action of columns in the Covering Troops districts was increased with comparative ease by the General Staff during the 1930s by further road building in the NWFP. Most work was carried out in Waziristan, but to pacify new areas, construction began on a further series of roads elsewhere in tribal territory in 1934, although it proved an expensive, time-consuming process and frequently provoked opposition. Henceforth punitive operations in tribal territory were normally combined with road construction to allow small, lightly-equipped columns to be supplied and operate in the hills as well as extending political control. Hand-in-hand with road building went the slow introduction into service in India of MT, tractors, half-tracks and fully tracked vehicles—Carden Lloyd Mark VI Armored Machine Gun Carriers and Mk 1A Light Tanks—with much improved cross-country performance.

It proved far more difficult to improve the off-road mobility of imperial troops in mountainous terrain, although this was addressed by reducing or lightening personal clothing, arms and equipment, decreasing the scale of supporting weapons and changes in training. Many Indian battalions replaced their heavy ammunition boots with *chaplis* and substituted lightweight clothing in place of the normal issue. Amounts of ammunition and equipment carried by each soldier were also reduced, and from 1934 a considerably lighter and more reliable replacement for the cumbersome Lewis gun, with its attendant mule, began issue. Yet despite continued criticism of the new machine gun company, the number of Vickers MMGs in each battalion was increased during 1931 by two weapons, to maintain uniformity with the rest of the British army. The administrative tail of Indian columns was successfully "docked" by cutting down superfluous pack animals and the number of troops required for their care and protection. However, despite being regarded as anachronistic by many officers, pack mules and camels still remained essential in all operations mounted beyond a road head in tribal territory. Air supply was also carefully examined as an alternative means of maintaining troops and reinforcing isolated posts, now that two Bomber Transport aircraft were in India. Despite the potential demonstrated by air supply on two occasions in 1930, the General Staff remained skeptical because of the limited number of aircraft available, the expense, and their inability to evacuate casualties.

The General Staff made no radical changes in the system of periodic relief of units stationed in the NWFP or the training methods used by the Army in India apart from greater emphasis on light-infantry training. By the mid-1930s Indian Army regiments were highly proficient in frontier warfare. Most now contained a large cadre of officers, NCOs, and other ranks with both practical experience and training in frontier warfare, enabling them to quickly achieve a high standard of efficiency when they returned to a border station. In comparison, British regiments were the "natural prey" of the tribesmen as most of their training was predicated on conventional "open warfare" or internal security duties. An intermittent one-year tour of duty in the NWFP prevented them from accumulating a cadre of "frontier hands," placing even greater reliance on theoretical instruction and on-the-job training. To a large extent the performance of British units depended upon their willingness to adapt and learn from those with greater experience. A combination of cap-badge rivalry between regiments, rapid changeovers in personnel, the comparative "amateurism" of British officers, professional arrogance, and racism often militated against the assimilation of military skills required on the frontier from experienced Indian units.

Training of British officers, NCOs, and men was facilitated by the publication of an unofficial textbook in 1932, written by General Sir Andrew Skeen and specifically directed at junior British army officers "as he is less likely in his wider range of service to be trained for the local problem which all officer in India have to keep in mind." *Passing it On: Short Talks on Tribal Fighting on the North-West Frontier of India* provided a detailed source of clear and comprehensive information in an easily readable form regarding the trans-border Pathan tribes, tactics, and administration in hill warfare, based on the author's extensive experience.[20] It assumed an authoritative position, running to three editions, and was widely read in Britain and India. Two copies were specially issued to British army officers' and sergeants' messes and one copy to other British and Indian combatant units in India at the orders of the Commander-in-Chief, Sir Philip Chetwode, to allow British soldiers to benefit from the tactical and administrative guidance provided by perhaps the Indian Army's most experienced frontier soldier.

The Mohmand Campaign, August–September 1935

The Mohmand country provided a practical test of the various changes introduced during the early 1930s, after local tribesmen carried out a series of major raids and other acts of open hostility against the government of the NWFP. To punish them, a punitive column advanced deep into tribal territory, constructing behind it a road both to facilitate military operations the advance and to open the area to trade and peaceful development. A combination of cutbacks in personal equipment and light-infantry training speeded up piqueting and improved cross-country mobility, but the MMG company in each battalion remained a serious brake on mobility. Perhaps the most striking feature of the campaign was the willingness of Indian commanders to undertake large-scale night operations, enabling them to seize the initiative, upset tribal plans, and avoid the delay inherent in mounting deliberate attacks. As a result, columns penetrated deeper into tribal territory before they had to return to the security of a perimeter camp each night. New equipment also made its debut. A single tractor-drawn battery of 18-pounders supplemented the mountain artillery, whose longer-ranged and more powerful guns could support several widely separated Indian columns. Perhaps of greater significance was the successful deployment of a single company of Mk II light tanks, whose invulnerability to rifle fire and cross-country mobility quickened the pace of operations. Although it required careful ground reconnaissance by cavalry, and engineers had to construct tank crossings over nullahs and improve the track across the Nahakki Pass, the terrain in Mohmand country did not present an appreciable obstacle nor did an attempt by the tribesmen to impede movement by digging pits and strewing the roads with rocks and boulders.

"Mohforce" was heavily dependent on large quantities of ancillary units throughout the fighting, which had both tactical and administrative implications for frontier warfare. A large number of noncombatant signallers, field ambulances, engineer parks, ordnance depots, and motor vehicles accompanied Mohforce, and each day MT carried ammunition, supplies, and water to a roadhead, from where pack transport carried it to the forward troops. To encompass the large number of vulnerable vehicles and noncombatant troops, perimeter camps grew in size and complexity. It often proved difficult to find a flat space large enough for all troops and equipment and their construction took much time and required considerable labor. The amount of manpower required for their defense, also was considerable; but as the proportion of infantry to other arms had fallen, it was often difficult to provide sufficient troops. A heavy consumption of ammunition made it vital to maintain and protect a permanent line of communication along the Gandab road to service growing logistical requirements, facilitate the movement of reinforcements, and evacuate casualties. Armored cars regularly patrolled the Gandab road, but the burden of protection, as always, fell to the infantry. Permanent piquets were constructed in the Karappa Pass, but the intricate and relatively low-lying land between Kialgai and Karappa meant a new system based on mobility and offensive defense, employing lightly equipped fighting patrols, was employed to deny tribal marksmen good positions on either side of the road.

The lessons learned in Mohmand country had clearly convinced the General Staff in India and many other British officers that both the tactical and administrative conduct of hill warfare had undergone major changes since 1925. A detailed section discussing this campaign in the *A. H. Q. India Training Memorandum* for the 1935–36 collective training season began:

> The recent Mohmand operations showed marked advance in the conduct of operations of this nature and the methods employed. Apart from the advantages of a L. of C. with a road for M.T., which was effectively maintained, and of efficient administrative arrangements, the rapid and complete success obtained in this campaign may be attributed to enterprising leadership, development of existing methods, and the introduction of innovations.

Units throughout India were ordered by the Commander-in-Chief to follow guidelines laid down in this publication during the forthcoming training season, which incorporated various lessons learned regarding the employment of night operations, light tanks, and armored cars and the protection of the lines of communication. Sufficient practical experience of the impact of changes in the tactics, training, organization, and equipment on the conduct of hill warfare had now been gained to prompt the military authorities to begin preparation of a long awaited replacement for *The Manual of Operations on the North-West Frontier of India*.[21]

The improving state of interservice relations in India, following the appointment of Air Marshal Edgar Ludlow-Hewitt as AOC (after years of divisive argument), meant the RAF also took a greater interest in tactical cooperation with the army in mountain warfare after years of neglect. Under his command in April 1935 the Air Staff in India had issued instructions that RAF training in the subcontinent should henceforth be directed solely towards efficiency in tribal warfare, although primarily employing independent bombing operations. This decision strengthened the conviction of Wing Commander John Slessor—Commanding Officer of No. 3 (Indian) Wing)—that a radical change should be made in the system of army cooperation used in India, as the existing "Aldershot model"—devised for conventional European warfare—was largely ineffective in mountainous terrain.[22] Writing on April 10, 1936, he urged:

> The great cry now-a-days seems to be co-operation—the balanced use of all arms and Services in Frontier warfare…I should have thought there could be no better way of ensuring that good co-operation than by having a combined manual on which we all work, containing the description of all methods of Frontier warfare.[23]

During the summer, "Tactical Exercises Without Troops" were held near Rawalpindi to demonstrate the effectiveness of close air support and study the inherent problems from the viewpoint of ground troops, while the Vickers-Bomb-Lewis (VBL) ground attack method was developed at Peshawar. The 2nd (Rawalpindi) Brigade and aircraft from No. 3 (Indian) Wing took part in a large combined exercise at Khanpur between November 17–25, 1936, to develop and test close air support tactics in mountain warfare, based on a provisional close-support manual written by Slessor and a draft of the new frontier warfare manual. These maneuvers (simulating tribal opposition to an Indian column engaged in road construction) conclusively demonstrated the practicalities of close support and indicated the importance of RAF liaison officers at column headquarters to direct operations, as well as an effective means of communication between the aircraft and forward troops and between columns and airfields.

The Lessons of the 1936–37 Waziristan Campaign

The Waziristan Military District provided the RAF and Army in India with an immediate opportunity to test the effectiveness of their new fighting methods when hostilities broke out in the Khaisora Valley in November 1936. Inspired and led by the Faqir of Ipi, this serious revolt directly challenged the "hearts and minds" and road-building policy implemented in the area since 1923 and provoked a major British response. This fighting, ultimately involving 61,056 regular and irregular troops, dragged on during 1937 as imperial forces endeavored to bring to battle an estimated 4,000 hostile tribesmen, whose elusive *lashkars* offered serious resistance in the still undeveloped mountainous areas bordering the frontier with Afghanistan and carried out small-scale raids into the settled areas of the NWFP.

Most of the lessons learned during the Mohmand operations were confirmed, indicating that there was no need for a radical change in imperial tactics. It also provided further important practical experience about light tanks, medium artillery, and aircraft in frontier warfare. But infantry remained the predominant arm during frontier fighting, now divided into two main categories: operations by columns operating in rugged, mountainous areas; and operations associated with road protection.

The infantryman and the pack mule still remained vital in all operations in mountainous terrain impassable to wheeled transport and where limited scope existed for tracked vehicles. However, in November 1936 the Khaisora operations graphically demonstrated that the maximum distance a fully equipped Indian column could march, taking full precautions and allowing sufficient time to establish a perimeter camp before nightfall, was limited to 8–10 miles. Despite reducing number, the factor that above all dictated the speed of movement and circuit of action of a column remained the protection of the masses of pack transport still required to carry supplies. Only by reducing piqueting below an acceptable margin of safety, or by neglecting sufficient supporting artillery and machine gun fire, was it possible to move further or faster. To provide security, all commanding terrain features up to 1,500 yards were occupied by a full platoon to provide Indian columns on the march or troops halted at night with protection from snipers. Perimeter camps were also justified when a massed assault was made on 2nd (Rawalpindi) Brigade on the night of April 27, 1937. Night operations were once again thoroughly vindicated, reducing tribal resistance and increasing mobility in the border hills, but they needed surprise and careful planning to prevent confusion. Two companies of Mk II and Mk IIb light tanks were employed when ground permitted in sections or subsections to carry out reconnaissance, protect flanks, cover withdrawals, and directly attack *lashkars*, adding to the strength and quickening the pace of movement.[24] Yet while the weight of firepower provided by machine guns, artillery, light tanks, and aircraft proved highly effective against large concentrated *lashkars* in the opening phases of the operations, it conversely exacerbated the problem of bringing the elusive tribesmen to battle. Moreover, the unrestricted employment of superior firepower was now a thing of the past, as the political restrictions associated with the "hearts and minds" campaign in Waziristan exerted a powerful influence on the fighting. As one British officer later described: "We were usually denied a soldier's greatest weapon—aggression, the first shot. Again, the government remembered its object, the re-establishment of tranquility, and reminded us that there would be no tranquillity among these proud and fierce people...if we fought the campaign on unnecessarily ruthless lines."[25]

It was clear that the Army in India was now more dependent than ever on roads that increased the mobility of units in Waziristan and facilitated the supply of imperial columns. Lorries were employed on an unprecedented scale, allowing a considerable reduction in the number of pack animals and noncombatants. The circular road allowed lightly equipped imperial troops to quickly concentrate and operate off a secure line of communication, greatly simplifying the whole problem of transport and supply as well as reducing the size and unwieldiness of columns. MT delivered troops, pack animals, and supplies to the point where columns left the roads, refilled supply echelons, and dumped stores at road heads; and to that extent, they were able to increase the radius of action of accordingly lightly equipped Indian troops. Roads also allowed heavy weapons to be deployed in Waziristan. Five batteries of mechanized field artillery, as well as a section of the 20/21st Medium Battery, equipped with a mixture of 18-pounder, 4.5" and 6" guns firing a heavier weight of shell than normally used in frontier warfare, supported columns within range and road protection troops.

Road protection was the main task carried out by imperial troops deployed in Waziristan as reliance on MT increased. A full infantry brigade was normally required to piquet 10–12 miles of road with mobile reserves held in each sector ready to respond to tribal raids. The stereotyped tactics most units employed for "Road Open Days"—normally held three days a week—allowed little opportunity for personal initiative or any variation in minor tactics when positions of tactical importance had to be repeatedly occupied. Most road protection schemes employed in Waziristan also surrendered the initiative and provided hostile tribesmen with an idea of the time, direction, method, and destination of each detachment as they piqueted a road each day, making them vulnerable to attack. Armored cars and on occasion light tanks proved an effective and economical means of patrolling roads, escorting convoys, and providing fire support to road protection troops. A clear lesson of the campaign following the ambush of a convoy in the Shahur Tangi, however, was that MT was still highly vulnerable to sniping and ambushes in hilly areas outside the security provided by static protective piquets.

Perhaps the most outstanding feature of the Waziristan operations was the close cooperation achieved between the RAF and the Army in India at the tactical level, although independent bombing operations were also carried out. Six squadrons—equipped with Westland Wapiti, Hawker Audax, and Hawker Hart aircraft—were used in the largest air operation ever undertaken in India, operating under detailed restrictions imposed by the political authorities intended to prevent the death of noncombatants and attacks on friendly tribal sections. Daily reconnaissance sorties located hostile *lashkars* and enabled column commanders to determine the number and location of piquets and perimeter camps in advance, and to direct long-range artillery fire. Bomber Transport Aircraft frequently dropped supplies to imperial columns, maintained isolated posts, and evacuated casualties. This increased the administrative, and hence the tactical, mobility of columns to the extent that following the Khaisora operations, it was proposed that supply drops of food, fodder, and ammunition should form a normal component of military operations in tribal territory to reduce the amount of pack transport required, remove the need for a permanent line of communication, extend the circuit of action of ground columns, and increase both their speed and mobility. Throughout 1937 the close-support tactics developed at Khanpur formed an integral part of most operations in Waziristan, with aircraft engaging hostile tribesmen in contact with imperial troops and those advancing or retiring in "proscribed" areas in advance or along the flanks of columns. As had been anticipated, close communication between pilots and the forward troops was essential. Radio telephony between aircraft and mule-pack sets accompanying column headquarters formed the basis of communication, while a simple "XVT," "Close Support Intercommunication Code" enabled forward troops to indicate their position and targets to supporting aircraft.

The 1936–37 Waziristan campaign demonstrated once again the necessity of a high standard of specialized training in frontier warfare for units in the Covering Troops and elements of the Field Army detailed as immediate reinforcements. During 1937 the recent lessons learned in tribal territory were included in reports issued by Northern Command and the annual report on collective training distributed throughout India.[26] The *Manual of Operations on the North-West Frontier's* planned replacement was not immediately available to these troops, however, despite agreement between the General Staff, Air Staff in India, and the Foreign and Political Department regarding its contents. When the first draft was submitted for approval in February 1936, General Sir William Bartholomew, the CGS, observed:

> It is most comprehensive and much larger than the old manual, but I think that it is right that this should be so. It is intended primarily for the use of officers of both services at Home and in India who have no knowledge of the Frontier or of Frontier fighting.[27]

Controversy over the politically sensitive sections dealing with aerial bombing, however, prevented publication when the Secretary of State for India decided they should be issued separately.[28] This decision bitterly disappointed Major-General Claude Auchinleck, who had drafted the manual and secured agreement between the RAF, army, and political authorities in India and it took General Sir Robert Cassels, the Commander-in-Chief in India, personal intervention to prevent the "emasculation" of the manual.[29] As a result the entire manual was finally reclassified as "For Official Use Only," although further differences over air operations delayed its approval for publication until November 1938. During this period a small section on frontier fighting was included in the *A. H. Q. India Training Memorandum* issued in July 1938, although the information it contained was deliberately kept limited pending the arrival of a new training manual.[30] Perhaps the most important means of disseminating information regarding the recent fighting was the service press. Many officers eagerly recorded their experiences and discerned lessons from the recent operations, although not all expressed satisfaction with the current tactics or training.[31]

Frontier Warfare (Army and Royal Air Force) 1939 was issued to British and Indian units and RAF squadrons during March 1939, providing them with a detailed and up-to-date formal written doctrine of frontier warfare. With 20,000 copies printed, it formed the basis of training for companies and higher formations for the remainder of British rule. Considerably larger than its predecessor, the manual codified the existing doctrine of frontier warfare in use in India at that time, modernized to the extent of discussing the use of aircraft, light tanks, and heavy artillery in tribal territory. Its contents reflected the greater understanding and cooperation between the Indian Army and the RAF that emphasized the need for cooperation of land and air forces and their dependence on each other. It described, in considerable detail, how aircraft could perform air blockades, proscriptive air action, destructive air action, and ground/air cooperation in mountain warfare. Despite growing criticism, the manual still emphasized the continued importance of the established orthodox methods of frontier warfare, columns, protective piquets, and perimeter camps, but it did warn officers against the dangers of operations becoming too stereotyped. The manual encouraged officers encouraged to read histories of military operations, and it included a bibliography of books dealing with both the frontier and frontier warfare.[32] Other sources of unofficial guidance complemented the new manual during 1939. Perhaps the most significant addition to this literature was a fourth revised edition of *Passing it On: Short Talks on Tribal Fighting on the North-West Frontier of India of India,* which contained a new chapter written by several Indian Army officers discussing the 1936–37 Waziristan operations.[33]

The North-West Frontier remained an unsolved problem for the local politiical administration and military liability for the Army in India until the end of British rule in the subcontinent, tying down large numbers of regular and irregular troops. Indeed, at the height of the Second World War some 48 battalions and two Indian Air Force squadrons and irregulars of the civil armed forces were deployed in the NWFP, despite the Japanese threat to India. Throughout the war, frontier warfare remained a key element of training for these units, with occasional skirmishes and small-scale operations against "hostiles." ensuring that a high level of readiness was maintained. Indeed, the "greatest training ground in the world" played an important part in honing the general military skills of units later despatched to North Africa, Southern Europe, and Southeast Asia to play their part in defeating conventional German, Italian, and Japanese troops.

Conclusion

As the General Staff in India faced a definite, long-term military problem, it adopted a far more pragmatic approach than the War Office (which directed military training elsewhere in the British Empire) that recognized the paramount importance of an officially sanctioned specialized doctrine and a system of training for frontier fighting. Following the disastrous 1919–20 Waziristan Campaign, it again acknowledged that the inherent difficulties of frontier fighting—exacerbated by improving tribal military effectiveness—meant imperial troops could not be left to "make it up as they went along" or rely on "on-the-job training" without running the risk of incurring significant casualties. Accordingly, it devoted considerable time and effort to collating, analyzing, and disseminating lessons learned by imperial troops fighting in tribal territory. These were passed on in new specialized training manuals (intended to complement the more general *FSR),* annual training memoranda, and standing orders that incorporated new developments. Outside official channels, the service press, textbooks written by serving or retired officers, and a large cadre of experienced men within units also provided an important means of "passing on" information. This was an important reflection of military professionalism directed toward colonial military requirements rather than an imitation of European practice.

The effectiveness of the Army in India on the North-West Frontier is open to question. Much criticism was directed by British service officers at the so-called anachronistic methods employed in tribal warfare. Yet Indian Army officers were not dyed-in-the-wool conservatives clinging to long-outdated methods. This approach to frontier warfare still remained remarkably effective, as it was determined more by the unchanging factors of the mountainous terrain and tribal military characteristics than by any other reasons. It must also be remembered that frontier warfare was not the sole task performed by the Army in India, and the training, organization, and equipment for its other roles directly affected both its tactical effectiveness during operations in tribal territory and its training approach. Both British and Indian units serving in India were always primarily organized, trained, and equipped for conventional military operations against a second-class opponent (either in Asia or as part of an imperial expedition); secondarily, frontier warfare; and finally, Internal Security duties. As a result of these disparate tasks, it often proved difficult to achieve the correct balance between time devoted to training for conventional operations and that for frontier warfare or Internal Security duties, especially during peacetime when local day-to-day military requirements always loomed larger in the minds of Indian Army officers.

Following the First World War, the conflicting and often contradictory requirements of frontier fighting and conventional warfare became explicit as modern weapons and equipment, intended for "civilized warfare," were adopted and dependence on supporting arms and services increased. As a result the relative mobility of Indian columns operating in the hills progressively declined and they were tied to fixed lines of communication. While the construction of roads in tribal territory considerably eased supply and administrative difficulties, allowed heavy weapons to be used in their immediate vicinity, and facilitated the deployment of units with higher scales of equipment, they did not affect the essential problems encountered by imperial troops when they moved off road. Apart from light tanks, the mountainous terrain afforded little scope for mechanization or heavy weapons, and pack mules and infantry remained essential when columns operated in the hills. As it was simply impossible to reconcile the heavy scale of equipment carried by regular troops and the attendant first-line mule transport with rapid cross-country movement, the tactical flexibility and mobility evident in prior frontier campaigns progressively declined. While the commitment to tribal control reduced its effectiveness in conventional military operations, at the same time the army's normal preoccupation with conventional war made it less fit for its frontier mission. The various discussions regarding the relative merits of resuscitating the PFF in the 1920s and 1930s reflected widespread recognition that specially trained and lightly equipped localized troops would be much more efficient and mobile than regulars on periodic tours of duty. However, such proposals were unacceptable to the military authorities as long as Afghanistan remained the most likely theater of operations for the Army in India, as tribal territory provided invaluable practical experience of the terrain and tactics likely to be encountered across the Durand Line. In any event, the Scouts and various militias now performed the policing and, to a lesser degree, many of the military tasks previously carried out by the frontier force when it had been under civil control.

CHAPTER 5

The Indian Army in the First World War, 1914–1918[1]

David Omissi

Introduction

When the King-Emperor George V declared war on the Central Powers in August 1914, he did so on behalf of the whole British Empire.[2] As a result, India was automatically involved. At the outbreak, British officials were concerned about the likely Indian attitudes, but these worries proved to be unfounded, at least in the early stages of the war. Expressions of loyalty came from all sections of Indian society. The Indian princes vied with each other to offer their services. The nationalist politicians fell silent, or proffered their support. Even the veteran extremist B.G. Tilak felt obliged to make sympathetic noises for fear of political isolation.[3]

At the outbreak of war, the Indian Army was an all-volunteer force of about 159,000 Indian officers and men, and about 2,300 British officers who occupied the middle and higher echelons of command.[4] There were 39 regiments of cavalry and 118 infantry battalions, recruited in India, and 20 battalions of Gurkha Rifles, recruited in Nepal. Apart from 12 mountain batteries, all the artillery was British, as it had become official policy since the 1857 "Mutiny" to keep heavy weapons in British hands, in case of another, similar outbreak. Along with about 68,000 British troops stationed in the subcontinent, these forces were collectively known as "the Army in India."

As a result of the reforms carried out by Lord Kitchener while Commander-in-Chief (1902–9), the Army in India was deployed in three roughly equal portions: the Internal Security troops supported the police "in aid of the civil power," or in the event of a major rebellion; the Covering troops defended the North-West Frontier and the lines of communication to it; and the Field Force formed a mobile reserve, principally intended to fight a war with Afghanistan. In 1914, only the Field Force was immediately ready to move outside India.

The Indian Expeditionary Forces preparing to leave Indian ports in the summer of 1914 would face many challenges, for some of which they were not fully prepared. By the war's end, Indian troops would have fought and died in France and Flanders, in Mesopotamia and Palestine, at Gallipoli and Salonika, and in Egypt, the Sudan, and East Africa. The war would raise important questions for the Indian military:

How effective would the Indian Army and the wider Indian military system prove to be, particularly in combat against European forces? What would the Indian soldiers make of their service overseas, especially in Europe, and how would they react or adapt to service conditions? What would be the war's wider political significance for India?

The Indian Army on The Western Front, 1914–15

The outbreak of war rapidly led to a crisis for the Allies on the Western Front. The German advance seemed unstoppable. Britain had sent the few divisions of the British Expeditionary Force (BEF) to support the French and the Belgians, but these formations were soon forced to fall back. The bad news from France made it clear that there was a desperate need for trained reinforcements. The countries of the "White" Commonwealth—Australia, Canada, Newfoundland, and New Zealand—would eventually provide many troops; but the peacetime Dominion armies were small, and their new forces had to be embodied and trained. India was the only source of further trained units that could immediately be sent to France.[5]

The decision to use Indian troops in Europe was controversial. Indian troops had not been used during the South African War of 1899–1902, largely for racial reasons (the British had not wanted to antagonize the Cape Dutch by using brown troops against their Boer "racial cousins"), but this discrimination had been far from popular with either the Indian Army or the Indian military communities.[6] In 1911, the Committee of Imperial Defence had discussed the possibility of using Indian troops in Europe; but at a meeting of the War Council on August 5, 1914, Lord Roberts, a former Commander-in-Chief in India, deprecated the idea of sending for the Indian soldiers (although he later changed his mind).[7] Both the king and the Viceroy of India, Lord Hardinge, however, wanted the Indian troops to serve.[8] They thought that bringing an end to the color bar would be popular in India, so in late August 1914 the Lahore and Meerut infantry divisions were diverted from Egypt and redirected to France.[9]

Who were these Indian soldiers? Particularly from the 1880s, initially as a result of the policies pursued by Lord Roberts, they had been recruited according to the doctrine of the "martial races," which classified the Indian population into "warlike" and "unwarlike" peoples.[10] This classification drew partly on the Indian caste system and on the martial self-image of some communities, such as the north Indian Rajputs, but it also derived from imported European racial notions linked to social Darwinism. As a result, over half the Indian Army in 1914 was recruited from the single "warlike" Indian province of the Punjab, and much of the remainder hailed from Nepal, the United Provinces and the North-West Frontier Province.[11] The Indian regiments were normally segregated by religion and language, with each company or squadron (or occasionally battalion, in the case of Gurkha, Garwhali, and some Sikh and Dogra units) being recruited from a particular community. Most of the men were from the middle peasantry, as the Indian Army had a policy of recruiting in rural areas, preferably fairly backward ones. The British authorities had no wish to enlist men who might have had contact with political nationalism, while the educated elite were either disinclined, or were not permitted, to serve in the regular Indian Army.

The Expeditionary Force that came to Europe was fairly typical of the Indian Army, although Gurkhas—often considered "crack" troops—were overrepresented. It included six battalions of Gurkhas, two battalions of Garhwalis from the Himalayan foothills, and four battalions of Sikhs. Most of the remaining units were mixed battalions, typically with separate companies of Sikhs, Dogras, Punjabi Muslims, Rajputs, Pathans, or Mahrattas. The Indian divisions included both Indian and British units; typically each infantry division contained three brigades, each consisting of three Indian and one (later two) British battalions. Each division also had an attached Indian cavalry regiment, an Indian pioneer battalion, and British artillery support.[12] The force included cavalry units, which eventually formed two further divisions.

After halting for a few days in Egypt, the Indian troops went on to southern France, where they arrived from late September 1914, reequipping with a more recent model of rifle as they did so. By the time they reached the front, the "Miracle of the Marne" had thwarted the Schlieffen Plan in its original form; but the Germans were still attempting to turn the Allied flank during the so-called "race to the sea." The Indian regiments were thrown piecemeal into the desperate actions around Ypres in late October and early November 1914, often attached to British

Muslim sepoys of the Indian Army in Belgium, 1914 (Courtesy of the Imperial War Museum)

formations.[13] By the end of 1914, almost one-third of the BEF in France and Belgium was drawn from India,[14] and these divisions helped to swing the balance in the Allies' favor. The Indian units suffered very heavy losses. The average Indian battalion was 764 men strong when it landed in France, but by the beginning of November 1914 this figure had fallen to 550.[15]

Indians had become eligible for the Victoria Cross (VC) in 1911, and the first Indian VC of the war was won by sepoy Khudadad Khan (1888–1971), a Pathan of the 129th Baluchis. He was a machine gunner, and he was decorated for his courage in an action of October 31, 1914,[16] during which, although wounded, he continued to fire after the other five men of his detachment had all been killed.[17]

How did these soldiers from rural India react to their first experience of industrialized combat on the Western Front? Historians now have a rich understanding of the experience of Indian soldiers in France, partly because some of the soldiers' correspondence has survived in the form of translated excerpts in British censorship reports. A censorship was set up towards the end of 1914 at the sorting office in Boulogne.[18] Initially intended to prevent seditious literature reaching the troops, this was later used to monitor their morale, which was causing concern. The first chief censor of the Indian mails was Captain (later Sir) Evelyn B. Howell (1877–1954), an official of the Indian Civil Service who had been attached as an Urdu-French translator to an Indian cavalry regiment. He was assisted by a small team, mainly retired Indian Army officers and ICS men. The censor's weekly reports, together with attached translated excerpts from a hundred or so letters, summarized the mood of the troops.[19]

The conditions and the losses at the front had come as a great shock to the Indian soldiers, who were more used to the small-scale skirmishes of colonial campaigning. The commander of the Indian Corps, General Sir James Willcocks (1857–1926), reported his men as unreliable in early November: he claimed that they might "go" at any minute.[20] The Indians' morale had begun to falter during the winter of 1914–15, particularly among the recovering wounded. The men were suffering from cultural disorientation and homesickness, and the loss of long-familiar officers also contributed to their dismay.[21] Soldiers began writing home, urging their relatives not to enlist, some of them using coded language in an effort to evade the censorship.

The soldiers' principal grievance was that the lightly wounded were sent back into action once they had recovered. "We are like grain that is flung a second time into the oven, and life does not come out of it," was a typical cry. A petition addressed to the King-Emperor from the wounded Indian soldiers in hospital expressed their concerns:

> England. The Emperor. Let no one except the King open this. From the Indian sick in hospital...Your Majesty's order was that a man who had been wounded once should be allowed to return to India; or that if he had recovered he should not be made to serve again. The heart of India is broken...The Indians have given their lives for eleven rupees. Any man who comes here wounded is returned thrice and four times to the trenches. Only that man goes to India who has lost an arm or a leg or an eye.[22]

As a result of the petition (passed on by the censors), the policy of returning the wounded to the front line was eventually modified.

As evidence of their poor morale, it has been suggested that Indian soldiers on the Western Front were particularly prone to self-inflicted wounds, mainly to the left hand. What is the evidence either way? On balance, it seems likely that self-wounding was, at least briefly, a problem. One inquiry found that 57 per cent of the 1,848 Indian soldiers admitted to the hospital up to November 3, 1914, had been wounded to the hand.[23] There also appear to be some coded references to self-inflicted wounds in Indian soldiers' letters.

The welfare of Indian soldiers soon became an object of charitable concern in Britain, especially among influential people with Indian connections.[24] The Order of St John of Jerusalem set up an Indian Soldiers' Fund to provide comforts to the troops. The fund's committee included Lady Willcocks (the wife of the Commander-in-Chief of the Indian Corps), Lord Curzon (a former viceroy), Lord George Hamilton (a former Secretary of State for India) and General Sir O'Moore Creagh (a former Commander-in-Chief in India). Subscribers included members of the British royal family, a number of Indian princes, and some businesses with Indian connections. Lord Curzon generously lent his London home in Carlton Terrace as a headquarters. Including a small government grant, the fund had raised the impressive sum of £167,000 by the end of November 1915. In addition to practical items such as warm clothing and trench periscopes, and luxuries such as cigarettes, sweets, and tea,[25] it also provided religious items, such as Korans, Brahminical threads, and Sikh daggers, combs, and bracelets. The fund also paid for the 500-bed Lady Hardinge Hospital, based at Brockenhurst in Hampshire. Evidence from soldiers' letters suggests that its work was greatly appreciated.

In all, just over 14,000 Indian troops were treated in British hospitals,[26] principally in Brighton, where the Pavilion and workhouse were converted for the Indian wounded. The authorities took great care to ensure that the troops in these establishments received food appropriate to their religious beliefs.[27] In general, soldiers' letters about England, the English, and the hospitals were positive. There had been some concern that sending Indian troops to Britain, with the resulting contact between white women and Indian men, might have damaged British prestige in India. Overall, however, the experiment of sending some of the Indian wounded to Britain was considered a success.[28]

By early 1915 the Indian troops were back in the line in the Ypres-La Bassée sector. The terrain was flat, cut with ditches and canals, and overlooked by the low rise of the Aubers ridge, held by the Germans. The main action of the Indian Corps on the Western Front was at Neuve Chapelle, on March 10–12, 1915, when the Indian Corps and the British IV Corps attacked the German lines.[29] The operation was a success, gaining approximately 1,000 yards of ground on a front of two miles; but the losses, about 12,800, were shattering.[30] During the battle, the Indian Corps lost about 20 percent of its strength and 27 percent of its British officers.[31] A Muslim soldier, clearly shell-shocked, wrote home to his brother shortly afterwards:

God knows whether the land of France is stained with sin or whether the Day of Judgement has begun in France. For guns and of rifles [*sic*] there is now a deluge, bodies upon bodies, and blood flowing. God preserve us, what has come to pass! From dawn to dark and from dark to dawn it goes on like hail. . . But especially our guns have filled the German trenches with dead and made them brim with blood. God grant us grace, for grace is needed. Oh God, we repent! Oh God, we repent![32]

Some Indian soldiers came to suspect that they were being deliberately sacrificed to spare British lives.[33]

The Lahore Division was diverted to Ypres in April 1915, in response to a German attack on April 22, using chlorine gas discharged from cylinders, against one French colonial and one French territorial division.[34] (The use of gas was in defiance of the Geneva Convention, to which Germany was a signatory.) The attack had created a gap in the line to the left of the Canadians.[35] Lahore made a grueling 30-mile forced march north in order to counterattack. During the battle, the division's Jullundur Brigade lost 1,385 of its 2,250 men, and the Sirhind Brigade could muster only about 300 men per battalion after a few days of fighting.[36] As a result of his actions during the battle, Jemadar Mir Dast, a Muslim soldier from what is now Pakistan, was awarded a VC. Despite being badly wounded and gassed, he rallied his men, who held their positions against German attacks until ordered to retire; and after the retirement, he helped bring in eight wounded British and Indian officers. He was the fourth Indian to be awarded the VC. His brother, Mir Mast, a Jemadar in Vaughan's Rifles, is thought to have deserted with a group of Pathans on the night of March 2–3, 1915.[37]

The Indian Corps remained on the Western Front for most of 1915. They suffered heavy losses while attacking German positions in front of the Aubers ridge and at Festubert in May.[38] At the Battle of Loos (during the first major British gas attack), which began on September 25, 1915, the Meerut Division mounted a diversionary attack.

Towards the end of October 1915, the two Indian infantry divisions were ordered to depart for the Middle East.[39] It is not entirely clear why. Possibly there were problems with morale. The Indian troops were surely depressed at the prospect of another winter in the mud, rain, and slaughter of Flanders. There were also plausible strategic reasons for moving them. The Canadian and New Army divisions were arriving in France, so the Indians' presence had become less vital than it had been in the autumn of 1914.[40] It also made sense to concentrate India's war effort in a region that would be easier to reinforce and to supply from Indian ports. Total Indian losses on the Western Front had been terrible. On landing in France, the Indian battalions had numbered in total about 220 British officers, 325 Indian officers, and 14,000 other ranks. Including reinforcements, they had suffered losses of almost 500 British officers, 500 Indian officers, and over 20,000 other ranks.[41]

The two Indian cavalry divisions remained on the Western Front until early 1918. After 1914, when some of them fought in the trenches on foot, there was not much frontline employment for cavalry, and the divisions stayed mainly in reserve. In July 1916, however, the Secunderabad Brigade made a successful charge on the Somme, killing a dozen or so Germans with swords and lances. The Indian cavalry also saw action during the German retreat to the Hindenburg Line and at the battle of Cambrai in the autumn of 1917.[42] In the spring of 1918, the cavalry were transferred to the Middle East to support General Allenby's forthcoming offensive in Palestine.[43]

The Indian soldiers' perceptions of Europe are particularly well documented. The troops were understandably homesick, but otherwise they seemed to have had a very positive image of France and of their grateful French hosts. They were struck by the wealth of the inhabitants, which they attributed to widespread literacy; and they admired the fine brick dwellings and prosperous farms.[44] As a result of visiting Europe, the soldiers began to reconsider India and Indian mores. Some of them wrote home suggesting to their families that they adopt certain European customs, such as the education of women and the practice of parsimony in marriage ceremonies. The soldiers were, however, critical of some aspects of European life, such as the familiar relations between the sexes and the apparent emptiness and superficiality of the Christian religion.

Other Theaters, 1914–16

In addition to the Indian troops in France, other Indian Expeditionary forces were sent to Africa, Egypt, and Basra. In East Africa, the Indian Army was given the task of mopping up the German colonies. However, an attack by two brigades of the Indian Expeditionary Force "B" on the German port of Tanga on November 4, 1914, was repulsed with 800 casualties, and the British were to remain on the defensive in East Africa for over a year.[45]

In the Middle East, where the Ottoman Empire still retained a loose suzerainty over most of Arabia, the British and Indian authorities were concerned about a possible German-Turkish attack on the South Persian oil installations, as well as potential efforts to raise jihad—a holy war of Muslims against nonbelievers—among the Arab and Muslim populations.[46] The Indian Army landed a brigade at Bahrain on October 23, 1915, to show the flag in a traditional area of Indian interests. When Britain declared war on Turkey in early November 1915, an Indian Expeditionary Force (Force "D") quickly captured and occupied the oil refineries at Abadan, in Turkish territory, and the city of Basra, the main outlet of the oil fields.[47] The Force sealed the Persian Gulf and fought off Turkish counterattacks.

In early 1915, the Allies tried to knock Turkey out of the war by forcing the Dardanelles and capturing Constantinople. An initial attempt to force the narrows with warships alone failed in February and March 1915 (as most naval officers thought it would), so Allied troops landed on the Gallipoli peninsula in April 1915. Reinforcements were soon needed, and the 29th Indian Brigade—three battalions of Gurkhas and one of Sikhs—was detached from the 10th Indian Division in Egypt in April 1915 and committed to the operation. The Indians acquitted themselves well, but the wider operation was not a success, and all Allied troops withdrew from the peninsula between December 1915 and January 1916. About 1,700 Indians had lost their lives.

It was Mesopotamia, however, that became India's main military undertaking from 1915 to the end of the war, and it was there that most Indian troops who served outside India were engaged—a total of approximately 675,000.[48] The troops were first intended to protect British interests in the Gulf, then to occupy the *vilayet* of Basra. Their mission was then extended to the capture of Baghdad 300 miles upstream, to maintain British prestige in the East in order to distract attention from the failures at Gallipoli.[49] The climate and conditions in the region were far from congenial. Mesopotamia was one of the hottest regions in the world in summer, while heavy rains in winter from the end of December caused flooding, making much of the country almost impassable. Communications were poor, and there was no railway between Basra and Baghdad.[50]

Initially, Indian operations in Mesopotamia were successful, as the British-Indian forces advanced up the line of the Tigris and Euphrates. An advance to Kut-al Amara, on the Tigris south of Baghdad, was approved on July 20, 1915, and Kut was captured on September 29. General Nixon, in overall command in Mesopotamia, hoped to push on to Baghdad, and Lord Hardinge was optimistic about what could be achieved. The British Cabinet authorized the advance on October 23, 1915,[51] provided that General Townshend, who commanded the force that would make the advance, was satisfied that the conditions were right. In the meantime, the two Indian infantry divisions from France were on their way to offer support.

Some signs were ominous. There were supply problems, and medical conditions were poor. The restricted diet of many Indian soldiers meant that they began to suffer from deficiency diseases, such as beri-beri and scurvy. There was a shortage of medical officers and of river transport to evacuate the sick.[52]

Turkish reinforcements were soon brought in from Gallipoli, and the Allied advance was checked before a strong Turkish position at Ctesiphon on November 22–24, 1915, with a loss of nearly 4,600 out of 13,756 men. Townshend was forced back to Kut-al-Amara by early December, where he was encircled by Turkish forces and besieged. At first the Indian authorities hoped that his forces could be relieved. Three attempts, on land and on river, were made in January, March, and April.[53] All failed. On April 29, 1916, after his men had run out of food, Townshend surrendered with approximately 3,000 British and 6,000 Indian troops. Hostile comment in the press and Parliament forced the British government to set up inquiries into the twin disasters of Gallipoli and Kut. The Mesopotamia Commission, chaired by Lord George Hamilton, would make its report the following year.

The fate of the Indian prisoners in Turkish hands was grim. Although Townshend spent the rest of the war in comfortable exile in a villa in Constantinople, his men were not so fortunate. They were marched (in oppressive heat) from Kut to Turkey, via Baghdad and Mosul. Many suffered from starvation, and more than half would die in captivity.[54]

India's War More Broadly, 1914–16

From the early stages of the war, the losses at the front stretched the capabilities of the prewar reserves of the Indian Army—only 34,767 strong—of whom many were elderly or unfit. Units in the field could therefore be reinforced only by cross-posting men from regiments still in India, a policy that tended to undermine the esprit de corps of the regiments at the front. Enlistments in the rural recruiting grounds fell off at harvest time, and some men wrote home advising their relatives not to enlist. The authorities had to introduce recruitment bonuses and other incentives, such as free rations and uniforms.

It was also difficult to find enough suitable British officers. Each Indian battalion normally had about 12–13 British officers; but many of these soon became casualties. There were only 40 prewar reserve British officers for the Indian Army,[55] and it was hard to find enough British men who could speak the appropriate Indian languages. The officer problem was compounded by the fact that Lord Kitchener had commandeered all the Indian Army officers on leave in Britain in 1914 as instructors for the new armies.[56]

If Indian opinion had broadly supported the war effort at the beginning, the growing losses at the front encouraged the feeling that India should receive some political concessions as a reward. The main Indian nationalist parties, Congress and the Muslim League, temporarily settled their differences with the Lucknow Pact of 1916, and Congress began to demand some form of "home rule" for India.[57]

The Turkish declaration of jihad had the potential to strain Muslim-British relations, as the Germans were well aware. German strategy in India aimed at subversion, in particular by exploiting the religious feelings of India's 66 million Muslims—about one-fifth of the population of the Indian Empire.[58] German agents and propaganda did achieve some influence, but British countermeasures, such as the Defence of India Act of 1915, were generally effective. The war with Turkey posed a potential problem of torn loyalties for Muslim troops, who formed around a third of the Indian Army.[59] The pull of pan-Islamic, or pro-Turkish, sentiment did indeed have some impact on discipline and cohesion. There were some desertions on the Western Front, mainly of small groups of Transfrontier Pathans—men who were recruited over the Indian border in Afghanistan. As a result, the British authorities eventually stopped recruiting from this community.

There were also some minor "mutinies," again mainly the result of the demands that the war with Turkey made on the religious sensibilities of some Muslim troops.[60] At Rangoon in January 1915, three companies of Pathans refused to embark to fight against the Turks. Seven of these men were condemned to death, and 197 sentenced to various terms of transportation.[61] On February 23, 1916, an Indian cavalry regiment, the 15th Lancers, mutinied at Basra in Iraq. The unit was recruited entirely from Muslims, mainly in what is now the Multan district of Pakistan. The men refused to march from Basra against the Turks near the holy places of Islam (especially Karbala), although they pleaded to be allowed to fight the King's enemies in other places, such as Europe, where they had already served with distinction.[62] In all, 429 men were arrested and disarmed. Tried by court-martial, they were sentenced to long periods of transportation to the Andaman Islands.[63] As a gesture of clemency, all except the "ringleaders" were released on King George V's birthday in 1917.[64]

The most significant, and most violent, Indian mutiny of the war occurred at Singapore in February 1915, when four Muslim companies of the 5th Light Infantry rose up and killed their British officers and any Europeans who happened to be nearby.[65] There had already been problems in the unit, in which there was a history of misunderstanding between officers and men. Some of the men seemed to believe that the Kaiser had converted to Islam. They feared they were going to be sent to fight against the Turks, and they had heard about the heavy casualties in Europe. The mutiny was also partly prompted by the declining visibility of British power in the region; the havoc wreaked by the German warship *Emden* in the Bay of Bengal had tarnished British prestige locally. During the mutiny about 30 Europeans were killed.[66] As a punishment, over 40 soldiers were executed, and 165 others were sentenced to various sentences of imprisonment or banishment. The mutiny, and its aftermath, would have a long-term effect on race relations in Malaya and Singapore.

The Later War Years, 1917–18

During the later war years, India's efforts had to be scaled up as the Allied situation became more difficult. The pressures were such that some regions of India (notably the Punjab) began to develop a significant "home front."[67] In 1916, the British authorities even began to consider the introduction of conscription in India, but instead decided to adopt a system of recruitment "quotas" according to Indian province and district. Previously, the Indian Army had relied entirely on volunteers motivated by the prospect of financial gain, or by a martial self-image, or both. Indian officials now had to apply this new and unpopular policy, at the risk of losing their posts if they failed. Their efforts produced more men, but some of these were "volunteers" in name only, and the policy was to inflict some postwar political damage in the recruiting grounds.

After the German offensives began on the Western Front in March 1918, Lloyd George appealed to India to become:

> The bulwark which will save Asia from the tide of oppression and disorder which it is the object of the enemy to achieve.[68]

In April, an all-India War Conference summoned by the viceroy in Delhi promised 500,000 more troops in the coming year, of which the Punjab was to provide 200,000.[69] In August alone, 51,705 combatants and 29,047 noncombatants were recruited.[70] To meet these numbers, the government of India had to broaden the basis of recruiting beyond the traditional "martial races' to groups with few traditions of military service.

In Mesopotamia, meanwhile, the War Office took control of military operations in February 1916.[71] The military administration was overhauled and made more efficient. Lieutenant-General Sir Stanley Maude (1864–1917) was appointed to command; and the Allies renewed their offensive in December along the Tigris, recapturing Kut al-Amara the following February. The Allies then skillfully maneuvered the Turks out of their defenses south of Baghdad. These successes in Mesopotamia were crowned by the capture of the city itself in early March 1917. Several Indian soldiers alluded to the event in their letters, Muslims being particularly glad that they could now pray in shrines previously inaccessible.[72] More prosaically, the victory also gave Indian troops better access to locally grown fresh fruit and vegetables, which improved their health.[73] At the end of September the advance resumed, and by early November Tikrit, almost halfway between Baghdad and Mosul, was occupied.[74]

In the meantime, in June 1917, the Report of the Mesopotamia Commission had appeared.[75] Broadly critical of nearly all who had been involved in the buildup to the disaster at Kut, the report's main targets were the consequences of the division of responsibility between Simla and Whitehall. The supply system had proved inadequate and the medical arrangements had virtually collapsed. The report was also very critical of the prewar atmosphere of economy, which had hampered military preparations in India. The prewar Indian military system had simply been unable to cope with the maintenance of a major expeditionary force overseas.

By the later war years, "political" India was increasingly demanding some reward for India's sacrifices, and the prospect of political difficulties prompted British concessions. The incoming secretary of state for India, Edwin Montagu (1879–1924), began his tenure of the India Office with his liberal-sounding declaration in the House of Commons on August 20, 1917, that:

> The Policy of His Majesty's Government, with which the Government of India are in complete accord, is that of the increasing association of Indians in every branch of the administration, and the gradual development of self-governing institutions, with a view to the progressive realization of responsible government in India as an integral part of the British Empire.[76]

After a subsequent tour of India, and discussions with the viceroy, Lord Chelmsford, the resulting Montagu-Chelmsford Report of 1918 promised concessions to the nationally-minded Indian parties.[77] These promises, once made, would probably have to be honored, strongly suggesting that there would be political movement in India after the war.

In the Middle East, the Allies went on the defensive in Mesopotamia in order to concentrate their offensive efforts in Palestine, where in June 1917 General Sir Edmund Allenby (1861–1936) had taken command.[78] Lloyd George had told him that the British people would like Jerusalem as a Christmas present. Allenby obliged. The Turks abandoned the city in early December 1917, Allied forces took over on December 9, and Allenby entered the city (on foot) two days later.[79]

The German offensive in France in the spring of 1918 meant that Allenby had to send most of his British infantry to the Western Front in exchange for Indian cavalry, so a further offensive in Palestine was delayed until September 1918.[80] Two Indian cavalry divisions took part in Allenby's offensive against the Turks in Palestine, which was a great success. The Turkish line in Palestine was broken in mid-September. The two Indian cavalry divisions joined the pursuit, driving the Turks before them into Syria. Allied forces captured Damascus in early October, and Beirut and Aleppo soon afterward.[81] The defeated Turks signed an armistice on board a British dreadnought at Mudros on the island of Lemnos on October 30.

In Mesopotamia, the Indian Army was also prominent in the Allied advance, and the war there ended with the capture of the strategically significant, oil-rich province of Mosul; Allied forces entered Mosul city shortly after the Turkish armistice.[82] The British campaign in the Middle East had ended in almost complete success. The Ottoman Empire had collapsed, and Britain was in a strong negotiating position in the region, particularly vis-à-vis her wartime ally and long-standing colonial rival France. By the early 1920s, the British Empire had reached its greatest extent thus far; and the Indian Army had played a significant part in the victory. On November 1, 1918, the Indian Army provided no fewer than 13 of the 17 British and Imperial divisions in Palestine and Mesopotamia.[83]

The Indian Army retained an important presence in the Middle East well after 1918, as the new territories of Palestine, Transjordan, and Iraq (awarded to Britain as mandates of the League of Nations) still had to be guarded.[84] The postwar British army suffered significantly from imperial "overstretch," so the Indian Army provided most of the garrisons in the 1920s.[85] Up to 85,000 Indian troops were employed in suppressing the Iraq rebellion in the summer and autumn of 1920.[86] All this caused

Lewis Gun manned by Indian troops, Mesopotamia, 1918 (Courtesy of the Imperial War Museum)

further problems with morale. The Indian troops were increasingly homesick, and the prospect of a harsh peace with Turkey was unpopular with Muslim soldiers.[87] After the war, Indian politics increasingly impinged on the use of the Indian Army outside India, as the nationalists vociferously objected to the army being used as an imperial "fire brigade."

Conclusion

India's contribution to the war in men, money, and supplies had been impressive.[88] At the Armistice, 943,344 Indian troops were serving overseas.[89] Most Indians had served outside the decisive theater of Western Europe, but they had freed British and Dominion divisions to fight there. Indian losses are difficult to establish exactly, but official figures suggest that between 62,000 and 64,449 Indian soldiers were killed or died of wounds. These losses were similar to those of Australia (59,000) or Canada (57,000), although as a proportion of the total Indian population of over 300 million, they were much smaller than those of the Dominions. It should be remembered, however, that more than half the Indian dead were from the single province of the Punjab.[90] Among the many decorations won during the war by Indian soldiers were 11 Victoria Crosses.

A balance sheet might consider that India provided a vital contingent of trained troops during the emergency of 1914 and subsequently made a large-scale effort, especially in the Middle East, throughout the war. The Indian home front had remained broadly loyal, and India became an important resource for the war economy. On the other hand, the Indian military system had failed early on in Mesopotamia and had encountered some discipline problems, including one violent mutiny. The prewar Indian system had perhaps been asked to achieve more than it realistically could. After the war, the government of India began an extensive enquiry into military reform.

The impact of the war on India was varied. Politically, the war strengthened the claims of the nationalist movement to a greater degree of Indian self-government—that India's relationship with Britain and the wider "British world" should tend increasingly to be one of partnership rather than subordination.[91] This claim had significant military implications, most notably that Indians should be allowed to achieve higher levels of command in the Indian Army. Wartime inflation and overzealous methods of obtaining troops had produced dissent in the recruiting grounds, and ex-soldiers were involved in the disturbances that affected postwar northern India, notably in the Punjab. In the city of Amritsar, Indian ex-servicemen may have been among the 379 protestors shot dead, on British orders, by troops of the Indian Army in April 1919.

Indian soldiers were commemorated much like those of other Commonwealth nations—the general principle being that all should be remembered where they fell, and in their home countries. Accordingly, there were cemeteries and memorials in the Middle East, including Iraq. Most of the few Indians who died in hospitals in Britain were cremated (if they were Hindus or Sikhs) on the South Downs, or buried (if they were Muslims) in the grounds of Woking mosque. On the Western Front, there are many Indian names on the Menin Gate at Ypres. The principal Indian war memorial in Europe is at Neuve Chapelle, the site of the Indian Army's most famous, and most costly, battle in 1915. Designed by Sir Herbert Baker, it was inaugurated in the autumn of 1927 by Lord Birkenhead, then secretary of state for India, and a former officer of the Indian Corps.[92] The memorial is a graceful structure, with circular walls on which are inscribed the names of over 5,000 Indian and British dead from Indian units.[93] In India, the main memorial is the massive arch of India Gate, which anchors one of the main avenues of New Delhi. On it is carved the name of every Indian soldier then known to have died on active service.

CHAPTER 6

Grudging Concessions: The Officer Corps and Its Indianization, 1817–1940[1]

Chandar S. Sundaram

Officering the Indian Army

Like everything else about the Army in India, its officering was complex. Initially, standards were low, with some European officers not even being able to read and write. This changed during the crisis of the 1740s, when the East India Company's (EIC) army had to drastically expand to meet the twin challenges of first the French, who had their own East India Company; and then the Indian rulers, some of whom had substantial and well-equipped armed forces, which were trained by Europeans. Efforts were made to recruit well-born Englishmen of the gentlemanly classes into the officer corps of the EIC's military service, the idea here being the chivalric one that aristocrats and gentlemen were predisposed by birth to be leaders of men, in peace and in war. But as the EIC forces grew, so too did their need for professional officer training. To meet this need, a military "seminary" was founded at Baraset, near Calcutta, in 1809. It was not a success: the cadets were too rowdy, and the staff was too small to control them effectively. The Baraset seminary lasted only three years. However, from 1809 to 1861, an EIC military academy operated at Addiscombe, south of London. After its abolition, all new officers of the Army in India were expected to have graduated from either Sandhurst, the military college of the British Army, or Woolwich, the training Institution of the British (Royal) Artillery and Engineers.[2]

Until 1917, only British officers could be King's Commissioned Officers (KCOs), which allowed them to command both British and Indian troops. Yet there were Indian officers too, occupying an officer grade below the British officers and above the Indian troops. They were initially called "Native Officers", but after 1858 became known as "Viceroy Commissioned Officers" (VCOs). Within the battalion or regiment, VCOs were the crucial liaison between the British officers and the sepoy rank-and-file. Every battalion had 20 VCOs, who performed the duties of company officers and platoon commanders. There were three VCO ranks: the *jemadar*, who functioned roughly as the lieutenant; the *subedar*, who had the duties of a captain;

and the *subedar-major,* who was the senior VCO of the battalion or regiment. In Indian cavalry units, these ranks were called *daffadar, rissaldar,* and *rissaldar-major,* respectively. However, in the Company's early days, the rank of Native Commandant existed. This rank was abolished in the reorganization of the 1760s. when sepoy battalions were placed under the overall command of British officers.[3]

VCOs were not commissioned in the usual sense. They did not go through a training course. Rather, they rose from the ranks in the units they first joined, as ordinary *sepoys* or *sowars.* Since recruitment of the Indian component of the army was always based on ethnicity, VCOs always came from the same communities as the troops they commanded. This gave them a unique role within their respective units. Not only did their British superior officers look upon them as their eyes-and-ears, but they were also keenly attuned to the needs and aspirations of the sepoy rank-and-file. Yet, even the most senior *subedar-major* was junior to the newest English subaltern, fresh off the boat from the British Isles. Promotion was another problem: it was by strict seniority, and, except for wartime attrition, was extremely slow. In the Bengal infantry, for example, sepoys who joined at the age of 16, became *naiks* after 20 years, *havildars* 15 years after that, *jemadars* nine years after that, and *subedars* six years later. This meant that most *subedars* were in their sixties.[4]

British officers of Indian units quite liked this mode of officering. First, it meant that they did not have to perform many of the routine bureaucratic tasks undertaken by junior officers in wholly British units. Secondly, it gave young British officers in Indian units far greater opportunities to see action than their colleagues in wholly British units had.[5]

Although the first King's Commissioned Indian Officer (KCIO) was not commissioned until the early 1920s, the issue of Indianization—admitting Indians into the Indian Army's commissioned officer ranks in the same grades as British officers—was debated, in some form or another, since the early nineteenth century. This debate revolved around two related questions. First, did Indians possess the necessary leadership qualities to become officers on a par with British officers? Second, if it was proven that they did, how were Indians to be integrated into the army's officer corps in a way that would not threaten the character of the Indian Army and the continuance of British India itself? Three main elite groups were involved in this debate as it unfolded, especially after 1885. In India, there were the officials of the British Government of India, headed by the Viceroy; the officers of the Army in India, headed by the Commander-in-Chief; and Indian nationalists of the moderate school, who became increasingly more important in the period 1917–40. In England, there was the India Office, headed by the Secretary of State for India, who was a member of the British government; other government departments, such as the War Office, and the Colonial Office, also intervened in the debate. Generally speaking, for the Indian nationalists, the answer to the first question of whether Indians had "the habit of command" was a resounding "yes," and the second question was unimportant, because it was a given that any Indian KCO would be a loyal subject of the Crown. For British officers and officials, again speaking generally, both questions were important; however, the second became more central post-1917, as Indianization began to be haltingly introduced.[6]

The Debate before 1857

An early Indian advocate of higher commissions for Indians was the famous Bengali intellectual and public figure, Rammohan Roy. To Roy, writing in the early nineteenth century, higher commissions were part of his general proposal to liberalize British rule over India by Indianizing the bureaucracy. However, Roy did not go into specifics on Indianizing the army's higher ranks.

At about the same time, some British officers were also interested in Indianization, which they saw as mainly professionalizing the native officer class and attracting a "better class of Indian" into its ranks. In 1817, Sir Thomas Munro worried that the character of the native officer class could not be improved as long as they could not attain any rank higher than that of *subedar*. In the 1820s, Sir John Malcolm suggested that native officers' sons be placed on a "boy establishment," under which they would receive training before joining the native army. General Sir Thomas Bradford, the Commander-in-Chief of the Bombay Army from 1826 to 1829, thought that the way to attract a better class of "native gentleman" would be to directly commission them into the native officer ranks. They would be thus able to avoid the chore of serving in the sepoy ranks.

But these were only vague ideas. In 1836, Lieutenant-Colonel John Briggs, a Madras Army officer, proposed the first detailed scheme aimed at improving the native officer class. He too advocated the entry of Indian gentlemen, whom he defined as well-educated "natives" of good families, into the native officer class. His scheme was a compromise between direct commissioning and promotion by seniority. Qualified Indian gentlemen would be granted volunteer appointments by the Commanders-in-Chief of the Presidency Armies, which would entitle them to be "fast-tracked" into the native officer ranks after serving only six years as sepoys. Briggs also thought the professionalism of the native officers could be improved through the creation of cadet colleges. At these colleges, native gentlemen and the sons of serving native officers would undergo a three-year training course. Upon the completion of this course, and after two years' service as Indian noncommissioned officers, they would enter the native officer grade as *jemadars*. But although it was only limited to native officers, Briggs's plan was not implemented.[7]

Before the 1857 Indian Mutiny, Henry Lawrence was the British official who came closest to advocating Indianization. In an 1844 essay, he maintained that there existed in the ranks of the native army more than a few men with the ability to attain the "European" officer ranks. These men's aspirations, thought Lawrence, should be addressed "with justice and liberality." Such a policy would forge far stronger bonds between Indian and Briton than would a "suspicious and niggardly" one.[8] Such a policy would also help prevent British-trained sepoys and sowars from quitting the Presidency Armies and hiring themselves out to the armed forces of any of the Indian rulers, where there was no bar on advancement. Lawrence mentioned two former sepoys who had risen to the very top of the Sikh and Awadhi armies respectively. Although Lawrence did not follow up these ideas with a concrete proposal, his ideas, especially regarding Indianization's innate justice, would be cited by its later advocates.

Chesney vs. Roberts

As a result of the Indian Mutiny of 1857, the British Crown abolished the EIC and took over direct control of India, including its armed forces. Though sepoys still formed the majority of the Army in India, the white element, consisting of units of the British Home Army, was considerably increased. The uprising, sparked as it was by the mutiny of sepoys of the Bengal Army, also killed any talk of Indianization for a good 30 years. During this interval, India saw the rise of a small but vocal English-educated Indian intelligentsia who gained employment as lawyers, teachers, journalists, and low-level officials in the bureaucracy of "Anglo-India"—a term coined by the British ruling classes and expatriates in India to describe themselves. By the 1870s and 1880s, members of this intelligentsia, schooled in the values of English political liberalism, were openly criticizing some of the more authoritarian practices of the colonial state. They particularly accused the British of not honoring the 1858 Royal Proclamation on India, which promised that all of Queen Victoria's subjects "...of whatever race or creed, be freely and impartially admitted to offices in our service, the duties of which they may be qualified, by their education, ability, and integrity, duly to discharge."[9] To the Indian intelligentsia, these "offices" included higher commissions in the army.

General Sir George Chesney,[10] Military Member on the Viceroy's Executive Council—the highest decision-making body in British India—was sympathetic to the Indians' concern regarding Indianization, and was eager to address it before Indian political agitation gathered steam. Between 1885 and 1891, Chesney proposed Indianization plans four separate times. Taken together, these plans made three proposals: the Indianization of the officer cadre of one or two regiments; the institution of an Indian military college in India to train Indians for higher commissions; and the professionalization of the VCO grade. These proposals were important, for they set the template for all future discussions and official policy initiatives on Indianizing the officer corps until 1921.

Chesney was quite clear about the class of Indians he preferred to see become officers. They were not men of the intelligentsia—now derogatorily referred to as *babus*. Rather, they were men of the Indian "princely, aristocratic, and gentlemanly classes" who either lived in the approximately 500 Princely States scattered over South Asia, or were important local landowners and magnates of rural North India, such as the "Oudh Taluqdars." In post-1857 India, British policy-makers and ideologues—often the same people—held that these classes constituted the "real" India, with whom the colonial state could cooperate and collaborate against the rising *babus*. Moreover, it was thought that these classes were "martial" as opposed to the "effeminate and bookish" *babus*.[11] Therefore, they were deemed good officer material.

Aware that what he was proposing was highly radical from the British perspective, he proposed that one Indian commissioned officer be admitted to the regiment in question on a trial basis, as the most junior lieutenant. If that officer performed well, then another Indian lieutenant would join that regiment, and so on, until eventually the whole regiment would be officered by Indians. The reason for this glacial deployment was to reassure Anglo-India that no British officer would have to serve under an Indian officer "for a great many years to come."[12]

Chesney's Indian Military College plan was clearly a response to the rising nationalism of the Indian intelligentsia, who formed the Indian National Congress (INC) in 1885. In 1887, the INC passed a resolution calling for an Indian military college to be established in India to train Indians for higher commissions. But whereas the INC resolution included all Indians, Chesney's military college was only meant for the Indian aristocrats and VCOs.[13]

All Chesney's proposals failed, mainly because they were strenuously opposed by the then Commander-in-Chief of the Army in India (CinC India), General Frederick Roberts. To Roberts, Indianization was pure folly, because military leadership was racially determined: the British had it; the Indians, brave though they undoubtedly were, did not. Roberts also pointed out that British officers and soldiers would balk at serving with, or under, an Indian officer. These two "facts" alone would be dangerous, because they would undermine a unit's military effectiveness. Another "danger" would be that Indian commissioned officers might be disloyal to the Crown and sell military secrets to Russia, then seen as Britain's main adversary in Asia. He also believed that the demand for Indianization was frivolous, because it did not come from members of the martial races or the Indian aristocracy—who really mattered—but only from "the misguided Englishmen and Hindus who direct[ed] the machinations of the [Indian] National Congress."[14] However, if it was found that a start had to be made with respect to Indianization, Roberts recommended that Indian cadets be trained in England, so as not to make it too easy for them.

The Maharaja of Cooch Behar and the Imperial Cadet Corps

The Indianization issue lay dormant for much of the 1890s. It was revived in 1897 by the Maharaja of Cooch Behar. British officials could not ignore his interest, for, as a member of the Indian aristocracy, he represented precisely the class of Indian that they deemed tolerable to become higher officers. The Maharaja wrote directly to Lord George Hamilton, the India Secretary, to inquire about the possibility of his son gaining a higher commission after undergoing the regular officer training course at Sandhurst. Though the Maharaja's request was not approved, this time due to opposition from the War Office and the Colonial Office, Hamilton sympathized with the Maharaja. He was also impressed by the Indian princes' support for Britain's imperial wars in China and South Africa, and was therefore eager to ". . .soften the racial bar. . .which exist[ed] in the Army."[15]

Hamilton found a willing partner in the new Viceroy, Lord George Curzon. Curzon viewed the Indian princes as "...the only class in India who are bound to us by every tie of self-interest, if not of loyalty."[16] Together, they came up with the Imperial Cadet Corps (ICC). This was a small institution, designed to give the rudiments of military education to between 20 and 30 young Indian men of princely and aristocratic lineage at any one time. The course of study was to be two years long. However, those "few cadets" who showed promise of being good officers, would undergo a third year of training, and receive officer commissions. But these were not regular King's Commissions. Rather, they were commissions in His Majesty's Native Indian Land Forces (HMNILF), which did not confer powers of command over either British or Indian troops of the Army in India, but only "extraregimental billets": posts on the staffs of some generals.

Twenty-four cadets joined the ICC in 1901, but the intake was never again that high. Some heirs to princely *Gadis* (thrones) attended, but did not complete even the two-year course. The ICC had three basic functions. First, it acted as a sort of "public school," because in the early terms, a large part of the curriculum was devoted to reading and writing English, and mathematics. Second, it had a ceremonial function. Cadets had an opulent dress uniform that they wore on occasions of state, such as the Delhi Durbar of 1903, which Curzon organized to celebrate the coronation of King Edward VII. Third, it was to provide the cadets with a military education, but it delivered only a partial one. Most of the instruction was in surveying and mapmaking, with drill and rifle practice thrown in. Cadets were not taught the core subjects of the Sandhurst course, like military writing, voice procedure, and military law. They also did not participate in any simulations or staff rides.[17]

Future employment of the cadets was also a matter of concern, both to the cadets themselves and to the British authorities.[18] After much discussion, it was agreed that, besides extraregimental billets, ICC graduates could be employed in the Imperial Service Troop (IST) contingents. These were the armed forces maintained under British supervision by various princely states. In 1914, of the 11 graduates of the ICC, two were serving in the IST contingents, five were attached to regular Indian Army regiments, two were aides to generals, and one was attached to the Indian Political Service, the Anglo-Indian government's agency dealing with the princely states. These were "...unimportant posts that did not give... [the ICC graduates]...meaningful professional military experience—and they knew it!"[19]

By 1912, it was clear that the ICC had failed. Early that year, a high-level conference was held in Calcutta to discuss its problems. General Sir O'Moore Creagh, the CinC India, argued that the ICC be turned into a proper officer training facility for Indians, and that it be fully under the jurisdiction of the Military Department, as opposed to the Foreign Department. But the Viceroy, Charles Hardinge, and representatives from the War Office insisted on Sandhurst training for all Indians desiring a King's Commission. A deadlock had been reached. With the outbreak of war in 1914, the ICC was shut down.[20]

World War I and the 1917 Declaration

Three considerations spurred British officials to declare, in 1917, that Indians were eligible for the King's Commission. First, India's contribution to the Allied war effort in World War I, was huge. India raised about 1.4 million men, 800,000 of whom saw action in France, Mesopotamia, Palestine, and East Africa. This was all the more significant because the Indian Army was an all-volunteer force. Second, Indian politicians grew impatient with government pledges of political reform *after* the war. Sir Satyendra Sinha made Indianization a key part of his presidential address at the 1915 INC session, pointing out that, although Indians were fighting bravely on various fronts, and were winning Victoria Crosses, ". . .not one of them can receive a commission in His Majesty's Army—irrespective of birth, education, or efficiency." Third was the official desire to work out a political reforms package that would forestall the formation of a united front against them by the INC and the other main Indian political party—the Muslim League—which was then in the works. Indianization was seen as a natural corollary of these reforms. Though Sir Austen Chamberlain, as India Secretary, was Indianization's prime mover, the actual declaration was made by his successor, Sir Edwin Montagu, on August 20, 1917: "The Government have [*sic*] decided that the bar which has hitherto precluded the admission of Indians to commissioned rank in His Majesty's Army should be removed."[21]

Towards the Eight-Units' Scheme

Montagu's declaration was in many ways a wartime expedient, because it did not lead to any immediate and wholesale Indianization. A sure sign of this was the closing down, in 1919, of the officer cadet course at Daly College, Indore. This course, which lasted only a year, managed to graduate 39 KCIOs. After its closure, the only avenue open to Indians wanting the King's commission was to attend Sandhurst, where 10 places yearly were reserved for them. Yet, even for these places, there was a definite preference for "selected representatives of families of the fighting classes which have rendered valuable services to the State during the [last] war."[22]

The Indian Army's top brass might have left matters at that had it not been for the sustained interest shown in Indianization by Indian moderate politicians sitting in the newly minted Indian Central Legislative Assembly (CLA). In March 1921, responding to the findings of the Esher Committee on future Anglo-Indian military policy, Sir P. S. Sivaswamy Aiyer tabled a set of 15 resolutions in the CLA. Two of these resolutions, concerning Indianization, sparked considerable debate. Resolution Seven proposed that Indians, including those of the Indian intelligentsia, should be encouraged to enter the commissioned ranks of the army, provided they met the "prescribed standards of fitness." It also proposed that, as an initial step, not less than 25 percent of the total King's Commissions granted every year from Sandhurst should go to Indians. Resolution Eight proposed that adequate preparatory training be given in India to youths so as to fit them for Sandhurst entry. The eventual aim of setting up an Indian Sandhurst was also voiced.[23]

The Sivaswamy Aiyer resolutions, which set the tone for all future discussions, passed by the slimmest of margins, but only after Resolution Seven had been significantly amended to favor the martial races. General Rawlinson, the CinC India, immediately formed an Indian Military Requirements Committee to implement them. Rawlinson's motives here were devious. To him, the "Indian races...[were]... a lot of sheep,"[24] with no military leadership aptitude whatsoever. Therefore, he only supported progressive Indianization proposals because he was sure London would reject them. A responsible CinC, fully supportive of the proposals, might have cooperated with Indian politicians to work out a scheme acceptable to London.

In any case, he was right: the India Office rejected the proposals. General A.S. Cobbe, the Military Secretary there, instead proposed the creation of a Dominion Army (DA), to exist alongside the regular Indian Army. DA units would be composed of Indian troops recently demobilized. They would be wholly officered by Indians, who would hold Dominion Commissions, which would confer powers of command only over Indian troops. If the experiment worked, then additional DA units would be created and the regular wholly British-officered Indian Army would be correspondingly downsized. Cobbe argued his plan held certain advantages: first, the Indian Army's military efficiency would be maintained; and second, no British officer would have to serve under an Indian.[25]

Delhi did not see it that way, on the grounds that India could not afford a Dominion Army on top of the already expensive Indian Army. Perhaps more importantly, not even the most moderate, loyalist Indian politician would accept the Dominion Army, quite rightly viewing it as a second-rate force.[26] Rawlinson now formed a new committee to submit a new proposal, which it did in early 1922. Seemingly a radical departure, this proposal called for *complete* Indianization, to be achieved in three 14-year stages. In stage one, 27 units would be Indianized; in stage two, 47, and in stage three, 41. If stage one proved successful, the later stages could be shortened to nine and seven years, respectively, allowing the scheme to be completed in 30 years instead of 42. Thus, if started in 1925, complete Indianization would be potentially possible by 1955![27]

Again, this proposal was a sop to nationalist Indian opinion and was sure to fail in London. It did. There, the Indian Military Requirements Sub-Committee of the Committee for Imperial Defence was prepared to allow the Indianization of only four units. After protests from the Viceroy, Lord Reading, that even the most moderate Indian nationalists would be insulted by the Indianization of so few units, it was agreed to Indianize eight units—six infantry battalions and two cavalry regiments. Thereafter, all KCIOs graduating from Sandhurst would be posted only to these units. They were, in effect, segregated. Only a very few British officers would have to serve with them, and certainly none under them.[28]

Indians at Sandhurst, and as Officers

By mid-1923, 52 Indian cadets had been admitted to Sandhurst after undergoing an exceedingly stringent nine-stage selection process, involving, among other things, an interview with the Viceroy himself! Leaving aside the 24 who were still being trained there, only 14 had successfully passed the course and had been granted the King's Commission; the rest either withdrew or died. Moreover, two cadets had resigned their commission, and one even had it cancelled because he was late in reporting for duty.[29]

Worried by the Indian cadets' high failure rate, and the bad press it would get in India, Delhi decided to put into effect resolution 8a of the Sivaswamy Aiyer resolutions, which called for the establishment of a school to prepare Indian youths for entry into Sandhurst. Accordingly, the Prince of Wales Royal Indian Military College (POWRIMC), opened at Dehra Dun in 1922. The college was organized and administered on military lines, and its aim was essentially that of a British public school. It was to "...imbue...cadets...with...those qualities which are essential if they are later to fill successfully their positions as officers and leaders of men." These qualities included: "...a sense of loyalty, patriotism, manliness and a self-effacing spirit of Service, together with a healthiness of mind and body such as will render them true and useful servants and citizens of India and the Empire."[30]

But Indians did not have an easy time of it either at Sandhurst or later, when they were posted to their units. This was undoubtedly due to the racial prejudice that had so long barred them from the "British" officer grades. At Sandhurst, a British officer was appointed to act as a guardian to the Indian cadets. It was thought that this would help ease the culture shock that these young men would face in the "alien" British culture and society. Yet Indian cadets complained that the guardian—a retired lieutenant-colonel who had served in India—was quite moody, aloof, and brusque. Apparently, he did not develop a true mentoring relationship with the cadets and showed no sympathy for their desires and concerns. Indian cadets especially resented that the guardian discouraged them from going to London or any other city where they could mix freely with English people and white women. Perhaps the guardian felt justified in taking this attitude, because of a rather spectacular case of a cadet from a princely state who was dismissed because he: was absent without leave; had bought an expensive motorcycle, which he had blithely told the dealer, would be paid for by the India Office; and had contracted a venereal disease from prostitutes at an English seaside resort. But then again, had the guardian been truly sympathetic to the Indian cadets, he should not have generalized from just one case.[31]

For those Indians who were successfully commissioned as KCIOs and posted to their units, things were not any easier. Put simply, the notion of having Indian KCOs went against the "traditions" of every cantonment. This came as a rude shock to the KCIOs and caused much resentment among them. Indian officers complained of never once being invited the homes of their British COs for even so much as a cup of tea. According to one of them, KCIOs lived in "virtual isolation" from their British counterparts.[32]

In the CLA, pro-government members stated that mixing between KCIOs and British officers would lead to "social difficulties". To this, the nationalist member Mohammed Ali Jinnah—who later became Pakistan's founding father—responded that the only social handicap KCIOs would face in a regimental mess would be that they would not be able to keep up with the alcohol consumption of their British colleagues.[33]

The Indian Sandhurst (Skeen) Committee

Not satisfied with these measures, Indian nationalist MLAs kept up the pressure. In February 1925, the CLA passed a resolution calling for an increased rate of Indianization and the establishment of an Indian Sandhurst. The Government of India responded by creating the Indian Sandhurst Committee (ISC). The ISC was chaired by General Andrew Skeen, the then Chief of General Staff India, and included among its members nationalist heavy-hitters like Motilal Nehru and Mohammed Ali Jinnah, as well as two Indians who had graduated from the ICC. Indian MLAs were disappointed that the ISC was tasked not with increasing the rate of Indianization, but only with improving the supply of Indian candidates and exploring the possibility of opening an Indian Sandhurst.[34]

After interviewing 122 witnesses and deputing a subcommittee to conduct a fact-finding trip to the military academies of Britain, France, Canada, and the United States, the ISC completed its report in late 1926. The report went far beyond the ISC's terms of reference, proposing a wholesale extension of Indianization. It made seven recommendations: the immediate doubling of the reserved places at Sandhurst for Indians from 10 to 20; the establishment, by the early 1930s, of an Indian Sandhurst to cater for 100 cadets on a three-year course; the expansion of the POWRIMC to cater for 250 cadets, and the setting up of a similar preparatory institution elsewhere in India; abolishing the eight-unit scheme in favor of unrestricted Indianization; that Indians be made eligible to become KCIOs in the Royal Artillery and the Royal Air Force; that the selection process for Indians applying for Sandhurst or the future Indian military academy (IMA) be made less stringent, arduous and forbidding; and that there should be more publicity in India about officer prospects and careers in the Army. If all these measures were implemented, and if the pass rates at the various training institution were good, the report contended that by 1952, there would be 1,169 serving KCIOs, constituting fully half of the Indian Army's officer establishment.[35]

As expected, nationalist MLAs warmly accepted the ISC report. However, Delhi rejected it on the grounds that the committee had overstepped its terms of reference. But because British officials realized that its complete rejection would be unacceptable to Indian opinion, they offered small concessions. The reservation of places at Sandhurst for Indians would be increased from 10 to 25, and a small number of Indians would be admitted to Woolwich and the Royal Air Force academy at Cranwell.[36]

Increasing the places for Indians at Sandhurst would soon create an oversupply of KCIOs for Indianizing units, which were still limited to eight. Delhi sought to solve this problem not by increasing the number of Indianizing units, but by changing the officering of the Indianizing units. Whereas, until then, they had been officered on the Indian pattern of between 19 and 20 VCOs and 12 and 14 KCOs/KCIOs, they would now be officered on the British pattern of between 23 and 28 KCOs/KCIOs, thus eliminating the VCO class entirely. Indian lieutenants would now begin their careers as platoon-commanders rather than as company 2-in-cs, the level at which KCOs in Indian regiments began. Therefore, the career advancement of KCIOs would be slowed. Delhi and London justified this by saying that since KCIOs were Indian, they would not need the liaising services of the VCOs.[37] However, their motive here was also to influence the martial races in the army to turn against Indianization. The martial races' main path to career advancement was the VCO grade. Therefore, it is safe to assume that their representatives would not support any measure that would mean the extinction of VCOs—something that Indianization, if carried out on the British pattern, surely would.

Indian Politics and the Road to the Indian Military College

By the end of the 1920s, it was clear that a higher rate of Indianization could not be delayed much longer. In 1929 for the first time, more than 10 Indians qualified for Sandhurst entry. By 1930, 77 KCIOs had been commissioned, of whom 68 were still serving in the army. On the political front, too, things were moving. In 1928, London appointed an Indian Statutory Commission—which, ironically, contained no Indian member—to report on Indian constitutional development. On Indianization, the commission's proposal was quite similar to Cobbe's Dominion Army scheme of 1922. This was rejected by the Congress, who, in their "all-Parties" report—a response to the Statutory Commission generally—reiterated their demand for an Indian military college and greater Indianization.[38]

The deadlock on the Indian constitution was broken by the Viceroy's 1929 offer of Dominion Status for India. This was significant because this status had been reserved until then for Britain's white colonies. That the very idea was now on the table was undoubtedly due to the coming to power in London of a Labour Party government which was more sympathetic to Indian self-government than its Conservative Party rivals. The Viceroy also had come around to the belief that the time for greater Indianization had arrived. The first step was the announcement, in April 1931, of the extension of Indianization from a mere eight units to a whole combat division of 15 units—12 infantry battalions and three cavalry regiments. Also, the Round Table Conference that took place in London that same year to negotiate Dominion Status for India recommended the formation of a committee to consider starting an Indian Military College.[39]

The so-named Indian Military College Committee (IMCC) first met in May, 1931, and submitted its report that July. Chaired by the CinC, General Chetwode, it had among its 20 members some prominent Indians such as Sivaswamy Aiyer and Surendra Nath Mukarji, principal of the prestigious St. Stephen's College in Delhi. The IMCC's major recommendation was the establishment of an Indian Military College (IMC). The training was to be three years long, and the annual intake was to be 60 cadets. Upon graduation, cadets would be called Indian Commissioned Officers (ICOs) as opposed to KCIOs. The IMCC proposed that, after the IMC opened, no more Indians be allowed admission into Sandhurst or Woolwich. British committee members justified this by assuming that having Sandhurst-trained KCIOs serving with IMC-trained ICOs in the same unit would lead to social friction and a loss of unit efficiency. This clearly reflected British attitudes, where officers of the British Home Army tended to look down their noses at officers of the Indian service. But it is also highly plausible that the Sandhurst and Woolwich authorities, never exactly enthusiastic about having Indians in their midst, quite approved of the IMC as a way to get rid of the Indians. This might have especially been the case in the 1930s when the increased number of units undergoing Indianization would have necessitated more Indians at Sandhurst and Woolwich, thereby changing the "racial complexions" of these institutions.

Wedded to the martial races ideology the IMCC proposed that half the IMC cadetships be reserved for soldiers serving in the Army, and that the CinC be allowed to nominate a further six candidates who had obtained borderline marks in the entrance examination. Thus only 24 places yearly were to be filled by open public examination. Babus would always be a minority.[40]

Even these recommendations proved too radical for Anglo-India. The Royal Indian Military Academy (RIMA) opened at Dehra Dun in October 1932, with an annual intake of only 40 cadets. Fifteen cadets were selected from the VCO grade of the Indian Army, and cadetships were filled from the Indian States' Forces, as the ISTs were now called. Only 15 places were filled by open competitive examinations. The tone of the IMA's syllabus generally mirrored that of Sandhurst, though the course was twice as long. It aimed at, firstly developing in the cadet the qualities of leadership, discipline, and physical fitness. The second, though no less important, aim was to make certain that the ICO would be able to carry out a platoon-commander's duties upon joining his unit. However it is interesting to note that, as opposed to Sandhurst, IMC cadets were not given much training in staff duties. According to Brigadier L.P. Collins, the IMC's first Commandant, staff work was not as important for the ICO as the development of platoon-level leadership skills.[41]

Indianization's Progress to 1940

The progress of Indianization in this period was slow and halting. This was due to a number of factors. Firstly, feelings of inequality existed between KCIOs and ICOs. This stemmed not only from the fact that overseas-trained KCIOs had more status and prestige than Indian-trained ICOs, but because KCIOs received twice or three times the pay and allowances than did their ICO colleagues. Promotions were also a source of ICO discontent. According to an ICO who later had a command-role in India's 1971 victory against Pakistan, KCIOs and especially ICOs were frequently passed over when it came to sought-after appointments. The fact that the ICOs had not received training in higher staff work might have been a reason for this. There was also some talk of further segregating the ICOs by giving them messes separate from the KCIOs and British officers. But this idea was soon abandoned, because it was realized that such segregation would result in ICOs not getting the respect from their men that was so essential for effective command. It is little wonder then that throughout the 1930s, there was a steady decrease in the number of Indians competing for RIMA entry by open competition, from 274 in 1932 to a mere 128 in 1938. When British officials cited these numbers as "proof" that Indians were not interested in careers as army officers, Indian MLAs like S. Satyamurthy shot back, saying that it was widely known that ICOs were treated as inferiors. It was therefore not surprising that "the best [boys] in the country" did not choose a military career.[42]

As war loomed closer in the late 1930s, Indian nationalists increased their pressure on defense matters, including Indianization. In September 1938, the CLA passed a resolution calling for the immediate creation of a committee whose task would be to recommend ways of increasing Indianization. The radical wing of the Congress Party denounced Indianization policy as a sham, and called for complete Indianization in 15 years. In the light of subsequent events, their desire would prove prophetic.

Bowing to such pressure, Delhi appointed an Indianization Committee under General C.J.E. Auchinleck in May 1939. Part of the Auchinleck Committee's job was to interview and obtain the views of serving KCIOs and ICOs. One of the Indian officers thus interviewed was Major K.M. Cariappa, a senior KCIO from a martial family, who had wide experience with Indianizing units, and who later became the first head of independent India's army. Cariappa confidently spoke his mind. He criticized the slow pace of Indianization, which had produced only 550 KCIOs and ICOs in 20 years. He also maintained that KCIOs and ICOs could be every bit as good at the regimental officer level as British KCOs, and that to use them as platoon-officers was like "using a Rolls-Royce to do the work of a Ford car." Moreover, he maintained that inevitably, KCIOs and ICOs in Indianizing units would grow to resent having to do the same work as that done by VCOs in non-Indianized units. Another defect of the Indianizing units, according to Cariappa, was that there was an imbalance in their officer establishments: the very few British officers were usually very senior, with the rest—all Indians—being very junior. Such an age disparity meant that there was little chance to develop the feelings of comradeship essential for military efficiency. The Auchinleck Committee seemed sympathetic to Cariappa's points, but the Second World War intervened before it could make concrete recommendations.[43]

The outbreak of war in 1939 resulted in the wholesale expansion of the Indian Army. As more units were raised, more officers were needed to command them. And British officers were in short supply. Bowing to the inevitable, Delhi declared on June 17, 1940, that the policy of posting ICOs to certain purely Indianized units was to be abolished. ICOs would therefore be "available for posting throughout the Indian Army, where their services can best be used."[44] Indianization, debated in various forms for over a century, had begun in earnest. This time, there would be no turning back.

Grudging Concessions

This chapter has demonstrated that the Indianization of the Indian Army's officer corps was one of the central issues debated in the corridors of the Raj's power for over a century. The reason for the protracted length of the debate was that Indianization was not merely a military issue, but one that had political and ideological overtones as well.

For Anglo-India, the debate, and the schemes issuing from it, were informed by the concepts of "similarity" and "difference." Put simply, some Anglo-Indians thought that Indians were essentially similar to Europeans. These people thought Indians were capable of being "trained-up" to European standards of "civilization". Other Anglo-Indians, particularly after 1857, deeply believed that Indians were different from Europeans, an inferior "race," incapable of improvement. Therefore, the only government suitable for them was a paternal one that was strongly authoritarian.[45] But similarity and difference coexisted in the Indianization debate: Chesney and Skeen believed in the former, while Roberts and Rawlinson believed the latter to be true, and either vehemently opposed, or tried to hold back, Indianization.

Political and military expediency also impelled Indianization. Politically, there was the Anglo-Indian need to continue collaboration with the Indian moderate politicians—the main class pressing for Indianization—as a way of counteracting Gandhian mass nationalism.[46] Militarily, one must note that Indianization's actual adoption was made during wartime, when the need for Indian manpower and resources was great. Similarly, the decree accepting unlimited Indianization was also made during wartime, when Britain's defense was in an even more perilous state. So, in a very real sense, the demands of modern, twentieth-century war necessitated Indianization, but its advent was slow and grudging.

Surveying the record of the Indianization of the Indian Army's officer corps in October 1940, General Auchinleck wrote that

> We [British] have been playing a losing hand from the start in this matter of "Indianisation". The Indian has always thought, rightly or wrongly, that we never intended the scheme to succeed and expected it to fail. Colour has been lent to this view by the way in which each new step has had to be wrested from us instead of being freely given. Now that we have given the lot, we get no credit because there was little grace in our giving.[47]

Looking at the issue some 66 years later, it is hard to dispute his assessment.

CHAPTER 7

A Force Transformed: The Indian Army and the Second World War

Daniel P. Marston

The Second World War was a period of unprecedented expansion for the Indian Army. Between 1939 and 1945, the army expanded from 200,000 to more than 2.5 million men and officers, even though conscription was never imposed. The Indian Army began the war as the "Imperial Reserve" for the British government. By the end of the war, it had played the leading role in the destruction of the Imperial Japanese Army in Burma, as well as significant supporting roles in the defeats of the Italian and German forces in North and East Africa and Italy. Indian Army forces played a role in the occupation of the important oilfields within Iraq and Iran. During all of these engagements, the Indian Army also continued to maintain its traditional duties of frontier defense on the Northwest Frontier and the Aid to the Civil Powers in India.

Throughout the Second World War the Indian Army also faced fundamental questions about its existence and formation. The Indianization of the officer corps reached new heights during this period, signaling the end of the British officer corps in the postwar era. Recruitment also expanded to include South Asian ethnic groups that had long been dismissed as being "non-martial."[1] The army's rapid expansion in response to the needs of the war raised additional questions concerning the quality of troops and officers.

Through all this upheaval, the Indian Army's officers and men kept focused on the need to learn from the mistakes that were inevitable for any force finding itself in new situations and environments, with inexperienced personnel. The army had a number of teething troubles as it grew in strength and experience, but it was always able to point with pride to its ability to learn from mistakes and adapt to conditions. By the beginning of 1944, the Indian Army had reached a level of performance characterized by consistent and reliable professionalism in an impressive variety of types and theaters of warfare.[2]

North and East Africa, 1939–40[3]

When war broke out in Europe in September 1939, the Government of India offered to expand the Indian Army to help deal with the threat. The British government refused the offer, envisioning the coming crisis as a solely European war. (The Indian Army's significant contributions to the war effort during the First World War appeared to have been forgotten in London.) The defeat of France in 1940, along with Italy's entry into the war, changed the strategic map, and the British government reversed its decision and called for the Indian Army's expansion. By 1941, the army had expanded to more than 1.5 million men, organized into more than 10 divisions.[4]

Equipment shortages were widespread throughout British forces in 1939 and 1940. As a result, only a few Indian formations were equipped to deal with mechanized warfare. These units were organized into the 5th and 11th Indian Infantry Brigade groups and deployed in August and September 1939 to safeguard the defense of Egypt. The 7th Indian Infantry Brigade group followed in 1940, and the three brigades formed the nucleus of the 4th Indian Division.

The 4th Indian Division was the first Indian Army unit to see active service in the Second World War. During the period prior to Italy's declaration of war on June 8, 1940, the division spent its time training. General Sir Geoffrey Evans, then brigade major in the 11th Indian Infantry Brigade, recalled: "we were sent out into the desert…and since our training for desert warfare had been hard and continuous, we were fit, we were tough and we were ready for battle."[5]

The Italians made the first moves in the North African theater. With 14 divisions in Libya, they began to move against Egypt and the strategically vital Suez Canal. Their offensive was cautious, and by September 1940 it had slowed down south of the town of Sidi Barrani, 250 miles west of Alexandria. The British forces in the area were the 4th Indian Division and the 7th Armoured Division (also known as the Desert Rats). General Sir Archibald Wavell, Commander-in-Chief of Middle East land forces, decided to confront the Italian threat rather than wait for it to come to him.

Wavell's forces knew the area in and around Sidi Barrani and were operating at peak efficiency. British forces had previously carried out a series of training exercises to the east of Sidi Barrani, and the Italians did not suspect the British and Indians were preparing for battle. The British massed 31,000 troops, 120 guns, and 225 tanks against 80,000 Italian soldiers, 250 guns and 120 tanks. In late November, senior officers of the 4th Indian and 7th Armoured were advised of the battle plan, and on December 6 the formations moved out for more "training." The following evening, the divisions were informed that the exercise was not training, but indeed the real thing. The first attack against the Italians took place on December 8, at Nibeiwa. Surprise was key, and was effectively achieved; one eyewitness account recalled that "in one hour and 25 minutes from the firing of the first shell, this huge camp was in our possession."[6] Despite this immediate success, the battle lasted three days, and the Italians were soundly defeated. More than 20,000 prisoners were taken, and close to four Italian divisions were destroyed. By comparison, the 4th Indian Division suffered fewer than 700 casualties.[7] The British forces continued to advance across Cyrenaica, but the 4th Indian Division was pulled out and sent to the Sudan to deal with the Italian threat there.

Italian forces in Abyssinia (Eritrea) advanced into British-controlled Sudan in July 1940 and captured Kassala and Gallabat. Italian troops also attacked and overwhelmed British Somaliland (present-day northern Somalia). In September 1940, the 5th Indian Division arrived in the Sudan from India; in late December, they were joined by elements of the 4th Indian Division. The Italians realized that the arrival of the 4th and 5th divisions meant that they would have to withdraw into Abyssinia, a task that occupied them throughout January 1941. They judged that an Indian advance into Abyssinia would involve extremely difficult mountainous terrain, while the Italian defense was concentrated around the strategic positions at Keren. Not all Indian and British units were battle hardened at this stage. As Colonel G. R. Stevens noted, "the enemy began shelling us with light artillery. It was the first time that I had been under fire and I was quite surprised at first—rather feeling that the enemy was cheating using live rounds on manoeuvres."[8]

Entrance into the plains around Keren depended upon penetrating the Donogolaas Gorge. Anticipating this, Italian engineers had set off explosives in the gorge, blocking the road with rubble. This left the Indian troops no option but to seize the surrounding peaks. The irony of the situation was that the Indian troops had been expert mountain warriors due to their experiences on the Northwest Frontier. They had, however, been mechanized and retrained for conditions in North Africa, so they had lost most of the equipment and some of the skills necessary for successful mountain warfare. To make matters worse, units needed to be maintained with supplies in an area that was well forward of most supply depots, as well as being difficult hilly terrain. As General Evans noted, "every drop of water, round of ammo and tin of food had to be laboriously carried up on men's backs."[9]

The first phase of the battle for Keren was an attempt to dislodge the Italians from the west; the focus then switched to the east, and then back to the west side of the gorge. Most of the fighting centered on the western side, along what became known as Cameron Ridge. After the first attacks of February 4–12, the 5th Indian Division withdrew to the rear to resupply and undertake further training in mountain warfare. The second attack, on March 15, involved both divisions in attacks along the ridges, trying to find a breakthrough. Bitter fighting ensued; the Indian divisions seized the vital ridges and held on against an Italian counterattack. By March 27, the Italians were withdrawing from their defenses, and Keren fell without a fight. The two Indian divisions followed up the Italian withdrawal and captured the vital port of Massawa on April 8. Shortly thereafter, the 4th Indian Division was withdrawn to North Africa to contend with the Italian and German counterattacks. The 5th Indian Division continued the fighting in Eritrea, and the Italians surrendered on May 19.

North Africa, Iraq, Syria, and Persia (Iran), 1941

The successes of late 1940 and early 1941 in North Africa were short-lived for British and Commonwealth forces. The Italians reinforced their Libyan army, and the Germans intervened when General Erwin Rommel arrived with the Afrikakorps in February. Rommel launched a major counteroffensive on March 24, not long after the 3rd Indian Motor Brigade arrived in North Africa. Some of the best troops of the British forces had been redeployed elsewhere, principally Greece and East Africa. The Germans and the Italians smashed into the British forces left in the region and pushed them back across Libya. The 3rd Brigade carried out an excellent holding action at El Mechili to give Australian forces time to build up the defenses at Tobruk. The German offensive was flawless, bottling up two divisions in Tobruk while the British managed to muster only one armored brigade and various infantry brigades to defend Egypt.

North Africa was not the only theater troubling British forces in 1941. Iraq, which had become an independent state in 1930, suffered a military coup d'etat in March 1941. The British government considered the Iraqi Army pro-German, and this situation, combined with threats in North Africa and the Balkans, motivated London and GHQ India to act. The 20th Indian Brigade, 10th Indian Division, was earmarked to land at Basra in April. One junior officer described the advance into Basra: "[I]n the event there was no opposition. As we approached Basra I remember clearly passing an Iraqi Army barracks with a parade ground. A medium machine gun unit with its British-made Vickers was on parade. The guns were lined up with their locks open, as if to show there was not hostile intent." This was important, as he noted that "fortunately we were not called up to defend the place [the RAF base at Shaiba] because the battalion were woefully inexperienced."[10] The 21st and 25th brigades shortly arrived in Basra, and the 10th Division, once completed, moved towards Baghdad. They struck north, seizing the valuable oil fields in and around Mosul. The 21st Indian Brigade then moved into western Syria to support British efforts there. At the same time the campaign in Iraq was getting under way, the 5th Indian Brigade, 4th Indian Division, had been sent to Palestine to aid in the capture of Vichy Syria. The attack into Syria began in May, and ended within three weeks with the capture of Damascus.[11]

Wavell, in North Africa, waited for the remainder of 4th Indian Division to arrive, as well as replacement tanks for the 7th Armoured Division, before launching the British counterattack, Operation Battleaxe, on 15 June. The offensive failed, and units of the 4th Indian and supporting tanks from the 7th Armoured Division were forced back to their original positions. The lifting of the siege of Tobruk would have to wait. In July 1941, Wavell was replaced as Commander-in-Chief for the Middle East by General Sir Claude Auchinleck. Meanwhile, Afrikakorps and British and Commonwealth forces gathered strength for the offensives that would be inevitable in the autumn. The British Western Desert Force was renamed the Eighth Army as planning for the campaign got underway.

The oilfields of Persia (Iran) also became a strategic consideration during the summer of 1941. The Germans had placed agents in Teheran, as they had done in Iraq the previous spring. The British and the Soviets decided to mount a joint invasion of Persia, to begin on August 25, 1941, in the hope of safeguarding the oilfields and potentially establishing supply routes through Persia. The Soviets planned to invade the northern regions, along with the 8th and 10th Indian divisions from Iraq. The British, meanwhile, seized Teheran, effectively completing the invasion. One veteran described the reasons for the invasion as "justifiable only on the grounds of war-necessity."[12] To safeguard the conquests of Persia, Syria, and Iraq, PAIFORCE (Persia and Iraq Force) was born. Nearly two and one-half Indian divisions performed internal security duties in the occupied territories over the remainder of the war. Both the 8th and 10th Indian divisions would eventually be shifted to the Middle East fighting.

Auchinleck waited for reinforcements to arrive before he ordered another offensive in North Africa. Operation Crusader was scheduled to begin in November. The main axis of attack to relieve Tobruk was XXX Corps. The 4th Indian Division, commanded by Major General Frank Messervy, was part of XIII Corps, who were ordered to attack the major enemy defensive positions (known as the "Omars") to support the main drive of XXX Corps.

Units of the 4th Indian Division had been reconnoitering the area since September. Lessons from Operation Battleaxe, as well as earlier campaigns, had been compiled and disseminated via the Army in India Training Memoranda (AITM). Reports from the 4th and, later, the 5th Indian divisions were regularly disseminated throughout the army for training purposes.[13]

The general offensive began on the night of November 18–19. XXX Corps crossed the frontier and headed northwest, hoping to destroy Axis forces between Tobruk and the frontier. The 7th Brigade, 4th Indian Division, headed towards the Omars. The other two brigades (5th and 11th) were in reserve, due to the lack of transport available. By November 22, XXX Corps and the rest of XIII Corps were pushing hard to reach their objectives. The Central India Horse (CIH) cut off the road communications for the "Omar" positions, and the 7th Brigade was in position to attack. The 1st Royal Sussex were to attack Omar Nouva, the 4/16th Punjabis, the Libyan Omar, and the 4/11th Sikhs to mask Cove to the north.

The first attack, against Omar Nouva, went according to plan. The position was taken and the Punjabis moved through to attack Libyan Omar, supported by two tank squadrons. This time, the Germans inflicted massive damage on the tanks and hit the Punjabis hard as well. By evening, the Punjabis had managed to seize the eastern portion of the box; one officer recalled that "they battled forward bravely taking one line of trenches after another but suffered so many casualties that at last they stopped."[14]

The attack by the Punjabis ceased altogether on November 23, due to circumstances elsewhere in Operation Crusader. The attack by XXX Corps was being heavily engaged by the Germans and Italians. A large gap had opened between XXX and XIII corps, which General Rommel made haste to exploit. Auchinleck sacked the

Eighth Army commander, General Cunningham, and replaced him with General Neil Ritchie. Confusion reigned within the British and Commonwealth forces as reports circulated about German panzers on the move. The 4th Indian Division, supported by both the 5th and 11th brigades, decided to hold their lines and build up their defensive positions in the Omars. The field artillery of the 4th Indian, with supporting infantry, held their lines and destroyed various German attacks for more than two days. The German attack to link up with the "Omar" positions and force the British back from Tobruk failed. Rommel's tanks needed fuel, and the Allied depots had not been seized.[15]

On 25 November, the Allies counterattacked. The 2nd New Zealand Division moved towards Tobruk, while the 4th Indian continued the attacks against the last remains of the German and Italian defenders in the Omars. By November 30, the Omars had been cleared, and the Axis forces began to retreat on all fronts. The siege of Tobruk was lifted, and the Germans and Italians withdrew across Cyrenaica once again. This time the retreat was orderly, allowing them to inflict substantial damage upon the British forces on their heels. The CIH seized Benghazi before Christmas, followed closely by the rest of the 4th Indian Division.[16]

While units of the 4th Indian Division were stationed[17] in western Cyrenaica in late 1941, Rommel struck. The 4th Indian Division was under the command of Major General F. I. S. Tucker[18] and had been split up—the 7th Brigade was in Benghazi, the 5th was in the rear in Barce and the 11th was in Tobruk. With Rommel moving towards Benghazi, confusion reigned. Tucker received orders to withdraw, and then to attack. Further reports indicated German tanks to the north and east of Benghazi; it became apparent that the Germans had created a large gap between the 1st Armoured and the 4th Indian in Benghazi. On January 27, Tucker and his command staff left Benghazi, and the 7th Brigade was ordered to hold in the town. The 5th Brigade was ordered to withdraw further to the east to avoid the German advance.

The 7th was fighting for its life, encircled and cut off from the roads to the north. Brigadier Harold Briggs,[19] in a bold stroke, decided to break out. He divided his brigade into three groups, and they cut behind the Germans and Italians, before striking into the open desert and making their way to the British lines at El Mechili.[20] The rest of the 4th Indian Division had already met up with units of the 5th Indian Division[21] in Barce. Serious fighting ensued as the German and Italian forces came up against the British forces withdrawing back towards Tobruk. They arrived at Acroma, south-west of Tobruk, on February 4, 1942, and began digging defenses to hold the line.

March to May 1942 was a stalemate in North Africa. The 4th Indian Division[22] was relieved and the three brigades were shipped to Cyprus, Palestine, and the Suez Canal Zone. The 5th Indian Division, under the command of Major General Briggs, took over their positions. The 10th Indian Division[23] was also sent to North Africa to support the British and Commonwealth defenses.

On May 27, 1942, Rommel struck once again, hitting the British positions along the Gazala defense lines. The main attack crashed into the 3rd Indian Motor Brigade box formation. Within three hours, the brigade had suffered such casualties that it ceased to exist as a formation. Scattered elements were able to escape to fight another day. In response, the British threw in all their reserves to stop the advance. The 5th Indian Division was sent in when they heard reports of the 3rd Brigade's engagements. British forces fought the ensuing battle attached to whatever formation needed them most at the time. An official historian wrote that "from this point [5th Division's move] no record will be given of the multiplicity of formations in which the Indian and British units of the Indian Divisions found themselves. The 5th Indian Division for instance never functioned as whole. Sometimes it had two brigades, sometimes one, and on occasions none at all. Brigades of the 4th and 10th Indian Divisions also came under command, only to disappear again."[24]

The fighting was confused and bitter. On June 20, 1942, Tobruk fell to the Germans,[25] and the British began to retreat back into Egypt. Elements of the 10th Indian Division put up a stalwart defense at Mersa Matruh, only to have their flanks exposed and then receive orders on June 28 to break out to the east. By the end of June, the British had withdrawn to the final defense lines west of El Alamein. The 18th Indian Brigade put up a valiant defense against Rommel's advance at the foot of the strategically important Ruweisat Ridge, stopping the advance in early July. On 14 July, the 5th Indian Brigade, 5th Indian Division, successfully attacked in and around the Ruweisat Ridge, which would form a centerpiece to the defense. Rommel counterattacked almost immediately, but failed to gain any ground. Over the course of the month, the rest of the 5th Indian Division reinforced the area. Rommel attempted another attack on August 30, but called it off after two days. The front had been stabilized, and more troops, along with new tanks, artillery, and supplies, began to arrive in Egypt.[26]

General Alexander replaced Auchinleck as Commander-in-Chief, Middle East, and General Bernard Montgomery became Eighth Army commander. The 4th Indian Division relieved the 5th Indian Division on the ridge; the 5th left North Africa for Iraq and was later ordered to India to undergo jungle warfare training for deployment to Burma in 1943. The 10th Indian Division was withdrawn for garrison duty in Cyprus for nearly two years. The 4th Indian remained as the sole Indian formation for the coming Allied victory in North Africa. General Tucker carried on with compiling lessons learned in battle and training instructions for his division.[27]

Malaya and Burma, 1941–42

The Indian Army expanded from about 200,000 men and officers to more than one million between 1939 and 1941. As a result of this rapid growth, many units lacked properly trained officers and men. To compound this problem, any training and planning that was undertaken by Indian troops at depots in India emphasized the type of fighting that was typical of North Africa—open spaces and large mechanized formations.[28]

Under the circumstances, it is perhaps not surprising that the 1941 campaign in Malaya[29] ended in unequivocal defeat. Many of the reasons for the defeat were beyond the control of the troops themselves, and in many cases they rested on decisions made by strategic planners in the 1920s and 1930s. Their performance was conclusively undermined by their lack of training in general, and lack of training in jungle warfare techniques in particular. As Tim Moreman stated: "The British garrison of Malaya, however, was still far from ready in December 1941 for war....[They] paid a heavy penalty in northern Malaya for the limitations of their organisation and equipment and the failure of pre-war training to fit them for the war in the jungle."[30]

The III Indian Corps, comprising the 9th and 11th Indian divisions and supporting brigades, formed the main defensive line in northern Malaya. On December 8, 1941, the Imperial Japanese Army landed veteran troops along the coast, and struck hard at the Indian troops. The Japanese, while not jungle experts, were able to use the terrain to their advantage and constantly outflank III Corps. Within days, Indian troops were in retreat, spending most of their time trying to forestall the Japanese advance. To make matters worse, units in Malaya received very few replacements, and those who did arrive were generally half-trained officers and men who did not know how to fight in the terrain. The campaign was over in seven weeks when Singapore surrendered on February 15, 1942. The Japanese had captured more than 100,000 Australian, Indian, and British officers and men during the campaign.

The Japanese offensive into Burma (First Burma Campaign) began on December 11, 1941.[31] As with Malaya, the Indian forces in Burma were heavily "milked,"[32] and any training given was for open-style warfare. One junior officer remembered his CO asking a staff officer about training; the reply was "training—you can't do any training because it is bloody jungle."[33] The collective training for the two divisions, the 1st Burma and 17th Indian, had been minimal as well. Unlike Malaya, however, many veterans from the Burma campaign escaped to Assam, bringing with them valuable experiences and lessons.[34]

The First Burma Campaign can be divided into two significant parts: first, the fighting to the Sittang Bridge and loss of Rangoon; and second, the retreat to Assam.[35] The Japanese were able to outflank their road-bound and half-trained enemy during the first phase. The 17th Indian Division was below 40 percent strength after the heavy fighting to the Sittang River during January and February. Following the loss of defenses along the river, changes were made within the campaign command structure. Lieutenant General William Slim, as Burma Corps (BURCORPS) commander, and Major General "Punch" Cowan arrived to take over the 17th Indian Division. The last reinforcements arrived in Rangoon as Japanese forces set out to destroy the British, Burmese, and Indian units. Rangoon fell on March 9, cutting off BURCORPS from the outside world.[36]

BURCORPS was forced to retreat as the Japanese were reinforced and increased the pressure to entrap and completely destroy the British and Indian formations, as well as the Nationalist Chinese forces that had intervened in the eastern Shan states. As the units were forced relentlessly north, BURCORPS finally decided on April 28 to formally abandon Burma and withdraw to Assam. The last troops entered the

Imphal Plain by late May. This was the longest retreat in British military history, more than 900 miles. The only saving grace was that the Japanese had failed to completely destroy BURCORPS. Those who had survived would use their knowledge to create a reform movement that would eventually produce the Imperial Japanese Army's single worst defeat.

El Alamein and the Drive to Tunisia, 1942–43

Following the heavy fighting of the spring and summer of 1942, the 4th Indian Division and other formations in the 8th Army were resupplied and rested for a coming offensive. The 4th Indian Division carried out lesson discussions and training directives during this period.[37] On the eve of battle, Brigadier A.W. Holworthy, 7th Indian Brigade, was not optimistic: "D-day—what is to be the outcome? I do not expect too much but keep this to myself."[38]

The role of the 4th Indian Division was to provide support to the main effort. The division was stationed in the southern area of the defensive line and was ordered to carry out raids and tie down the Axis forces in the area. As General Tucker noted to his officers and men on the first day of the battle (October 23), "this is to be a hard fight and prolonged battle. None of us thinks it will be otherwise...no position will be given up. Surrender is shameful."[39] For 10 days, as the battle ebbed and flowed to the north, the 4th Indian Division applied pressure along their defense lines. With Rommel's tanks being cornered towards the coast, on November 1 orders were given for Operation Supercharge. The 5th Indian Brigade was ordered to cut a line in the Axis defenses, to allow the 7th Armoured and 2nd New Zealand divisions to cross out and destroy the Axis forces. The brigade achieved its goal, and the Allied divisions thrust forward to destroy the Afrikakorps. The 4th Indian Division began to round up Axis soldiers in and around the defensive positions, but the pursuit of the Afrikakorps was done by other troops. General Tucker was outraged at the plan to use the 4th Indian Division as a mop-up force, and sent his objections to XXX Corps. Lieutenant General Horrocks agreed and passed along his thoughts to General Montgomery. He emphasized: "There is no doubt that this [4th Indian] is an experienced division, more experienced probably than any other division in the Middle East."[40]

As the Afrikakorps withdrew towards Tunisia, the Eighth Army followed. The terrain in Tunisia was dramatically different from the open desert, and specialist skills were required to overcome the Axis defensive line positions at the Mareth Line.[41] The 4th Indian Division was moved forward in March 1943, and its units conducted raids and reconnaissance patrols assessing the German and Italian defenses. Following a series of unsuccessful attacks by the 50th Division, a revised battle plan was called for. By the end of March, with valuable support from the 4th Indian, the 2nd New Zealand Division had enveloped the Mareth Line from the west, forcing the Axis to withdraw to a series of hills to the north.

In April, the 4th Indian was assigned a diversionary role in the clearance of the Wadi Akarit positions. The attack involved two brigades, and the fighting was bitter.[42] Eventually the British succeeded in turning the Axis forces from their defenses. An officer from the 4/16th Punjabis described the scene: "After a while I saw the platoon advancing across the valley, turn west across a road, then in open formation, return to attack another strongly held feature. I could not stop them....[A]ll we could do was provide supporting fire. What a sight! Twenty-five men attacking a high hill, studded with enemy trenches....[The enemy] threw down their arms and surrendered—300 or more of them." The Germans and Italians withdrew again as Allied forces, First Army, entered the battle from the west. On May 11, 1943, the German commander of the Afrikakorps and Italian troops surrendered to Lieutenant Colonel L.C.J. Showers of the 1/2nd Gurkhas, ending the war in North Africa. Montgomery's comment on the Indian Army's performance in North Africa was succinct. "I sent the First Army my best," he said, "7th Armoured and 4th Indian."[43]

Far East, 1942–43

The period following the defeats in Malaya and Burma was trying for the Indian Army. During the summer of 1942, the Indian National Congress Party called for the "Quit India Movement." The movement caused considerable disruptions for the Indian Army, as more than 60 battalions were called out in the Aid to the Civil Power role. Many units continued to assess and teach the valuable lessons learned in the fighting in both Malaya and Burma, but there was still no centralized system to coordinate all the efforts.[44]

Around this time, the 14th Indian Division was ordered to begin an operation to clear the Japanese from the Arakan region of Burma in the autumn of 1942. The division had carried out some jungle warfare training and had several veteran officers with jungle warfare experience, but it was not sufficiently trained to undertake this mission. And because no centralized training system had been established, any reinforcements that arrived had not received any jungle warfare training. The division advanced slowly, but by the end of 1942 it was close to the end of the peninsula. The advance ended outside Donbaik and Rathedaung near the end of January 1943, and from there the British launched numerous unsuccessful attacks against the Japanese positions. A battle of attrition ensued, and more and more British and Indian brigades were sent to battle. The Japanese, meanwhile, built up their reserves in the area, preparatory to launching a counterattack in mid-March. The British and Indian units, caught off guard, were forced to retreat once again. By the end of April, the British and Indian units, fighting for their lives, had withdrawn all the way to their original starting positions.[45] General Wavell, CinC India, reflecting on the campaign, commented that "we still have a great deal to learn about jungle fighting."[46]

The defeat in the Arakan finally convinced GHQ India to confront the Indian Army's tactical limitations in the terrain of the Far East. The Infantry Committee, formed in June 1943 to assess the situation, criticized the practice of "milking" regiments, which had left many units below strength and deprived of their best officers and men. The Infantry Committee called for a centralized doctrine and training system. They also addressed a number of other issues which are outside the scope of this chapter.[47]

As a result of the Infantry Committee's recommendations, the 14th and 39th Indian divisions were organized as jungle warfare training divisions. Doctrine, in the form of the *Jungle Book,* was created and disseminated to enable officers and men to understand the tactics of jungle warfare. Initiatives and practices relevant to training, operational lessons, and constant performance assessment began to permeate the whole of the Indian Army from mid-1943. The army's war in the Far East was also reorganized. South East Asia Command was created in August 1943 under the command of Admiral Lord Louis Mountbatten; 14th Army was the land component, led by General Slim, while General Auchinleck headed up India Command. More formations arrived to bolster the war effort in the east.[48]

The Indian Army's training transformation was underway. By the end of 1943, the 17th and 23rd Indian divisions, both of whom had instituted assessment and jungle warfare programs, were holding the line in the Imphal region of Assam.[49] The 5th and 7th Indian divisions were sent to the Arakan region to start another offensive along the Mayu Range.[50] The Japanese, for their part, failed to notice that the forces arrayed against them in late 1943 and 1944 were not the same as those they had faced in the past.

Indian troops carry out jungle training (Courtesy of the Imperial War Museum)

Italy 1943–45[51]

Some senior officers and politicians expected that a campaign in Italy would be easy, referring to it as "the soft under-belly of the Axis." In July 1943, the Allies landed on Sicily, with the Indian Army providing a few battalions as "beachhead" units. The campaign ended quickly, and by September the Allies had crossed to mainland Italy. The Italians had surrendered in early September, so the Germans decided to defend the peninsula themselves. Italy's mountainous terrain, numerous rivers, and fortified villages were perfect for military defense, and the Germans knew that they could tie down the Allied forces with relatively few troops. The Italian topography, combined with the skill of the German defenders, made the conquest of Italy a long and bloody campaign that ended only with the surrender of the German forces in other regions.

The 8th Indian Division landed at Taranto, between the heel and toe of the boot of Italy, in September 1943. The Eighth Army, meanwhile, was moving north along the Adriatic coast. The Germans began to fall back towards their first major defensive position, the Gustav line north of Naples, destroying bridges and road systems as they went. In early November, the 8th Indian Division began its first major action, crossing the Trigno River. It took three days of fighting to clear the Germans from their positions, after which the division moved forward to confront the Sangro River defenses. The division crossed the Sangro on November 25 and began to fight its way through a series of fortified villages en route to join up with other divisions and cross the next river, the Moro. The crossing was successful, and on the other side the units were involved in more heavy fighting in the villages. By the time the Allies had cleared the area, winter had set in, slowing the campaign to a series of raids on both sides of the front. The 8th Indian Division spent the winter months snowbound.[52]

The 4th Indian Division had left North Africa for Palestine in the summer of 1943 for rest and training. During this six-month period, General Tucker and his commanders set out to create training exercises emphasizing the lessons learned from the recent North Africa campaigns. In early December, the division was ordered to Italy. Arriving in the Adriatic sector of the front, they immediately set out to learn from the formations around them. Tucker called for a series of lectures and training packages focusing on better armored cooperation and the important "Town and Village Fighting."[53]

Early in February 1944, the division was sent, with the 2nd New Zealand Division, to serve under the command of the U.S. Fifth Army and to seize the town of Cassino and the surrounding hills. This action would involve the two divisions in a prolonged, bloody, and attritional battle for just one section of the Gustav line. The fight for Cassino encompassed four major battles.[54] The U.S. troops had failed in the first attack in January. The 4th Indian Division took part in the defeats of the second and third battles. The German troops in and around Cassino were some of the best troops in the German order of battle and had the advantage of excellent defensive arrangements, centered around Cassino itself and the mountains and monastery overlooking the town.

Italy. Map artwork by The Map Studio, ESS 48, "The Second World War (4) The Mediterranean."
© Osprey Publishing, Ltd. www.ospreypublishing.com.

Tucker was replaced, due to illness, just before the division went into battle. The 4th Indian Division took over positions from the U.S. troops in the area. The first battles for the 4th centred chiefly around the fighting for Pt. 593 en route to the monastery. As with Keren, only a brigade could be maintained in the area, due to the mountainous terrain. Two battalions were thrown at the ridge over the course of four days. All the attacks failed. No ground was taken. The New Zealanders, in the town, fared no better.[55]

Gurkhas from the 4th Indian Division among the Italian mountains (Courtesy of the Imperial War Museum)

The third offensive was called for March 15. The 4th Indian would attempt to seize the monastery and the northern part of town from a different direction. The fighting centered around Castle Hill, which the 4th Indian had taken over from the 2nd New Zealand Division, and the heroic efforts of the 1/9th Gurkhas, who succeeded in reaching the Hangman's Hill, just below the monastery. Realizing the danger they were in, the Germans attacked the Gurkha positions, and heavy fighting ensued. By March 23, a stalemate had developed once again. The General Staff officer grade 1 for the division, Colonel J. K. Shepheard, noted that "morale is very low in many units."[56] The two major battles had cost the division more than 4,000 dead and wounded.

The final battle involved the 8th Indian Division, along with other formations from the Eighth Army that were to be used in two major flank attacks. The 4th Indian Division had returned to the Adriatic sector, and the 8th Indian and

4th British divisions were to breach the German defenses along the Gari River to the south of Cassino. The attack began on the evening of May 11–12, as Allied artillery pounded the German defenses. The crossing was a bitter struggle, but by midday on the May 12 various toeholds had been created. The Germans put up a stiff resistance in and around the town of St. Angelo. After a few days of fierce fighting, it was finally cleared.[57]

The formations that crossed after a series of heavy fights were able to pierce the Gustav defenses, opening the road to Rome. Allied troops successfully completed the linkup with the Anzio beachhead, and Rome fell on June 4, 1944. The 8th Indian Division continued to pursue the Germans towards Perugia; they had advanced more than 200 miles since crossing the Gari River.[58]

The 10th Indian Division arrived in the Adriatic sector of Italy in March 1944. Before their deployment, the formation had been carrying out training, using lessons from the grueling fighting in North Africa and Italy. The commander of the 25th Indian Brigade recalled that "in Cyprus our training was chiefly on elementary and individual standard....We...returned to Lebanon to complete a mountain warfare course before going out to Italy."[59]

Major General Denys Reid, commander of the 10th, was, like many of his counterparts in the Indian Army of 1944, convinced of the need for training directives based upon lessons learned in combat.[60] When the division arrived in Italy, their sector was quiet, enabling units to undertake further training and patrolling activities, to learn different styles of fighting, and to hone their skills. In May, after the bloody battles of Cassino, the 4th Indian relieved the 10th Indian, allowing the 10th to carry out higher-level exercises in mountain warfare. This continued until the division was ordered to move on June 10 to relieve the 8th Indian Division outside Perugia.[61]

On June 30 the division began to push towards Florence. The fighting in northern Italy was similar to earlier campaigns—countless river crossings; the taking of hills, mountains and fortified villages; and ferocious fighting all the way. The Germans had been busy building a second major defensive line, called the Gothic Line, to the north of Florence. This line, like the Gustav line, ran right across the Italian peninsula. By August, the 8th Indian Division had joined the 10th, and the two formations reached Florence in mid-August. They pressed on to the Gothic line positions in early September, when the 10th was moved back to the Adriatic sector to support the 4th Indian against German defenses in the Foglia valley.[62]

Overall, the Allied effort in Italy was suffering a manpower shortage in late 1944. Nearly seven divisions had already been withdrawn to fight in France,[63] and in late September the 4th Indian Division followed suit, redeployed to Greece to intervene in the civil war erupting there in the wake of the German withdrawal.[64]

The remaining Indian divisions continued the advance and constant attritional fighting of patrols and raids throughout the rest of 1944 and into 1945 in the Adriatic sector of the front. Allied commanders recognized the abilities of the Indian divisions; the 8th Indian Division served as a fire brigade, and at one point moved in to replace the U.S. 92nd Division when it encountered problems holding the front.

The final offensives in Italy began in April 1945. The 8th and 10th divisions were involved with the crossing of the Senio River. The attack began on April 9, when the 8th crossed the river. As with all the previous river crossings, the fighting was bitter as the Germans made the Allies pay. When the Germans finally began to give ground, the 10th Indian Division and 43rd Gurkha Lorried Brigade took part in the pursuit. The 10th was ordered to storm the Idice River, the last river crossing before the Po River. After yet more ferocious fighting, the Indian units managed to hold on to their small bridgeheads, while other formations stormed through. The Germans withdrew, the Po Valley opened up, and the war in Italy came to an end.[65]

Burma 1944–45

In 1944, the formations that fought in the 14th Army had been transformed. Early in the year, the Japanese decided to launch Operation Ha-Go in the Arakan to offset British advances in the area and distract attention from their major offensive in the Imphal region. By early February, the Japanese 55th Division was on the move, intending to destroy the 5th and 7th Indian divisions, XV Corps. But these British and Indian units did not break and run as their predecessors had; they stood and fought their ground, ensconced in their new box formations and patrol bases.

The fighting was vicious. One account, of an action by the 1/11th Sikhs, is indicative: "C coy was hit hard in the flank from unseen Japanese trenches....A naik (corporal) named Nand Singh crawled forward and attacked three Japanese trenches in intense hand to hand fighting. He single-handedly cleared all three trenches, allowing the rest of the platoon to come forward."[66] Nand Singh was awarded the Victoria Cross for his actions. Some mistakes were made during the opening phase of battle, but British and Indian units were able to correct the situation, and within a few weeks they had neutralized the Japanese threat. By early March, the Indian Army was on the counteroffensive.[67]

Around the same time, General Slim began to receive reports that the Japanese were on the move in the Assam region. The IV Corps, 17th, 20th, and 23rd Indian divisions and various brigades, were stationed in and around the Imphal region. The Japanese had amassed more than three divisions, with orders to destroy IV Corps and seize the important supply depots in the area. Operation U-Go began on March 9, when the 17th Indian Division made contact along the Tiddim Road. The 17th and 20th Indian divisions were ordered to withdraw to the Imphal Plain. The 17th Indian found it more difficult to extricate itself from the Japanese advance, but eventually succeeded in withdrawing to the plain. The 20th Indian's withdrawal was more orderly.[68] At the end of March, British and Indian units had returned to Imphal. The road network to the north, via Kohima, had been cut off by the Japanese advance.

The fight for Imphal and Kohima became a battle of attrition as British and Indian units held their ground against countless Japanese attacks. Major R. S. Noronha, an Indian Commissioned Officer (ICO), in a situation characteristic of the campaign, was ordered to hold an area to the "last man, last round." A company of 4/3rd Madras Regiment, under Noronha's command, was repeatedly attacked by

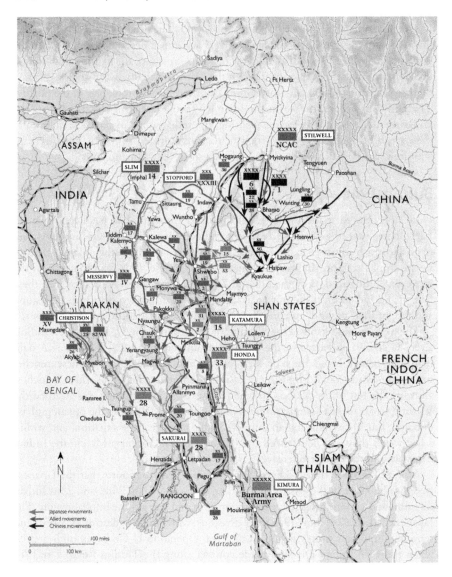

Reconquest of Burma. Map artwork by The Map Studio, taken from *The Pacific War Companion.*
© Osprey Publishing, Ltd. www.ospreypublishing.com.

Japanese along its positions at Sita for seven days and nights. The company held its
ground against every assault, and Noronha received the Military Cross.[69]

Troops in such situations were reinforced with air-dropped and air-landed
supplies and troops.[70] The British/Indian counteroffensive began from the north,
as elements of the 5th and 7th Indian, along with the 2nd British Division, fought
and destroyed the Japanese forces in and around Kohima, linking up with the Imphal

garrison on June 22. The Japanese refused to accept defeat until July 9, when they ordered a withdrawal to Burma. By that time, however, it was too late, and IV Corps, seizing the advantage, carried on with a counteroffensive.

The 14th Army had not been idle either. As the 5th Indian and 11th East African divisions continued the advance to destroy the Japanese withdrawal during the monsoon season, other formations sat down to assess lessons from the operations of 1944 and make improvements in training and deployment. Assessment also identified the fact that, when the army advanced into Burma, the terrain would change, offering new challenges that would need to be examined and discussed. The divisional commanders, as their counterparts in Italy had done, expected officers and men to write down experiences, identify lessons, and assess mistakes. These assessments were incorporated in divisional lessons and training exercises, as well as in the official doctrine written by GHQ India and embodied in the AITM and Military Training Pamphlets (MTPs).[71]

Operation Extended Capital[72] brought about the final destruction of the Imperial Japanese Burma Area Army. By late November 1944, Slim and his commanders were ready to begin the advance into Burma. The offensive began in early December, when the 19th and 20th Indian divisions crossed the Chindwin River and advanced on Japanese forces stationed on the other side. The Japanese, however, had placed only rearguard troops on the Shwebo Plain; most of their forces had withdrawn to the far side of the Irrawaddy River. Their defensive line followed the river from north of Mandalay south towards Nyaungo. Realizing that his original plan was not going to work, Slim altered it accordingly.

Under the revised plan, IV Corps was earmarked to carry out a secret route march that would end up opposite the thinly defended river area near Nyaungo. There they would cross and strike towards the important Japanese supply network based at Meiktila. Meanwhile, XXXIII Corps was earmarked to cross the Schwebo Plain and draw the Japanese into a battle in and around Mandalay. General Slim theorized that "If we took Meiktila while Kimura [Japanese commander] was deeply engaged along the Irrawaddy about Mandalay, he would be compelled to detach large forces to clear his vital communications. This would give me not only the major battle I desired, but the chance to repeat the hammer and anvil tactics [used previously at Imphal and Kohima]...[with] XXXIII Corps the hammer from the north against the anvil of IV Corps at Meiktila and the Japanese between."[73]

Slim's plan worked, but fighting in the bridgeheads was ferocious. The 1/11th Sikhs, as part of the 7th Indian Division's bridgehead, encountered Japanese forces determined to destroy their positions before the division could launch a strike towards Meiktila. The Japanese launched repeated attacks, and the brutal conditions are indicated by the story of 1/11th Sikhs' Jemadar Parkash Singh. Jemadar Singh, of C Company, rallied his men repeatedly and carried ammunition between posts. He was wounded three times before a grenade killed him. He died in the arms of his company commander and was later awarded the Victoria Cross.[74]

Despite the best efforts of the Japanese, Meiktila was in British hands by early March 1945, and the Japanese were regrouping to defend against the British and

19th Indian divisional artillery at Mandalay (Courtesy of the Imperial War Museum)

Indian bridgeheads in and around Mandalay. Fierce fighting ensued in and around Mandalay and Meiktila and along the Irrawaddy River. One machine gun company noted counting more than 250 dead Japanese outside their perimeter after three nights' fighting.[75] The Japanese began to withdraw on March 24, unable to hold their positions against the aggressive British and Indian forces. A Japanese commander commented that "since 2[8]th of February allied tanks [thrust] deep into our positions every day.... [I]n this fighting the co-operation among allied infantry, artillery and tanks was made admirably."[76]

With the area firmly under British and Indian control, the race to Rangoon began. The 14th Army's professionalism was demonstrated as its units quickly adapted to new conditions; some units executed open-style and mechanized warfare, while others reverted to jungle tactics, as the Japanese were systematically destroyed along the banks of the Irawaddy and the road to Rangoon. Rangoon fell to an amphibious assault on May 3, ending the war in Burma for all intents and purposes. The Burma campaign, which had begun as the longest retreat in British military history, ended as the Imperial Japanese Army's most conclusive defeat.

Indianization and Recruitment Expansion

The Indian Army ended the war as the largest all-volunteer force the world had ever seen—more than 2.5 million men. The only way for the army to expand to these levels rested with two innovations that were nothing short of revolutionary in the historical and political context of British India. The first was the rapid expansion of the "Indian" officer class, and the second was the expansion of recruitment policies to include men from the so-called "non-martial" races.

The chief architect of these critical reforms was General Sir Claude Auchinleck, Commander-in-Chief of the Indian Army in 1941, and again from 1943 to 1947. Auchinleck did not agree with the racial prejudices that were widespread in British India before the Second World War, and he set out to eradicate them from army policy as quickly as he could. His influence was widely felt and made him an object of respect throughout the army, particularly among Indian personnel; one Indian ICO, writing to Auchinleck late in the war, stated: "I know who is behind all these moves [reform of the officer class] and the ICOs thank you for your kindness you have showed them during your command."[77]

Indian officers had traditionally been restricted to positions in which they could not command British officers. This policy ended in 1940, and from then on Indian officers were assigned throughout the army as needed. They could command British officers and would later serve on courts-martial of British soldiers and officers. (Issues surrounding pay inequality, however, remained unresolved until 1945, despite Auchinleck's efforts.) In 1941, British officers outnumbered Indian officers in the Indian Army 12–1; by 1945, this ratio had dropped to 4.2–1. The first Indian officer to command a combat unit was Lieutenant Colonel D.S. Brar, 5th Mahratta Machine Gun Battalion, 8th Indian Division, in late 1943. By the end of the war, several Indian lieutenant colonels as well as three brigadiers commanded infantry, cavalry, and artillery units. Many of these had been decorated for bravery in the field. The most highly decorated Indian Army battalion in the war, the 2/1st Punjab Regiment, included one ICO who received the Distinguished Service Order (out of five awarded to the battalion) and seven ICOs who received MCs (out of twelve awarded to the battalion).[78]

A number of groups, including the Madrassis, Ahers, M&R Sikhs, Baluchis, Chamars, and Gujars, all of whom had previously been dismissed as "non-martial," were heavily recruited during the war. Attempts to expand the army to include people who had been excluded took time, and the prewar preference for recruits from "martial" races persisted in some quarters. Despite such obstacles, troops from the newly recruited groups performed well in the war in various theatres. One such group, the Sikh Light Infantry (SLI), received high praise from their divisional commander, Major General Cowan, after the fighting in Meiktila: "I can best describe them by saying that, in my opinion, the SLI are absolutely first class." In recognition of their performance, the postwar Indian Army continued to recruit men and officers from these groups.[79]

The Indian Army went through some growing pains during the Second World War. It made many mistakes, but its great strength as an organization was its ability to learn from those mistakes. By the middle of 1945, it was a professional, modern military force, capable of waging war in the jungle, in the mountains, on the open plains—even as an amphibious assault force. The need to learn from defeat had been drilled into the minds of the Indian Army's officers as they learned their trade in North and East Africa to eventually lead troops in Italy and the Far East.

The success of the Indian Army's reforms is most clearly demonstrated in its victory over the Imperial Japanese Army in 1945. A more subtle indication of the changes brought about is evident in a quote from *The Road Past Mandalay*, the memoirs of John Masters, a Gurkha officer:

As the tanks burst away down the road to Rangoon . . . it took possession of the empire *we* had built. . . . Twenty races, a dozen religions, a score of languages passed in those trucks and tanks. When my great-great-grandfather first went to India there had been as many nations; now there was one—India. . . . It was all summed up in the voice of an Indian colonel of artillery. The Indian Army had not been allowed to possess any field artillery from the time of the Mutiny (1857) until just before the Second World War. Now the Indian, bending close to an English colonel over a map, straightened and said with a smile, "O.K., George. Thanks. I've got it. We'll take over all tasks at 1800. What about a beer?"[80]

CHAPTER 8

The Indian National Army, 1942–1946: A Circumstantial Force[1]

Chandar S. Sundaram

Origins and the First INA

The story of the Indian Army in World War II cannot be told without reference to the Indian National Army (INA), a force raised to fight for India's independence, which was "allied" to the Japanese. This is because the INA's nucleus was the nearly 45,000 *jawans* (soldiers) of Britain's Far Eastern Command, captured by the Japanese when Singapore fell in early 1942. While it is undeniable that a substantial portion of the nearly 40,000 *jawans* who joined the INA in 1942 did so to gain better treatment from the Japanese, recent research has revealed incidents of discontent, disaffection, and outright mutiny among the Indian troops garrisoning the two major stations of the British Far East, at Singapore and Hong Kong, prior to the Japanese attack. This, compounded with the inept British handling of the Malayan campaign, shook the loyalty of the *jawan*.[2]

Besides these soldiers, the formation of the INA involved the Imperial Japanese Army (IJA) and the politically minded Indian expatriate community in Japanese-occupied Southeast Asia. The IJA sought to exploit the above-mentioned disaffection of Indian troops by suborning their loyalty to the Raj. The Indian expatriates, operating on the principle "your enemy's enemy is your friend," thought that by allying themselves with the Japanese, they would help hasten the British departure from India.[3]

Despite their initial promises, the IJA was never entirely comfortable with the INA. To them, the fact that the core of its personnel had surrendered made it automatically worthless, since under the Japanese *Bushido* code, surrender represented dishonor and an irredeemable loss of face. Also, despite their "Asia for Asians" rhetoric, many IJA officers and men were racist and looked down upon other Asians, as their treatment of the Chinese since 1931 had clearly demonstrated.[4]

There were two INAs in the Far East. The first was commanded by a Sikh former prisoner of war (POW)—Captain Mohan Singh, a regular Indian Army officer who had graduated from the Royal Indian Military Academy at Dehra

Dun. He had progressive ideas. For instance, to foster nationalism and solidarity among INA's rank-and-file, he instituted a common mess in the INA, as opposed to the separate religiously-based messing then prevalent in the Indian Army. But he quickly became frustrated that the Japanese only allowed the formation of one INA division of 16,000 men. Singh also resisted attempts of both the IJA and the Indian Independence League (IIL), the political organization of the Indian expatriate community, to limit the INA's independence and autonomy. In December 1942, matters came to a boil as the Japanese ordered Mohan Singh's arrest. In retaliation, Singh ordered the INA to disband, and all INA personnel promptly complied.[5]

Subhas Chandra Bose

The Japanese, however, wanted to keep the INA alive for its great propaganda value. For this they needed it to be led by an Indian with an established political stature. Subhas Chandra Bose fit the bill perfectly. A famous Indian nationalist from Bengal, Bose was in the same league as Mahatma Gandhi and Jawaharlal Nehru. However, Bose disagreed with these leaders' nonviolent, noncooperationist nationalism and favored an outright armed struggle against the Raj. In 1940, he escaped from British custody and made his way to Berlin. There, Nazi leaders were lukewarm to his idea of leading an army to liberate India from British rule. Despite this, Bose managed to form the 3,000-man Free India Legion, composed of Indian POWs captured by Axis forces in North Africa. Some of these *jawans* saw action against Allied troops invading France in 1944. While in Europe, Bose also spent time broadcasting anti-British propaganda to India.[6]

Bose realized that the Japanese takeover of Southeast Asia offered more scope for the formation of a liberation army and immediately wanted to go there. Eventually, in mid-1943, Bose was transported to Southeast Asia by submarine. Along the way, at the suggestion of one of his aides, he adopted the title "Netaji" ("revered leader," in Bengali). Once in Singapore, Bose galvanized the Indian expatriate movement by forming the Provisional Government of Free India (Azad Hind). He also expanded the INA to three "divisions"—each about the size of an Indian Army brigade—the first composed entirely of Indian ex-POWs, the second of Indian ex-POWs and local Indian civilian recruits, and the third entirely of Indian civilians. He even formed a womens' unit, the Rani of Jhansi Regiment, named in honor of the Indian heroine of the 1857 uprising.[7] Significantly, however, Bose made little attempt to rehabilitate or consult with Mohan Singh.

Bose also began negotiating with the IJA about a combat role for the INA in the planned Japanese offensive into Northeastern India. Bose envisioned a grandiose "March on Delhi"—*Chalo Dilli* in Hindustani—with the INA in the vanguard. He believed that Indian Army *jawans,* once they encountered the INA, would immediately join it, thus becoming an irresistible force against the British. This was not as farfetched as it may seem, for during the Malayan campaign of 1941–42, cells composed of IJA intelligence operatives and members of a Sikh expatriate extremist political organization had effectively induced *jawans* to defect.[8] The IJA, however, had other ideas. They merely intended to shore up the Japanese Empire's western perimeter by destroying the Allied buildup on the Indo-Burmese frontier. In these plans, the INA had no combat role; however, Bose insisted that it have one. After much wrangling, a compromise was reached. One INA brigade— the Bose Brigade—would be deployed in the forthcoming offensive, along with INA intelligence and special service detachments.

Chalo Dilli Goes Bust: The INA in Battle

INA units saw action on three fronts: in the Arakan and at Imphal in 1944, and on the Irrawaddy–Central Burma front in 1945. Contrary to the accounts of some Western and Indian writers,[9] their combat performance was far from stellar. Units were deployed in piecemeal fashion and in support roles. For example, the First Battalion, Bose Brigade, under Major P.S. Raturi, was deployed along the Kaladan River, on the extreme east of the IJA front in the Arakan. And rather than being a vanguard, it was more of a rearguard, reaching its positions in April 1944, well after the launching of the Japanese offensive. There, it fought against British West African troops and planted the Indian Tricolor flag on Indian soil, after taking the village of Mowdok (now in Bangladesh), just inside the border. But Mowdok had only a symbolic importance. It had no strategic value, and Raturi's men abandoned it in September 1944.[10]

The rest of the Bose Brigade, commanded by Lieutenant-Colonel Shah Nawaz Khan, was not faring any better. Deployed in the Chin Hills, a very quiet sector on the IJA's line of communications, Shah Nawaz's men were put to work, building and repairing roads and running supplies to frontline IJA units—but not fighting. Shah Nawaz complained to Bose, who managed to secure a promise from the IJA of a combat role for Shah Nawaz's men—but only after two weeks' hard bargaining. But the combat role never came. Moreover, the INA's logistics, never good, now broke down completely. The twin specters of disease and starvation haunted the INA *jawans* in the Chin Hills. Not surprisingly, in July 1944, companies of the Third Battalion, Bose Brigade, surrendered to the British.[11]

Apart from the Bose Brigade, approximately 400 men of the INA's Intelligence and Special Service groups were deployed in the Arakan. They were tasked with intelligence-gathering, raiding Allied communications, and trying to win over Indian Army *jawans*. They were not very successful, especially in the last task, because the Indian Army was now a very different animal from what it had been in 1941–42.[12]

Despite the fact that they had only agreed to the frontline presence of the Bose Brigade, the Japanese reluctantly gave way to Bose's constant pestering, allowing the INA's First Division to be deployed on the Imphal sector. Here, it was to operate under the IJA's 33rd Division. Its only operation of note was the attack on the Palel airbase, on April 30, 1944. This was a disaster. The INA commander, Colonel M.Z. Kiani, was told that the Allied forces were on the brink of surrendering and was ordered to take the airbase in a swift attack. But the British and Indian

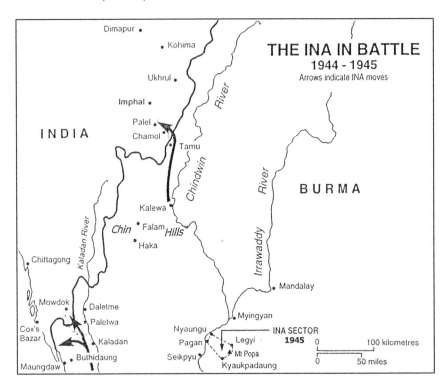

The INA in battle, 1944–1945 (Courtesy of *War and Society*)

forces there were well fed and well armed, and repulsed the INA's flimsy assault. Here too, Indian Army *jawans* held the INA in contempt.[13]

Mass desertions caused withdrawal of the Azad and Gandhi brigades of the First INA division from the front by July 1944. When interrogated by Allied military intelligence, these men reported that they had deserted because they had to endure severe privations and because of high-handed treatment by IJA personnel. By mid-August 1944, the Japanese offensive had failed, and they were in full retreat, taking the First INA Division with them. A total of 9,000 INA *jawans* had been deployed—1,500 in the Arakan and 7,500 in the Imphal battles. It had suffered about 1,000 killed and wounded, and between 2,000 and 3,000 dead from sickness and starvation.[14]

Defeat on the Irrawaddy

Meeting with his senior commanders in October 1944, Bose was shocked by the difficulties they had faced in combat and in their relations with IJA frontline command. However, instead of trying to dissociate the INA from Japanese war plans—which any military commander with a concern for his men would have done—Bose sought a greater role for the INA in the Japanese defense of Burma. Because of Bose's persistence, the IJA agreed to Bose's demand that the INA be allotted an independent sector in which it could operate in a unified way. Accordingly, Second Division INA was given a small sector along the eastern bank of the Irrawaddy River, between the IJA's 15th and 28th armies. Here, it was to guard against Allied river crossings, help fortify the Mount Popa–Kyaukpadaung sector, and patrol the upper reaches of the Irrawaddy towards Mandalay.[15]

The INA's experience in this sector was extremely similar to what it had been subjected to in the Arakan and Imphal fighting of 1944. In spite of Bose's insistence on the INA's operational integrity and autonomy, the officer commanding the Japanese 15th Army decided that the INA's Nehru Brigade be put under his command. He then ordered it to the villages of Nyaungu and Pagan, where it was to act as a flank guard. Furthermore, in early February, 1945, the entire Second Division INA was placed under IJA command and ordered to build fortifications. Symbolically, its radio link with the Japanese 15th Army was terminated.[16]

Matters were about to get a lot worse. On February 14, the Allies launched their main attack across the Irrawaddy, at the junction of the IJA's 15th and 28th Armies. The Nehru Brigade, caught in the crosshairs of the 7th Indian Division, was overrun. Two hundred and fifty of its men surrendered. A joint INA-IJA counterattack on February 16 fought hard, but failed to stem the tide. By that evening, the Nehru Brigade was retreating, having lost a majority of its men through desertion.[17]

The INA's dismal performance and desertion rate—900 in February alone—greatly alarmed Bose. He even tried to visit the front to boost INA morale, but the IJA prevented him from doing this. However, he did increase his morale-boosting pronouncements. He also instituted capital punishments for INA deserters, and offered monetary rewards for INA *jawans* who captured Allied personnel. These punishments/inducements proved somewhat effective. In March and April 1945, INA units fought better. Another reason for this improved performance was that most of the men of the INA units were now Tamils, recruited from the Malayan Indian civilian community. Both the IJA and the British thought the Tamils fought better than the overwhelmingly "martial race" Indian ex-POWs. The British thought this was because the Tamils had nothing to lose, as opposed to the ex-Indian POWs, who desperately wanted to get back to India.[18]

The INA lost 637 men in combat in the Irrawaddy battles, but nearly twice that number—1,100—had deserted, or had surrendered without firing a shot. By May 1945, the INA's retreat had become a disorderly rout, and mass surrenders of INA men became frequent. When Allied forces took Rangoon that month, the last remnants of the INA's frontline troops—7,000 men—capitulated. But where was Bose? He had left with the evacuating Japanese. Some have criticized him for doing this.[19] However, their criticism is misplaced, as Bose was a political leader and not a military commander, although he did like wearing uniforms. Would Churchill, had he been at Tobruk when Rommel's tanks came charging in, have surrendered with his men? I think not. In August 1945, Bose embarked on a rather fantastic scheme to reach the Soviet Union. He never got there, dying instead when his plane crashed on take-off from Taipei.

Controversy continues to surround Bose's death. As recently as May 2006, an Indian inquiry commission appointed in 1999 published its finding that Bose "... did not die in a plane crash and the ashes in the Renkoji Temple [in Japan] were not those of Netaji." This is buttressed by the fact that the Taiwanese government categorically stated in 2005 that "...there were no plane crashes at Taipei between August 14 and September 20, 1945 [the timeframe during which Bose's plane is supposed to have crashed.][20] It is an unsolved mystery, which adds to Bose's heroic allure.

The INA Trials and Their Impact

After Japan's surrender, British authorities in India decided to put the INA—or "Japanese Indian Forces" (JIFs) as they called them—on trial, for the treasonable offense of "waging war against the King-Emperor." Some of them were also charged with murder and abetment to murder, because they had been involved in trying and executing INA jawans whom they had caught deserting. The trials were to take place in the full glare of publicity, at the Red Fort in Delhi.[21]

The British believed that, in staging the trials in such a way, they would demonstrate their power, and the INA's impotence, to the Indian public. They miscalculated, badly. First, holding the trial in the Red Fort was deeply offensive to Indians. It was the same place where, 87 years before, the British had tried the Mughal emperor, Bahadur Shah, for his part in leading the Indian uprising of 1857. Thus the choice of venue legitimated the INA in Indian eyes by linking its exploits with 1857, which some Indians at the time were characterizing as India's "first war of independence."[22]

A second factor promoting the Indian public's support for the INA was religion. The first INA defendants were a Muslim, Shah Nawaz Khan, a Hindu, Prem Kumar Sahgal, and a Sikh, Gurbaksh Singh Dhillon. Considering that these three faiths accounted for nearly 99 percent of India's population, and considering that religion was and still is an extremely important touchstone in South Asia, it is easy to see why this aroused the ire of Indian public opinion.

A third factor was the exploitation of the issue by the Indian National Congress. During the war, Congress leaders like Nehru, while acknowledging the sincerity of the INA's efforts, had staunchly come out against it, as it was totally opposed to their own nonviolent beliefs. However, at the war's close, Congress leaders, including Nehru, had just been released from detention. They needed an issue that would once again propel them into the limelight, where they needed to make up any ground lost to the Muslim League, an organization now pushing for the creation of Pakistan. The INA was just such an issue. Besides organizing an INA defense committee, which included Nehru himself, Congress actively promoted public Indian opposition to the trials. At first, these were mere peaceful protests, but rioting soon followed, with Indians attacking white Allied service personnel. Moreover, there were signs that

Hindus, Muslims, and Sikhs were uniting over the issue. More alarming for the British were indications that Indian armed forces personnel were supporting the INA defendants. In February 1946, mutinies occurred in the Royal Indian Navy and Royal Indian Air Force. Sentiment against the INA trials, while not the main cause of these disturbances, was certainly a factor in many of the mutineers' minds.[23]

All this pressure forced the British to adopt a lenient policy. The Commander-in-Chief, Auchinleck, commuted the sentences of transportation for life in the first trial, essentially setting the defendants free. In April 1946, it was decided to terminate all INA trials, but that those few already found guilty would serve out their terms. After India gained independence, Nehru made a pledge to grant INA personnel veterans' pensions. In deference to opinion within the army, however, he strictly forbade INA veterans from rejoining the Indian armed forces.

The INA: A Circumstantial Force?

The INA existed because of a special set of circumstances. Its raw material—the nearly 45,000 *jawans* who formed the core of its manpower—was the result of disastrous Allied defeat in Malaya and Singapore. Its formation resulted from circumstantial collaboration between IJA intelligence officers and Indian underground nationalist organizations. For a leader, it had Subhas Bose, a prominent Indian nationalist with fascist leanings who was eager to seize the circumstantial opportunity offered by the INA. Congress' involvement too was circumstantial. In 1945, it needed an issue, and the INA trials could not have been a better one. After independence, successive Congress governments ignored INA veterans, favoring instead their established, stable, and apolitical armed forces.

Militarily, we must honestly admit that the INA was a disaster. This assessment stems from three basic considerations. First, if at all Tokyo considered the INA, it was only as a propaganda tool. Second, the IJA, from its high command all the way to its field command level, regarded the INA with suspicion and contempt. This was because the core of the INA consisted of men who had surrendered, the very idea of which was an absolute anathema to the Japanese. Also, it was very clear that the IJA's and the INA's conceptions of logistics were poles apart. Third, we must question Bose's leadership. Yes, he was a fervent believer in India's freedom, and yes, he was a brilliant organizer; but he was a politician, not a soldier. He lacked the devotion to his men that is the mark of a good officer. In this light he comes off rather badly in comparison with Mohan Singh. When the Japanese were high-handed, Mohan Singh stood his ground, even to the point of dissolving the INA. Bose, it seems, went along with the Japanese, arguing for an independent INA sector when the experience of the disastrous Imphal-Kohima campaign should have told him that his force was a "paper tiger" rather than the springing one he so wished it to be. Had he known that, and it is inexplicable that he did not, he might have stood his ground, laying down certain requirements to be met before the INA would fight. These requirements included the proper arming and supplying of his men, proper medical care of his men, and the status of an allied army. Objectively speaking, then, he is far from being "...the greatest military hero of India's modern history," which is how he is commonly depicted in modern Bengal and, curiously, by a recent historical monograph on British Asia in World War II.[24]

But the INA's real significance lay in what it did to the Raj. The very fact that about 35,000 men had joined the INA, and that a large portion of them were Indian POWs, surely shook the confidence of the British. It also directly questioned their ability to rule India in a way that had not been attempted since 1857. Indeed, Auchinleck, the last Commander-in-Chief of the "old" Indian Army, by adopting a lenient policy towards the INA defendants, tacitly acknowledged that for the Raj, the end was nigh.

CHAPTER 9

End of the Raj, 1945–1947[1]

Daniel P. Marston

The postwar period brought new and difficult challenges for the British Indian Army. Many of the difficulties resulted from political decisions taken in New Delhi and London. These left the army facing massive demobilization, threats upon morale, political and communal violence, the thankless task of occupation duties in Southeast Asia,[2] and the most difficult task, the division of the Indian Army by the summer of 1947.

The Indian National Army

The Indian National Army (INA) was born from the defeats in Malaya and Burma in the early years of the Second World War. Indian prisoners of war were encouraged or coerced to fight on the side of Japanese forces—ultimately, as they believed, to free India from British imperialism. See Chapter 8 for a more detailed discussion of the INA. At the end of the war, Indian Army troops suspected of involvement in the INA were brought back to India to face the consequences of their actions.

In the end, only seven officers and viceroy commissioned officers (VCOs) were put on trial for INA involvement. General Sir Claude Auchinleck was primarily responsible for this decision. He decided to limit the trials to minimize the repercussions, primarily within the Indian Army but also within the civilian population. He gave as his reason the fact that "the evidence reaching us now increasingly goes to show that the general opinion in the Army is in favor of leniency."[3] Auchinleck further commented: "As soon at it became known to the public that trials were about to commence, all the main political parties, especially [the Indian National] Congress [Party], made the INA a prominent political issue."[4] Later, in November 1945, Auchinleck elaborated: "the present INA trials are agitating all sections of Indian public opinion deeply and also have provided the Congress with an excellent election cry."[5] Jawaharlal Nehru in particular used the situation to his advantage, contradicting his wartime sentiments, when he categorically stated that "they [INA] had put themselves on the wrong side and were functioning under Japanese auspices."[6]

The first INA trial was held in the Red Fort from November 3 to December 31, 1945. Fearing that a closed trial would be dismissed as illegitimate, Auchinleck therefore decided to make the trial public. This was a serious mistake, as the trial sparked a public and press frenzy. The three defendants[7] were a Hindu, a Muslim, and a Sikh. All were found guilty, but the death sentences were commuted in recognition of the political climate. However, the men were sentenced to cashiering, forfeiture of pay, and banishment for life.

What was the effect upon the Indian Army? One report, published in January 1946, stated that: "the events of the past quarter [three months] have brought the army into closer contact with Indian politics...than ever before. The main reason has been the exploitation by the political parties of the INA court martial....The soldiers who [are] normally disinterested in political matters [have] been forced to consider the questions."[8] Intelligence reports commented: "first impressions are that [the INA trial] has had little effect on the opinion of the bulk of the rank and file and may have if anything enjoyed a slight decline in interest."[9] Auchinleck, feeling the pressure, decided to send out questionnaires throughout the army to assess feeling about the INA. The findings were thought-provoking. The opinions of officers, for example, could be summed up as follows:

> the vast majority [ICOs], however much they may like and respect the British, are glad and relieved because of the result of the trial. Most of them admit the gravity of the offence and do not condone it, but practically all are sure that any attempt to enforce the sentence would have led to chaos in the country at large and probably to mutiny and dissension within the army culminating in its dissolution probably along communal lines....[T]hey realise that if their future is to be at all secure, discipline and loyalty must be maintained....[VCOs] in many units apparently [displayed] little interest...in the INA trials....[Ironically] the effect on British officers has been bad, and has led to public criticism which has not been in accordance with the traditional loyalty I am entitled to expect....[M]oreover, they forgot, if they ever knew, the great bitterness bred in the minds of many Indian officers in the early days of Indianisation by the discrimination, often very real, exercised against them, and the discourteous, contemptuous treatment often meted out to them by many British officers who should have known better.[10]

Mutinies and Disturbances

The Royal Indian Navy (RIN) mutiny, which erupted near Bombay on February 18, 1946, arose out of concerns about prospective demobilization. The disturbance was handled quickly and contained by a platoon from the Ajmer Regiment.[11] A small contingent of Indian Army logistical support troops took part in this disorder; they were caught and tried for their activities. The effect on the army appeared to be negligible.[12] Indeed, the Indian Army received great praise for its handling, both of the mutiny and of the civil disturbances that occurred in Bombay. One report recounted how "during the RIN mutiny in Bombay and subsequent civil disturbances in the city, the morale of the Indian troops employed in settling the mutiny and in assisting the civil power was reported to have been high. Men carried out their duties efficiently and impartially."[13]

Despite the Indian Army's performance, nationalist attempts to subvert Auchinleck's authority compelled him to set out the army's role clearly. He did so in a letter to his officers on March 28, 1946. The letter was addressed to "Every Officer of the Indian Army." He emphasized that the "Great Duty" was to let the Indian Army guard its good name and that the army was the anchor of the country. It further emphasized that all officers "remain disciplined: efficient: and LOYAL TO WHATEVER GOVERNMENT MAY BE IN POWER....THUS MAY THE INDIAN ARMY LEAD THE WAY."[14]

Calcutta Riots

As the subcontinent moved closer to independence, political and communal violence steadily increased. In August 1946, the Indian Army was called in to contend with serious communal violence in Calcutta. The army was not called in until August 17, several days after violence had erupted. By August 19, they had the situation under control, but more than 10,000 people had died during the "Great Calcutta Killing." One report evaluating the army's performance during the riots stated that "all ranks employed in Calcutta during and after the riots are reported to have behaved in an exemplary manner and have received praise for their hard work, fairness and impartiality. The Calcutta calamity seems if anything to have drawn Indian soldiers of different communities closer together."[15] The adjutant general of the army, General Sir Reginald Savory, wrote to his wife: "I find it all intensely interesting as I am fairly closely involved in things so far as the army alone stands between order and chaos just now."[16]

Senior Indian officials such as Sardar Baldev Singh, cabinet member of the interim government and representative on the defense committee, stated mixed views: "[T]he army had been well disciplined up to now and there had been no difficulty with Indian troops in Calcutta, but if bigger communal riots occurred some parts of the army might be affected."[17]

Demobilization and Division of the Army

From the end of the Second World War until June 1947, the Indian Army went through a major reorganization. At the end of the war, the army stood at some 2.5 million men. As soon as peace was declared, the Indian and British governments moved quickly to demobilize most of the army, mindful of costs. As one officer stated, "planning for the composition and size of the army had been going on for the past two years, but the basis of planning had to be changed...in order to fall in line with the financial resources likely to be available."[18] The fear of a demobilized and militarized society began to surface in March 1946. One intelligence report highlighted disaffection within the Jat Sikh ranks, who wondered why they were being demobilized and expressed anger at such a move.[19] Numerous proposals were put forward in an attempt to slow plans for demobiliszation; meanwhile, General Auchinleck feared that too many issues remained unresolved on the political side and believed that the Indian Army would be required to serve as the backbone of a secure society. Matters, however, had been taken out of the army's hands. By October 1946, there were just 800,000 soldiers in the army;[20] this number was scheduled to decrease even further, to 387,000 men, by April 1947. General Auchinleck felt that this number was too small to carry out the myriad duties of an army, especially one with as many internal security responsibilities as the Indian Army.[21] Senior commanders fretted that "the army cannot be looked upon by the civil power as an enormous reservoir....[O]fficers are noting that their numbers are too low to carry out all their duties and General Messervy [GOC Northern Command] stated that many units are below strength."[22]

The first formal discussions about dividing the Indian Army took place in London in March 1947, with General Geoffrey Scoones representing the Indian Army and Auchinleck. Those present decided to create a secret plan to divide the army along communal lines, fearing that morale would suffer if the army found out too soon.[23] The British Chiefs of Staff went into greater detail about the potential division of the forces, but asserted that "in any event, there must be no splitting of the Indian armed forces while we [British] are responsible for the defence of India....The Indian armed forces must therefore remain efficient [to deal with civil strife] and under unified control until the time of handing over power."[24] It is interesting to note how quickly these views would change. Some members of the interim government called for the army to be divided up along communal lines as soon as possible.[25] Auchinleck, meanwhile, advised the Viceroy of India, Lord Mountbatten, that it might take years to plan and carry out such a split in the army. For just one example, many Muslim officers did not reside in the territory that would become Pakistan.[26]

Mr. Baldev Singh, defense minister, was one of the few politicians who seemed to understand the army as an entity. He wrote: "The armed forces as a whole have been built upon a non-communal basis. They have, fortunately for India, remained free from communal complications up until now....[I]f even the mere indication of splitting the armed forces is allowed to gain ground at this stage, it will result in creating chaotic conditions in the ranks and disintegration will set in almost immediately....[I]n the communally surcharged atmosphere...such a contingency would be too disastrous to contemplate."[27] Throughout the month of May, both Mr. Singh and Auchinleck attempted to forestall movement on or even discuss the proposed division of the armed forces.

On June 3, Mountbatten informed Auchinleck unequivocally that it would be necessary to divide the armed forces. Adjutant General Savory wrote that "the political leaders of India are intent on splitting the Indian Army as rapidly as they possibly can, irrespective of the cost, and they will do it at the fastest rate."[28] On June 4, Mountbatten announced a further complicating factor: Independence was now to be granted on August 15, 1947, instead of June 1948 as originally planned. Auchinleck had officially stated only four days previously that it would take three years to undertake the division properly. In response, he had been given less then three months.

Punjab Violence: February–September 1947

The communal violence that erupted in the Punjab in February and continued into October 1947, with varying degrees of intensity, tested the Indian Army at the same time that major changes occurred in its structure. To complicate the situation still further, a large percentage of the army still recruited heavily in the province.

The earliest reports from this period indicate that communalism within the ranks was still not apparent, even after a month's work in internal security duties.[29] General Frank Messervy, GOC Northern Command, in a major paper discussing the disturbances in the Punjab, highlighted issues that would come to the fore during August 1947. For example, he identified significant concerns concerning the professionalism of the Punjab Police.[30] (It must be said that the police force did not, in fact, collapse, although there were many reports of their collusion or failure to stop violence against one part of the community.) He reported that, while "the army has been steady and disciplined throughout...there have been a few cases of Muslim troops not acting with [the] energy or alacrity with which they should have done." He also documented two cases of ICOs who had been accused of bias and the ongoing investigation into those cases. General Messervy's report also highlighted the need to make clear within the province that any "[army] pensioners engaged in the disturbances, or not co-operating with the Government to prevent them, [will] lose their pensions." He warned that "the districts affected are as heavily recruited as any in India. There is little doubt, I fear, that ex-soldiers and pensioners, some of the latter even including VCOs, have been heavily involved in many areas. In others they did very well and helped to save many of the minority community."[31]

Messervy's comments confirmed, in many senior officers' minds, their fear of a large, demobilized, militarized society with no loyalty except to their communal leaders. One of the last intelligence reports, written in June 1947, focused on the same themes: "reports from units employed on IS duties continue to stress impartiality shown by the troops in carrying out their duties.... [U]nfortunately many VCOs who were on leave or pensioned took no action to prevent the disturbances in their villages or in a few cases went to the extent of participating."[32]

A letter written by a senior officer to Governor Sir Evan Jenkins provided an uncomfortable picture of what the future was likely to hold: "[M]any of the loyal supporters of law and order in the employ of either the ICS, [the] police, [or the] IA are inevitably looking over their shoulders and wondering how their actions will be construed.... [A]lthough the loyalty of the army has remained outwardly unshaken by communal disturbances and political events...it would not be unrealistic to question the loyalty in the event of an unpopular order by HMG."[33]

In the midst of the Punjab violence, the army closely monitored the reactions of the men serving there, particularly those regiments that recruited heavily from the region. Infantry battalions were required to send in quarterly reports discussing various matters, including morale issues. Many commanding officers commented that morale remained high within the units. One report stated that "during the period of review a high state of morale has been maintained. Recent disturbances in the

Punjab caused concern and anxiety but fortunately the affected areas only had an indirect effect." The same report, however, noted that releases "[had] caused considerable upset in the battalion, the change over in officers [had] been partially drastic and the hasty clearing of British ECOs [had] not been to the benefit to the battalion."[34] Other battalions reported that morale was high and "the trouble in the Punjab has been strongly denounced by...PMs and Jats and Rajputs."[35]

Punjab Boundary Force

On July 17, 1947, the Partition Council decided to create a Punjab Boundary Force (PBF) to contend with the problems that were expected to arise in that region in the course of partition. The PBF, initially made up of five brigades,[36] was expected to patrol 12 districts[37] within the Punjab, comprising 37,500 square miles and 14.5 million people. The population of the Punjab was 55 percent Muslim, 25 percent Hindu, and 20 percent Sikh.[38]

On August 1, Major General Pete Rees gathered his senior commanders and other officers. He said, in part:

> We are going to [be] the last representatives of the old Indian Army. The honour and integrity of the Indian Army of which we are so proud is at stake and in our hands and you and I, officers, VCOS, and men have got to ensure that we uphold and maintain our tradition....We are a neutral force, operating in a defined area, holding the scales of justice impartially under the direct orders of the Supreme Commander, Field Marshal Auchinleck. We will continue to operate after the 15th of August for as long as shall prove necessary to maintain law and order and there is no question of units being ordered off to Pakistan or India....[There is an] absolute necessity for law and order, and in carrying out of our duties, if we came in conflict with people who defy law and order and use violence, we will use force....I promise officers and men that provided they act in all honesty of purpose I will back them up completely.[39]

The violence in the Punjab continued throughout July, and escalated as August 15 approached. The PBF, composed of troops from the 4th Indian Division, had already been serving in the area for several months. The units, spread throughout the province, began reporting problems with intelligence gathering almost immediately. They recorded that "in late July and early August it was exceedingly difficult to get information as to the scale and type of trouble to expect....[I]t is very necessary for the fighting services to be aware of the problems of the civil service."[40] Major Riches concurred that HQ believed that the Punjab Police were not viable, and hence intelligence was drying up all around the districts. As he put it, from August 2, "the PBF was a reaction force—it could not pre-empt many of the attacks."[41] It was quickly apparent that the PBF was going to have a difficult time of it.

The first major escalation in the level of violence occurred when a well-organized Sikh gang surrounded two Muslim villages, burned them to the ground, and killed all the inhabitants. An officer who witnessed the violence described how "women and children had their limbs hacked off and their breasts amputated before being killed. Pregnant mothers were sliced open. Babies were left impaled on upright spears dug into the ground. Burnt corpses littered the narrow streets....[S]uch scenes were our daily sights combined with even worse horrors as we were directed by brigade to follow up incidents."[42]

In a letter dated August 8, Sir Evans Jenkins, Governor of the Punjab, wrote to Mountbatten that communal violence had erupted in nine of the 12 districts of the Punjab. Initial reports stated that casualties appeared to be at least 100 a day. Reporting by the police, however, had fallen off due to transfers. Sir Jenkins wrote that the "police in the East Punjab are unsteady and Moslem policemen in Amritsar intend to desert to West Punjab on the 15th August."[43] He also cited problems with the PBF, chiefly insufficient numbers of soldiers. While there were five brigades, they were under strength, and in reality there were only 7,500 rifles to control the 12 districts. The situation reached a crisis point on the eve of Independence. Some units appeared to be having real problems, but the PBF seemed to be holding together. Sir Jenkins, in one of his last letters as governor, wrote to Rees on August 14:

> [B]efore I leave I must thank you and the 4th Indian Division and PBF for all the help you have given us during this difficult time. Troops can seldom have had a more arduous and unpleasant task as the aid to the civil power....[H]ow deeply we are in your debt, and what confidence we have had in your troops and in yourself.[44]

After August 15, things did indeed get worse. By the end of the month, there would be accusations of troops firing upon one another.

Military commanders held politicians on both sides largely responsible for the communal violence. General Rees reinforced this view: "[W]e are having heavy communal propaganda levelled at our officers and men...but I am combating it through the ICOs, Subedars and VCOs and they and the men realise and agree that unlimited bloodshed and terror would have been reigning in the central Punjab today...if they were not standing firm and rock like as the IA always [is] when called upon."[45]

When the Joint Defence Council met on August 25, members called for the end of the PBF and final division of the units to Pakistan and India. At the same time that the JDC was calling for an end to the PBF, the 5th Indian Brigade accused Mr. Baldev Singh, the JDC member, of providing weapons to Sikhs in the fighting. Civil-military relations were suffering.[46] On the same day, a *Times* correspondent openly accused Hindu and Sikh soldiers of standing by while violence was perpetrated against Muslims.[47] The *Hindustan Times* took its cue from the *Times* and printed an article on August 27, claiming that British officers of the PBF and British ICS had not risen to the occasion, but had allowed the atrocities to go on.[48]

The decision was made to disband the PBF on the evening of September 1–2, and General Rees issued a final memo to his troops on August 31. His summary offers an interesting response to his critics:

[W]hen we set forth upon our present duties I told you it was going to be a difficult task....[O]fficers and men have worked loyally and without sparing themselves. I know the strain and fatigue that you have been subjected to and I know the strains and tugs of loyalties involved. We have been accused of partiality by both parties and that in itself is good evidence of the practical measures of overall impartiality which you have achieved in circumstances of unparalleled difficulty....[I]t will be agreed that you in the PBF have ultimately upheld the honour of the old Indian Army, by your devotion to duty.[49]

The Indian Army maintained its discipline and professionalism throughout this period.[50] While there were minor issues, especially when dealing with the division of the Punjab, the army performed beyond the expectations of many, both critics and supporters. The maintenance of a professional officer corps, both British and Indian, was a critical factor in maintaining organizational stability, as was the solid leadership provided by Field Marshal Sir Claude Auchinleck, as Commander-in-Chief, and his subordinate commanders.

CHAPTER 10

The State of War with Pakistan

Bhashyam Kasturi

Introduction

India is in a state of perpetual war with Pakistan. Apart from the military wars fought in the plains of Punjab and Kashmir in 1947, 1965, 1971, and 1999, a continuing war of nerves is being fought on every front by the two countries. This chapter attempts to paraphrase the historical chart of conflict between India and Pakistan, two South Asian neighbors whose mutual hostility has thus far prevented the growth of a South Asian identity. This refers to emergence of a SAARC-style regional identity that focuses on economic integration.

Apart from the actual wars fought, there have been near-warlike crises when both sides have mobilized their fighting resources to the fullest. The crisis over Exercise Brasstacks in 1987, the nuclear crisis in 1990–91, and the Parakram standoff in 2001 are instances of military mobilization that, for one reason or another, led to heightened tensions between the two countries. It is possible to trace the roots of such near war to the 1950s, when the spillover of refugees from East Pakistan led to a near conflict.

In the aftermath of partition, in 1949–50, there was violence and riots in the border territories of West Bengal and Tripura. The cause of the violence was mainly ethnic violence against Muslims and Hindus, wherever each was a minority. Then there was the mass movement of refugees from East Pakistan into India. In an attempt to get the refugees back across the border into West and East Pakistan, and to secure her frontiers, India deployed troops, which caused great alarm in Karachi.[1] This situation generated the momentum for the Nehru-Liaqat Ali Pact in April 1950.

A survey of the extant literature on India-Pakistan wars shows that both sides tend to defend their positions and blame each other for starting the conflict. There is another way of viewing this. If, in 1971, the Pakistan Air Force (PAF) began the war on December 3 by bombing Indian Air Force (IAF) bases, the war had unofficially begun on November 22, when troops from both sides clashed.

A battalion-strength Pakistani force with some tanks entered Indian territory on the pretext of chasing the Mukti Bahni in the Boyra area. The engagement between the two sides lasted for two days, during which the Pakistanis lost 13 tanks. The next day, the scene of action was also in the eastern sector, a few minutes' flying time away from Kolkata. The provocation was the repeated intrusion by groups of PAF F-86

Sabres into a salient inside Indian territory—Bangladeshi Mukti Bahini had been using the Boyra salient to launch attacks inside East Pakistan. The job of tackling the Mukti Bahini was given to the PAF Sabres, which began intruding into Indian airspace, did their strafing, and then slipped back into Pakistani airspace. On November 23, three PAF Sabres were shot down.

Actually by October 1971, the Mukti Bahini were already waging a guerrilla war and had even temporarily captured airstrips at Lalmonirhat and Shalutikar. In return, while carrying out "hot pursuit" of the Mukti Bahini guerrillas, the Pakistan Army did enter India several times causing ever-increasing skirmishes, most notably at Kamalpur (between October 20 and 22), at Boyra (on November 22), and Hilli (between November 26 and 28). Thus perceptions vary on when the war actually started. Broadly speaking, any attempt to analyze the military conflicts between India and Pakistan has to necessarily balance the various points and counterpoints.

While one can debate the validity of certain historical assertions based on available data, it is clear that India-Pakistan wars can be classified as basically being of short duration, being limited in time and space. Problems of logistics, terrain, and finally external influences have tended to limit the scope of conflict. Most of the India-Pakistan wars have been dominated by land battles, and this is not surprising since the respective armies have always sought and received the lion's share of the military budget. Their military doctrines have also been dominated by land-warfare doctrines. More relevant has been the armor fixation on both sides, with tanks and associated support elements forming the core of the strike formations on both sides. Being land-dominated means that little thought has been given to joint command-and-control and joint operations. The air forces on both sides remain dedicated to close air support and ground attack operations, while the navies have been tasked with protection of the sea-lanes of communication and protection of vital maritime interests.[2]

The other aspect is that in most of the India-Pakistan wars, Jammu and Kashmir has been the bone of contention and has witnessed battles, both direct and covert, for its possession. Both in 1947–48 and in 1965, Pakistan chose to begin the conflict by initiating a proxy war, by irregulars and tribal lashkars, into J&K territory from Pakistan-occupied Kashmir (POK), and this subsequently led to general war. In 1971, the war was fought mainly in the eastern theater, with the intention of taking Dhaka at the earliest. But the battles in the southern salient of Jammu and Kashmir, in Chhamb and Shakargarh, also reflected the importance of this theater of operations.

In 1999, Pakistan violated the Line of Control (LoC) in Kargil and hoped to interdict the Leh-Srinagar road. For some time, the Indian forces were oblivious to the intrusions, and when they did wake up to the fact, considerable area was in Pakistani hands. What began as an intrusion soon turned into a full-scale war with both sides mobilizing all their forces. India, being on the back foot, had to employ air power to offset the disadvantage of attacking the enemy in fortified positions on the heights.[3]

It is important to remember that both sides today possess nuclear weapons, and the logic of nuclear deterrence is that conflict is prevented because of the presence of these weapons. Despite the knowledge that India has possessed some sort of weaponry since its "Peaceful Nuclear Explosions" (PNE) in 1974, Pakistan did not stop its attempt to infiltrate into the Kargil region of Jammu and Kashmir along the LoC in 1999. Therefore, there is a need to question assumptions and seek answers to a large number of queries rather than just look at the state of war between India and Pakistan.

The two countries have militaries with colonial pasts, and while in the case of India civilian control over the military has sustained, in Pakistan the military has effectively controlled the nation since 1947. Therefore, the manner in which the militaries think and act is conditioned by this factor.[4] This factor has determined the wars that have occurred and will determine future conflicts, too.

The Pakistani state has vowed to bleed India through a thousand cuts, and the aim is to wear down the Indian state to a point at which military victory becomes irrelevant. Pakistan continues to pursue military and covert options to wage war against India. In the last 50 years there have been regular wars from time to time, interspersed with spells of peace. But by using covert means, Pakistan has continued to wage war against India. The Inter-Services Intelligence of Pakistan (ISI) has aided and abetted terrorist organizations like the Lashkar-e-Toiba (LeT) who engage in a war against the Indian state in Jammu and Kashmir.

This proxy war has been on since 1989 and is ongoing. It now has an all-India dimension. This war has the benefit of keeping Pakistani troops in the barracks while making India utilize all her resources to counter the proxies that Pakistan sends across the borders. Thus, for example, military deployment in Jammu and Kashmir on long-drawn counterinsurgency operations, though useful for keeping the Indian forces fighting fit, takes them away from their primary task of preparing to fight conventional wars.

India and Pakistan has have fought military wars on four occasions. First, immediately after the partition of the subcontinent in 1947–48; then again in 1965; and then in 1971. Between 1971 and 1999 there was a spell of peace, even though there were occasions when war seemed pretty close, like when the two sides engaged in brinkmanship over Exercise Brasstacks in 1987–88. In 1999, Pakistan chose to attempt a realignment of the Line of Control in the Kargil sector in Jammu and Kashmir. This resulted in near total war because India refrained from crossing the LoC.

Then in 2001, after the attack on the Indian Parliament on December 13, Indian troops were amassed on the international border with Pakistan in readiness for an attack, but this remained an exercise in ineffective diplomacy. For almost a year the armed forces remained in a state of readiness, but in the end there was no war, only an extensive and wasted deployment of Indian troops. The Pakistani deployment too was prolonged and with no result, but it needs noting that it was India's initiative to take the war into the enemy's camp and it did not do so. There is a contention in New Delhi that the then Chief of Army Staff General S. Padmanabhan received permission to cross the LoC in Jammu and Kashmir during Operation Parakaram, but he did not avail of the opportunity.[5]

In between, India mounted an airlift operation on the Saltoro Ridge in the northern reaches of Kashmir, in 1984 (Operation Meghdoot) to ensure that Pakistani troops did not occupy the heights overlooking the Siachen Glacier. This is the route of ingress into Ladakh, and is thus important for India. Even in 1999, during the Kargil war, Pakistan had an opportunity to threaten Ladakh, but they did not do so.

There is a need here to look at the overall trends rather than get bogged down by tactical detail, much of which has been covered by scholars elsewhere.[6] In terms of actual wars, it can be safely said that both countries, which inherited colonial armies, retained their fighting skills and officer cadres intact for the first 20-odd years of their existence. Only later, in the case of Pakistan, did the influence of U.S. military doctrine and, in the 1960s, Chinese influence lead to shifts in doctrinal thinking. In the Indian case, the British impact on the armed forces remained for a long time, while in doctrinal and operational terms more so. What changed things was the induction of Soviet weaponry in the 1960s, creating space for a movement towards self-reliance.

The War in Kashmir, 1947–49

The first test for the Indian armed forces came shortly after independence with the first Indo-Pakistani conflict (1947–48). The military was called upon to defend the borders of Jammu and Kashmir when tribals and some regular Pakistani troops "on leave" attacked from the northwest reaches of the state on October 22, 1947. India's 161 Infantry Brigade was deployed and thwarted the advance of the tribal forces. The brigade, hastily assembled on an ad hoc basis and operating with light equipment, managed first to hold and then to beat down the tribal main body, thus giving the campaign a flying start. In early November 1947, the 161 Brigade counterattacked and successfully broke through enemy defenses. Despite early successes, the Indian Army suffered a setback in December because of logistical problems. The problems enabled the irregular and regular forces of Pakistan to take the initiative and force the Indian troops to retreat from the border areas.[7]

Throughout the winter of 1947, the road from Jammu through Akhnur and Naushera to Jhangar was the target of Pakistani irregulars. On February 6, 1948, a fierce battle took place for control of Naushera, in which the attacking Pakistani force was estimated to be 15,000. Indian forces eventually prevailed. Pakistan also launched operations through the northern areas of the state, with the aim of advancing to the Indus River. After a long haul, the garrison at Skardu surrendered. As a result, India lost Gilgit and Baltistan. By the end of May 1948, Indian forces had captured Tithwal on the Kishenganga River and were only eighteen miles from Muzaffarabad. On November 1, 1948, an Indian brigade supported by 7 Cavalry broke through Zoji La to drive the Pakistanis out of Ladakh.[8] Then on January 1, 1949, the United Nations–brokered cease-fire came into effect.

The IAF was very active during the war, providing airlift to troops into the valley from October 27, 1947, onwards. An entire brigade was flown into the valley in the next five days. Tempest fighter-bombers flew close-air support and ground attack missions. And it must be mentioned that an IAF Dakota bombed the Kohala bridge along the Rawalpindi-Srinagar highway.[9]

No doubt fearing that the war might move into Pakistan proper, regular units of the Pakistan Army became more actively involved by early 1948. Pakistan admitted to the United Nations Commission for India and Pakistan (UNCIP) in July that they had three brigades in Jammu and Kashmir in May 1948. Actually, by March–April 1948 Pakistan's 7 Infantry Division had joined the battle. Then on June 9, Frontier Division was inducted into the Uri-Tithwal sector. Besides these regular formations, there were many thousand troops of Azad Kashmir, fully equipped and trained by Pakistan. As the conflict escalated, the Indian leadership quickly recognized that the war could not be brought to a close unless all Pakistani support for the forces in occupied Kashmir could be stopped. In all, 1,500 soldiers died on each side during the war.

Leadership on both sides showed that lessons learned during the Second World War were put to good effect. Both militaries had officers who had trained and fought under the British during the Second World War. Indian officers had until then little experience in the higher planning and direction of war. These officers utilized the experience gained in ad hoc operations, movement of troops, and providing of logistic support to operations. The officers made the best use of the limited experience gained in tactical warfare during the Burma campaign and in Europe in the Kashmir war in 1947–48. This proved useful in terms of both man management and operational art.[10] On the Indian side, the ad hoc operation to save the state of Jammu and Kashmir was a success, and it provided the grounding for future battles. Not all the lessons learned were incorporated for future strategic planning, however. This was perhaps inherent to the newly formed Indian state that it did not have in place a system for long-term planning, though Lord Ismay had brought into being the very organizations needed for such planning like the Joint Planning Staff.[11]

For Pakistan it was the start of a long haul against India. It set in place a chain of thought that irregulars combined with regular troops could prove useful in a situation of asymmetry. While the real reason for using irregulars was to obviate the need to become directly involved, this proved a boon in the long run, when the United Nations began the process of mediation in the conflict. This mediation proved unsuccessful particularly because of the sympathy in the West, in the United Kingdom especially, for Pakistan.[12]

The Second Round, 1965

The second war began in April 1965, when fighting broke out in the Rann of Kutch, a sparsely inhabited region along the Pakistan–India border. It started in January when the Indian Police found that their counterparts across the border were using tracks a mile and half inside Indian territory. In April, troops from both sides were sent to the area, and on April 24, Pakistani troops attacked Indian positions with something less than a division. The attack was contained with considerable casualties to the Pakistan Army.[13]

The Kutch affair gave the Pakistanis the chance to test the new weaponry they had acquired from the United States. This included the M-47 Patton tank and Sabre jets, which the Pakistani establishment thought would give them an edge over their Indian counterparts. The Pakistan Navy had also leased one submarine from the United States and purchased two from France. They wrongly assumed that India had been defeated, and similarly an adventure in Jammu and Kashmir would be met with success. Thus began Operation Gibraltar, followed by Operation Grand Slam, the attack on Chhamb.

India, on the other hand, adopted a twofold strategy in this war. First, India decided to raise the stakes of the Pakistani invasion by crossing the international border (IB). Thus when Pakistan attacked Chhamb, India crossed the IB with a view to threatening Lahore.[14] Secondly, the Indian military was given a relatively free hand to conduct operations. The impact of the 1962 border war with China was felt in 1965 in terms of the conduct of the war. But while the army could conduct operations as it saw fit, it did not necessarily follow that higher defense organization in India managed to secure the cooperation of all three services, or that they planned for it together accordingly. In fact, separate plans were drawn up by each service with no joint consultation.[15]

In August, fighting spread to Kashmir and to the Punjab, and in September 1965 Pakistani and Indian troops crossed the partition line between the two countries and launched air assaults on each other's cities. The 1965 war broadly took place in five phases. The first phase was the infiltration of guerrillas into Jammu and Kashmir and their consequent unsuccessful attempt to generate a revolt in the valley. The second phase witnessed the Pakistani attack on Chhamb. This was followed by the Indian riposte towards Lahore and Pakistan's attack in Khemkaran region of Punjab. The fourth phase saw the Indian offensive in Chawinda, and finally the second round actually witnessed a war in the air between the two air forces.[16]

The second war in 1965 was also fought over Kashmir and started without a formal declaration of war. It is widely accepted that the war began with the infiltration of Pakistani-sponsored guerrillas into Jammu and Kashmir on August 5, 1965. Skirmishes with Indian forces started as early as August 6 or 7, and the first major engagement between the regular armed forces of the two sides took place on August 14. The next day, Indian forces scored a major victory after a prolonged artillery barrage and captured three important mountain positions in the northern sector. Later in the month, the Pakistanis counterattacked, moving concentrations near Tithwal, Uri, and Punch. Their move, in turn, provoked a powerful Indian thrust into POK.[17]

The infiltration into Jammu and Kashmir was planned and controlled by Pakistan's 12 Corps, commanded by Major General Akhtar Hussein Malik. But this plan failed because the people of Jammu and Kashmir were not for Pakistan. Throughout August, Pakistan kept up infiltration under the cover of artillery shelling. By the end of the month, India decided to attack the bases from which infiltration was taking place. The capture of Haji Pir pass on September 10 was one such operation. Similar operations were launched in the Tithwal sector to capture Pir Saheba, an important hill feature.

The Indian gains led to a major Pakistani counterattack on September 1 in the southern sector, in Punjab, where Indian forces were caught unprepared and suffered heavy losses. The sheer strength of the Pakistani thrust, which was spearheaded by seventy tanks and two infantry brigades, led Indian commanders to call for air support. Pakistan retaliated on September 2 with its own air strikes in both Kashmir and Punjab. The Pakistani attack on Chhamb was brilliant in conception but poor in implementation. While Pakistan made some initial gains, it was halted by Indian troops. As an answer to this, India decided to drive up to Lahore. What probably saved Pakistan was the Ichhogil Canal and the failure of Indian intelligence to reveal the existence of Pakistan's 1st Armored Division that was brought up to the canal to face the Indian forces.[18]

While both sides were almost equal in military strength (though the Indian Army had more manpower) the IAF had an edge over its Pakistani counterparts in numbers. The IAF had 500 combat aircraft, while the PAF had only some 200. The moment Pakistan attacked Chhamb, air support from the IAF was called in. Some 28 sorties were flown from Pathankot for ground attack missions, and these stalled the Pakistan offensive. The PAF had planned preemptive strikes against Indian airfields, particularly forward airbases in the Punjab, Jammu and Kashmir, and Rajasthan. Only 32 aircraft carried out this strike, and it did not have a major impact.[19]

The IAF in return used its Hunters and Canberras to good effect and attacked the Pakistani bases at Sargodha, Chaklala, Peshawar, and Kohat. Since this did not prove effective, the IAF switched to operating on deep-strike missions in Pakistan, launching its bombers supported by Gnats on road and rail targets in the Lahore and Sialkot sectors. At the end of the war, both sides claimed large numbers of kills, but in the fog of war it was difficult to determine the exact number of losses on either side. Pakistan claimed to have shot down 110 IAF aircraft, while India claimed it had shot down 73 PAF aircraft. Actual figures may vary, but India claimed to have lost only 35 aircraft while Pakistan lost only 20.[20]

After threats of intervention by China on Pakistan's side had been successfully opposed by the United States and Britain, Pakistan and India agreed to a UN-sponsored cease-fire and withdrew to their pre-August 1965 lines. Indian Prime Minister Lal Bahadur Shastri and Pakistani President Ayub Khan met in Tashkent, USSR (now in Uzbekistan), in January 1966 and signed an agreement pledging to continue negotiations and to respect the cease-fire conditions. The Indian side lost 3,000, while the Pakistani side suffered 3,800 battlefield deaths. The Soviet-brokered Tashkent Declaration, signed on January 10, 1966, required that both sides withdraw by February 26, 1966, to positions held prior to August 5, 1965, and observe the cease-fire line agreed to on June 30, 1965.[21]

Command and control of forces on the Indian side under Prime Minister Shastri was clear, and objectives were defined well. In the case of Pakistan the politico-military objectives were vaguely defined, and no thought was given to finishing the battle. Instead, operational military orders tended to be rhetorical rather than commands, which led to confusion. On both sides officers were sacked or moved during operations, and leadership that had served in the first Kashmir war was sometimes found wanting.[22]

Strategic miscalculations by both nations ensured that the result of this war remained a stalemate. The Indian Army failed to recognize the presence of heavy Pakistani artillery and armaments in Chhamb and suffered significant losses as a result. According to the *Official History of the 1965 War* (which is available online and has not been officially released by the government of India), on September 22, 1965, when the Security Council was pressing for a cease-fire, Prime Minister Shastri asked the army chief, General J. N. Chaudhuri, if India could possibly win the war, were he to hold off accepting the cease-fire for a while longer. The general replied that most of India's frontline ammunition had been used up and the Indian Army had suffered considerable tank losses. It was found later that only 14 percent of India's frontline ammunition had been fired, and India still held twice the number of tanks than Pakistan did. By this time, the Pakistan Army itself had used close to 80 percent of its ammunition.

The Liberation War, 1971

The origins of the third Indo-Pakistani conflict in 1971 were different from the previous conflicts. Pakistan's failure to accommodate demands for autonomy in East Pakistan in 1970 led to secessionist demands in 1971. In March 1971, Pakistan's armed forces launched a fierce campaign to suppress the resistance movement that had emerged, but encountered unexpected mass defections among East Pakistani soldiers and police. Pakistani forces regrouped and reasserted their authority over most of East Pakistan by May. Civil war erupted in Pakistan, pitting the West Pakistan Army against East Pakistanis demanding greater autonomy. The fighting forced 10 million East Pakistani Bengalis to flee to India.[23]

The Indian leadership, in the absence of a political solution to the East Pakistan crisis, fashioned a strategy designed to assist the establishment of the independent nation of Bangladesh. As part of this strategy, India signed a 20-year Treaty of Peace, Friendship, and Cooperation with the Soviet Union in August 1971. Given the U.S.-China link, this was the best way for India to ensure that any threat to it from forces other than Pakistan would be dealt with, at least diplomatically. Simultaneously, India organized, trained, and provided sanctuary to the Mukti Bahini, the East Pakistani armed resistance fighters. The former Chief of Staff with Eastern Command, Lieutenant General J. F. R. Jacob, states that the Mukti Bahni were a "key factor in the liberation struggle." Despite limitations of training and lack of junior leadership, they contributed substantially to the defeat of Pakistani forces in East Bengal.[24]

On December 3, 1971, Pakistan launched an air attack in the western sector on a number of Indian airfields, including Ambala in Haryana, Amritsar in Punjab, and Udhampur in Jammu and Kashmir. The attacks did not inflict substantial damage.

The Indian Air Force retaliated the next day and quickly achieved air superiority. On the ground, the strategy in the eastern sector marked a significant departure from previous Indian battle plans and tactics, which had emphasized set-piece battles and slow advances.

Pakistan had two armored divisions, 12 infantry divisions, and one independent armored brigade. The Pakistan Air Force had 14 fighter squadrons and three bomber squadrons, but only one squadron of Sabre fighters in East Pakistan. The Indian Army was organized into one armored division, 13 infantry and 10 mountain divisions, and a number of independent armored brigades. The IAF had a strength of 625 aircraft, including seven squadrons of MiG-21s. The Indian Navy was built around the carrier INS *Vikrant* and several Russian-built fast-attack craft.[25]

The Indian aim was to hold a defensive action in the west while carrying out swift operations in the east. In the east, the aim was to achieve air superiority with a swift land campaign to take Dacca. Pakistan took a rigid posture of prepared defense along the most likely routes of ingress along the border with hardly any central mobile reserves, a policy that led to the dispersal and dissipation of forces along the periphery. They also took up positions to defend the main roads leading to Dacca, leaving the countryside open to quick movement with little or no resistance.[26]

India deployed six infantry divisions and various supporting troops on all sides of East Pakistan. Supporting the Indian force were eight battalions of Mukti Bahini and many irregular Bengali soldiers. To force a quick decision, India had to strike deep toward Dacca. Since the accessibility of most of the region is poor, the combat forces were lightly equipped, but they were well trained and were reinforced with engineers to assist in river crossings.

The strategy adopted was a swift, three-pronged assault of nine infantry divisions with attached armored units and close air support that rapidly converged on Dhaka, the capital of East Pakistan. Lieutenant General Sagat Singh, who commanded the 8, 23, and 57 divisions, led the Indian thrust into East Pakistan. As these forces attacked Pakistani formations, the Indian Air Force rapidly destroyed the small Pakistani air contingent in East Pakistan and put the Dacca airfield out of commission. In the meantime, the Indian Navy effectively blockaded East Pakistan. Dhaka fell to combined Indian and Mukti Bahini forces on December 16, 1971, bringing a quick end to the war.[27]

Action in the western sector was divided into four segments, from the cease-fire line in Jammu and Kashmir to the marshes of the Rann of Kutch in northwestern Gujarat. On the evening of December 3, the Pakistan Army launched ground operations in Kashmir and Punjab. It also started an armored operation in Rajasthan. In Kashmir, the operations were concentrated on two key points, Punch and Chhamb. The Chhamb area witnessed a particularly intense battle in which the Pakistanis forced the Indians to withdraw from their positions. In other parts of Kashmir, the Indians made some small gains along the cease-fire line. The major Indian counter-offensive came in the Sialkot-Shakargarh area south and west of Chhamb. There, two Pakistani tank regiments, equipped with U.S.-made Patton tanks, confronted the Indian 1 Armored Corps, which had British Centurion tanks. In what proved to be the largest tank battle of the war (the battle of Basantar), both sides suffered considerable casualties. Pakistan is said to have lost over 66 tanks, while India lost only 23.[28]

Though the Indian conduct of the land war on the western front was somewhat timid, the role of the Indian Air Force was both extensive and daring. During the 14-day war, the IAF's Western Command conducted some 4,000 sorties. There was little retaliation by the PAF, partly because of the paucity of non-Bengali technical personnel. Additionally, this lack of retaliation reflected the deliberate decision of the PAF to conserve its forces because of heavy losses incurred in the early days of the war.[29]

The 14-day war was the first full-scale Indian naval war. India's fleet was much superior to that of Pakistan and was well prepared when war was declared on December 3. The Indian Navy was able to defend the coast while blockading East Pakistan and attacking shore targets in support of ground operations. Pakistan's surface fleet had neither air cover nor the weapons to defend itself against India's missile boats. Therefore, it stayed in Karachi harbor while submarines were given the task of destroying India's aircraft carrier and cruiser. They were unsuccessful; on December 4, a Dafne-class Pakistani submarine was sunk by a carrier escort in the Bay of Bengal, while a second was sunk off Visakhapatnam harbor. The only Indian loss was the frigate INS *Khukri,* sunk by a Pakistani submarine in the Arabian Sea on December 9.

On December 8, an Indian Navy task force headed by Rear Admiral Kuruvilla attacked oil installations in Karachi harbor and some ships. This created absolute panic in the Pakistan Navy, which remained bottled up in the Karachi area for the rest of the war. But India's main naval effort was in the Bay of Bengal where a carrier task force blockaded the sea approaches to East Pakistan. Six merchant ships and "numerous" small craft were captured. Carrier-based aircraft struck assembly points of small boats in the Ganges delta area, preventing the escape or reinforcement of Pakistan Army elements. The establishment of air superiority early in the war allowed the ships freedom to maneuver to and attack shore targets at Chittagong, Cox's Bazar, Chalna, Kulna, and other economic and military targets. These actions had a significant effect on the collapse of East Pakistan.[30]

The major problem with the Pakistani military was that they needed air superiority and they failed to achieve it. The PAF tried a preemptive attack on the IAF, but they failed to strike Indian airfields in sufficient numbers or depth. IAF operations were never seriously challenged. The PAF did not provide sufficient sorties to gain even local air superiority to support the ground forces, even though aircraft was available. Apart from the early losses of aircraft, the PAF command thought it prudent to conserve aircraft so that these could be used to counter a possible Indian offensive into West Pakistan.

The Pakistan Army attacked along a very broad front of the western Indian border. But they never massed sufficient forces to ensure a rapid breakthrough. Generally, the points of attack were in terrain unsuited for wide maneuver, and hence mobility and speed could not be developed to gain a significant amount of Indian land. Although battles were fiercely contested at battalion and brigade level, the attacks were only loosely coordinated at the corps and army level, and hence lacked unity.[31]

The most effective way to disconnect West Pakistan from East Pakistan was a naval blockade, and the Indian Navy managed to do this. Combined with Indian domination of the air, there was no possibility of reinforcing or withdrawing army forces in East Pakistan. This only further reduced morale and the will of the soldiers in East Pakistan to resist. Also, the Indian Navy was able to carry the war directly to Karachi while the Pakistan Navy could not venture out without risking irreplaceable losses.[32]

The Pakistan Navy was simply not equipped to take on the missiles and aircraft of the Indian fleet in order to protect its own navy or commercial ships. Thus, West as well as East Pakistan was isolated from their major sea supply routes. The state of the navy was indicative of the neglect of reality on the part of the military government in Islamabad.

Lastly, Pakistan underestimated the ability of the Indians to move forces through the sodden terrain of Bengal. The Pakistanis had deployed in strength in the towns while leaving the rural areas relatively unprotected. The Indian Army, supported by Bengalis with local knowledge, quickly outflanked these strong points. With no strategic reserve available, the Pakistanis could not block the Indian advance. When the strong points were surrounded, there was simply no place for the defenders to go, and they surrendered in thousands. The speed of the Indian advance helped relieve the Indian logistic effort of improving roads, bridges, and railways necessary to move large quantities of supplies for slower, more deliberate operations. Indian forces were lightly equipped to move quickly through to Dacca.[33]

The Kargil War

Both India and Pakistan have had a nascent nuclear capability, but in 1998 it became overt. It was and is argued that the presence of nuclear weapons in South Asia would prevent another war.[34] This did not, however, stop Pakistan from attempting to realign the LoC in 1999, when regular and irregular forces occupied a large number of posts in the Kargil sector of Jammu and Kashmir. There was a twofold aim here: first, to realign the de facto border between the two countries; and second, to be able to place observers on the heights on the LoC so that artillery fire can be directed at the national highway connecting Srinagar and Leh. There is also a suggestion that Kargil was revenge for India's actions in Siachen in 1984.[35]

In winter 1998, over 1,000 Pakistan-based militants and Pakistani regulars crossed the LoC into the Kargil area of Jammu and Kashmir and seized Indian Army outposts that had been vacated for the season. Pakistan took advantage of the fact that in winter, Indian troops in the sector vacated their posts. Therefore, by the end of 1998, Pakistani forces were well entrenched in Indian posts. But it was not until the first week of May 1999 that their presence was discovered.[36]

The Indian Army eventually regrouped and attacked, driving the Pakistani forces back. In the end, U.S. diplomacy helped persuade Pakistani Prime Minister

Nawaz Sharif to pull his troops out of India and temporarily headed off a full-scale war. Months later, on October 12, 1999 General Pervez Musharraf, widely held to be the architect of the Kargil offensive, deposed Sharif. The Kargil War signifies the first war that was imposed on India in the background of the nuclear environment. It resembled the low-level border conflicts that occurred in 1969 between the Soviet Union and China in the Ussuri River dispute that had the potential of turning nuclear.[37]

The intruders from Pakistan on the heights of Kargil were an amalgam of professional soldiers and mercenaries. They included the 3rd, 4th, 5th, 6th, and 12th battalions of the Pakistan Army's Northern Light Infantry (NLI). Among them were many Mujahedin and members of the Pakistani Special Services Group (SSG). It was initially estimated that about 500 to 1,000 intruders occupied the heights; but later, it is estimated, the actual strength of the intruders may have been about 5,000. The area of intrusion extended across a 160-km area. The Pakistan Army had set up a complex logistical network through which the intruders across the LoC were well supplied from the bases in POK. The intruders were well armed with AK-47/56s, mortars, artillery, antiaircraft guns, and Stinger missiles.[38]

The Indian Army detected the intrusions between May 3 and 12, 1999. From May 15 to 25, 1999, military operations were planned, troops were inducted into attack locations, artillery and other equipment was moved in, and the necessary equipment was purchased. The Indian Army's offensive, named Operation Vijay, was launched on May 26, 1999. Indian troops inched towards Pakistani-occupied positions at heights ranging from 14,000 to 18,000 feet with air cover provided by aircraft and helicopters. The main sectors in which battles were fought is given below.

Batalik Sector
Eastern Section

Located between the Shyok and Indus rivers, this sector was responsible for about half of the Indian casualties. The eastern section of the Batalik sector consists of Chorbat La, Turtuk, and Pt. 5287. The Ladakh Scouts captured the ridge of Chorbat La on the Indian side and preempted the Pakistani forces from occupying the area. This was the first Indian victory in the sector and resulted in heavy Pakistani losses. Turtuk is an important peak and the location of several important villages in the valley as well a link to Siachen Glacier. Eleven Rajputana Rifles recaptured Turtuk on June 16, 1999, while the Ladakh Scouts recaptured Pt. 5287 on July 5. The eastern section was recaptured on July 6 after 38 days of fighting.

Jubar Ridge is located at the western end of the Batalik sector and is several kilometers from the LOC. Jubar Ridge and the neighboring peaks were the site of some of the fiercest battles during the conflict. The battle raged for 40 days, ending on July 8, 1999; it involved hand-to-hand combat and heavy casualties. Eventually, 1 Bihar of the Indian Army prevailed over the enemy forces.

Central Section

The Central Section of Batalik Sector consists of Muntho Dhalo, Kokarthang and Pt 5285. Initial attacks by the Indian Army in this area were unsuccessful. The 1 Para and 11 Gorkha Rifles units pressed on and were able to take back all of the peaks in the region.

Dras Sector

Dras Sector is the westernmost of the intruders' positions. It is adjacent to the Srinagar-Leh Highway (NH 1), making this sector strategically important, as traffic on the highway was vulnerable to enemy firing. The main positions of the intruders were the Tololing Top, Tiger Hill, Pt. 4875, Pt. 4590, Pt. 5100 and Pt. 5140.

Tololing Peak is the dominant high point in the sector, as it directly overlooks NH 1. The attack on Tololing, initially carried out by 18 Grenadiers on May 22, was unsuccessful. Subsequently, 1 Naga, 15 Garhwal, and the Grenadiers took up the task but also failed to recapture the peak. Eventually 2 Rajput was given the task of capturing the peak, and they did so on June 13. The next day the same battalion was successful in capturing Pt. 4590. Pt. 5410 located east of Tololing and closer to the LoC, was captured by 1 Naga. Pt. 5100, located close to the LoC, was a major supply route for enemy forces. Its capture on July 1, 1999, was instrumental in the recapture of Tiger Hill.

Tiger Hill is also a major peak located along the highway. Initial attempts by 8 Sikh were unsuccessful. Tiger Hill is also the location of the downing of the Mi 17 helicopter on May 28, 1999. Eventually Tiger Hill fell to a combined attack from three sides, which resulted in the cutting of supply lines of the intruders. Tiger Hill was recaptured on July 3, and cleared on July 9. Pt. 4875, the third of the major peaks located along the highway, was taken by 8 Jat and 16 Grenadiers on July 5.

Kaksar Sector

This sector is located between the two dominant sectors of Batalik and Dras. As the peaks in this area do not over look the highway, it was not a priority sector unlike other sectors. The major point of intrusion was Bajrang Post, located on Pt. 5299. Operations in this sector were undertaken after the Dras sector was secured. The task of recapturing Bajrang Post fell to 1 Naga and 16 Grenadiers, and it was successfully retaken on 12 July 1999.

Muskoh Valley and Other Sectors of the LoC

The Mushkoh Valley is located west of the Dras Sector but does not overlook the Srinagar-Leh highway. Operations to recapture the area were mobilized after the Dras sector was retaken. On July 9, 1999, Pakistan agreed to pull back its intruders, and the Indian Army moved forward to reoccupy the vacated land.

The Kargil war was fought in the high mountain ranges of Kashmir. It was an expensive war of men and material. To take a target, the Indian Army had to have a ratio of at least 1–10—i.e., for every Pakistani soldier, 10 Indian soldiers were needed to capture a location.

No doubt the regiments of the Indian Army gained valuable experience in mountain warfare during the Kargil war. But was that not the lesson of the 1962 war, which led to the creation of such divisions in the first place? Intelligence gathering and assessment at all levels, both civil and military, failed to provide decision makers with proper real-time information. This led to Indian forces being caught by surprise. War by infiltration and negotiation under pressure has been Pakistan's strategy since 1947, and it nearly succeeded in Kargil in 1999.

The Pakistani air force played a largely supportive role, with logistics support being the main task. The IAF, on the other hand, was called in early on in the conflict to provide offensive air support and attack missions, at heights at which they were not used to operating. Mi-24 gun ships could not operate at that height and combat aircraft and their pilots had to adapt to the new situation as they went along. The IAF adapted to high-altitude flying and bombing using the MiG-21s and, on occasions, the Mirage-2000. The loss of a MiG-21 and a MiG-27 (and a helicopter) early in the war meant that the IAF had to reorient its tactics to suit the situation. Softening of targets (which the infamous FH-77 Bofors guns also did admirably), striking at Pakistani logistic dumps on the LoC, and generally giving the boys on the ground the required air cover was the main task for the IAF.[39]

Diplomacy

Both sides tried to build up a world consensus for their side. Pakistan issued statements condemning India's counterattack and falsely claiming that the fighters on the heights of Kargil were Mujahedin and/or Kashmiri freedom fighters. Pakistan also falsely claimed that the Line of Control separating the two sides was not clearly defined. This was false, as the LoC was clearly delineated by the two sides in 1972.[40]

Pakistan tried to use Kargil as a way to project the Kashmir conflict as a potential nuclear showdown, thereby encouraging international intervention that might favor Pakistan. Similarly, Pakistani leaders visited China, an ardent ally, to shore up support for their cause and simultaneously pressure India.[41]

However, despite early success, much of Pakistan's diplomatic overtures failed. The world saw proof of Pakistan Army involvement in Kargil. India likewise tried to use the international media to make its case known. India was successful in showing the world that the LoC was clearly delineated, and that both sides possessed copies of the maps. Second, India demonstrated that the Kargil conflict was orchestrated and executed by the Pakistan Army, working with the Mujahedin. Indian restraint and limitation to restrict the operations to Kashmir allayed fears that the conflict would spiral out of control and result in nuclear war. It successfully thwarted Pakistani attempts at "nuclear" blackmail. The ultimate triumph of diplomacy occurred as Pakistani Prime Minister Nawaz Sharif traveled to Washington, DC, in early July 1999 to negotiate a settlement of the conflict. At this time, defeat of the Pakistani occupying forces was assured as the Indian armed forces had recaptured almost all of the peaks in their respective sectors. The only remaining occupied peaks were the ones closest to the LoC, where Pakistani artillery fire could provide cover to the invaders. In a negotiated settlement, Pakistan decided to withdraw its troops from the remaining locations in a set time frame.

The most valuable lesson from the Kargil war for India was that Pakistan, despite attempts at peace, would not end the use of its military option in Kashmir. Pakistan had since the late 1980s been using an indirect military option against India by sending terrorists across the LoC to generate instability in the Indian state of Jammu and Kashmir. Kargil, a more direct military option, was used to bolster the morale of its forces and to achieve political and tactical gains. However, after the initial shock, the operation for Pakistan was a failure. It failed to achieve the desired political gains, as Pakistan stood isolated within the international community. And it failed in its tactical objective, as any gained territory was lost.[42]

The morale of Pakistani forces, despite early euphoria, was badly damaged; many units of the NLI were destroyed, and many of the dead were never brought home and, worse still, not acknowledged. India also learned another valuable lesson—that its military needed more funds and equipment to maintain a state of readiness against a cunning enemy. India also realized that its intelligence organizations needed to be better organized so that information and evidence would reach the proper authorities. Another important lesson was the Indian military and intelligence system needed a system of accountability for its failures.

The Kashmir Factor

It is not often realized that in analyzing India-Pakistan wars, Jammu and Kashmir has been a major theater of conflict. Except in 1971, all the wars fought by the two sides have focused, in one way or another, on Jammu and Kashmir. This stems partly from the Pakistani urge to take the state by force. They tried to do so by a combination of irregular and regular forces in 1947–48, and again in 1965. In 1965 the Pakistan tried to cut off Kashmir from the rest of India by attacking Chhamb. They also tried in 1971 to take parts of the Kargil sector on the LoC, but failed. In fact, in 1965, India had taken Haji Pir, an area of vital strategic importance that, had it remained in Indian hands, could have played a pivotal role in any counterinfiltration strategy that India would have adopted post-1989, when the Pakistan-sponsored insurgency in Jammu and Kashmir erupted.

The ifs and buts of history apart, the fact remains that for the last 20-odd years, until the Kargil war was fought on the LoC in Jammu and Kashmir, the proxy war was the main weapon that Pakistan had in its armory to offset India's conventional capabilities. Pakistan continues to use proxy war as part of its military's strategy against India. This continues post-Kargil also. The main problem is that the military on both sides is engaged heavily in Kashmir; be it in Siachen, on the LoC, or on the international border. The profiles on both sides are slightly different.

For India, troops are needed for counterinfiltration and to keep the LoC safe throughout its length. For Pakistan, the LoC is an area of infiltration and thus it actively uses its artillery to this end. Thus for Pakistan, the Kashmir theater is for offensive operations, while for India it is one for defense. To keep a watch on both Pakistan and on China, it was forced to create a new corps in the aftermath of Kargil; this was the 14 Corps.

Kashmir is in this sense central to the conflict for both sides. In military terms, it is a difficult logistic proposition. The nature of the terrain and weather precludes swift military campaigns. The nature of the militaries and their experiences in Kashmir does not suggest that they are likely to change their mind-sets of the essential capacities in terms of armor fixations, and to move to lightly equipped troops with enhanced firepower that could be used in the mountains to good effect. On the Indian side, military counterinsurgency operations on the LoC continue, with army presence playing a key role in the operations. On the Pakistani side, there is a continued military presence on the side of Kashmir that they occupy. This presence is aimed more at maintaining internal security and ensuring that dissent does not raise its head. It is also there on the LoC to help the infiltration of terrorists to the Indian side in the larger efforts of the Pakistani state to promote proxy war against India.

Select Bibliography

General Sources

Bajwa, Major General Kuldip Singh. *Jammu and Kashmir War, 1947–48: Political and Military Perspectives.* New Delhi: Har-Anand Publications, 2003.

Bleoria, Sudhir S. *Battles of Zoji La, 1948.* New Delhi: Har-Anand Publications, 1997.

Dasgupta, Chandrashekhar. *War and Diplomacy in Kashmir, 1947–48.* New Delhi: Sage Publications, 2002.

Khan, Akbar. *Raiders in Kashmir.* Karachi: Pakistan Publishers, 1970.

Prasad, S.N., and Dharam Pal. *Operations in Jammu and Kashmir, 1947-48.* Delhi: History Division, Ministry of Defence, Government of India, 1987.

Sen, L.P. *Slender Was the Thread.* New Delhi: Orient Longman Ltd., 1969.

1965 War

Ahmed, G. *Pakistan Meets Indian Challenge.* Lahore: Islamic Book Foundation, 1986.

Brines, Russell. *The Indo-Pakistan Conflict.* London: Pall Mall Books, 1968.

Chakravorty, B.C. *History of the Indo-Pak War 1965.* Armed Forces of the Indian Union, History Division, Ministry of Defence, Government of India. Available at http://www.bharat-rakshak.com/LANDFORCES/Army/History/1965War/PDF/index.html.

Khan, M. Asghar. *The First Round: Indo-Pakistan War, 1965.* New Delhi: Vikas Publishing House, 1979.

Khan, Mohammed Musa. *My Version: India-Pakistan War 1965.* New Delhi: ABC Publishing House, 1983.

Mankekar, D.R. *Twenty-two Fateful Days: Pakistan Cut to Size.* Bombay: Manaktalas, 1967.

Mohan, P.V.S. Jagan, and Samir Chopra. *The India-Pakistan Air War of 1965.* New Delhi: Manohar Publishers.

Singh, Lt. Gen. Harbaksh. *War Despatches 1965.* New Delhi: Lancer International.

1971 War

Jacob, Lt. Gen. J.F.R. *Surrender at Dacca: Birth of a Nation.* New Delhi: Manohar Publishers and Distributors, 1997.

Niazi, A.A.K. *The Betrayal of East Pakistan.* New Delhi: Manohar, 1998.

Palit, Major General D.K. *The Lightning Campaign: Indo-Pak War 1971.* New Delhi: Thompson Press India Ltd. 1972.

Qureshi, Hakeem Arshad. *The 1971 Indo-Pak War: A Soldier's Narrative.* Reprint, Karachi: Oxford University Press, 2004.

Roy, Vice Admiral Mihir K. *War in the Indian Ocean.* New Delhi: Lancer Publishers and Distributors, 1995.

Singh, Major General Sukhwant. *The Liberation of Bangladesh.* New Delhi: Vikas Publishing House, 1980.

———. *Defence of the Western Border.* New Delhi: Vikas Publishing House, 1981.

1999 Kargil War

Kargil Review Committee, *From Surprise to Reckoning: The Kargil Review Committee Report.* New Delhi: Sage Publications, 2000.

Krishna, Major General Ashok (Retired) and P.R. Chari, eds. *Kargil—The Tables Turned.* Published under the auspices of the Institute of Peace and Conflict Studies, New Delhi. New Delhi: Manohar Publishers and Distributors, 2001.

Malik, General V.P. *Kargil: From Surprise to Victory.* Harper Collins, 2006.

Singh, Amarinder. *A Ridge Too Far: War in the Kargil Heights.* Patiala: Moti Bagh Palace, 1999.

Singh, Jasjit. *Kargil 1999: Pakistan's Fourth War for Kashmir.* New Delhi: South Asia Books, 1999.

Tellis, Ashley J. *Limited Conflicts Under the Nuclear Umbrella: Indian and Pakistani Lessons from the Kargil Crisis.* Santa Monica, CA: Rand, 2001.

Indian and Pakistani Civil-Military Relations

Cohen, Stephen. *The Pakistan Army,* 2nd rev. ed. Karachi: Oxford University Press, 1998.

Kadian, Rajesh. *The Indian Army.* New Delhi: Vision Books, 1990.

Kukreja, Veena *Contemporary Pakistan: Political Processes, Conflicts and Crises.* New Delhi: Sage Publications, 2003.

———. *Civil Military Relations in South Asia: Pakistan, Bangladesh and India.* New Delhi: Sage Publications, 1991.

Malik, Iftikhar H. *State and Civil Society in Pakistan.* New York: St. Martin's Press, 1997.

Rosen, Stephen Peter. *Societies and Military Power: India and Its Armies.* Ithaca, NY: Cornell University Press, 1996.

India-Pakistan Wars

Bajpai, Kanti, P.R. Chari, et al. *Exercise Brasstacks.* New Delhi: Manohar, 2000.

Barua, Pradeep. *The State of War in South Asia.* Lincoln: University of Nebraska Press, 2005.

Chari, P.R. *Indo-Pak Nuclear Standoff: The Role of the United States.* New Delhi: Manohar, 1995.

Cloughley, Brian. *A History of the Pakistan Army: Wars and Insurrections.* 2nd ed. Karachi: Oxford University Press, 2000.

Das, Major General Chand N. *Hours of Glory: Famous Battles of the Indian Army, 1801–71.* New Delhi: Vision Books, 1997.

Ganguly, Sumit. *Conflict Unending: India-Pakistan Tensions Since 1947.* New York: Columbia University Press, 2001.

Lal, Air Chief Marshal P.C. *My Years with the IAF.* New Delhi: Lancer International, 1986.

Praval, Major K.C. *Indian Army after Independence.* New Delhi: Lancer International, 1995.

Rao, General K.V. Krishna. *Prepare Or Perish: A Study of National Security.* New Delhi: Lancer, 1991.

Singh, Major General Joginder. *Behind the Scene: An Analysis of India's Military Operations, 1947–71.* New Delhi: Lancer International, 1993.

CHAPTER 11

A Bad Knock:
The War with China, 1962

Srinath Raghavan

The historiography of the Sino-Indian war of 1962 is sharply polarized. The early accounts tended to portray India as the victim of Chinese betrayal. India's defeat was usually attributed to Prime Minister Jawaharlal Nehru's naïveté and negligence of military necessities. Within a decade came the revisionists, who argued that Nehru willfully pushed the military to fight a war they could only have lost.[1] Even today discussions on the war tend to generate more heat than light. This chapter attempts to push the tiller in the direction of a synthesis. Drawing upon a range of sources, it offers a brief account of the causes, conduct, and consequences of the war with China.

The origins of the war lay in two intertwined issues: the boundary dispute and Tibet. The Sino-Indian boundary is usually divided into three sectors. The western sector consists of the boundary of Ladakh with Sinkiang and Tibet. Here both India and China claimed the area of Aksai Chin. The eastern sector comprises the boundary between Tibet and India's North East Frontier Agency (NEFA). India claimed that the boundary ran along the McMahon Line, agreed upon in the 1914 Simla conference between India, China, and Tibet. On this occasion, the Chinese representative had initialed the map depicting the McMahon Line as the boundary. Later the Chinese government had repudiated the Simla conference. When the dispute arose, the Indians argued that the Chinese had rejected the conference owing to differences on the boundary between Tibet and mainland China, and not on account of the McMahon Line. In any case, it did not matter, for Tibet exercised treaty-making powers at that time. The Chinese, however, held that they had never assented to this alignment, and that Tibet had no right to conclude agreements with British India. The dispute in the central sector, along the boundary between Himachal Pradesh and Uttar Pradesh, and Tibet was a minor one.[2]

Closely related was the question of Tibet. During their rule in India, the British had sought to maintain Tibet as a buffer state, free of external influences, particularly Russian. Hence, they only acknowledged China's "suzerainty" over Tibet as opposed to "sovereignty." In practice this meant maintaining direct diplomatic links with Tibet and enjoying other privileges such as maintaining armed detachments in Tibet.

China-India Border: Western Sector

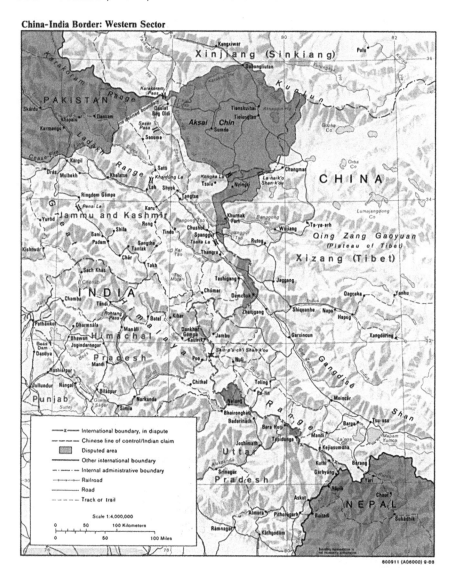

China-India border: Western Sector (Courtesy of the University of Texas Libraries, The University of Texas at Austin)

Following the Chinese annexation of Tibet, India signed an agreement with China in 1954, agreeing to forego these prerogatives, and also recognizing Tibet as a "region of China." Neither side sought to raise the boundary issue during the negotiations for this treaty. Differences in the central sector soon emerged, but both countries refrained from bringing up the other two sectors. In 1956, China began constructing

China-India Border: Eastern Sector

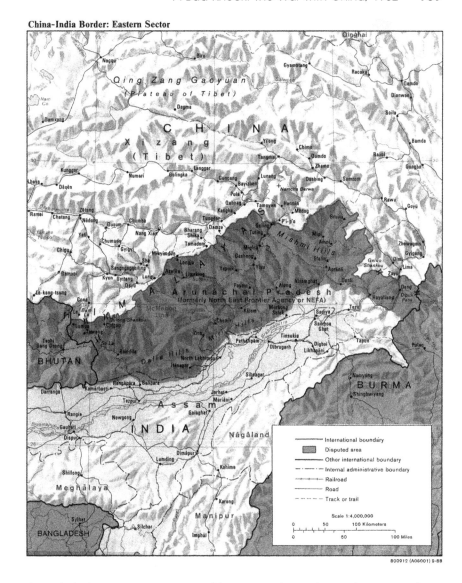

China-India border: Eastern Sector (Courtesy of the University of Texas Libraries, The University of Texas at Austin)

a highway through Aksai Chin, connecting Tibet and Sinkiang. This would become a link of strategic importance to the Chinese in maintaining their control over Tibet.

By the time the boundary dispute came to the fore in early 1959, an anti-Chinese rebellion was raging in Tibet. The Chinese mistakenly thought that India was abetting the rebels in an effort to detach Tibet from China and turn it into a buffer state. Delhi's decision to offer political asylum to the Dalai Lama enraged Beijing and imposed heavy strains on their relationship. In their quest to subdue the rebellion, Chinese troops moved up to the frontier with India. The Indians, too, were engaged in strengthening their position in these parts. Not surprisingly clashes occurred. Following a serious incident in Ladakh in October 1959, Prime Minister Nehru decided to hand over control of the frontiers to the army.

The army chief, General K.S. Thimayya, recommended that 4 Division—deployed in Punjab—be immediately shifted to NEFA. In preparing contingency plans, the General Staff aimed to offer only token resistance at the frontier and confront the Chinese deep inside Indian territory. Given the poor state of border communications at that point, it made much sense. However, the force levels envisaged by the General Staff catered only for a limited attack. Thimayya admitted that "the measures would not be adequate to contain a major invasion."[3] The requirements for a larger invasion seem to have been neither considered nor requested.

In April 1960, the Chinese premier came to Delhi for discussions with Nehru on the boundary dispute. The summit failed to achieve anything beyond the appointment of official teams to examine the legal-historical record. When pressed to specify their claims during these exchanges, the Chinese advanced a new claim line in Ladakh, incorporating an additional 2,000 square miles. In the summer of 1960, the Indian Intelligence Bureau (IB) began reporting Chinese activity, including road building, closer to their new claim line. Nehru and the defense minister, V.K. Krishna Menon, were keen to commence patrolling to prevent further ingress by the Chinese. The army headquarters, however, acted cautiously and left it to Western Command to decide whether patrolling should be undertaken. The civilians considered this a dilatory attitude on the part of the military. The General Staff responded that owing to logistical difficulties, additional troops had not yet been inducted into Ladakh; hence sufficient resources were not available for these tasks.

The civilian bureaucracy undoubtedly underestimated the issue of logistics, but part of the problem also lay with the military. The latter's approach to their tasks is evinced from the Chiefs of Staff Paper of January 1961.[4] To meet the threat from China, the chiefs recommended an increase of two infantry divisions and a brigade. Having given out their requirements, the chiefs added:

> Should the nature of the war go beyond that of a limited war...it would be beyond the capacity of our forces to prosecute war...beyond a short period, because of limitation on size, the paucity of available equipment and the lack of adequate logistical support.

The chiefs assumed that they would only have to prepare for a limited conflict and the question of countering threats across a spectrum was overlooked. In particular, the problem of dealing with territorial incursions did not loom significantly in their thinking. Assuming that they would have to prepare for a limited war, the chiefs projected only a modest increase in resources. And they went on to state the lack of resources as a constraint in waging a higher intensity conflict, or indeed in implementing existing plans. The paper displayed a remarkable lack of strategic judgment on part of the professional military.

Forward Policy

The chiefs' inability to formulate specific proposals to meet such incursions left the initiative for planning in the hands of civilians. In a meeting presided by Nehru in January or early February 1961, Menon suggested the idea of "zigzagging"—placing posts in areas claimed but not occupied by China.[5] This would prevent the Chinese from establishing another "line of control" west of the existing one. No action was initiated presumably because of the logistical difficulties faced by the army. By mid-1961, a new team of officers had taken over at the army headquarters. Thimayya had retired and was replaced by General P. N. Thapar; Lieutenant General B. M. Kaul took over as his Chief of General Staff (CGS). Kaul was an odd choice, for he had no operational experience, having served for most of his career in the supply corps. However, Kaul was close to Nehru and well attuned to the political atmosphere of Delhi. It is often claimed that Thapar and Kaul were "courtier soldiers" handpicked by Nehru and Menon, as opposed the "old-guard professionals."[6] It is possible that the government chose its top military advisors for political pliability. Nevertheless, it was the military system that brought to the top generals like Kaul and Thapar, who proved to be either incapable of offering the civilian leadership real alternatives, or too eager for consensus to lay out sharp choices for them to make.

The decision to adopt the so-called forward policy was taken at a meeting chaired by Nehru on November 2, 1961. The idea was to establish Indian posts as far forward as possible to deter Chinese incursions. This would, however, be done without getting involved in any clashes. The decision was based on a note from the IB that the Chinese would not move into any area where Indian personnel had established themselves. More importantly, Nehru believed that the Chinese would not launch a major attack on India, owing to the possibility of U.S. intervention in such a conflict. Besides, he thought that the Soviet Union would diplomatically restrain the Chinese.

During this meeting, Thapar observed that the new posts could not be supported tactically or logistically; nor could the Indians keep up in a race with the Chinese. But these arguments were not presented forcefully. Moreover, Kaul and the Director of Military Operations (DMO), Brigadier D. K. Palit, were inclined to agree with the IB's assessment of Chinese behavior. The military leadership thus went along with the civilian advocates of forward policy despite reservations. In this instance, as in subsequent ones, personality and proximity to political leadership only partially account for their stance. The fundamental problem was that they had no alternatives to offer, no unanimous professional judgment that applied to the situation. Criticism of top military commanders for not "standing up" to civilians—a recurrent theme in writings on the war—largely misses the point.

Notwithstanding protests from Western Command, posts with barely 10 to 20 troops were sited ahead of the Chinese claim line in Ladakh. Thinking that the Indians were "nibbling" Chinese territory, Beijing decided to establish its own posts encircling the Indian ones. Thus, in the spring of 1962, Indian and Chinese posts were established overlooking and crisscrossing each other. Despite inducting a fourth battalion into Ladakh, the Indians could not match China's numerical and logistical superiority. The Chinese posts were also qualitatively superior, for they had constructed a serviceable network of roads leading right up to the forward areas. The Chinese thus sited most of their posts on dominating heights, whereas the Indians had to establish theirs on valley floors where dropping zones were available.

On May 6, about 100 Chinese troops "in assault formation" advanced towards an Indian post in Chip Chap valley, but eventually pulled back without attacking. A couple of months later, the Chinese surrounded a platoon-sized post in Galwan valley, cut off withdrawal routes, and came within 100 yards of it. In Delhi, the Chinese ambassador was warned of serious consequences should Chinese troops come any closer. The Chinese did pull back slightly but continued to surround the post. The escalation in violence worried Nehru, who thought that the situation was "drifting badly." He therefore initiated diplomatic moves aimed at resuming discussions. Krishna Menon met the Chinese foreign minister, Chen Yi, at Geneva. The two sides negotiated seriously and wanted to issue a joint communiqué calling for further discussions. Menon referred the proposal to Nehru, but owing to a delay in communication, Nehru's approval was not received before Chen Yi's departure.[7] By the end of August, Beijing was convinced that India was not sincere about seeking a negotiated solution. The Chinese also viewed the forward policy as aimed at forcing them to relinquish the Aksai Chin road—an important step in India's attempt to make Tibet an independent, buffer state. On August 29 the major Chinese buildup of supplies and troops began.

Meanwhile, in NEFA an additional 34 Assam Rifles posts were established close to the McMahon Line. 4 Division had only two brigades: 7 Brigade, headquartered in Tawang, and 5 Brigade, for the rest of NEFA. The divisional commander, Major-General Niranjan Prasad, considered the platoon-sized Assam Rifles posts of little tactical value. It would be better to establish company or battalion-sized positions in the rear. Further, given the lack of roads and requisite airlift capability, it would be a logistical nightmare to support these forward posts. Prasad's immediate superior, 33 Corps Commander, Lieutenant-General Umrao Singh, agreed with his assessment. But CGS Kaul told Prasad that the prime minister himself had ordered the setting up of these posts and that he would allow no foot-dragging in this matter.

As part of this hasty drive to "plug gaps," a post was set up close to the NEFA-Bhutan-Tibet trijunction. Sited in the valley of the Namkachu River, it was overlooked by the Thagla ridge. This was a sensitive area, for the Indians and the Chinese had differed on the interpretation of the McMahon Line in it. Prasad thought that if the area did belong to India, it made more tactical sense to occupy the Thagla ridge itself. Accordingly, he sought permission to occupy the ridge pre-emptively. By the time the army headquarters got back, the Chinese had occupied the Thagla ridge on September 8. The following day, 7 Brigade was ordered to move to Dhola. Hitherto, the brigade had the task of defending Tawang, which was the designated "vital ground"; pushing it ahead only served to unravel the existing plans. At a meeting led by Menon, it was decided to use force to evict the Chinese from south of Thagla. Thapar, Sen, and the deputy CGS thought that the Chinese strength near Dhola approximated 600, whereas they would soon have a brigade. They also felt that adequate supplies were available and that the brigade could be maintained by air.

Commanders down the echelon considered any such action utterly infeasible. In a conference in Tezpur (33 Corps headquarters) on September 12, the corps commander, Umrao Singh, urged pulling back the Dhola Post. After a heated exchange, Sen demanded that Umrao and his subordinates produce an operational plan with the utmost speed. The plan was prepared by the divisional and brigade Commanders, Prasad and John Dalvi. Incredibly, the plan was a make-believe one, expressly designed to show the impossibility of throwing the Chinese out of the Namkachu area. Umrao handed it to the army commander on September 29, with his comments that the operation was totally impracticable. Sen responded that the commanders seemed to have gotten cold feet. He refused to accept that the projected logistical buildup was truly necessary, and argued that airlift could be used to improve the situation.

At a meeting in Delhi on October 2, Sen held Umrao responsible for the delays in launching the operation. He claimed that unless a new corps commander was appointed, they might be let down at a critical moment. Thapar concurred with Sen, and asked Menon for permission to replace Umrao. The following day it was decided that instead of removing Umrao, 33 Corps would be divested of responsibility for NEFA; instead a new formation, 4 Corps, would be raised. The new corps would be commanded by Kaul, who would continue to act as CGS. Kaul, of course, would have no additional troops apart from the two brigades of 4 Division.

Upon arrival in NEFA, one of Kaul's first actions was to push forward two battalions and the headquarters of 7 Brigade towards Namkachu. From the beginning Kaul was fixated on the Prasad-Dalvi plan. Prasad explained its genesis and unfeasibility, but Kaul was determined to execute it. On October 9, Kaul sent a small patrol ahead of the Namkachu. The next morning, the Chinese attacked the patrol and mauled it seriously. Kaul abandoned bravado and intimated to army headquarters that "a grave situation" had developed. He sought permission to fly to Delhi to present his case. On receiving approval, Kaul departed after instructing Prasad to hold the present positions along the Namkachu.

In a meeting on October 11, Kaul explained the situation beneath Thagla. Nehru stated that he did not want to jeopardize the troops, and asked the military to decide whether to hold Namkachu or fall back. Oblivious to ground reality, Sen and Thapar felt that a brigade could hold existing defensive positions against an enemy division. They urged that the positions along the Namkachu be held, even if the plan of evicting the Chinese were shelved. Nehru confirmed this decision. Kaul returned to his headquarters at Tezpur on October 13. Two days later, Prasad requested the withdrawal of 7 Brigade from its present positions; Kaul's staff officers backed this suggestion. In response to Kaul's entreaty, Thapar ordered Kaul to carry out aggressive patrolling and to forward his requirements for commencing the eviction operation at the earliest. Thus, despite the discretion vested in him by the prime minister, Thapar was keen to jump-start the offensive.

The following morning, Menon, Thapar, and Sen met Kaul at Tezpur. Kaul strongly argued that Namkachu positions were untenable. After three hours of discussion, the civilians left the room to let the military commanders arrive at a decision. Considering Thapar's orders to Kaul the previous day, it is not surprising that the generals decided against any withdrawal. Thapar agreed to provide additional supplies, equipment, and troops. Shortly thereafter, Kaul became seriously ill due to his exertions in high altitudes. He was evacuated to Delhi on October 18, but, rather unusually, continued to command from his sickbed. At Namkachu, Indian troops watched pathetically as the Chinese openly prepared for the attack. On the night of October 19, Chinese troops began to infiltrate Indian positions along the river. At the crack of dawn the Chinese onslaught commenced.

The Offensive

Within a few hours the Chinese had overrun the defenses of 7 Brigade. Dalvi requested and obtained permission to pull back to Tsangdhar, only to find it already seized by the Chinese. The remnants of the brigade were forced to head westward to Bhutan and make their way into Indian territory. Dalvi himself was taken prisoner on October 22. Apart from Dhola, the Chinese attacked western NEFA at Khinzemane and Bum-la with Tawang as the major objective. At the eastern end of NEFA, the Indian positions at Walong were assaulted.

In concert with the operations in NEFA, the Chinese commenced an offensive in Ladakh. Here they sought to systematically eliminate Indian posts ahead of their claim line. Indian positions in Chip Chap and Galwan valleys were attacked almost simultaneously. The puny "forward policy" posts stood no chance and were swiftly wiped out. Some of the posts, which were not attacked initially, were withdrawn. In the next couple of days the Chinese attacked in the Chang Chenmo valley and Pangong Lake. By October 24 they effectively controlled territory up to their claim line in northern and central Ladakh. The Chinese then overwhelmed Indian posts around Demchok on October 27 before pausing to consolidate their positions.

Until October 22, both the army commander and chief were keen to defend Tawang. In Kaul's absence, Sen flew to Tawang and instructed the troops to hold on at all costs and promised reinforcement by two brigades. The divisional commander, however, was convinced that Tawang was untenable and that the reinforcements could not arrive in time to make an effective stand. Prasad urged Sen to permit him to withdraw south and concentrate his forces at Se-la. Sen reluctantly authorized Prasad to act as he deemed fit and left Tawang. Concurrently, at the army headquarters, DMO Palit sought to convince his superiors of the imperative of evacuating Tawang and concentrating at Se-la. During his tenure as 7 Brigade commander a few years previously, Palit had been convinced that Tawang was tactically unsuited for waging a defensive battle. Thapar felt that the government would not accept the abandonment of such an important town as Tawang.

At a meeting presided by Nehru on October 23, Thapar asked Palit to explain his views. Briefing from a map, Palit pointed out that the Chinese could use numerous tracks to bypass Tawang and head straight for the plains of Assam via Manda-la. Hence, it was important to pull back from Tawang and hold the dominating Se-la massif. Nehru unhesitatingly left the decision to the army chief: "It is a matter now for the military to decide—where and how they should fight."[8] Thapar decided to fly down to Tezpur to personally convey the decision to hold Se-la. The army head-quarters also commenced preparations for rapidly stocking Se-la with ammunition and supplies for four to five battalions for 14 days.

In the meantime, the staff at 4 Corps headquarters had issued orders for 4 Division to withdraw to Bomdi-la, 60 miles south of Se-la. In their opinion, Bomdi-la was the farthest point to the north where they could build up faster than the Chinese; it would be logistically impossible to build up sufficiently to fight a battle at Se-la. The issue was discussed that evening when Thapar and Palit visited Tezpur. Logistics aside, the problem was that though Se-la was the most dominating feature in the area, a track leading south from Poshing-la to Bomdi-la bypassed Se-la entirely. If the Chinese managed to come down this trail, the stronghold at Se-la would be rendered irrelevant. Palit, however, vociferously advocated holding Se-la with a brigade, to be built up to two. He suggested that as additional troops became available, a brigade could be located at Bomdi-la to guard the approach from Poshing-la. Palit was aware of this problem, but felt that the Poshing-la approach was a difficult one, over which no sizeable force could be maintained. In the event, Thapar and Sen were persuaded. Sen spoke to Prasad, who had already reached Dirang, and ordered him to return to Se-la. Tawang was evacuated on October 23, and two days later the Chinese entered it unopposed. In NEFA, the Chinese paused after occupying Tawang.

The Interlude

Over the next few days, a number of command changes occurred within NEFA. Kaul was persuaded to step down, and Lieutenant-General Harbaksh Singh was appointed instead. Kaul agreed to do so after stipulating that he should be reinstated once he had been declared medically fit. Sen, meanwhile, decided that Prasad had to be removed, and replaced him with Major-General Anant Pathania. Although a highly decorated soldier, Pathania was moved from a cushy job in Delhi to com-manding a division at NEFA. Commanders of 62, 65, and 5 Brigade were also replaced. Incredibly, the rationale behind these changes was to get decorated soldiers to command in NEFA. Battalions too were shifted and cross-posted until no brigade in NEFA had its original units under command.

The assumption of command by Harbaksh was a healthy development. An impos-ing personality with a soldierly demeanor, Harbaksh's presence proved inspiring to the troops. Harbaksh undertook immediate reconnaissance and set about making his appreciations. The defensive plan conceived by Harbaksh appears to have drawn upon the ideas articulated by Palit. According to this plan, Se-la would be 4 Division's vital ground, with a division less a brigade. It would be backed up by a brigade-sized strong point at Bomdi-la. Both positions would be stocked by road and air for a 15- to 20-day siege. Crucially, "the road between them was to be discarded before it became the target of Chinese infiltration tactics."[9] Harbaksh was particularly keen to avoid Dirang, the lowest point on the road between Se-la and Bomdi-la. The plan sought to replicate the successful use of "box" formations by the Indian Army during the campaign against the Japanese in the Second World War. Harbaksh himself had been trained in the use of boxes in Malaya during the war—an interesting example of lessons passed on from the colonial army. By the evening of October 25, preparation of Se-la defenses were proceeding apace.[10]

The army headquarters also decided to raise a new formation, 2 Division, with two brigades, 5 and 11 (from 4 Division), with responsibility for eastern NEFA. As opposed to the close supervision in NEFA, the army headquarters gave Western Command greater leeway in reorganizing the defenses in Ladakh. Long before the commencement of hostilities, the Western Army commander, Daulet Singh, had drawn up a contingency plan to meet a large-scale attack. Based on a war game conducted in October 1960, Daulet had estimated that an entire division would be required to cater to this scenario. The plan envisaged inner and outer rings for the defense of Leh. The outer ring would consist of the Daulat Beg Oldi, Chushul, Dungti, and Phobrang areas, held by at least a battalion each. The inner ring would entail holding the approaches to Leh, with adequate troops in Leh itself.[11]

Following the October offensive a modified version of this plan was implemented, for Daulat Beg Oldi had been abandoned. Chushul was identified as the vital ground in Ladakh: if the Chinese sought to advance to Leh, the Spanggur gap, in which Chushul lay, would provide the obvious route. Consequently, 114 Brigade with an artillery regiment and a troop of tanks was inducted into the area by mid-November. Although the Chushul town and the airstrip were beyond the Chinese claim line, the defense of Chushul necessitated holding outposts on the hills to the east, across their claim line. Some of these were at altitudes of over 16,000 feet, where defenses could not be dug and the frozen ground had to be blasted. Despite such inordinately tough conditions, Indian troops managed to create positions with some defensive capability. As part of these moves, two brigades were also transferred to Ladakh from the line of control with Pakistan in Kashmir. Thus, prior to the reopening of Chinese attacks, Daulet Singh had managed to induct and support almost a division in his theater of operations.

The alacrity and decisiveness of moves in Ladakh sharply contrasted with the muddle on the eastern front. Just as Harbaksh Singh had settled in and set in motion his plans, Kaul was abruptly restored as 4 Corps commander on October 28. Ever since his removal a few days before, Kaul had lobbied hard to be reinstated. He argued that "unless he went back to the front, he would not be able to rehabilitate himself either in the army circles or in the public eye."[12] Krishna Menon was apparently sympathetic to Kaul's entreaties. In any case, Kaul seems to have convinced Nehru that he ought to be back in command.

Kaul's reinstatement, as the IB observed, had a demoralizing impact on troops in NEFA. The momentum built up by Harbaksh slackened and Kaul proved incapable of restoring it. Worse still, Kaul refused to be briefed by Harbaksh on the operational situation and consequently tampered with the defensive plan drawn up by the latter.

After Kaul returned to Tezpur, the 4 Division commander, Pathania, complained of high-altitude headaches and requested permission to shift his headquarters from Se-la to Dirang. Kaul's approval of this move was a crucial departure from the Harbaksh plan. It can be attributed only to Kaul's own lack of operational experience and his disinclination to be briefed by Harbaksh. Even more egregiously, Pathania pulled back a brigade from Se-la for the defense of his own headquarters at Dirang. The army headquarters was apparently not apprised of these moves until the Chinese offensive commenced.

During the lull in battle two important decisions were made. First, the government decided to approach several Western countries for military equipment-principally America and Britain. Nehru acknowledged past negligence on this aspect. As he wrote to Menon, "we have been found lacking and there is an impression that we have approached these things in a somewhat amateurish way."[13] By early November the first consignment of weapons started arriving from the United Kingdom and the United States, but the bulk of Western assistance would arrive only after the cease-fire. The other decision was to remove Menon from office. Shortly after the war began, there was a groundswell of criticism of Menon by members of the Congress Party, who held him culpable for the reverses. Besides, it was felt that Menon's standing with the Americans was at its nadir and that he could not effectively procure military supplies from them.[14] Nehru was compelled to accept Menon's resignation and assume the charge of defense himself.

The Finale

The Chinese utilized the pause in operations to construct a motorable road from Bum-la to Tawang by early November. Thereafter, they began to improve the road from Tawang to Se-la. The Chinese did not await completion of the road to begin applying pressure on Se-la. Indian patrols reported movements in areas north and southwest of Se-la. Evidently the Chinese were attempting to use various tracks—especially the Poshing-la axis—to outflank Se-la and sever the road connecting Se-la and Bomdi-la. On November 7, a frantic Kaul called Palit at army headquarters asking for an additional division. The Chinese, he said, were skirting Se-la in large numbers. Kaul was especially concerned about an attack on Bomdi-la from the north. Palit assured him that so long as Se-la held, there could be no major attack. He urged Kaul to take measures to disrupt Chinese supply columns bypassing Se-la. The General Staff rightly felt that Kaul was overestimating enemy capabilities: despite the road to Tawang, the Chinese could not logistically sustain a three-divisional offensive in NEFA. Ultimately, it was decided that an additional brigade would be allotted to 4 Corps.

During the lull in fighting, the Chinese had continued to probe the defences at Walong. Initially this sector had been the responsibility of 5 Brigade; when 2 Division was raised, it was allotted 181 Brigade for Walong. The divisional commander, Major-General Mohinder Pathania (a cousin of the other Pathania) wanted 181 Brigade to be replaced, and was allotted 11 Brigade. Thus within a span of

10 days, the battalions had served under three brigade headquarters. By the time 11 Brigade had settled down, the Chinese had managed to creep ahead and occupy two heights named "Green Pimple" and "Yellow Pimple," both overlooking Indian positions in Walong.

During his brief tenure in NEFA, Harbaksh had felt that Walong was untenable as a main defensive position, owing to the existence of a route bypassing it. Besides, wind conditions at Walong airstrip would impede a rapid buildup of forces. Harbaksh had planned to hold Walong with covering troops, and had identified Hayuliang—further to the rear—as the main defensive position. Kaul was apparently unaware of Harbaksh's assessment. Thus when the divisional commander recommended a local counterattack to retake Yellow Pimple, Kaul consented. Pathania thought that if an additional battalion could be inducted into Walong, the Chinese could be pushed back to the McMahon Line. Kaul's staff at 4 Corps headquarters differed from this assessment: they estimated Chinese strength just across the McMahon Line as one division. Nonetheless, Kaul decided to go ahead with the attack. The additional troops requested for the attack began to be airlifted to Walong on November 13. Even though the buildup was not complete, the attack was launched as scheduled the next day. The unseemly haste has been explained in several ways; the most plausible is that from their positions on Yellow Pimple, the Chinese had begun to direct accurate artillery fire on Indian defenses and thus were better positioned to launch their own offensive. The Indian attack was halted short of the crest, and the Chinese managed to push back the survivors.

On November 16, the Chinese launched their assault on the Indian positions. Within a few hours, the brigade's position became untenable. When the brigade commander turned to Kaul for instructions (both Kaul and Pathania were present at Walong), Kaul gave permission for the brigade to withdraw. The actual orders given by Kaul are interesting. The commander was to hold his present position to the best of his ability; if it became untenable, he was to take up an alternate position and hold it. Should the alternate position also become untenable, he was to continue holding a series of such positions. In effect, the order sought to place the responsibility for the decision to withdraw on the brigade commander. It would not be the last time that Kaul gave such an equivocal order to a subordinate commander. In attempting to withdraw, 11 Brigade quickly disintegrated into small parties, which trickled back to the plains over the next three weeks, suffering serious losses at the hands of the pursuing Chinese. The following day, Kaul sent a desperate signal imploring the government to "get such armed forces to come to our aid as are willing to do so without which... it seems beyond the capacity of our armed forces to stem the tide."[15] An alarmed Thapar took the signal directly to Nehru, and decided to rush to Tezpur immediately.

Upon arriving, Thapar and Palit were informed by Sen that the Chinese had launched an offensive against Se-la. By November 17, 4 Division had considerable resources available for defending the Se-la–Bomdi-la sector. 62 Brigade was deployed at Se-la with five battalions; 48 Brigade held Bomdi-la with two battalions; in between, at Dirang, was the division headquarters with 65 Brigade, comprising two battalions. Se-la was stocked with rations for a week, and the division had a sufficient complement of supporting arms, including heavy mortars, artillery, and some light tanks. Thus 4 Division should have been capable of holding the Chinese at bay until the onset of winter. Nevertheless, the box strategy had already been partially compromised by the decision to locate the division headquarters at Dirang; for this necessitated ensuring that the road between Se-la and Bomdi-la was not cut off. Hence, small bodies of troops had to be deployed to prevent Chinese infiltration. Furthermore, sitting in Dirang, Pathania could neither comprehend the situation at Se-la fully, nor could he effectively direct that crucial battle.

Soon after first light on November 17, the Chinese had attacked a battalion deployed as covering troops ahead of Se-la. The battalion repulsed five consecutive attempts to overrun the position, inflicting a large number of casualties in the process. The 65 Brigade commander, Hoshiar Singh, decided to pull back the battalion to the main defenses as a major attack on Se-la was clearly in the offing. Concurrently, the Chinese began to advance from the northeast via Poshing-la. In his appreciation of October 28, Pathania had identified the threat from this axis and the need to position a battalion to meet it. But he failed to take timely action to secure the pass. Although troops were dispatched in driblets from Bomdi-la starting on November 4, the bulk of them reached Tembang (south of Poshing-la) only on the morning of November 17. Attacked at noon, the battalion held the Chinese for three hours. The 48 Brigade commander, Gurbux Singh, decided to withdraw the battalion to Bomdi-la ostensibly because they were running out of ammunition. This hasty decision threw open the Se-la–Bomdi-la road to the Chinese. Owing to darkness and the thickly forested terrain, control was lost and the battalion disintegrated. Less than a company of troops managed to reach Bomdi-la, and the rest reached the plains over the next few weeks. By last light the Chinese had established a roadblock between Dirang and Bomdi-la.

That evening Pathania spoke to the staff at 4 Corps, describing the situation of the Se-la brigade and his own headquarters as precarious. He importuned for permission to withdraw to Bomdi-la. A little later Pathania called and spoke to Thapar and Sen. Both the chief and the army commander declined to give him any instructions until Kaul returned. By this time a heated debate had ensued at the corps headquarters. Sen favored the idea of a withdrawal from Se-la on the hope that the division could get away intact. Palit staunchly opposed it. He rightly argued that Se-la was capable of withstanding Chinese onslaught; a withdrawal into the Dirang valley made no tactical sense and would only end in a rout. Pathania, meanwhile, instructed Hoshiar Singh to prepare for the withdrawal of 62 Brigade on the same night. The brigade commander reportedly demurred that he could hold out if supplied by air, but was overridden by Pathania. He nevertheless convinced Pathania that the withdrawal ought to be done on the following night, to avoid confusion and panic.

The testy discussion at the corps headquarters continued after Kaul's return at about 7:00 PM. Kaul also spoke to Pathania, who reiterated his request. For reasons not quite clear, Kaul sent a signal instructing 4 Division to "withdraw to Bomdi-la."[16] When Palit was informed of this order, he beseeched the chief to reconsider it. After further consultations the order was rescinded. Kaul then issued another, characteristically temporizing order: "You will hold on to your present positions to the best of your ability. When any position becomes untenable I delegate the authority to you to withdraw to any alternative position you can hold."[17] As before, Kaul sought to shift the onus of decision onto a subordinate. Kaul also spoke to 48 Brigade Commander at Bomdi-la and ordered him to clear the roadblock. Gurbux argued that the defenses of Bomdi-la were already depleted to six infantry companies. Moreover, it would be reckless to attempt evicting the Chinese on a foggy night. Kaul agreed to withhold his order until the next morning, when two more battalions would reach Bomdi-la.

Kaul's ambiguous signal did not reach 4 Division headquarters until the early hours of the next day. But later that night Kaul, in the presence of Thapar, spoke to Pathania and told him to "hang on" to his defenses and "have another chat" in the morning.[18] Such unusually casual instructions could have hardly bolstered Pathania's flagging resolve. By this time, the 65 Brigade commander had prepared plans for withdrawal the following night, and had conveyed these to his battalion commanders. At about 10:30 PM, instructions were issued to the battalion occupying an important position on the periphery of Se-la to pull back to another position just behind the pass, to cover withdrawal of the brigade the following night. The rationale behind this sudden move was apparently that the Chinese were preparing to assault the battalion the next morning, and it would be difficult to extricate it under fire.

It is not entirely clear whether this move was ordered by Hoshiar or Pathania: given Hoshiar's reluctance to withdraw, it seems unlikely that he would have made the decision. In any case, it proved disastrous. The unexpected rearward passage of troops appears to have unnerved the other battalions. The problem was compounded as the Chinese followed the withdrawing troops, occupied the vacated positions, and opened fire. In the ensuing pandemonium, the other battalions also began to withdraw. Realizing that the eastern side of Se-la was completely denuded of troops, Hoshiar ordered a general withdrawal to a position just behind Se-la. As the Chinese brought to bear effective fire on the retreating columns, the brigade splintered into small groups, which individually made their way for the plains. Many such groups were ambushed en route; Hoshiar Singh himself was killed on November 27.

At 5:30 AM on November 18, Pathania reported to Kaul that 62 Brigade had begun to withdraw; only then did Kaul formally grant permission. More importantly, Kaul did not give any instructions on whether Dirang should be held or the entire division should reel in to Bomdi-la. The initiative thus lay with Pathania, who was already concerned that the Chinese were blocking the retreat of the brigade from Se-la. Further, his own headquarters was coming under fire from positions as near as a thousand yards. He ordered 65 Brigade to withdraw to the plains and instructed the tanks to attempt to fight through to Bomdi-la. Pathania departed for the plains post haste, leaving no one in charge, and without even informing the corps headquarters. He would later claim that he had intended to reach Bomdi-la by a circuitous route, and had moved southward only after learning of its fall.

By mid-morning on November 18, 48 Brigade at Bomdi-la was the only remaining defensive formation in NEFA. Six companies occupied a position designed to hold twice the number; hence there were many gaps. Nevertheless, the troops waited in prepared positions backed by heavy mortars, field guns, and four light tanks. At about 10:40 AM, Kaul ordered the brigade commander to send a column towards Dirang, to link up with the main division. Kaul, of course, was unaware that Dirang had been abandoned. Gurbux was loathe to weaken his defenses further; for apart from the roadblock, a second Chinese column was reported to be advancing towards Bomdi-la from the west. Kaul categorically ordered Gurbux to dispatch the column regardless of the consequences to Bomdi-la. Kaul appears to have been influenced by his concern for Dirang and his confidence that two more battalions would reach Bomdi-la shortly.

Two infantry companies with a couple of mountain guns and tanks were formed into a column and began to head towards Dirang. Even as they moved out, Chinese troops hiding in the wooded slopes advanced to occupy the vacated positions. The column traversed only a short distance before being ambushed. Soon an assault on Bomdi-la commenced. After several hours of fighting, the Chinese had captured bunkers along the perimeter, and Indian counterattacks had failed. As yet there was no sign of reinforcements except for the advance party of one battalion. At about 4:00 PM, Gurbux decided to withdraw from Bomdi-la and make a stand eight miles south, at Rupa, hoping that the reinforcements would have reached there already.

Gurbux, however, does not seem to have made his intentions clear; for shortly after his departure, one of the reinforcing battalions arrived at Bomdi-la. Gurbux himself returned to Bomdi-la later that night. At an officers' conference, the idea of counterattacking was considered. But it was felt that unless the fresh troops had conducted reconnaissance, it would be inadvisable to launch an attack. In the early hours of November 19, the battalion was ordered back to Rupa. By the time the troops could get into position, the Chinese opened up fire from features all around Rupa, forcing Gurbux to withdraw further south. Adding to his problems were contradictory orders issued by the staff at 4 Corps headquarters and by General Kaul, who had gone forward. The remnants of 48 Brigade finally broke up under fire from the pursuing Chinese at Chako. By about 3:00 AM on November 20, 4 Division ceased to exist as a fighting force.

During the second phase of operations, the Chinese also attacked Indian positions in Ladakh. Artillery bombardment of the airfield, Indian positions in and ahead of Chushul commenced after midnight on November 18. At first light, the Chinese assaulted the key Indian outposts at Gurung Hill and Rezang-la. The occupation of the former would pose a direct threat to the airfield, while taking the latter would enable the Chinese to cut off the road connecting Chushul with Leh, forcing the garrison to rely on a mule track. After a failed frontal attack on Rezang-la, the Chinese moved to envelop it from the rear and a flank. Rezang-la witnessed some of the most bitter fighting of the war. No quarter was asked and none given: a mere three soldiers of the company of 112 returned to the battalion headquarters.

When an Indian party reached Rezang-la three months later, they found the rest of the company frozen in their positions, with weapons in hand.

The initial attack on Gurung Hill was also broken up. Indian troops resolutely resisted the follow-up assault, taking a heavy toll on the attackers; but they too suffered serious casualties. Consequently, the brigade commander pulled back the remainder and regrouped them in previously identified positions in the hills west of Chushul. The Chinese did not press on to attack Chushul; having suffered a large number of casualties, they seem to have been deterred by the strong Indian positions. Besides, Chushul itself lay beyond their claim line. In the western sector, the Indian Army gave a much better account of itself as compared to NEFA. Although the Chinese managed to push the Indians beyond their claim line, they had to pay dearly for the territory they won.

Cease-fire and After

By the evening of November 19, the Indian Army stood seemingly helpless to withstand further Chinese onslaught. In the west, the Chinese were shelling the Chushul airfield and appeared likely to advance to Leh. In the east, they were poised to enter the plains; the loss of large portions of Assam seemed ineluctable. Nehru now decided to approach the United States for air cover. Writing to President John F. Kennedy, he described the situation as "really desperate" and requested immediate despatch of at least 12 squadrons of fighter aircraft. Until the Indians were trained, these would be manned by American pilots to protect Indian cities, and to assist the Indian Air Force in any battles within Indian airspace. Action against the Chinese elsewhere would be undertaken solely by the Indian Air Force. For Nehru, who had staked so much on nonalignment, it was a crushing acceptance of failure.

The American Ambassador, J.K. Galbraith, disagreed with the Indian assessment of the situation. Besides, he thought that the Indian Air Force could not stem the Chinese drive. Galbraith recommended that vessels of the Seventh Fleet be dispatched urgently to the Bay of Bengal.[19] Kennedy, however, was more forthcoming and offered to send a high-level team immediately to assess India's needs.[20] In any event, the cessation of hostilities by the Chinese, not American aircraft, precluded further disaster. On November 21, Beijing announced a unilateral cease-fire, to be followed 10 days later by the withdrawal of Chinese troops to the north of the McMahon Line in the east, and the "line of actual control" in the west, with police posts in the withdrawn areas. In effect, the Chinese would retain control up to their 1960 claim line in Ladakh. Delhi refused to accept the cease-fire proposals as it was felt to be tantamount to granting legitimacy to a line established forcefully by the Chinese. The Indians, however, tacitly accepted the situation. Indeed, the status quo persists to date.

Following the debacle at NEFA, the army chief, General Thapar, stepped down. Kaul, too, subsequently tendered his resignation. The war with China had considerable impact in shaping India's outlook towards its defense policy. As Nehru put it, Chinese aggression was a "permanent piece of education." In the immediate aftermath of the war, it was decided that the army should raise 10 mountain divisions within a decade. In the budget for 1963–64, the allocation for defense was twice that of the previous year. The proportion of the budget assigned for defense rose sharply from the previous average of roughly 15 percent to 28 percent in 1963. A five-year defense plan was introduced aimed at expansion, modernization of weapons and equipment, boosting of defense production, and creation of an operational infrastructure along the borders. Eventually, the Indian Army increased in strength to over 21 divisions, and the air force to 45 squadrons. Reforms were also undertaken to enhance the operational performance of the forces. In particular, rigorous and realistic training methods were introduced to improve their capability to operate in jungles and high altitudes. The defeat of 1962 thus set in motion the process whereby India became the preeminent military power in South Asia.

Select Bibliography

Dalvi, J. P. *Himalayan Blunder.* New Delhi: Thacker, 1969.

Galbraith, J. K. *Ambassador's Journal.* Boston: Houghton Mifflin, 1969.

Gopal, Sarvepalli. *Jawaharlal Nehru: A Biography,* Vol. III. Cambridge, MA: Harvard University Press, 1984.

Hoffmann, Steven. *India and the China Crisis.* Berkeley: University of California Press, 1990.

Johri, S. R. *Chinese Invasion of Ladakh.* Lucknow: Himalaya Publishers, 1969.

———. *Chinese Invasion of NEFA.* Lucknow: Himalaya Publishers, 1968.

Kaul, B. M. *The Untold Story.* New Delhi: Allied Publishers, 1967.

Kavic, Lorne. *India's Quest for Security: Defense Policies, 1947–1965.* Berkeley: University of California Press, 1967.

Khera, S. S. *India's Defence Problem.* Bombay: Orient-Longman, 1968.

Lamb, Alastair. *The China-India Border: The Origins of the Disputed Boundaries.* London: Oxford University Press, 1964.

———. *The McMahon Line,* 2 vols. London: Routledge and Kegan Paul, 1966.

———. *The Sino-Indian Boundary in Ladakh.* Columbia: University of South Carolina Press, 1975.

———. *Tibet, China and India.* Hertfordshire: Roxford Books, 1989.

Macfarquhar, Roderick. *Origins of the Cultural Revolution 3: The Coming of the Cataclysm 1961–1966.* Oxford: Oxford University Press, 1997.

Mankekar, D. R. *The Guilty Men of 1962.* Bombay: Tulsi Shah Enterprises, 1968.

Maxwell, Neville. *India's China War.* New York: Doubleday, 1972.

———. *China's "Aggression" of 1962.* Oxford: Court Place Books, 1999.

Mehra, Parshotam. *An "Agreed" Frontier: Ladakh and India's Northernmost Borders, 1846–1947.* New Delhi: Oxford University Press, 1992.

———. *The McMahon Line and After.* New Delhi: Macmillan, 1974.

Mullik, B. N. *The Chinese Betrayal.* New Delhi: Allied Publishers, 1971.

Palit, D. K. *War in High Himalaya: The Indian Army in Crisis, 1962.* London: Hurst, 1991.

Prasad, Niranjan. *The Fall of Towang.* New Delhi: Palit & Palit, 1981.

Saigal, J. R. *The Unfought War of 1962.* New Delhi: Allied Publishers, 1979.

Sinha, P.B. and A.A. Athale, *History of the Conflict with China, 1962.* India: History Division, Ministry of Defence, 1992.

Smith, Louis J., ed. *Foreign Relations of the United States, 1961–1963,* Vol. XIX. Washington, D. C.: U.S. Government Printing Office, 1996.

Vertzberger, Yaakov. *Misperceptions in Foreign Policy Making: The Sino-Indian Conflict, 1959–1962.* Boulder, CO: Westview Press, 1984.

Peace through Military Parity? The Tamil Tigers and the Government Forces in Sri Lanka

Channa Wickremesekera

The war between the Liberation Tigers of Tamil Ealam (hereafter LTTE) and the Sri Lankan state is one of the longest and most intractable conflicts in the region. Since 1983 it has taken the lives of more than 60,000 Sri Lankans and displaced over 300,000 people. It had caused widespread destruction to government and civilian property and turned valuable agricultural land into a no-man's-land. As of this writing, a cease-fire signed in 2002 is holding, but war clouds have not completely drifted away.

For the greater part of the conflict, both sides have used their military power as a means to force a negotiated settlement under favorable conditions. What has made this "search for a negotiated settlement by military means" so prolonged and agonizing has been the inability of the two sides to realize their major military objectives. For both the LTTE and the Sri Lankan forces (hereafter SLF) this has been their failure to "liberate" all of the north and the east from their opponents. Ironically, this military failure has eventually led both sides to the negotiating table, albeit after immeasurable human and material loss. This chapter will look at the key developments in the military conflict that have led to this decisive military "parity" between the two sides.

Background to the conflict: Tamils in Sri Lanka and Tamil Nationalism

Tamils, who currently make up about 18 percent of Sri Lanka's population, have been part of Sri Lanka's ethnic makeup for centuries. Sri Lanka's proximity to south India, where Tamil kingdoms and empires have flourished from the pre-Christian era, meant that there was always the potential for an influx of Tamil-speaking people to the island. They arrived as merchants, immigrants, and invaders, the majority of them settling in the north and the east of the island. This movement intensified with the establishment of a Tamil kingdom in the north of the island in the thirteenth century, with Jaffna as its capital. In the south, several Sinhalese kingdoms remained dominant. The northern kingdom expanded and contracted in response to internal and external forces and was briefly conquered and ruled by the Sinhalese kingdom of Kotte from 1450 to 1467. Then, in 1619, the Portuguese who had taken over the southwestern coastline, conquered Jaffna and brought it under their direct control. From the Portuguese, Jaffna passed on to the Dutch and then, in 1796, to the British.

The British enhanced the Tamil presence in Sri Lanka through their plantation economy. Thousands of Tamil laborers were brought from south India to work in tea plantations.[1] The colonial rule in general also provided many opportunities for Tamils to advance. During European colonial rule, many educational institutions were set up in the coastal areas, which enabled many Tamils to obtain a Western-style education that a majority of the Sinhalese in the interior lacked. As a consequence, a disproportionate number of Tamils gained employment in the civil service under the British. Many Tamils also rose to be wealthy business-men using the opportunities provided by the colonial economy.

After independence in 1948, political parties led by Sinhalese politicians deriv-ing their support mainly from the Sinhalese majority came to rule the country. These governments faced considerable pressure to acknowledge the primacy of the Sinhalese in administration. In 1956 Sinhalese was made the official language, and state-sponsored colonization of the Tamil-dominated Eastern Province with predominantly Sinhalese farmers also began. Tamils became increasingly insecure about these developments, which led to Tamil leaders demanding greater autonomy for Tamil-dominated areas, namely the north and the east of the island.[2] The attempts to grant substantial autonomy were thwarted by Sinhala opposition in 1958 and 1965. In 1972, Sri Lanka became a republic. The new constitution fueled Tamil discontent by giving primacy to Buddhism, the religion of the majority of Sinhalese.

Rise of Tamil Militancy

By the early 1970s, the unsuccessful campaign for autonomy had frustrated many Tamils, particularly the younger generation. As a consequence, a number of militant groups emerged with the idea of using violence to achieve independence in the form of a state called Tamil Ealam. These groups were very small in number, and few were armed. Their activities included bank robberies and spearheading of militant demon-strations against the Sri Lankan state. Things took a more violent turn in 1975 when Alfred Duraiappa, the mayor of Jafna and a member of the ruling party, was gunned down. Another Tamil politician, M. Canegaratnam, suffered a similar fate in 1977 for switching his allegiance from the main Tamil political party, the Tamil United Liberation Front, to the then ruling party, the United National Party. In 1978 the CID inspector Bastianpilai, who had been appointed to investigate the militant movement, and four others were murdered. More policemen were killed in 1979–80, and in October 1981 the militants killed their first Sri Lankan soldier. The Tamil rebellion had begun.

The Emergence of the LTTE

At present, the LTTE is the only Tamil militant group in conflict with the Sri Lankan government. However at its formation in 1975, the LTTE was but one of many militant groups rebelling against the Sri Lankan state. Although they cooperated in many activities, things were never entirely harmonious between the groups. Matters came to a head in 1985 when the LTTE decided to go after the TELO (Tamil Ealam Liberation Organization) and PLOTE (People's Liberation Organization of Tamil Ealam), killing many members of the two groups. Soon, other groups to came to bear the wrath of the Tigers.

The LTTE's assault decimated the rival groups. It also pushed them all towards the Sri Lankan security forces for their own survival as well as a future avenue of revenge. Today many members of these groups are working alongside Sri Lankan security forces.

The Tigers vs. the Sri Lankan State: A Brief History

From the beginning of the armed struggle, the avowed aim of the militants was to "liberate" the "Tamil homeland" from the Sri Lankan forces. These forces were entrusted with the task of crushing the rebels and bringing the north and the east under government control. In the mid-eighties, the militants seemed to gain the upper hand, succeeding in confining troops to the barracks. The Sri Lankan forces made two major attempts to break free from this confinement in 1986 and 1987. Both efforts petered out in the face of stiff resistance.

The 1987 operation (code named "Operation Liberation") also came under heavy pressure from neighboring India. India had been watching the developments in Sri Lanka keenly. It had considerable geopolitical interests in the course of the war on the island. Home to 500 million Tamils, India did not wish to see a Tamil backlash at home over the Sri Lankan government's treatment of Tamils in Sri Lanka. Equally, if not more important, was India's concern about the conflict inducing the Sri Lankan government to forge an alliance with a country that had conflicting interests with India in the region.

Indian pressure and Sri Lanka's inability to crush the Tigers led to the signing of the Indo-Lanka Accord in July 1987. Under the accord, an Indian Peace Keeping Force (IPKF) arrived in the north and east of the island to take over from Sri Lankan forces and ensure the militants handed over their weapons. The government was to establish provincial councils in Sri Lanka that offered substantial autonomy to the provinces, including the north and the east.

Things worked well for a while in the north and the east. The Tamils welcomed the IPKF enthusiastically and the militants began to hand in their weapons.

But the honeymoon between the IPKF and the militants was short-lived. In October 1987 a dispute over the transfer of some LTTE prisoners from Jaffna to Colombo led to a rupture between the LTTE and the IPKF, resulting in the former turning its guns on the Indians. The peacemakers were forced to fight.

The Indians went straight for the jugular. They launched an assault on the LTTE's stronghold in Jaffna. Heavy armor and a massive troop concentration soon crushed the Tiger resistance, but not before the guerrillas had inflicted some stinging blows on the Indians. Small-scale resistance continued throughout the northern and eastern mainland, but the Tigers were clearly on the run.

The Tigers received a much-needed respite by the rising anti-Indian sentiment in the south of Sri Lanka. The Sri Lankan government, under pressure from its constituents and hopeful of a separate peace with the Tigers, now called for the withdrawal of the Indian troops. The Indians complied, happy to distance themselves from a war that had cost more than 1,000 Indian lives.

The Sri Lankan government's hopes for a settlement with the Tigers were short-lived. The withdrawal of the IPKF allowed the LTTE to move back into areas vacated by the Indians. They reestablished themselves in Jaffna and gradually began to consolidate their power in the eastern province. They eliminated their remaining rivals and established strongpoints within sight of police stations and army barracks.

In June 1990 fighting broke out again between the government and the LTTE. The SLF quickly dislodged the Tigers from the towns in the east and cleared the coast, but the LTTE withdrew to the thickly forested hinterland and continued its guerrilla operations. Regrouping, the Tigers now began to mount operations on an unprecedented scale, demonstrating an alarming capacity for conventional fighting. By 1994 the war had settled to a stalemate, with the forces holding much of the east and the LTTE running a de facto state in the north.

In 1994 a new government came to power in Sri Lanka and called for an immediate truce with the Tigers. The truce led to talks between the two sides. No major decisions on ending the war had been made when the LTTE broke off the talks in April 1995, citing frustrations with the slow progress of the talks as the reason.

This new war was fought on an unprecedented scale. The government launched a massive offensive to capture the Jaffna peninsula in May 1995 and succeeded in doing so in early the following year. The LTTE withdrew the bulk of its forces and its heavy weapons to the jungles of Wanni, where they established themselves. The security forces also consolidated their positions around the main Eastern Province towns of Trincomalee and Batticaloa, while the LTTE controlled the coast to the north of Trincomalee. Ferocious fighting displaced thousands of people in the north and the east and the Tigers intensified the pressure on the government by unleashing terror strikes on a range of targets in the south.

Although the army controlled much of Jaffna, supplies for more than 25,000 troops in the peninsula had to be sent by air and sea. These operations were vulnerable to Tiger attacks. In 1998 a major operation was launched to open a main supply route from Vavuniya to Jaffna. The campaign proceeded well for a while and the troops recovered a subtstantial area from the rebels. But in 1998 the Tigers hit back ferociously, recapturing much of the lost territory and capturing the major army base at Killinochchi. They followed up their success by capturing Elephant Pass. Buoyant Tigers pressed hard on Jaffna for the ultimate prize, but failed in the face of stiff resistance.

Things have virtually remained in this state until July 2001, when the LTTE launched one of their most successful operations—a devastating attack on the Katunayake International Airport.[3] In December of that year, the LTTE declared a unilateral cease-fire. The government, responded shortly and negotiations under Norwegian facilitation led to the cease-fire of 2002.

The Balance of Forces: Critical Features and Developments

The military events of this conflict have been dominated by some interesting operational and organizational developments in the forces on both sides. These developments, while making the war one of the most destructive in the region, has also made it hard for either side to achieve a decisive advantage.

Use of Terrorism

The LTTE is listed as a terrorist organization by a number of countries, including the United States. This has led to the organization being banned in many parts of the world. The reason for this is not hard to find: terrorism is one of the most effective weapons deployed by the LTTE in its struggle against the Sri Lankan state.

Like many "liberation organizations," the LTTE began its armed activities by carrying out operations against noncombatants, their first victims being Tamil civilians and politicians who did not toe their line. In the 1980s they graduated to carrying out massacres of Sinhalese and Muslim civilians in the northeast and exploding bombs in the capital, Colombo. One of the deadliest bombs exploded in central Colombo in April 1987, killing over a hundred people. There were a number of reasons for these operations. Some were carried out in retaliation for the military's atrocities against civilians in the north, while others were meant to cleanse the Tamil homeland of Sinhalese and Muslim civilians.[4]

Terrorist tactics continued to be a feature of the Tigers' campaign in the 1990s and the 2000s. However, the incorporation of new tactics increased the reach and power of terrorism. In the 1990s the Tigers perfected the use of suicide bombers, which now came to be their most deadly terrorist weapon. Specially chosen and trained cadres known as Black Tigers carried out the bombings. The method of delivery was either via an individual wearing a "suicide jacket" or by a vehicle rigged with explosives.

The targets of the suicide cadres were mainly key individuals and economic infrastructure of the country. Their victims included the Prime Minister of India,

Rajiv Gandhi, and the President of Sri Lanka, Ranasinghe Premadasa. The assassination of Gandhi showed that the reach of the bombers extended beyond the Palk Strait, but this was a rare occurrence. The suicide cadres, unlike the squads of killers that operated in the 1980s, carried out their attacks mostly in and around Colombo. It was a telling way of bringing the war to the south. They showed the people in the south, especially the Sinhalese majority, that they could not expect the war to continue without suffering some of its consequences.

The adoption of suicide tactics elevated the Tigers' terrorism to a new level of efficiency. Because they were willing to die, the suicide bombers could take greater risks in approaching their targets, thereby extending their reach. Even if detected, they could still cause harm by detonating their charges prematurely, causing havoc. Dealing with such a threat was unnerving for regular security forces, let alone the general populace.

The Emergence of the LTTE as a Conventional Force

Although the LTTE uses terrorist tactics very effectively, to reduce the LTTE's military strength to its ability to launch terror strikes is to miss the point completely. The LTTE's terrorism is only one part of its impressive military machine. The Tigers' military forces today also consist of thousands of personnel who are organized and armed along conventional lines and capable of taking on and defeating the Sri Lankan forces in conventional military encounters. A considerable number of these cadres are children, many of whom are forcibly recruited.[5] There is also a heavy presence of women, who figure prominently in combat.

The Tigers built up their regular forces gradually. In the early days the Tigers' military targets were limited to individuals or small groups in the security forces, especially the police. Then, in July 1983, the Tigers graduated from this type of minor skirmish to more substantial engagements with a deadly ambush of an army patrol.[6] After 1983 the separatist campaign gathered momentum with frequent attacks on security force patrols and outposts. The land mine now came to the fore as the Tigers' weapon of choice, taking a steady toll of Sri Lankan security forces on a regular basis. The militants were not just a terrorist group anymore. They were also a burgeoning guerrilla force.

Gradually, mounting attacks forced the security forces to curtail their movements between their camps and outposts. In some areas patrolling virtually ceased and any movement out of the camps turned into major excursions in force. Outside the military camps, the militants virtually ran the show in Jaffna.

In 1986 and 1987, the first major clashes between this increasingly assertive guerrilla outfit and the beleaguered security forces occurred. In two major operations, columns of soldiers thrust out of several bases on the Jaffna peninsula in an attempt to break the tightening noose and deliver a crushing blow to the rebels. The Tigers countered these operations with their now customary guerrilla tactics. Land mines and booby traps delayed the army's advance, which finally petered out without recovering much territory.

The Tigers confronted the IPKF with the same tactics they used against the SLF. Their tactics initially made some impression on the Indian soldiers, who ventured into unknown territory with little knowledge of the enemy. However, they soon found that the Indian Army possessed far greater firepower than the Sri Lankan forces could muster. In classic guerrilla mode, the Tigers melted into the countryside. Their main force shifted to the Vanni—the sparsely populated and thickly forested region on the mainland south of the Jaffna Peninsula. For two years the Tigers maintained a low-key guerrilla campaign against the IPKF. They caused the Indians many casualties but failed to gain any considerable hold over the Jaffna Peninsula.

When war resumed in 1990, the LTTE again resorted to guerrilla warfare, but not for long. In 1991, the Tigers, pushed out of the urban areas in the east, now regrouped to stage a counterattack of previously unimaginable proportions. Gathering thousands of cadres, they set siege to the Elephant Pass military base that straddles the little strip of land connecting the Jaffna Peninsula to the mainland. The objective was to eliminate the base and thereby ensure the isolation of the peninsula.

Even though the LTTE was defeated in the battle, the encounter demonstrated the startling graduation of the Tigers into a conventional force. At Elephant Pass, the Tigers departed from their usual hit-and-run approach to engaging the security forces and opted for a full-scale siege of a major military base. Issuing from a network of trenches that had taken months to dig, they launched attacks across open terrain and stood up to continuous bombardment from air, land, and sea for several days, withdrawing only after casualties had mounted beyond what they could reasonably sustain.

From this time onwards the Tigers displayed a consistent propensity for engaging Sri Lankan security forces in conventional warfare while maintaining the intensity of the guerrilla campaign. And they were rewarded with some spectacular successes. These included the capture of the Pooneryn base in 1993 and the Mullaitivu army camp in 1996. But perhaps their biggest successes came in 1998 and 1999, when they rolled back a major military offensive and captured the army base of Killinochchi. They crowned this achievement with the capture of Elephant Pass in 2000 and launched a massive assault on the supreme prize, Jaffna. The attack fizzled out in the early months of 2001, but the rebels remained alarmingly close to the heart of Jaffna until the cease-fire the following year.

The Tigers have planned their conventional operations meticulously, especially those against fixed targets. Detailed information about the target was obtained through careful and efficient reconnaissance, and the planning of the operation was carried out using models of the targets. Months were spent preparing assault positions around the target while carefully concealed from the enemy forces on the ground and in the air. The Tigers' assaults have been as swift as their planning has been meticulous; "human wave attacks," usually led by suicide cadres, have often been used to break the resistance of the enemy.

The Tigers' increasing predilection for conventional warfare has been accompanied by a steady acquisition of more powerful and sophisticated weapons. In the early 1980s the Tiger arsenal consisted mainly of an assortment of rifles and even shotguns. However, in the mid 1980s they acquired heavier weapons such as light and heavy machine guns and RPGs. They also manufactured mortars. In the 1990s the mortar—especially the 81-mm variety—emerged as the weapon of choice for battering defenses and shattering troop concentrations. But what really boosted their firepower was the capture of several pieces of long- and medium-range heavy artillery from the Sri Lankan forces. These included 120-mm howitzers, 120-mm mortars, and 130-mm and 150-mm guns. These were captured over several engagements, the spoils from one victory helping to obtain another.[7] In the mid-1990s the Tigers also added surface-to-air missiles to their arsenal and proceeded to bring down several fixed and rotary winged aircraft of the Sri Lankan air force. The possession of these weapons enabled the Tigers to pose a serious conventional threat to the SLF.

The "Sea Tigers"

The LTTE's military power does not rest only on its land forces—regular, guerrilla, or terrorist. The LTTE is perhaps the only guerilla organization in the world to have developed an effective naval arm—the "Sea Tigers." The naval arm had existed since the early days of the insurgency, but its initial role was little more than smuggling weapons for the guerrillas. In 1984 it was turned into a more offensive arm.

The Sea Tigers' fleet consists mainly of 15-m fiberglass boats of 250 horsepower mounted with light and heavy machine guns and grenade launchers. These boats are notorious for engaging the Sri Lankan navy (SLN) with multiple vessels in wolfpack-like attacks. They are also frequently rigged with explosives and used for suicide attacks. Up to date they have destroyed more than 30 SLN crafts.

Sea Tiger operations are facilitated by a flexible system of command. The commanders of Sea Tiger crafts are authorized to take decisions based on circumstances without authorization from the shore. This has given lower-ranking commanders greater initiative than in a regular naval force.

The Sea Tigers have been a thorn in the side of the SLF. The troops stationed in the Jaffna peninsula are supplied by air and sea. The Sea Tigers have played an important role in making the seas unsafe for Sri Lankan naval traffic and thereby applying indirect pressure on the land forces in the peninsula. In crucial campaigns, Sea Tigers also act as a deterrent against the landing of Sri Lankan forces. They have also facilitated the LTTE's land operations by transporting troops to crucial battlefields. A case in point is the induction of several hundred Tiger troops behind enemy lines during the investment of Elephant Pass in 2000. They have also taken part in attacks on major bases. In May 1995 the Sea Tigers led the successful assault on the island of Mandathivu off the Jaffna peninsula, and in 1996 they played a crucial role in attacking the coastal army base of Mullaitivu.

Apart from their smaller attack craft, the Sea Tigers also possess a number of larger merchant vessels. These ships are registered under the flags of several countries and are mainly used for carrying weapons and other equipment for the Tigers. The Sri Lankan air force and navy have destroyed several of these vessels, but the greater part of the merchant fleet remains intact.

The Sri Lankan Forces

The LTTE was not the only party to the conflict to acquire deadlier weapons and enhance its effectiveness. The Tamil insurgency also contributed immensely to the development of the Sri Lankan military forces.

After independence, Sri Lanka was left with a tiny military force with outdated equipment. The infantry was armed with .303 rifles and a few Bren guns, while the pathetically weak navy and air force possessed only a few aircrafts and boats. But, in the absence of any external threat and significant internal conflict, these forces were adequate; they were used mainly to aid the police in times of civil unrest and to provide disaster relief. However, under the stimulus of serious internal threats from the 1970s, the Sri Lankan forces gradually bolstered its strength in manpower, training, and equipment.

The first major increase in the Sri Lankan forces' capability occurred in 1971. Following an aborted youth uprising that year, the SLF received considerable military aid from a number of countries, amounting to training as well as equipment. The latter included a number of armored cars (Saladins and Ferrets) from the United Kingdom, artillery from Czechoslovakia, and several MiG fighters from the Soviet Union.

During the 1980s, the Sri Lankan forces combated the growing strength of the Tiger guerrillas with its motley collection of armored cars, helicopters, and planes. But things were also looking up. In the mid-1980s the air force bolstered its ground attack capabilities by acquiring several single-engine Siai Marchetti SF 260 training aircraft and fitting them with rockets and bombs. The army acquired more armored vehicles and artillery and also succeeded in arming the majority of its soldiers with Chinese AK-47 assault rifles. In the 1990s the forces' operational capabilities increased to counter the growing sophistication of the LTTE. The air force acquired F-7 s and Kfir fighters and a number of transport and attack helicopters. Armored personnel carriers arrived from South Africa, and in 1992 the army, for the first time, acquired 25 T-55 battle tanks from Poland. In the late 1990s, in response to the Tigers' pressure on Jaffna, the army acquired a number of multibarreled rocket launchers.

With the growing firepower, the army also expanded in numbers. By 1990 the strength of the army had grown to 55,000 from just a few thousand a decade ago. By the late 1990s, the strength had reached close to 100,000. The air force and navy also grew in numbers.

The personnel were also receiving better training. In the early 1980s the army was little more than a rabble of armed men, having little experience in combat and considered among the most undisciplined military forces in the world. Sri Lankan soldiers were implicated in numerous acts of violence towards Tamil civilians in the north. However, as the LTTE's campaign intensified, the Sri Lankan forces received better training and discipline that aimed to enhance their battle worthiness. The effect of this was already apparent in 1987 during Operation Liberation, when the army advanced under fire to the surprise of the Tigers. The army was also showing signs of greater tactical initiative; in 1991, during the siege of Elephant Pass, the army landed a relief force a few miles north of the base and successfully relieved the beleaguered garrison. The forces also began to demonstrate a greater awareness of their responsibilities towards the civilian population.

The challenge of guerrilla warfare also led the SLF to develop their special forces. Of particular significance was the establishment of a "deep-penetration unit," a highly trained group of men operating behind enemy lines, carrying out sabotage and ambushes on Tiger forces. In the early 2000s, this unit caused considerable disruption to the LTTE's movements inside territory controlled by them. Their operations came to a halt with the cease-fire in 2002.

The Military Balance

Despite this growing sophistication in their operational capabilities the Sri Lankan forces have not been able to deal a decisive blow to the Tigers. They have succeeded in capturing and holding Jaffna, the northern capital from the Tigers and in the eastern province the SL forces have established a measure of control. However, they have failed to make any significant inroads into the heart of Tiger control in the Wanni, allowing the Tigers plenty of space and scope for regrouping and reorganizing. Nor have the Tigers been able to land a knockout punch. True, they have overrun a number of large military bases and prevented the SLF from advancing into the Vanni, but they have failed to capture their main prize, Jaffna.

One of the interesting features of the war since its start in the 1980s is that both sides have been quite evenly matched on the ground. True, on paper, the LTTE lacks the firepower of the SLF. However, on the ground, a number of factors bridge this gap. The LTTE's ability to operate at different levels—conventional, guerrilla, and terrorist—enables them to carry out their operations in a way that the army cannot. It gives the LTTE an operational flexibility that enables them to gather intelligence and plan and execute devastating attacks, ranging from well-planned and coordinated assaults on army bases and ambushing patrols and convoys to the infiltration of major installations such as the Katunayake airport. The development of a naval arm and the adoption of guerrilla tactics in the sea have reduced the effectiveness of the Sri Lankan navy, while the acquisition of surface to air missiles has challenged the Sri Lankan air force's supremacy in the air.

At the same time, the operational practices of the SLF have made it hard for them to spring surprises on the Tigers. The SLF forces usually operate as conventional forces, with armor, artillery, and air support. Moving out of well- established camps, such large forces have failed to keep their intentions hidden from the enemy. This has enabled the LTTE to anticipate major attacks and take appropriate action. A case in point is the operation to open a main supply route to Jaffna in 1997–98. The SLF committed more than 20,000 troops to this operation along a well-designated axis, providing the Tigers' long- and medium-range weapons with an ideal target. Moreover, the use of conventional forces in built-up areas has displaced large numbers of civilians, creating a potential recruitment base for the Tigers. While the employment of special forces like the deep-penetration unit has caused considerable anxiety to the Tigers, its operations by themselves were not enough to thwart the LTTE's ability to carry out their war.

The Tigers also appear to have an edge over the SLF in the motivation of their cadres and leadership. The willingness of LTTE cadres to expose themselves to danger in major battles, especially in human wave assaults, has been one of the decisive factors. The LTTE has used propaganda very effectively to reach out to the populace in the north and the east, enhancing its image as a liberation organization and its war effort as integral to Tamil nationalism. The LTTE's authoritarian leadership and its insusceptibility to electoral politics has also helped to focus on the war with a single-mindedness that has enabled them to maintain clear strategic goals.

A major blow to the LTTE leadership's control over the organization came in 2004. Karuna, one of the toughest and most able commanders of the LTTE, broke away from the group, accusing the leadership of discrimination against cadres from the Eastern Province. The LTTE launched an assault on the breakaway faction and disbanded many of Karuna's men, but the renegade leader remains at large with what appears to be a core group of hardened fighters. Frequent clashes have taken place between the two sides, with death and injuries on both sides. The operation of the cease-fire has prevented the two sides from having an all-out confrontation and the Sri Lankan government from exploiting this serious rift in the LTTE's ranks.

On the other hand, the Sri Lankan forces have been plagued by a number of problems that badly affect their morale. A massive desertion rate runs into the tens of thousands.[8] Offers of amnesty have not succeeded in attracting many of the deserters back into service. Officers have been implicated in irregularities in arms procurement, and there has been little agreement among the major political parties in the south about the objectives of the war.

These factors have contributed to making the disparities between the forces on paper less real on the ground. As a consequence, the Sri Lankan forces have not been able to achieve its main military objective of "liberating" all of the north and the east from the grip of the Tigers. The Tigers, on the other hand, have failed to eject the army from the Jaffna Peninsula or to bring the Eastern Province completely under their control. The realization of this unwinnable nature of the war has been largely responsible for bringing the two sides to the negotiating table without continuing to pursue their military goals.

At the time of this writing, the cease-fire is holding. There is considerable pressure on both sides from hard-line elements to return to a military solution. However, sanity, brought about by the memories of futile campaigns for military supremacy and international pressure, seems to have prevailed among those who have the greatest power to decide between war and peace. It is hoped that this sanity continues to prevail for the sake of the millions of Sri Lankans who desire to live in peace.

CHAPTER **13**

India's Nuclear Policy

Rajesh M. Basrur

India has made a habit of surprising the world. In May 1974, it unexpectedly tested a nuclear device, then refrained from developing a nuclear armory. Twenty-four years later, defying a watchful world's pressure to roll back its nuclear program, it carried out a series of five more tests and declared itself a nuclear power. Perhaps the biggest surprise of all was to follow. Despite rising tensions with its long-time rival Pakistan, which had quickly followed suit, India held back from deploying its nuclear weapons. Two major India-Pakistan crises followed. Yet India persisted in seeking stable relations with both its nuclear adversaries, Pakistan and China. This chapter explains these surprises by examining its evolving nuclear policy both before and after the 1998 tests.

Nuclear weapons, we must recognize, are unique and even revolutionary in character. In the immediate aftermath of the Second World War, which killed some 40 million people, the atom bomb was regarded by many as simply a more destructive form of weaponry. But statesmen, scientists, and scholars alike soon realized that these were qualitatively different instruments of war: they were capable of such great and indiscriminate destruction in such a short time that their use was hard to contemplate without deep moral horror. They came to be regarded as "unusable," whether by nuclear powers against nonnuclear powers or between rival nuclear powers. The Cold War demonstrated repeatedly that no matter what the political stakes, the possibility of nuclear holocaust was too high a cost to permit war. Instead, those at the helm of affairs of state devoted a great deal of energy to finding ways and means of avoiding war through their own caution and through negotiations to reduce nuclear risks. The nuclear revolution, in effect, did two things: it led those who possessed this deadly technology to think of deterrence rather than victory, and it forced opponents to cooperate and stabilize their relationship.[1] Invariably, relations between hostile nuclear powers carry elements of cooperation as well as conflict. Similar patterns are discernible in the relationships between the United States and the Soviet Union, between the Soviet Union and China, and between India and Pakistan. Each pair has gone through one or more cycles of confrontation and compromise. The key issue in every case is how stable or unstable a relationship is.

Reluctant Nuclearization: The Evolution of India's Nuclear Policy

For the most part, countries that have obtained nuclear weapons have raced to do so. India's story is very different, marked by much hesitation and reluctance to go down the path of nuclearization. After independence, India's first Prime Minister, Jawaharlal Nehru, laid the foundation of nuclear policy. On the one hand, he was deeply uncomfortable with nuclear weapons because of their immense capacity for indiscriminate destruction; and on the other, he could not reject them entirely, for he recognized that "there is always a built-in advantage of defence use if the need should arise."[2] This mixture of idealism and realism became the hallmark of Indian nuclear policy. In 1964, when China demonstrated its nuclear prowess just two years after defeating India in a border war, Prime Minister Lal Bahadur Shastri approved a research program for an underground test, but did not give the green signal for an actual test. At that time, it may be recalled, there was not much international pressure against going nuclear. The Nuclear Non-Proliferation Treaty (NPT), which set in motion a tightening process of controls over the spread of nuclear weapons capability, came into force much later, in 1970.

Prime Minister Indira Gandhi did eventually carry out a test in 1974, when India seemed to be overly dependent on the Soviet Union for political support and military supplies. But, having demonstrated India's potential, Mrs. Gandhi did nothing to develop an armory of nuclear weapons or an organization for their deployment. She did, however, launch the Integrated Guided Missile Program, which led to the development of India's present crop of nuclear-capable and conventional missiles. The nuclear door was opened just a little wider, but there was little interest in making India a nuclear power. Thus was crystallized a strategic culture—a consistent pattern of thinking as well as practice—of reluctant nuclearization.

During the 1980s, as evidence of Pakistani nuclearization with Chinese assistance heightened Indian insecurity, the pressure to build nuclear weapons grew. Prime Minister Rajiv Gandhi, like his grandfather Nehru and his mother Indira, remained unenthusiastic about nuclear weapons. Instead, he repeatedly called for universal nuclear disarmament and presented his own plan toward this end at the United Nations General Assembly's Third Special Session on Disarmament in 1988. The plea ignored, Rajiv Gandhi authorized secret production of the bomb, but was content to keep his bombs in the basement; and, like Indira, he made no effort to build an organizational structure for them. Succeeding prime ministers—P. V. Narasimha Rao of the Congress, and H. D. Deve Gowda and I. K. Gujral of the United Front coalition—sustained the covert and incremental program to build a covert arsenal during the 1990s, until Atal Behari Vajpayee, who headed a coalition government led by the Bharatiya Janata Party (BJP) took the fateful decision to test in 1998.

What motivated Vajpayee and the BJP to go nuclear officially? There are three main explanations for why nations choose to acquire nuclear weapons.[3] They may do so (1) for security purposes, i.e., if they feel sufficiently threatened to require the bomb in order to deter an enemy; (2) if domestic interest groups, such as the armed forces, the scientific-technical bureaucracy, or a political party, press for nuclear weapons on behalf of their own interests; or (3) when the bomb offers a symbolic reward by bringing prestige to nations or reinforcing their identity as modern entities. In the Indian case, while all three explanations have some merit, the chief cause for the acquisition of nuclear weapons was security. In the aftermath of the Cold War, India felt isolated as its main source of strategic support, the Soviet Union, collapsed and its successor state, Russia, drew close to the United States. Viewing nuclear proliferation as the main threat to post–Cold War stability, the United States exerted enormous pressure on India to roll back its nuclear weapons program. The combination of a continuing threat from China and Pakistan on the one hand and the U.S.-led squeeze on the other placed India in a now-or-never position. The BJP chose now.

This decision was not led by domestic political interests. The armed forces and the nuclear establishment have always been under tight control. Nor did the BJP carry out the tests for immediate political gain. Everyone knew that Mrs. Gandhi had reeled under a storm of political opposition just a few months after the 1974 test. Besides, since its inception in the early 1980s, the BJP (and indeed its predecessor party, the Jana Sangh) had consistently advocated nuclearization as part of its political platform on security. While the 1998 tests certainly had symbolic value, this had never been strong enough to propel a vigorous drive for nuclear weapons. Indeed, when Prime Minister Morarji Desai's cabinet had debated a decision to go nuclear in 1979, Vajpayee, then Minister for External Affairs, had voted against it on the ground that it might aggravate relations with Pakistan.[4] The overall picture that emerges from a review of available evidence is that the process of going nuclear was long, slow, and reluctant, culminating in the 1998 tests when India felt compelled to break out of the tightening nonproliferation squeeze. This cautious approach to the bomb remains in place today.

Nuclear Doctrine and Posture after 1998

Nations opting for nuclear weapons have to decide how many they want, of what kind, and how they will employ these "unusable" weapons. Some, like the United States and the Soviet Union/Russia, choose to have large, sophisticated arsenals ready for instant use. They believe that deterrence—preventing an attack by posing a threat of nuclear retaliation—rests on the capacity to inflict massive damage on an enemy. Others, like Britain, France, and China, prefer more modest weapon stocks that can cause enough harm to a potential aggressor to make the cost of an attack unaffordable. The Indian strategic doctrine of minimum deterrence is a version of the latter position.[5] It reflects in many ways the strategic culture of reluctant nuclearization we have seen above. On the one hand, there is great caution with respect to the potential use of nuclear weapons. On the other, there is a continuing search for developing a variety of technical capabilities just in case they may be required. These capabilities are briefly reviewed here.

Estimates of the number of nuclear warheads or bombs in India's armory vary widely, from about 40 to about 100. These can be delivered to targets by attack aircraft such as the Jaguar, the Mirage 2000, the MiG-27, the MiG-29, and the Su-30; and by the slow-moving naval reconnaissance aircraft, the Tu-22M and the Tu-142. While Pakistan comes well within the range of Indian aircraft, most of China does not. To some extent, this is offset by the newly acquired air refueling capability of the Indian Air Force. The mainstay of the Indian arsenal is its array of missiles. Variants of the short-range Prithvi (150–300 km) are available to the army, the air force, and the navy. The Agni-I (700 km) and the Agni-II (2,000–2,500 km) have longer ranges, but major Chinese targets are still out of range. The Agni-III (3,500 km) is still under development. Also under development are a nuclear-powered submarine known as the Advanced Technology Vessel (ATV) and submarine-launched missiles for it. As is evident, India aims to build a nuclear "triad" of land-, air-, and undersea-based weapons. With Russian collaboration, India has also produced a short-range conventional supersonic cruise missile, the Brahmos (currently land-based, with air- and sea-based versions planned), which may at some time be extended in range and modified to carry nuclear weapons.

Other than the need to deter China with the forthcoming Agni-III, there does not seem to be a clear conception of how much more a minimum deterrence strategy requires. What exactly is the purpose of a triad? Are submarine-launched missiles really necessary? The orthodox view is that they are, since submarines, because they can go deep under the sea surface and are mobile, are the least vulnerable of weapons platforms. But this argument typically comes from the orthodox perspective of American and Soviet/Russian thinking, echoed by others, that rests on the belief that vulnerability matters a great deal. Why? Because a vulnerable weapon may be destroyed by a surprise enemy strike. This would give the enemy an advantage by reducing one's capacity to hit it sufficiently hard. The enemy's knowledge of its advantage would reduce one's ability to deter it. This sort of argument rests on the dubious belief that only the threat of "assured destruction" can deter effectively. Minimum deterrence not only requires much less destructive capacity, but does not compel one to be *certain* of inflicting unacceptable damage. It is enough to pose a risk of damage in order to deter an enemy. After all, the United States was deterred by a much smaller Soviet force during the Cuban Missile Crisis of 1962, and the Soviet Union likewise by a small Chinese force in 1969.[6]

Indian doctrine is neither clear nor consistent in this respect, doubtless because inhibitions about acquiring nuclear weapons have prevented a careful assessment of the practical requirements of deterrence. Following the 1998 tests, Prime Minsiter Vajpayee stated in Parliament that under the strategy of "minimum credible deterrence," his government would not be the first to use nuclear weapons, that further testing was not necessary, that India would adhere to export control norms on nuclear technology, and that his government was fully committed to arms control. In August 1999, India produced a Draft Nuclear Doctrine that called for a triad of nuclear forces and emphasized "survivability." The Draft was later dubbed "unofficial," but aspects of it are known to have been incorporated into official doctrine.

Details have not been made available to the public. A press release in January 2003 added that India would resort to "massive" retaliation if attacked with nuclear weapons and that the option could be exercised in response to chemical and biological attacks as well.[7] It also asserted that India reserved the right to a nuclear response to such attacks on its forces "anywhere," implying that Indian forces might be engaged in combat outside Indian territory. This aspect remains problematic, as we shall see in the next section, since it implies a belief that conventional war is feasible in a nuclear environment. An obvious criticism is that there is no discernible limit to the number and types of weapons that Indian forces may want to acquire in the future.

Some of the key elements of Indian thinking have not been aired at length. An important source for these is an interview given by then Minister for External Affairs Jaswant Singh to the newspaper, the *Hindu,* in November 1999.[8] Singh asserted that "parity is not essential for deterrence," which indicated that India was not interested in catching up with China. This clearly showed that the nuclear balance of power was unimportant, that India would not engage in arms racing, and that future attempts at arms control would not be bogged down by numerical calculations of who has how much. More important, Singh stated that "retaliation need not be instantaneous," which meant that India was content with a nonprovocative posture of undeployed weapons. So far, that has been the case. India has not only refrained from deploying its weapons, but kept its weapons platforms separate from warheads and maintained the warheads themselves in unassembled condition. A nondeployed posture is conducive to stability because it allows time for thoughtful reaction in the event of a crisis or a false alarm, and it keeps weapons secure from unauthorized launch or terrorist attacks. Perhaps the most remarkable feature of Indian nuclear practice is that despite serious crises with Pakistan, nuclear weapons have never been deployed. Finally, Singh declared that "we do not see nuclear weapons as weapons of war fighting." This meant that Indian nuclear forces would not add small tactical weapons to their stock. The possession of such weapons makes it easier to cross the threshold to nuclear war because they are relatively small and normally aimed at military targets. A small nuclear conflict could quickly escalate to a major nuclear war.

Confrontation and Cooperation after 1998

In the aftermath of India's 1998 tests, which were matched by Pakistan just weeks later, it was common wisdom that South Asia had become "the most dangerous place on earth." That anxiety has subsided somewhat, but still hovers in the background as Indian-Pakistani relations remain uncertain. An overview of India's evolving strategic relationship with its two current nuclear-powered adversaries, Pakistan and China, provides a more nuanced picture. The two relationships reveal different mixes of co-operation and conflict. While India and Pakistan have been dogged by high tension and recurrent crises followed by attempts at stabilization, India and China have been able to find much common ground even though mutual suspicions remain.

India and Pakistan

In 1947, British rule over India ended with the violent and bitter partition of the land into two entities: India and Pakistan. War immediately broke out in 1947 over the disputed territory of Kashmir, which was left divided between the two countries. This and later wars in 1965 and 1971 have left the dispute unsettled, and tensions have risen periodically. Without giving up its claim to the whole of Kashmir, India has been a status quo power, while Pakistan has been a revisionist one. The acquisition of nuclear capability by both countries in the late 1980s intensified the rivalry between them. A series of crises occurred before the 1998 tests (in 1986–87 and 1990) and after (1999, 2001–2). Like other hostile nuclear pairs before them (the United States and the Soviet Union, the Soviet Union and China), India and Pakistan went through cycles of bickering, maneuvering, confrontation, crises, and stabilization. At work was the "stability-instability paradox," under which nuclear rivals are unable for fear of holocaust to go to full-scale war, but engage in competition and low-level conflict, sometimes leading to marginal armed clashes, often to crises and the threat of war.[9]

In 1999, Pakistani troops in civilian garb crossed the mutually agreed Line of Control (LoC) into the Kargil region of the Indian-held portion of Kashmir and occupied large swathes of territory. The aim was to create a crisis without officially crossing the LoC—i.e., to obtain a military advantage while denying government responsibility. Pakistan hoped to invite international intervention by evoking a general fear of escalation from subconventional to conventional to nuclear conflict and to pressure India to negotiate on Kashmir. Instead, India replied with a large-scale counterattack, which eventually drove Pakistani forces back. U.S. President Bill Clinton did intervene, but did so on India's side and compelled Pakistan to bring the adventure to an early close. The episode is an instructive example of conflict between nuclear-armed states and has had only one precedent: the Sino-Soviet border clashes of 1969. Nuclear deterrence worked in the sense that both sides recognized the risk of war and restrained themselves at considerable cost. India refrained from crossing the LoC while counterattacking. Pakistan, on its part, did not back up its retreating forces. Both exercised circumspection in not widening the conflict to other sectors along their long border.

The Kargil crisis demonstrated that Indian leaders had not fully appreciated the strategic implications of the nuclearization of the subcontinent. After carrying out the 1998 tests, BJP leader L.K. Advani had claimed that Pakistan was no longer in a position to alter the status quo. Clearly, he and his colleagues had failed to anticipate the stability-instability paradox. The problem became worse for them as Pakistan intensified another tack it had taken since the 1980s: providing support to terrorist groups fighting to break Kashmir away from India.[10] As terrorist violence stepped up, Indian leaders felt paralyzed by the constraints imposed by nuclear weapons. In an attempt to break out of the straitjacket, they asserted that all war was not ruled out under the shadow of nuclear weapons. The options aired included hot pursuit of terrorists into Pakistani territory, limited strikes, special forces missions against terrorist camps in Pakistan, and an undefined conception of "limited war." But the options were never exercised for fear that they might lead to a larger conflict.

In December 2001, matters came to a head when terrorists launched an audacious assault on the Indian Parliament in New Delhi. Though the attack failed, it came close to precipitating a disaster as Parliament was in session and many members, including several ministers and the vice president of the country, were on the premises. For Vajpayee and his colleagues, this was the last straw. India recalled its high commissioner from Islamabad and stopped all traffic between the two countries. Threatening an unspecified form of military response, it launched Operation Parakram (meaning "valor"), a full-scale mobilization of its forces. Pakistan countered with its own mobilization and rhetoric was high. The United States, fearful of the consequences of war, pressed Pakistan to make concessions. President Pervez Musharraf did impose a ban on some terrorist groups and arrest some of their leading members, but Indian forces remained at the border as terrorists continued to cross into India and perpetrate acts of violence. Another major attack in May 2002, which involved the killing of 22 wives and children of soldiers of the Indian Army, caused a fresh crisis. This brought the two countries to the brink of war, but wiser counsel prevailed, and nothing happened.

The confrontation stretched on until October 2002, when Indian forces were given orders to relocate. Though tensions were extremely high, Indian policy was restrained, and no shots were fired. Notably, despite the carrying out of missile tests by both sides, there is no evidence that nuclear weapons were actually deployed. For India, the mobilization yielded no more than temporary and partial concessions on the part of Pakistan. Terrorists continued to cross the border and carry out attacks on Indian soil. Faced with the choice of carrying out its threat of war or withdrawing its forces, India backed down and demobilized.

Operation Parakram was an attempt to turn the stability-instability paradox around against Pakistan. It was also an attempt to exercise coercive diplomacy (or what strategic analysts call "compellence") against that country. Mirroring Pakistani strategy in Kargil, India invited external (mainly American) intervention on its side by raising the fear of nuclear war. The United States could not rebut the Indian position because it had just launched an invasion of Afghanistan in the wake of the September 11 terrorist attacks. But like Kargil, the 2001–2 crisis demonstrated that in a confrontation between nuclear powers, deterrence prevails. Neither side benefited much from the crises, and the essential problem of Kashmir and cross-border terrorism remained, as they do today. After each confrontation, India and Pakistan entered into negotiations. For pessimists, the next crisis lies in wait around the corner. Optimists prefer to believe that, like other nuclear rivals before them, India and Pakistan have learned their lessons. They may continue their contest as before, but they will be more prudent in the future. Since February 2004, they have been engaged in a multifaceted "composite dialogue" that covers a range of political and strategic issues. On nuclear matters, this has yielded two confidence-building measures as of spring 2006: an agreement to set up a hotline between their foreign secretaries, and an agreement to notify each other on impending missile tests. Still, the resolution of their basic political disputes seems distant. As things stand, the key question is whether they can set aside their territorial quarrel and gain from cooperation in other areas, as India and China have done.

India and China

India faces a second nuclear adversary, China, with which its strategic history is similar to that with Pakistan. The territorial dispute between them stretches across much of their long border. It led to a short war between them in 1962, which ended in a humiliating defeat for India. This left Indians distrustful of the Chinese for having "betrayed" their friendship. The relationship between the two countries was unfriendly for decades, but has since the late twentieth century improved significantly. However, 1962 is still alive in India's strategic memory, and the undercurrent of suspicion remains. The dispute too remains unresolved after endless talks, but this is different from Kashmir in that neither side is in a hurry to find a solution.

The China factor entered Indian nuclear-strategic thinking in 1964, when the Chinese tested their first nuclear bomb. As mentioned earlier, Prime Minister Shastri sanctioned a research program that took India close to a nuclear test. But neither he nor his successors considered China a sufficiently strong threat to require a full-fledged nuclear response. The threat of renewed conflict did appear in 1986–87, in the Sumdorong Chu valley in the Indian state of Arunachal Pradesh, which China does not recognize as part of India. As a local dispute swelled into a larger confrontation, China threatened to "teach India a lesson," and both sides mobilized several divisions. But war was averted by compromise, though the two sides fully withdrew their forces as late as August 1995. Again, in July–August 2003, a confrontation between border patrols at the Line of Actual Control (analogous to the India-Pakistan LoC) in Arunachal Pradesh was met with a diplomatic rather than a military response.

China was a major cause for India's decision to go nuclear officially, even though from the Indian standpoint, it did not pose a threat that was direct or immediate. After 1962, China had developed a close relationship with Pakistan with a view to containing India. Though Sino-Indian relations were improving, New Delhi saw evidence of China's assistance to Pakistan's missile and nuclear programs as strong indication of continuing Chinese antipathy.[11] In a letter to U.S. President Clinton, Vajpayee justified his decision to test a nuclear weapon by pointing to the threat from China, which India's Defense Minister George Fernandes publicly branded "potential threat number one." China reacted angrily when the letter was leaked to the American press, but relations remained on an even keel. Subsequently, though gradually concerned about the potential nuclear threat from India, China has taken a rigid stand on India's nuclear status, unfailingly urging it to accede to the NPT as a non-nuclear-weapon state. China's refusal to give ground on this issue has ruled out, for the time being, any nuclear stabilization measures with India. This in turn restricts the prospects for India-Pakistan arms control, as Indian leaders are likely to balk at one-sided stabilization beyond a point. India's growing closeness to the United States is another source of concern to the Chinese, though they are not yet alarmed by it. India's development of the Agni-III missile is an indication of the underlying tension between them.

Despite the undercurrents of tension, India and China have managed their relationship remarkably well. The border problem has been kept in abeyance through the mechanism of annual talks since the early 1980s. A joint working group was established in 1988 to look for avenues of cooperation. Notwithstanding the fracas over the 1998 tests, trade between the two countries has expanded briskly, growing from $1.1 billion in 1995 to nearly $3.5 billion in 2001 and $13.6 billion in 2004. In April 2003, Fernandes visited China and expressed "a deep sense of satisfaction and the conviction that this visit will be the beginning for drawing a road map for the near future." China and India have worked together on negotiations at the World Trade Organization and on the issue of global warming. They have also made some effort to cooperate rather than compete with respect to their global quest for energy resources. In effect, though significant problems remain, the India-China relationship shows a remarkable capacity to come to terms with a history of tension, war and territorial dispute.

Prospects

Might India surprise us again? The inconsistencies in its nuclear thinking and practice may cause it to go along one or the other of divergent trajectories. It may remain content with a minimal deterrence force and seek accommodation and stability with its main rivals. Or it may in the face of deteriorating relations with one or the other choose to rapidly build up and deploy an expanding force that it will seek to make ever more "credible" and less "vulnerable." Our review of India's history and strategic culture indicate that it will in all probability choose the former path. The inconsistencies in doctrine and practice will perhaps remain, but that should be no surprise. Human society is scarcely ever devoid of contradictions of this kind.

India's nuclear policy seems to fit unobtrusively with the historical trend in contemporary world politics. The world today is far less a Hobbesian state of war than it was but half a century ago. The last great war—the Cold War—was one that could not be fought on the battlefield, for the new generation of weapons had become so destructive as to be practically unusable. They had instead made the combatants mutually dependent on each other's restraint for survival. At the same time, nations and peoples around the globe had become more and more interdependent and integrated through networks of economic exchange that resisted the disintegrating effects of war. War today has become too costly for states. Most of the violent conflict in the present age occurs within states, not between them.[12] In this complex world of rising interdependence, nuclear weapons have no more than a small role to play in deterring adversaries who are very unlikely to use them, but just *might* do so. And it is undeniable that the small chance of their being used has enormous implications for the humanness of human society. India's adoption of a minimum deterrence doctrine and posture seems inherently sensible because it at once provides security against nuclear threats and, in doing so, projects the least possible threat against others. In both ways, it tilts the balance firmly against the possible use of nuclear weapons.

India today is in the process of emerging as a major power on the world stage. Like others before it, it has to contend with resistance from the established order. Nowhere is this resistance greater than in the sphere of nuclear weapons. As a non-signatory to the NPT, it has long been treated as an outcast by the privileged weapons states. Yet its commitment to liberal democracy and to nuclear responsibility has been widely recognized. The American initiative to build an alliance-like relationship with India and to bring it into the framework of nonproliferation as a responsible nuclear power represents a historic policy change. It goes beyond the rigid and formal NPT-based distinction between nuclear haves and have-nots to focus on the real issue of who constitutes a threat and who does not. Regardless of the outcome of this path-breaking effort, India is likely to be true to its history of embedded nuclear restraint and remain a cautious and prudent nuclear power.

Notes

Introduction

1. This was the formal name for the land forces of British India, which were informally called "The Indian Army." See Government of India, *The Army in India and its Evolution* (Calcutta: Superintendent Government Printing India, 1924), 1.

2. L. James, *Raj: The Making and Unmaking of British India* (London: Little, Brown and Co., 1997), 38–39. It is quite possible that this coercive technique was adopted from Indian practice. See T.G. Percival Spear, *A History of India, Vol. 2: From the Sixteenth Century to the Twentieth Century* (Harmondsworth: Penguin, 1978), 112.

3. The notion of "military fiscalism" has been derived from the work of John Brewer, *The Sinews of Power: War, Money, and the English State, 1688–1783* (Cambridge, MA: Harvard University Press, 1988). For its application to the East India Company's colonial state in South Asia, see Douglas M. Peers, *Between Mars and Mammon: Colonial Armies and the Garrison State in Early Nineteenth Century India, 1819–1835* (London: I.B. Tauris, 1995).

4. James, *Raj,* 42; Chandar S. Sundaram, "Reviving a 'Dead Letter'": Military Indianization and the Ideology of Anglo-India, 1885–1891," in *The British Raj and Its Indian Armed Forces, 1857–1939,* ed. P.S. Gupta and A. Deshpande (Delhi: Oxford University Press, 2002), 46–47; and D.G. Boyes, "From Assaye to 'the Assaye': Reflections on British Government, Force, and Moral Authority in India," *Journal of Military History* 63, no. 3 (1999): 643–68 passim.

5. UK Government, *Report of the Indian Statutory (Simon) Commission,* vol. 1 (Calcutta: Government of India Central Publications Branch, 1930), 362.

6. On the considerable impact of the INA on Indian public opinion, both civilian and military, see K.K. Ghosh, *The Indian National Army* (Meerut: Meenakshi Prakashan, 1969), passim.; Anita Inder Singh, *The Origins of the Partition of India, 1936–1947* (Delhi: Oxford University Press, 1987), 147–49; and John Connell, *Auchinleck* (London: Jonathan Cape, 1959), 945, 949. On the INA, see Peter Fay, *The Forgotten Army: India's Armed Struggle for Independence, 1942–1945* (Ann Arbor: University of Michigan Press, 1993); C.S. Sundaram, "A Paper Tiger: The Indian National Army in Battle, 1944–1945," *War & Society* 13, no. 1 (May 1995); Sundaram, "Seditious Letters and Steel Helmets: Disaffection among Indian Troops in Singapore and Hong Kong, 1940–1941, and the Formation of the Indian National Army," in *War and Society in Colonial India, 1800–1947,* ed. D. Ellinwood and K. Roy (Delhi: Oxford University Press, 2006).

7. André Corvisier, *L'Armee Français de la fin du XVIIe siècle au ministère de Choiseul: le soldat,* 2 vols. (Paris, 1964);. Michael Roberts, *The Military Revolution, 1550–1650* (Belfast, 1956); Theodore Ropp, *War in the Modern World* (Durham, NC: Duke University Press, 1959).

8. Geoffrey Best, gen. ed., *The Fontana History of European War and Society,* 4 vols. (London and Leicester: Fontana Paperbacks and Leicester University Press, 1982–88); John Keegan, *The Face of Battle: A Study of Agincourt, Waterloo, and the Somme* (London: Jonathan

Cape, 1976); Michael Howard, *War in European History* (Oxford: Oxford University Press, 1976); Frank Tallett, *War and Society in Early Modern Europe, 1495–1715* (London: Routledge, 1992); and Geoffrey Parker, *The Military Revolution: Military Innovation and the Rise of the West, 1500–1800,* 2nd ed. (Cambridge: Cambridge University Press, 1996).

9. Amiya Barat, *The Bengal Native Infantry: Its Organisation and Discipline, 1796–1852* (Calcutta: Firma K.L. Mukhopadhyay, 1962); V. Longer, *Red Coats to Olive Green: A History of the Indian Army, 1600–1974* (Bombay: Allied Publishers, 1974); R. Callahan, *The East India Company and Army Reform, 1783–1798* (Cambridge, MA: Harvard University Press, 1972); S.P. Cohen, *The Indian Army: Its Contribution to the Development of a Nation* (Berkeley: University of California Press, 1971); D. Ellinwood, "The Indian Soldier and National Consciousness, 1914–1939," *Quarterly Journal of Historical Studies* 27, no. 1 (1987); and Ellinwood and S.D. Pradhan, eds., *India and World War I* (Columbia, MO: South Asia Books, 1978).

10. S. Alavi, *The Sepoys and the Company: Tradition and Transition in Northern India, 1770–1830* (Delhi: Oxford University Press, 1994); Peers, *Between Mars and Mammon;* Peers, "The Habitual Nobility of Being: British Officers and the Social Construction of the Bengal Army in the Early Nineteenth Century," *Modern Asian Studies* 25, no. 3 (1991); P. Stanley, *White Mutiny: British Military Culture in India* (New York: NYU Press, 1998); Sundaram, "Reviving a 'Dead Letter': Military Indianization and Ideology of Anglo-India, 1885–1891"; D. Omissi, *The Sepoy and the Raj: The Indian Army, 1860–1940* (Basingstoke: Macmillan, 1994); K. Roy, "The Construction of Regiments in the Indian Army, 1859–1913," *War in History* 8, no. 2 (2001); Roy, "Logistics and the Construction of Loyalty: The Welfare Mechanism in the Indian Army, 1859–1913, in *The British Raj and Its Indian Armed Forces;* V.A. Kaul, "Sepoys' Links with Society: A Study of the Bengal Army, 1858–1895" in *The British Raj and Its Indian Armed Forces;* C. Wickremesekere, *The Best Black Troops in the World: British Perceptions and the Making of the Sepoy, 1746–1805* (Delhi: Manohar, 2002); A. Deshpande, "Hopes and Disillusionment: Recruitment, Demobilization and the Emergence of Discontent in the Indian Armed Forces after the Second World War" *Indian Economic and Social History Review* 33, no. 2 (1996).

11. Bruce Lenman, "The Transition to European Military Ascendancy in India, 1600–1800", in *Tools of War: Instruments, Ideas, and Institutions of Warfare, 1445–1871,* ed. J.A. Lynn (Urbana: University of Illinois Press, 1990); R.G.S. Cooper, "Wellington and the Marathas in 1803," *International History Review* 11, no. 1 (1989); Pradeep Barua, "Military Developments in India, 1750–1850," *Journal of Military History* 58, no. 4 (1994); and S. Gordon, "The Limited Adoption of European Style Military Forces by Eighteenth Century Rulers in India," *IESHR* 35, no. 2 (1998).

12. T.R. Moreman, *The Army in India and the Development of Frontier Warfare, 1849–1947* (Basingstoke: Macmillan, 1998); Moreman, *The Jungle, the Japanese and the British Commonwealth Armies at War 1941–1945: Fighting Methods, Doctrine and Training for Jungle Warfare* (Abingdon, Oxon: Frank Cass, 2005); and D.P. Marston, *Phoenix from the Ashes: the Indian Army in the Burma Campaign* (Westport, CT: Praeger, 2003).

Chapter 1

1. My thanks to Suhrita for commenting on an earlier draft.

2. To Captain Penny, Deputy Assistant Adjutant General, from W. Sage, 3rd Class Executive Ordnance Officer, Dinapore, June 21, 1830, Letter No. 65, Progs. No. 24, Military Board Progs., July 1830, Part I, National Archives of India (henceforth NAI), New Delhi.

3. Richard Holmes, *Sahib: The British Soldier in India* (London: HarperCollins, 2005), 214, 250.

4. Gerald Bryant, "Officers of the East India Company's Army in the Day's of Clive and Hastings," *Journal of Imperial and Commonwealth History* 6, no. 3 (1978): 218–19.

5. Estimate of the Expenses incurred by the East India Company in India on account of His Majesty's Troops serving there, above the Number chargeable to the Company by Acts of Parliament of the 28 & 31 of His Present Majesty, no. 6, Appendix no. 5, Report from the Committee on the Account between the Public and the East India Company, 26 June 1805, *Parliamentary Papers* (henceforth *PP*), Colonies East India Sessions 1805–10 (Shannon: Irish University Press, 1971), 112–13, 223.

6. Account of Sales for Ten Years, from 1798–89 to 1807–1808; distinguishing India and China, and the Species of goods from each, Charles Cartwright, Accountant General, East India House, May 10, 1808, Appendix no. 10, Reply to the Argument against the Company's claim for Reimbursement of the Expenses, *PP*, 1805–10, 237, 243.

7. *The Punjab Papers: Selections from the Private Papers of Lord Auckland, Lord Ellenborough, Viscount Hardinge, and the Marquis of Dalhousie, 1836–49 on the Sikhs,* ed. and annotated with an introduction by Bikrama Jit Hasrat (Hoshiarpur: V. V. Research Institute Press, 1970), 120–21.

8. On the Report of the Commissioners appointed to enquire into the Sanitary state of the Army in India, Extract, p. 19 of the Report, Minutes by Major-General H. W. Norman, 1863–76, NAI; Peter Stanley, *White Mutiny: British Military Culture in India, 1825–75* (London: Hurst & Company, 1998), 40–42.

9. Minutes of Evidence taken before the Select Committee on the Affairs of the East India Company, Military, *PP*, vol. 5, 1832, para. 1208–9, 1267, pp. 182, 187.

10. W. J. Wilson, *Historical Record of the Fourth Prince of Wales' Own Regiment Madras Light Cavalry* (Madras: Govt. Office, 1877), 3, 85, 87.

11. Pratul Chandra Gupta, ed., "John Macleod's Private Journal during the Maratha War: 1817–1818," *Bengal Past and Present* 101, parts I and II, serial nos. 192–93 (Jan.–Dec. 1982): 99.

12. Kaushik Roy, "Rockets under Haidar Ali and Tipu Sultan," *Indian Journal of History of Science* 40, no. 4 (2005): 635–50.

13. Frederick W. Kagan, "Russia's Wars with Napoleon, 1805–15," in *The Military History of Tsarist Russia,* ed. Kagan and Robin Higham (New York: Palgrave, 2002), 109.

14. Kaushik Roy, "A Military Revolution in Mysore? Technological Changes, Social Transformation and Military Modernization under Haidar Ali and Tipu Sultan between 1752–99," *Contemporary India* 3, no. 3 (2004): 27.

15. "The Diplomatic Vision of Tipu Sultan: Briefs for Embassies to Turkey and France, 1785–86," trans. by Iqbal Husain, in *State and Diplomacy under Tipu Sultan: Documents and Essays,* ed. Irfan Habib (New Delhi: Tulika, 2001), 23.

16. M. P. Sridharan, "Tipu's Drive towards Modernization: French Evidence from the 1780s," in *Confronting Colonialism: Haidar Ali and Tipu Sultan,* ed. Irfan Habib (New Delhi: Tulika, 1999), 146.

17. Ghulam Muhammad, ed., *The History of Haidar Shah alias Hyder Ali Khan Bahadur and of his son Tipu Sultan, by M.M.D.L.T.* (1855; reprint, Delhi: Cosmo, 1976), 281.

18. Kaushik Roy, *India's Historic Battles: From Alexander the Great to Kargil* (New Delhi: Permanent Black, 2004), 109–20.

19. Kaushik Roy, "Firepower-Centric Warfare in India and the Military Modernization of the Marathas: 1740–1818," *Indian Journal of History of Science* 40, no. 4 (2005): 610.

20. Kaushik Roy, "Military Synthesis in South Asia: Armies, Warfare, and Indian Society, c. 1740–1849," *Journal of Military History* 69, no. 3 (2005): 670.

21. *Poona Akhbars,* vol. 1, ed. R.M. Joshi (Hyderabad: Central Records Office Hyderabad Government, 1953), 2.

22. *Poona Akhbars,* vol. 3 (Hyderabad: Central Records Office, Govt. of Andhra Pradesh, 1956), 1, 3.

23. Foreign Department Secret Proceedings, Apr. 1–28, 1783, pp. 1297, 1300; NAI.

24. Herbert Compton, *A Particular Account of the European Military Adventurers of Hindustan from 1784 to 1803* (1892; reprint, Karachi: Oxford University Press, 1976), 45–46.

25. Quoted in *Wellington at War: 1794–1815, A Selection of His Wartime Letters,* ed. and introduced by Antony Brett-James (London: Macmillan, 1961), 80.

26. H. Helsham Jones, "The Campaigns of Lord Lake against the Marathas: 1804–6," *Professional Papers of the Corps of Royal Engineers* (1882), 115–20, College of Military Engineering, Poona.

27. Valentine Blacker, *Memoir of Operations of the British Army in India during the Maratha War of 1817, 1818 & 1819* (London: Black, Kingsbury, Parbury and Allen, 1821), 22.

28. G.S. Sardesai, ed., *Poona Affairs (Elphinstone's Embassy), Part II, 1816–1818,* vol. 13 of Jadunath Sarkar and Sardesai, gen. eds., *English Records of Maratha History: Poona Residency Correspondence* (Bombay: Govt. Central Press, n.d.), 306–309, 340.

29. Pratulchandra Gupta, ed., "John Macleod's Private Journal during the Maratha War 1817–1818," *Bengal Past and Present* 100, part 1, no. 190 (Jan.–June 1981): 75.

30. J.S. Grewal and Indu Banga, eds., *Civil and Military Affairs of Maharaja Ranjit Singh* (Amritsar: Guru Nanak Dev University, 1987), 108.

31. Fauja Singh Bajwa, *Military System of the Sikhs during the Period 1799–1849* (Delhi: Motilal Banarasidas, 1964), 36, 38–39.

32. Joseph Davey Cunningham, *History of the Sikhs: From the Origin of the Nation to the Battles of the Sutlej* (1849; reprint, New Delhi: Rupa, 2002), 246.

33. W.L. M'Gregor, *The History of the Sikhs,* vol. 2 (1846; reprint, Allahabad: R.S. Publishing House, 1979), 377.

34. J.G.A. Baird, ed., *Private Letters of the Marquess of Dalhousie* (1910; reprint, Delhi: Low Price Publications, 1993), 46–47.

35. George Bruce, *Six Battles for India: The Anglo-Sikh Wars, 1845–6, 1848–9* (Calcutta: Rupa, 1969), 299, 300–301, 305.

Chapter 2

1. A bibliography of the Mutiny would require a long essay in itself. Here I can mention only a few useful titles. Sir John Kaye's nearly contemporary account, continued by Colonel G.B. Malleson, still has great value: Malleson, ed., *Kaye's and Malleson's History of the Indian Mutiny of 1857–8,* 6 vols. (London: 1898). Kaye's two volumes are the more perceptive, but Malleson provides an immense amount of detail about a conflict whose military dimension was characterized by a multiplicity of small-scale encounters. The centenary of the Mutiny saw the publication of a quasi-official Indian account, S.N. Sen's *Eighteen Fifty-Seven* (New Delhi, 1957), which annoyed some nationalists by its moderation. T.A. Heathcote, *The Indian Army: The Garrison of British Imperial India 1822–1922* (New York, 1974), provides a great deal of useful information in a clear, succinct format. Philip Mason, *A Matter of Honour: An account of the Indian Army, its officers & men* (London, 1974), by a former officer of the Indian

Civil Service who knew the Indian Army well in its last days, is beautifully written albeit heavily anecdotal. A more recent account of the Indian Army from a different perspective is S. L. Menezes, *Fidelity and Honour: The Indian Army from the Seventeenth to the Twenty-first Century* (New Delhi, 2001). The author, a retired lieutenant general, joined the Indian Army in the twilight of the Raj. The most recent account, Saul David's *The Indian Mutiny* (London, 2002) is well researched, readable, and more candid about the savagery that accompanied the suppression of the Mutiny than Kaye and Malleson or, more surprisingly, Sen. Eric Stokes, *The Peasant Armed: The Indian Revolt of 1857* (Oxford, 1986), demonstrates how widespread popular revolt was in 1857—at least in the North-Western Provinces. Stokes left this work incomplete at the time of his death, and it was edited for publication by C. A. Bayly. Sometimes fiction catches what archives cannot. The Mutiny has found continuous reflection in British fiction, from Flora Annie Steele's Victorian best seller, *On the Face of the Waters: A Tale of the Mutiny* (New York, 1897) through John Masters's *Nightrunners of Bengal* (New York, 1951) to J. G. Farrell's Booker Prize–winning *The Siege of Krishnapur* (London, 1973). The relevant volume in the memoirs of Brigadier-General Sir Harry Paget Flashman, V.C., *Flashman in the Great Game* (New York, 1975), ably edited by George MacDonald Fraser, is in a class by itself.

2. It is an interesting reflection of the unease that the Mutiny still generates that in the relevant volume of the new, supposedly definitive *The Nineteenth Century,* ed. Andrew Porter, Vol. 3 of *The Oxford History of the British Empire* (Oxford, 1999), the chapter that ostensibly covers the Mutiny, D. A. Washbrook, "India, 1818–1860: The Two Faces of Colonialism," in fact gives it two skimpy paragraphs and then briskly moves on.

3. The "native officers," in addition to being debilitated by the application of seniority promotion (which they could not escape by secondment), were also deprived of any significant authority. Designed as a security measure, this practice by 1857 became a significant source of weakness.

4. There is an account of the Bengal officers' confrontation with the Company and the British government in Raymond Callahan, *The East India Company and Army Reform 1783–1798* (Cambridge, MA, 1972). The whole subject of Indian Army officers under the Company and the Crown as well as their relationship to their British Army counterparts could use much more study.

5. A very readable account of the British soldier in India is Richard Holmes's *Sahibs: The British Soldier in India 1750–1914* (London, 2005). Holmes does not, however, address the tensions between British and Company officers.

6. A perceptive study of Vellore and its significance is by Devadas Moodley, "Vellore 1806: The Meanings of Mutiny," in *Rebellion, Repression, Reinventaion: Mutiny in Comparative Perspective,* ed. Jane Hathaway (Westport, CT, 2001), 87–101.

7. H. T. Lambrick, *John Jacob of Jacobabad* (London, 1960), is a fine study of this innovative soldier, a member of a family that soldiered for over a century in India for Company and Crown and produced an Indian Army field marshal (Field Marshal Sir Claude Jacob, Commander-in-Chief, India, 1924).

8. Kaye and Malleson, vol. 1, 435. The Company's officer to whom the remark was made was Major General Sir Henry Lawrence, long a critic of some of the Company's "modernizing" innovations. He was the British administrator in the newly annexed Kingdom of Oudh when the Mutiny broke out, and he led the defense of the Residency at Lucknow until his death.

9. Mason, *A Matter of Honour,* 452.

10. Despite Eric Stokes's excellent work, it remains true that we have little with which to reconstruct the mental world of the Bengal sepoys. Records of interrogations and trials provide some information, filtered through Victorian British perceptions, but much is forever lost. What exactly were the 19th BNI cheering as they left Barrackpore? Hearsey personally? Their escape from the Company they had come to fear? We will never know. A new study, however, does attempt to penetrate the mind of the Bengal sepoy: Rudrangshu Mukherjee, *Mangal Pandy: Brave Martyr or Accidental Hero?* (New Delhi, 2005). I owe this reference to Chandar S. Sundaram.

11. J.A.B. Palmer, *Mutiny Outbreak at Meerut* (Cambridge, 1966) is definitive.

12. David, *The Indian Mutiny,* is the best recent general account.

13. After the Mutiny, the Indian Army lost all its artillery units except for the mule-carried mountain gun—Kipling's "screw guns." The first Indian field artillery unit was formed in 1935.

14. A colorful but well-informed account of the Company soldiers who did so much to shape the Punjab administration and then suppress the Mutiny is Charles Allen, *Soldier Sahibs: The Men Who Made the North-West Frontier* (London, 2000).

15. The Punjab column, some 3,200 strong, faced some 9,000 sepoys at Badli-Ki-Serai on June 8 as they approached Delhi. The sepoys, especially the gunners, fought well but were beaten primarily due to defective higher command, a very good example of the problem that would, as noted above, plague them throughout the Mutiny.

16. A sympathetic study of Canning is Michael Maclagan, *"Clemency" Canning* (London, 1962).

17. On this, see Peter Stanley, *The White Mutiny: British Military Culture in India 1825–1875* (London, 1998).

18. The Gurkhas have been the subject of perhaps more writing than any other part of the old Indian Army, an indication of their grip on the British imagination. The best general account is Tony Gould, *Imperial Warriors: Britain and the Gurkhas* (London, 1999).

19. On the reconstructed army, see David Omissi, *The Sepoy and the Raj: The Indian Army, 1860–1940* (Basingstoke, England, 1994).

Chapter 3

1. George Fletcher MacMunn and Alfred Crowdy Lovett, *The Armies of India* (London: Adam and Charles Black, 1911), 129.

2. The culture of the officer class has been explored in Douglas M. Peers, "'The Habitual Nobility of Being': British Officers and the Social Construction of the Bengal Army in the Early Nineteenth Century," *Modern Asian Studies* 25 (1991): 545–70.

3. Douglas M. Peers, *Between Mars and Mammon: Colonial Armies and the Garrison State in Early-Nineteenth Century India* (London: Tauris, 1995). See also David Omissi, *The Sepoy and the Raj: the Indian Army, 1860–1940* (London: Macmillan, 1994).

4. The presence of martial race theories in colonial Africa has been discussed by Anthony H.M. Kirk-Green, "'Damnosa Hereditas': Ethnic Ranking and the Martial Races Imperative in Africa," *Ethnic and Racial Studies* 3 (1980): 393–414; and for Ireland, see Terence Denman, "'Ethnic Soldiers Pure and Simple'? The Irish in the Late Victorian Army," *War in History* 3 (1996): 253–73, in which the often ambivalent view of the Irish as a "martial race" is discussed in some detail. Denman notes that many of the chief proponents of the martial races ideology were themselves Anglo-Irish or Scots-Irish.

5. "Lieut.-Gen. Sir George MacMunn," *Times* (London), Aug. 25, 1952, 8.

6. Cynthia Enloe has defined these recruits as "ethnic soldiers," See Enloe, *Ethnic Soldiers: State Security in Divided Societies* (Athens: University of Georgia Press, 1980).

7. Government of India to Secretary of State, Feb. 4, 1880, Army Organization Commission Report, Indian Army Reorganization, *Parliamentary Papers,* 1884, 24.

8. Douglas M. Peers, "Colonial Knowledge and the Military in India, 1780–1860," *Journal of Imperial and Commonwealth History* 33, no. 2 (2005): 157–80. See also Susan Bayly, "The Evolution of Colonial Cultures: Nineteenth-Century Asia," in *Oxford History of the British Empire: The Nineteenth Century* (Oxford, Oxford University Press, 1999), 448

9. Nicholas Dirks, *Castes of Mind: Colonialism and the Making of Modern India* (Princeton: Princeton University Press, 2001), 9.

10. On the contested issue of who constituted a Sikh, see Richard Fox, *Lions of the Punjab: Culture in the Making* (Berkeley: University of California Press, 1985); Harjot Oberoi, *The Construction of Religious Boundaries; Culture, Identity and Diversity in the Sikh Tradition* (Chicago: University of Chicago Press, 1994); and for the Gurkhas, see Lionel Caplan, "Martial Gurkhas: the Persistence of a British Military Discourse on Race," in *The Concept of Race in South Asia,* ed. Peter Robb (Delhi: Oxford University Press, 1995), and Mary DesChene, "Relics of Empire: a Cultural History of the Gurkhas, 1815–1987" (PhD. diss., Stanford University, 1991).

11. "Report of the Commissioners Appointed to Enquire into the Organization of the Indian Army; together with Minutes of Evidence and Appendix," *Parliamentary Papers* 1859, 1st sess., appendix, 58.

12. David Omissi, "'Martial Races': Ethnicity and Security in Colonial India, 1858–1939." *War and Society* 9 (1991): 4.

13. MacMunn and Lovett, *Armies of India,* 140. See the important contribution made by Heather Streets, *Martial Races: The Military, Race and Masculinity in British Imperial Culture, 1857–1914* (Manchester: Manchester University Press, 2004).

14. Susan Bayly, "Caste and 'Race' in the Colonial Ethnography of India," in *The Concept of Race in South Asia,* 165–218. Stephen P. Cohen has remarked in an early study of caste in the Indian Army that "class" was for the British often "synonymous with clan, caste, race or religion and comprised the unit of recruitment." See Cohen, "The Untouchable Soldier: Caste, Politics, and the Indian Army," *Journal of Asian Studies* 28 (1969): 454.

15. "Memorandum on Some of the Results of the Indian Administration during the Past Fifty Years of British Rule in India," *Parliamentary Papers,* 1909 (Cmd 4956), 34.

16. "Evidence of Major-General Mansfield, Report of the Commissioners Appointed to Enquire into the Organization of the Indian Army; together with Minutes of Evidence and Appendix," *Parliamentary Papers* 1859, 1st sess., appendix, 97.

17. William Sleeman. *Rambles and Recollections of an Indian Official* (London: Hatchard, 1844), 287–88

18. [W.D. Arnold], "Jack Sepoy," *Fraser's Magazine* 54 (1856): 360.

19. Douglas M. Peers, "Sepoys, Soldiers and the Lash: Race, Caste and Army Discipline in India, 1820–1850," *Journal of Imperial and Commonwealth History* 23 (1995): 211–47.

20. Brigadier John Jacob, *Tracts on the Native Army of India: Its Organization and Discipline* (London: Smith, Elder and Co., 1858), 7.

21. Channa Wickremesekera, *"Best Black Troops in the World": British Perceptions and the Making of the Sepoy, 1746–1805* (New Delhi: Manohar, 2002), 158.

22. Lieut. Col. John Briggs, *Letter* (London: privately printed, 1836), 20.

23. Cohen, "The Untouchable Soldier," 453–68.

24. Editor, "Address to Our Readers," *Addiscombe Magazine* 1, no. 1 (1846): 1–2.

25. "Memoirs Regarding the Native Infantry upon the Bengal Establishment," *East India United Service Journal* 3 (1834): 14–15.

26. "Recruiting the Native Corps of the Army," *East India United Service Journal* 2 (1834): 610–11.

27. Anon., "The Bengal Native Cavalry," *East India United Service Journal* 2 (1834): 596–97.

28. Seema Alavi, *The Sepoys and the Company: Tradition and Transition in Northern India, 1770–1830* (Delhi: Oxford University Press, 1995), 37.

29. Quoted in Stephen P. Cohen, *The Indian Army: Its Contribution to the Development of a Nation,* 2nd ed. (New York: Oxford University Press, 1991), 47–48.

30. On the British fascination with the Aryan roots of Indian civilization, see Joan Leopold, "The Aryan Theory of Race," *Indian Economic and Social History Review* 7 (1970): 271–97; and "British Applications of the Aryan Theory of Race to India, 1850–1870," *English Historical Review* 89 (1974): 578–603. See also Thomas R. Trautmann, *Aryans and British India* (Berkeley: University of California Press, 1996).

31. T.C. Robertson, "Memo on the Indian Army," 1827, PwJf 2584, University of Nottingham Archives.

32. [S.S.], "An Apology for the Indian Army," *United Services Journal* 8 (1832): 31.

33. For a fuller discussion, see Norbert Peabody, "Tod's Rajasthan and the Boundaries of Imperial Rule in Nineteenth-Century India." *Modern Asian Studies* 30 (1996): 185–220. See also Thomas R. Metcalf, *Ideologies of the Raj,* Part III, vol. 4 of *The New Cambridge History of India* (Cambridge: Cambridge University Press, 1994), 75; and Douglas M. Peers, "'There is Nothing More Poetical than War': Romanticism, Orientalism, and Militarism in J.W. Kaye's Narratives of the Conquest of India," in *Imperial Co-Histories: National Identities and the British and Colonial Press,* ed. Julie F. Codell (Madison, NJ: Fairleigh-Dickinson University Press, 2003), 273–99. .

34. MacMunn and Lovett, *Armies of India,* 130; Lieutenant Colonel Valentine Blacker, *Memoir of the Operations of the British Army in India during the Mahratta War of 1817, 1818, and 1819* (London: Black, Kingsbury, Parbury and Allen, 1821), 20.

35. E. Barrow, "Proposals for Raising Territorial Units in India," June 19, 1916, MSS Eur E420/8, Oriental and India Office Collections, British Library (hereafter OIOC).

36. "General Regulations of the Bengal Army," sec. xxxi, clause 6 (1855), in "Report of the Commissioners Appointed to Enquire into the Organization of the Indian Army, 77.

37. For a fuller discussion of this commission and its findings, see Omissi, *The Sepoy and the Raj.*

38. "Royal Commission to Inquire into the Organization of the Indian Army; together with Minutes of Evidence and Appendix," *Parliamentary Papers,* 1 (1859), appendix, 63. See also "Evidence of Sir George Clerk," 41; the Marquis of Tweedale, appendix, 226; and James Outram, appendix, 74.

39. "Royal Commission to Inquire into the Organization of the Indian Army," xiv.

40. Memo by General Airey, May 6, 1875, Eurasians and Native Christian Company of Artillery, 1875, L/MIL/5/673, OIOC.

41. Government of India to Secretary State for India, Nov. 2, 1892, "Further Papers Respecting Proposed Changes in the Indian Army System," *Parliamentary Papers,* 1893 (Cmd 6987), 4.

42. Tan Tai Yong, *The Garrison State: The Military, Government and Society in Colonial Punjab, 1849–1947* (New Delhi: Sage, 2005), 56.

43. Evidence of Colonel Sir Herbert Edwardes, *Report from the Select Committee on Army (India and the Colonies),* 1867 (Cmd 478), 228.

44. Nirad Chaudhuri, "The 'Martial Races' of India," *The Modern Review* (Feb. 1931): 225.

45. Joseph S. Alter, "Gender, Sexuality and the Transformation of Gender into Nationalism in North India," *Journal of Asian Studies* 53 (1994): 45–66. On the relationship between the rebellion and masculinity, see Alison Blunt, "Embodying War: British Women and Domestic Defilement in the Indian 'Mutiny,' 1857–8," *Journal of Historical Geography* 26, no. 3 (2000): 403–28; Nancy L. Paxton, *Writing under the Raj: Gender, Race, and Rape in the British Colonial Imagination, 1830–1947* (New Brunswick, NJ: Rutgers University Press, 1998); Jenny Sharpe, *Allegories of Empire: The Figure of Woman in the Colonial Text* (Minneapolis: University of Minnesota Press, 1993); and Mrinalini Sinha, *Colonial Masculinity; the "Englishman" and the "Effeminate Bengali" in the Late Nineteenth-Century* (Manchester: Manchester University Press, 1995).

46. George MacMunn, *The Martial Races of India* (London: Sampson Low and Co., 1933), 3.

47. Captain H. W. L. Hime, "Natural Selection in War," *Journal of the Royal United Service Institution* 21 (1877): 588–610.

48. Field Marshal Frederick Roberts, *Forty-One Years in India, from Subaltern to Commander-in-Chief,* 1st ed. (London: Macmillan, 1905), x.

49. Ibid., 499, 532.

50. Government of India to the Secretary of State, Nov. 2, 1892, L/MIL/5/697, OIOC.

51. Secretary of State to the Government of India, Dec. 21, 1893, L/MIL/5/697, OIOC.

52. Roberts, *Forty-One Years in India,* 532.

53. Streets, *Martial Races,* especially 121–33.

54. Roberts, *Forty-One Years in India,* 533.

55. Royal Commission to Inquire into the Organization of the Indian Army," appendix, 97.

56. Wood to Elgin, May 9, 1862, MSS Eur F83/2, OIOC.

57. Yong, *The Garrison State,* 74–75.

58. "Statement Exhibiting the Moral and Material Progress and Condition of India during the Year 1891–92, and the Nine Preceding Years," *Parliamentary Papers,* 1894, 249.

59. Prem Chowdury, "Customs in a Peasant Economy: Women in Colonial Harayana," in *Recasting Women: Essays in Indian Colonial History,* ed. Kumkum Sangari and Sudesh Vaid (New Brunswick, NJ: Rutgers University Press, 1990), 302–36.

60. Philip Constable, "The Marginalization of a Dalit Martial race in Late Nineteenth and Early Twentieth Century Western India," *Journal of Asian Studies* 60 (2001): 439–78.

61. Rosalind O'Hanlon, *Caste, Conflict and Ideology: Mahatma Jotirao Phule and Low Caste Protest in Nineteenth Century Western India* (Cambridge: Cambridge University Press, 1985).

62. "Lord Kitchener and the Indian Army," *Times* (London), Apr. 10, 1906, 4.

63. Stephen Peter Rosen, *Societies and Military Power: India and its Armies* (Ithaca, NY: Cornell University Press, 1996), 217.

64. Omar Khalidi, *Khaki and Ethnic Violence in India* (New Delhi: Three Essays Collective, 2003).

Chapter 4

1. While the inhabitants of tribal territory proudly call themselves Pathans, Pashtuns has become widely used in Western literature.

2. For a comprehensive survey of the evolution of frontier fighting, see T.R. Moreman, *The Army in India and the Development of Frontier Warfare 1849–1947* (London, 1998).

3. *Field Service Regulations, Part I Operations. 1909, (Reprinted with Amendments, 1912)* (London, 1912).

4. GOC Northern Command to CGS, May 2, 1917, L/P&S/10/373, Oriental and India Office Collections, British Library (hereafter OIOC).

5. See *The Third Afghan War 1919. Official History* (Calcutta, 1926), and Brian Robson, *Crisis on the Frontier. The Third Afghan War and the Campaign In Waziristan 1919–20* (London, 2001).

6. Waziristan Force Weekly Appreciation for week ending Jan. 13, 1920, WO 106/56, Public Records Office (hereafter PRO).

7. *Mountain Warfare School. Abbottabad, Synopsis of Lectures 1920 (Revised 1921)* (Rawalpindi, 1921).

8. *Notes on Mountain Warfare* (Calcutta, 1920).

9. *Wazirforce Tactical Notes* (Dera Ismail Khan, 1921).

10. See S.H.C., *Mountain Warfare Notes* (Poona, 1921), and "Frontier," *Frontier Warfare* (Bombay, 1921).

11. Colonel F.S. Keen: "To what extent would the use of the latest scientific and mechanical methods of warfare affect operations on the North-West Frontier of India?" *Journal of the United Service Institution of India* (hereafter *JUSII*) 53, no. 233 (1923): 415.

12. *Field Service Regulations Vol. II (Operations)* (London, 1924), 215.

13. *Manual of Operations on the North-West Frontier of India* (Calcutta, 1925)

14. See *Kohat District Standing Orders for War and for Local Columns* (Lahore, 1927) and *Landi Kotal Standing Orders for War 1936* (Landi Kotal, 1936).

15. The Scouts (the successors to tribal militias raised in 1899) were raised in the early 1920s from local Pathan tribesmen, commanded by British officers, to police tribal territory and support the local administration. In comparison, the Frontier Constabulary, led by police officers, were locally recruited to patrol the line of the administrative border and police the settled lowland areas.

16. *Memorandum on Army Training (India) Collective Training Period 1929–30* (Simla, 1930), 4.

17. *Report of the Tribal Control and Defence Committee 1931* (Delhi, 1931), 38–39, L/MIL/17/13/34, OIOC.

18. General Staff Criticism of the Tribal Control and Defence Committee, May 19, 1931, L/P&S/12/3171.

19. Light Infantry, "Mobility," *JUSII* 62, no. 266, (1932): 11 and 17.

20. Gen. Sir A. Skeen, *Passing it On: Short Talks on Tribal Fighting on the North-West Frontier of India* (Aldershot, 1932).

21. *A.H.Q. India Training Memorandum No. 12 Collective Training period 1935–36* (Delhi, 1936), 2–8.

22. Slessor to Sutton, Apr. 15, 1935, Slessor MSS, AIR 75/29, PRO.

23. Slessor to Peck, Apr. 10, 1936, Slessor MSS, AIR 75/31, PRO.

24. Gort to Inskip, Dec. 29, 1937, Inskip MSS, IWM INP 1/2; and Slessor 1956, 131.

25. John Masters, *Bugles and a Tiger* (London, 1956), 206.

26. Comments and Deductions on the Khaisora Operations, Waziristan, June 8, 1937, Rees MSS, Mss.Eur.F.274/4, OIOC; and *A. H. Q. India Training Memorandum No. 14 Collective Training Period 1936–37,* (Delhi, 1937), 8–12.

27. Bartholomew to Wilson, Feb. 1937, L/WS/1/257, OIOC.

28. Wilson to Auchinleck, May 18, 1937, and Auchinleck to Wilson, May 27, 1937, L/WS/1/257, OIOC.

29. Commander-in-Chief to Wilson, May 28, 1937, L/WS/1/257, OIOC.

30. *A. H. Q. India Training Memorandum No. 16 Collective Training period 1937–38* (Delhi, 1938), 1.

31. See Auspex, "The Dream Sector, L. of C.," *JUSII* 68, no. 291, (1938).

32. *Frontier Warfare–India (Army and Royal Air Force)* (Delhi, 1939).

33. Skeen, *Passing it On,* 4th ed. (London, 1939)..

Chapter 5

1. All documentary references are to the National Archives of India (NAI) in New Delhi, to the Oriental and India Office Collections (OIOC) in the British Library, London, or to the Public Records Office (PRO), Kew, London. For further references to the literature on the Indian Army in the Great War, see the footnotes to D. E. Omissi, "Europe Through Indian Eyes: Indian Soldiers Encounter England and France, 1914–1918," *English Historical Review* 122 (2007).

2. A. J. Stockwell, "The War and the British Empire," in *Britain and the First World War,* ed. J. Turner (1988).

3. C. E. Carrington, "The Empire at War, 1914–18," in *The Cambridge History of the British Empire: Volume III,* ed. E. A. Benians, J. R. M. Butler, P. N. S. Mansergh, and E. A. Walker (1959), 606; A. Rumbold, *Watershed in India, 1914–1922* (1979), 20; H. Cotton, "India: Now and After," *Contemporary Review* 107 (1915): 195 and 201.

4. F. W. Perry, *The Commonwealth Armies: Manpower and Organization in Two World Wars* (1988), 85–86; G. Corrigan, *Sepoys in the Trenches: The Indian Corps on the Western Front, 1914–15* (1999), 246.

6. H. Howarth, "Our Indian Troops," *The Nineteenth Century* (1900); D. E. Omissi, "India: Some Perceptions of Race and Empire," in *The Impact of the South African War,* ed. Omissi and A. S. Thompson (2002).

7. H. H. Asquith, *H. H. Asquith: Letters to Venetia Stanley,* ed. M. Brock and E. Brock (1982), Doc. 260.

8. Lord Hardinge of Penshurst, *My Indian Years, 1910–1916* (1948), 98–99.

9. M. Hankey, *The Supreme Command, 1914–1918,* vol. 1 (1961), 171.

10. For the "martial races" strategy, see the fine books by L. Caplan, *Warrior Gentlemen: "Gurkhas" in the Western Imagination* (1995), and H. Streets, *Martial Races: The Military, Race and Masculinity in British Imperial Culture, 1857–1914* (2004).

11. M. O'Dwyer, *India as I Knew It, 1885–1925* (1925), 216; I. Talbot, *Punjab and the Raj, 1849–1947* (1988), 41.

12. See D. E. Omissi, *Indian Voices of the Great War: Soldiers' Letters, 1914–1918* (Macmillan, 1994), appendices 1 and 2.

13. I. F. W. Beckett, *Ypres: The First Battle, 1914* (2004); J. Greenhut, "The Imperial Reserve: The Indian Corps on the Western Front, 1914–15," *Journal of Imperial and Commonwealth History* 12 (1983): 56.

14. Rumbold, *Watershed in India,* 23. His figure presumably includes British units serving with Indian divisions.

15. Greenhut, "The Imperial Reserve," 54–56.

16. A 1952 likeness in oils is reproduced in A. Guy and P. Boyden, eds., *Soldiers of the Raj: The Indian Army, 1600–1947* (1998), 302.

17. P. Mason, *A Matter of Honour: An Account of the Indian Army, Its Officers and Men* (1974), 415.

18. Note By Censor, Nov. 6, 1915, L/MIL/5/825/7/1179, OIOC.

19. Omissi, *Indian Voices of the Great War,* 5–7.

20. Beckett, *Ypres,* 109.

21. Guy and Boyden, *Soldiers of the Raj,* 163.

22. Petition to the King-Emperor from the Indian wounded, Milford-on-Sea, May 24, 1915, quoted in Omissi, *Indian Voices of the Great War,* 61–62.

23. Greenhut, "Imperial Reserve," 57.

24. Reports of the Indian Soldiers' Fund, MSS Eur., F.120/6–8, OIOC.

25. Corrigan, *Sepoys in the Trenches,* 201.

26. Lawrence to Kitchener, Mar. 8, 1916, MSS Eur. F.143/65, OIOC.

27. R. Visram, "The First World War and the Indian Soldiers," *Indo-British Review* 16 (1989): 19; H.D. Roberts, *A History of the Royal Pavilion, Brighton* (1939), 200.

28. Lawrence to Kitchener, Mar. 8, 1916, OIOC.

29. For the strategic background, see D. French, *British Economic and Strategic Planning, 1905–15* (1982), 142; and for the battle itself, see G. Bridger, *The Battle of Neuve Chapelle* (2000).

30. Corrigan, *Sepoys in the Trenches,* 168–70.

31. Greenhut, "Imperial Reserve," 65.

32. Amir Khan (Punjab Muslim) to Lance Naik Khan Zaman (84th Rifles, Rawalpindi District, Punjab), Mar. 18, 1915, quoted in Omissi, *Indian Voices of the Great War,* 43.

33. Omissi, *Indian Voices of the Great War,* 49 and 58; Fortnightly Report on the Internal Political Situation in the Central Provinces for the Second Half of April, 1915, Home Political, Deposit, May 1915, 49, NAI.

34. Corrigan, *Sepoys in the Trenches,* 185.

35. Carrington, "The Empire at War," 622.

36. Greenhut, "Imperial Reserve," 65.

37. Mason, *A Matter of Honour,* 416–18; Corrigan, *Sepoys in the Trenches,* 196.

38. Corrigan, *Sepoys in the Trenches,* 204–15.

39. Greenhut, "Imperial Reserve," 67.

40. Corrigan, *Sepoys in the Trenches,* 237.

41. Greenhut, 'Imperial Reserve," 68.

42. Quarterly Report by Censor, Dec. 7, 1917, L/MIL/5/825/705, OIOC.

43. Omissi, *Indian Voices of the Great War* 4.

44. Omissi, "Europe Through Indian Eyes," passim.

45. Carrington, "The Empire at War," 621; H. Strachan, *The First World War: A New Illustrated History* (2003), 84–85.

46. Strachan, *The First World War,* 98–99.

47. Carrington, "The Empire at War," 611.

48. Mason, *A Matter of Honour,* 411.

49. D. French, "The Dardanelles, Mecca and Kut: Prestige as a Factor in British Eastern Strategy, 1914–1916," *War and Society* 5, no. 1 (1987).

50. E. Cotes, "Mesopotamia: The Tragedy of an Impossible System," *The Nineteenth Century,* Aug. 1917, 276–77; Mason, *A Matter of Honour,* 431–32.

51. D. Goold, "Lord Hardinge and the Mesopotamia Expedition and Enquiry, 1914–1917," *Historical Journal* 19, no. 4 (1976): 929–31.

52. Goold, "Lord Hardinge and the Mesopotamia Expedition," 940.

53. F.J. Moberly, *The Campaign in Mesopotamia, 1914–1918,* vol. 2 (1923–24), chaps. 19–25 and appendices XI and XII.

54. Carrington, "The Empire at War," 616.

55. Moberly, *Campaign in Mesopotamia,* vol. 1, 63.

56. Perry, *The Commonwealth Armies,* 92.

57. J.M. Brown, *Modern India: The Origins of an Asian Democracy* (1985), 191; Carrington, "The Empire at War," 644.

58. L. James, *Mutiny: In the British and Commonwealth Forces, 1797–1956* (1987), 217; T. G. Fraser, "Germany and Indian Revolution, 1914–1918," *Journal of Contemporary History* 12, no. 2 (1977): 255–72; V. Chirol, "Islam and the War," *Quarterly Review* 425, no. 229 (1918): 489; R. Popplewell, *Intelligence and Imperial Defence: British Intelligence and the Defence of the Indian Empire, 1904–1924* (1995).

59. The most numerous "class" in the Indian Army was Punjabi Muslims, of whom 136,126 served during the war from British India. Omissi, *Indian Voices of the Great War,* 367.

60. Howell to Barrow, c. Feb.–Mar. 1915, L/MIL/7/17347, OIOC.

61. Viceroy to Kitchener, Jan. 29, 1915, Kitchener Papers, 30/57/69, PRO.

62. Memo by Kirkpatrick, 6 May 1916, WO 106/5443, PRO.

63. Notes from War Diary "D" Force, L/MIL/7/18327, OIOC.

64. D.E. Omissi, *The Sepoy and the Raj: The Indian Army, 1860–1940* (1994), 146; George V to Secretary of State for India, May 19, 1917, L/MIL/7/18327, OIOC.

65. I. Beckett, "The Singapore Mutiny of February 1915," *Journal of the Society for Army Historical Research* 62, no. 3 (1984); Mutiny of 5th Light Infantry, Singapore, 1915, L/MIL/17/19/48, OIOC.

66. James, *Mutiny,* 215, 220–23.

67. Tan Tai-Yong, "An Imperial Home Front: Punjab and the First World War," *The Journal of Military History* 64 (2000) 371–410.

68. Rumbold, *Watershed in India,* 30.

69. O'Dwyer, *India as I Knew It,* 225.

70. Rumbold, *Watershed in India,* 30.

71. Carrington, "The Empire at War," 616.

72. Risaldar Malik Mahomed Latif Khan, 28th Light Cavalry, Persia, to Jemadar Usaf Ali Khan, 19th Lancers, France, Apr. 15, 1917, L/MIL/5/827/3, OIOC.

73. Harrison, "The Fight Against Disease in the Mesopotamian Campaign," in *Facing Armageddon: The First World War Experienced,* ed. H. Cecil and P. Liddle (1996), 482.

74. Mason, *A Matter of Honour,* 433.

75. Cd.8610, 1917; Goold, 'Lord Hardinge and the Mesopotamia Expedition', p. 943; Carrington, "The Empire at War," 616.

76. *Hansard, HC Debs,* 1917, vol. XCVII, cols. 1695–96.

77. Brown, *Modern India,* 198; Indian Constitutional Reforms (the Montagu-Chelmsford Report), Apr. 22, 1918, CID 112–D, CAB 6–4, PRO.

78. Mason, *A Matter of Honour,* 433.

79. M. Hughes, ed., *Allenby in Palestine* (2006), 9–11.

80. Carrington, "The Empire at War," 639.

81. M. Hughes, *Allenby and British Strategy in the Middle East* (1999), 97–98.

82. P. Sluglett, *Britain in Iraq, 1914–1932* (1976), 9–14; Strachan, *The First World War,* 316.

83. Carrington, "The Empire at War," 641.

84. Note on Demobilization in Mesopotamia, Sept. 28, 1918, Foreign and Political External-B (Secret), May 1921, 70–133, NAI.

85. K. Jeffery, *The British Army and the Crisis of Empire, 1918–1922* (1984); and Jeffery, *Field Marshal Sir Henry Wilson: A Political Soldier* (2006), chap. 12.

86. The Situation in Mesopotamia, Memo. by Radcliffe, Dec. 7, 1920, CP.2275, CAB 24/116, PRO.

87. Viceroy to Secretary of State for India, Mar. 19, 1920, CID 119–D, CAB 6/4, PRO.

88. For further details see Brown, *Modern India,* 188–89.

89. R. Holland, "The British Empire and the Great War, 1914–1918," in *The Oxford History of the British Empire, Vol. IV: The Twentieth Century,* ed. J.M. Brown and W.R. Louis (1999), 117.

90. O'Dwyer, *India as I Knew It,* 226.

91. Cotton, "India: Now and After," 199–201.

92. Corrigan, *Sepoys in the Trenches,* 252.

93. Bridger, *Neuve Chapelle,* 124–26.

Chapter 6

1. I thank Daniel P. Marston, Susan Sinkinson, Steve Reels, and my father, Shri S.P. Sundaram, for their useful comments and suggestions on an earlier draft of this chapter.

2. See: G.J. Bryant, "Officers in the East India Company's Army in the Days of Clive and Hastings," *Journal of Imperial and Commonwealth History,* 6, no. 3 (Sept. 1978); Memorandum by Captain Charles Stewart, Oct. 15, 1809, in National Army Museum 6014/74/4: *Papers of Captain Charles Stewart, Commandant, Baraset Cadet College*; J.M. Bourne, "The East India Company's Military Seminary, Addiscombe, 1809–1858," *Journal of the Society for Army Historical Research* 57 (1979); British Library, Oriental and India Office Collections [hereafter: OIOC]: L/MIL/9/357: *A History of Addiscombe, 1809–1860*; H.M. Vibart, *Addiscombe: its Heroes and Men of Note* (London: A. Constable, 1894).

3. I thank Channa Wickremesekera for this point.

4. See: Amiya Barat, *The Bengal Native Infantry: Its Organisation and Discipline* (Calcutta: Firma K.L. Mukhopadhyay, 1962).

5. Mark H. Jacobsen, "The Modernization of the Indian Army, 1925–1939" (Ph.D. thesis, University of California, Irvine, 1979), 12–13.

6. For the details, see Chandar S. Sundaram, "A Grudging Concession: the Indianization of the Indian Army's Officer Corps, 1817–1917" (Ph.D. thesis, McGill University, 1996).

7. Perhaps interservice rivalry had something to do with this. Already by 1836, the Bengal Army began to look down on the armies of Bombay and especially Madras. See: A. Hervey, *A Soldier of the Company: Life of an Indian Ensign, 1833–43,* ed. C. Allen (London: Michael Joseph, 1988), 112.

8. Henry M. Lawrence, "The Military Defence of Our Empire in the East," *Calcutta Review* 2, no. 3 (1844): 50–51, quoted in Chandar S. Sundaram, "Reviving a 'Dead Letter': Military Indianization and the Ideology of Anglo-India, 1885–1891" in *The British Raj*

and its Indian Armed Forces, 1857–1939, ed. P.S. Gupta and A. Deshpande (Delhi: Oxford University Press, 2002), 48–49.

9.   On the Indian intelligentsia, see: S.R. Mehrotra, *Towards India's Freedom and Partition,* rev. and enlarged ed. (Delhi: Rupa, 2005), chaps. 1–2; and A. Seal, *The Emergence of Indian Nationalism: Competition and Collaboration in the Later Nineteenth Century* (Cambridge: Cambridge University Press, 1968). The full text of the Royal Proclamation of 1 Nov. 1858 is in C.H. Phillips and B.N. Pandey, eds., *The Evolution of India and Pakistan, 1858 to 1947: Select Documents* (London: Oxford University Press, 1962), 10–11.

10.   In 1871, Chesney gained a certain amount of fame by publishing *The Battle of Dorking,* a fictitious account of a German invasion of England, which started a whole genre of invasion-scare writing. See I.F. Clarke, *Voices Prophesying War, 1763–1749,* 2nd ed. (London: Oxford University Press, 1992).

11.   In its original meaning, the Bengali word *Babu* was a term of respect, like the English "esquire." However, in the later nineteenth century, the British began to use it to derisively describe the Indian intelligentsia, whom they felt were getting rather too "pushy" for their own good, what with their criticism of the colonial state and their desire for equality with the British. On *Babu* "effeminacy," see Mrinalini Sinha, *Colonial Masculinity: The "Manly Eng-lishman" and the "Effeminate Bengali" in the Late Nineteenth Century* (Manchester and New York: Manchester University Press, 1995).

12.   Sundaram, "Reviving a 'Dead Letter,'" 54.

13.   Ibid., p. 67; On the early INC, see J.R. McLane, *Indian Nationalism and the Early Congress* (Princeton, NJ: Princeton University Press, 1977).

14.   General Sir Frederick Roberts, Memorandum on the Inexpediency of substituting Native for British Officers in the Indian Army, Oct. 6, 1890, in OIOC: L/MIL/17/5/1615: *Confidential Correspondence of General Sir Frederick Roberts,* part 6, quoted in Sundaram, "Reviving a 'Dead Letter,'" 76.

15.   Cooch Behar was a small principality in northern Bengal. See Chandar S. Sundaram, "Preventing 'Idleness': the Maharaja of Cooch Behar's Proposal for Officer Commissions in the British Army for the sons of Indian Princes and Gentlemen, 1897–1898," in *South Asia,* New Series, 18, no. 1 (June 1995); Sundaram, "'Martial' Indian Aristocrats and the Military System of the Raj: the Imperial Cadet Corps, 1900--14," in *The Journal of Imperial and Commonwealth History* 25, no. 3 (Sept. 1997): 417.

16.   Lord Curzon's Memorandum of June 4, 1900, para. 32, in Government of India's Confidential Despatch no. 103 of July 19, 1900, in OIOC: L/MIL/17/5/1750.

17.   Sundaram, "'Martial' Indian Aristocrats," 417–23. The uniform's splendor can be clearly seen in a photograph of one of the Cadets, Kanwar Amar Singh of Kanota. See L.I. Rudolph, S.H. Rudolph, and M.S. Kanota, eds., *Reversing the Gaze: Amar Singh's Diary, A Colonial Subject's Narrative of Imperial India* (Boulder, CO: Westview, 2002), 265.

18.   In 1903–4, Major W.A. Watson, the ICC's first Commandant, wrote a series of memoranda proposing plans for the future employment of ICC graduates. See Employment for Imperial Cadets, Oct. 16, 1903; Employment of Imperial Cadets, Jan. 18, 1904; and Future Employment for Imperial Cadets, Apr. 18, 1904, in Government of India, Foreign Department, Secret I, Jan. 1905, Proceedings 36–37, National Archives of India.

19.   DeWitt Ellinwood, *Between Two Worlds: A Rajput Officer in the Indian Army, 1905–1921, based on the Diary of Amar Singh of Jaipur* (Lanham, MD: Hamilton Books, 2005), 459; Sundaram, "'Martial' Indian Aristocrats,", 429–33; Government of India, *Indian Army List, April 1914,* 200.

20. Details of the conference are in: "Note of a Conference held at Government House, Calcutta, on January 3rd, 1912," in *Papers of Charles, Lord Hardinge, 85/1/7a,* Cambridge University Library; and Sundaram, "A Grudging Concession," 255–60.

21. Sir S. P. Sinha, "Commissions for Indians in the Army," *Indian Review* 17, no. 2 (Jan. 1916): 113. The Victoria Cross is Britain's highest award for gallantry in battle. Great Britain, Parliament, *Debates (Commons), 1917, 5th Series,* vol. 97, column 1696. The only detailed study of the wartime debate is Sundaram, "A Grudging Concession," chap. 5, "The First World War and the Advent of Indianization, 1914–1917."

22. S. L. Menezes, *Fidelity and Honour: the Indian Army from the Seventeenth to the Twenty-First Century* (New Delhi: Viking, 1993), 314; Government of India, Central Legislative Assembly, *Debates,* vol. 1, no. 2 (1921): 1754.

23. The Sivaswamy Aiyer resolutions are reproduced in Gautam Sharma, *Nationalisation of the Indian Army, 1885–1947* (New Delhi: Allied, 1996), 59–62.

24. Jacobsen, "Modernization," 227–29; Stephen Cohen, *The Indian Army: its Contribution to the Development of a Nation,* 2nd ed. (Delhi: Oxford University Press, 1990), 79–82.

25. General A. S. Cobbe, Memorandum [on the Dominion Army], Sept. 14, 1921, in PRO CAB 16/38(II).

26. David Omissi, *The Sepoy and the Raj: the Indian Army, 1860–1940* (Basingstoke: Macmillan, 1994), 169–70; and V. Longer, *Red Coats to Olive Green: the Indian Army, 1600–1974* (Bombay: Allied, 1974), 190.

27. Government of India, Army Department, *Scheme for the Indianization of the Indian Army, 24 Jan., 1922,* IMR 59, PRO CAB 16/38.

28. The Committee of Imperial Defence was set up in 1904 to advise the British Prime Minister on defence and imperial matters. Subcommittees were convened from time to time to report on specific issues, such as Indian military requirements. See F. A. Johnson, *Defence by Committee: the British Committee of Imperial Defence, 1885–1959* (London: Oxford University Press, 1959). Reading's plea is in Viceroy to Secretary of State for India, Feb. 18, 1922, in PRO CAB 16/38(II). The eight units selected for Indianization were: 7th Light Cavalry, 16th Light Cavalry, 2/1st Madras Pioneers, 4/19th Hyderabad Regiment, 5th Royal Battalion/5th Mahratta Light Infantry, 1/7th Rajput Regiment, 1/14th Punjab Regiment, and 2/1st Punjab Regiment. See Government of India, Legislative Assembly, *Debates,* vol. 3, no. 4 (1923): 3364–65.

29. Government of India, *Report of the Indian Sandhurst Committee, 14 November, 1925* (London: HMSO, 1928), 8; Government of India, Legislative Assembly, *Debates,* vol. 3, no. 6 (1923): 4281; and vol. 5, no. 2 (1925): 1276. For details of the stringent selection process, see: Apurba Kundu, *Militarism in India: the Army and Civil Society in Consensus* (London and New York: Tauris Academic Studies, 1998), chap. 1.

30. Regulations of the Prince of Wales's Royal Indian Military College, 1946, appendix II, para. 2., in OIOC: L/MIL/7/19042.

31. Statements by Indian Cadets at Sandhurst regarding the Official Guardian, in OIOC:L/MIL/7/19086. For details of the cadet who went AWOL, see: OIOC: L/MIL/7/19157.

32. See: D. K. Palit, "Indianisation of the Indian Army's Officer Cadre, 1920–1947," in *The Indo-British Review: A Journal of History* 16 (1989). See also: Z. Masani, *Indian Tales of the Raj* (Berkeley: University of California Press, 1987), 90–93.

33. Government of India, Legislative Assembly, *Debates,* vol. 5, no. 4 (1927):4264–65.

34. Government of India, Legislative Assembly, *Debates,* vol. 5, no. 2 (1925): 1181–1272; Government of India, *Report of the Indian Sandhurst Committee, 14 November 1927,*London:

HMSO, 1928, pp. 1–2; Sir P.S. Sivaswamy Aiyer, "The Indian Sandhurst Committee Report," *The Indian Review* 28, no. 4 (Apr. 1927): 217–18.

35. Omissi, *The Sepoy and the Raj,* 178–79; and Sharma, *Nationalisation of the Indian Army,* chap. 5.

36. Sharma, *Nationalisation of the Indian Army,* 92–93.

37. Omissi, *The Sepoy and the Raj,* 181–82; Longer, *Red Coats to Olive Green,* 199.

38. UK Government, *Report of the Indian Statutory Commission* (Calcutta: Central Publication Branch, 1930), vol. 1, para. 124; Longer, *Red Coats to Olive Green,* 204; Sharma, *Nationalisation of the Indian Army,* 107.

39. Omissi, *The Sepoy and the Raj,* 184.

40. Government of India, *Report of the Indian Military College Committee, 15 Jul., 1931* (Simla: Government Superintendent of Publications, 1931), preamble; paras. 2, 15–18, 58–59. Conversations with Lt.-Col. Gautam Sharma, New Delhi, July 15, Aug. 8, and Oct. 22, 1997.

41. Brigadier L.P. Collins, "Lecture given to the United Services Institution of India," n.d. but before October 1934, in *Journal of the United Services Institution of India* 64 (Jan.–Oct. 1934): 520.

42. Masani, *Indian Tales of the Raj,* 25; Omissi, *The Sepoy and the Raj,* 187; Government of India, Legislative Assembly, *Debates,* vol. 2 (1939): 2108.

43. Sharma, *Nationalisation of the Indian Army,* 165–67.

44. Government of India, Defence Department, *Official Communiqué, 17 June, 1940,* in OIOC:L/MIL/7/19112.

45. Metcalf, *Ideologies,* chaps. 2–3.

46. The literature on Gandhian mass agitation is voluminous. Very good introductions are: David Hardiman, *Gandhi in His Time and Ours* (New Delhi: Permanent Black, 2003), and Bikhu Parekh, *Gandhi: a Very Short Introduction* (New Delhi: Oxford University Press, 2005).

47. General C.J.E. Auchinleck to Leo Amery, Oct. 12, 1940, in OIOC: L/MIL/7/19156.

Chapter 7

1. See Chapters 3 and 6 for background to the issues surrounding martial races and the Indianization of the officer corps.

2. See Daniel P. Marston, *Phoenix from the Ashes: The Indian Army in the Burma Campaign* (London: Praeger, 2003), and Tim Moreman, *The Jungle, the Japanese and the British Commonwealth Armies at War 1941–1945: Fighting Methods, Doctrine and Training for Jungle Warfare* (London: Frank Cass, 2005).

3. The performance of the Indian divisions in the North African campaign remains largely unexamined. A comparative analysis with other Commonwealth forces is needed.

4. Rapid expansion meant that various regiments and battalions within these formations lacked equipment as well as proper training for war. Many units had lost professional officers and VCOs to new units. Much of the training was in open-style desert warfare; this was the main theater envisioned for the Indian Army at this juncture, although troops were stationed in Malaya and Burma. There were also two minor incidents during this period in which troops refused orders. In 1940, men in the RIASC (based in Egypt) refused to be used as porters, as they believed this was "coolie" work. Later the same year, the Central India Horse was ordered to embark for Egypt. The Sikh squadron refused, because they did not want to leave India. Official reports asserted that both issues could have been avoided if the officers had been in

better touch with their men. Each division had three brigades of infantry; each brigade was made up of two Indian battalions and one British battalion. The division also had the support of artillery and engineers.

5. General Sir Geoffrey Evans, *Desert and Jungle* (London: William Kimber, 1959), 17.

6. *Tiger Kills* (HMSO, 1942), 25.

7. *Fourth Indian Reflections* (privately published, 1987), 12.

8. Colonel G.R. Stevens, 67/31/1 [32], Imperial War Museum (IWM).

9. General Sir Geoffrey Evans, "Battle of Keren," *History Today* 16 (1966): 266.

10. Ken Ross, "With the 2/8th Gurkhas in Iraq 1941–1942" *Red Flash,* no. 22: 55.

11. Still one of the best sources for the reasons and the operations in both Iraq and Persia (Iran) was written in 1948. See *PAIFORCE: The Official Story of the Persia and Iraq Command, 1941–1946.*

12. Charles Chenevix-Trench, *The Indian Army and the King's Enemies, 1900–1947* (London: Thames and Hudson, 1988) 159.

13. See War Diary entries, WO 169/3289 "Defence Notes," Public Records Office (PRO), as well as AITM, nos. 2–9. The future commander of 4th Indian, Major General Francis Tucker, created more than 40 "training instructions" for his units during his two years as commander. See Tucker MSS, IWM, 71/12/2.

14. "Attack by the 4/16th Punjabis," *Fourth Indian Reflections* (privately published, 1988), 23.

15. Refer to *Tiger Strikes* (HMSO, 1944), 27–46; and WO 169/3289, 4th Indian Division, Dec. 1941, PRO.

16. *Tiger Strikes,* 46–47; and WO 169/3289, Dec. 1941, PRO.

17. Tucker specifically stated that training must continue. Jan. 14, 1942, Subject: Training: "it is unfortunately true that the standard of individual training in the division has shown signs of deterioration and this must be put right." Tucker MSS, IWM, 71/12/2.

18. Messervy went on to command the newly arrived and unseasoned 1st British Armoured Division. General Tucker led the 4th Indian for the next two years and began a major process of "lessons learned" and training directives. See Lt. General Sir Francis Tucker Papers, IWM, 71/12/2.

19. Briggs went on to command the 5th Indian Division from May 1942 and led the division during the hectic fighting in North Africa and, later, the important fighting in the Arakan and Imphal regions in Assam in 1944. He also became the Director of Operations in 1950 during the Malayan Emergency, where he created the "Briggs Plan" for which he remains famous.

20. WO 169/7529, Jan. and Feb. 1942, 4th Indian Division, PRO; and *Tiger Strikes.*

21. After Eritrea, it had gone to Iraq and Cyprus.

22. Even while the division was split up, General Tucker carried out lesson discussions with his officers and created training instructions. As he stated on March 13, "as future moves of this division have not been settled, division command has decided that individual training will begin." Later, in April, he wrote: "battle group training will be continued and two months of training will begin." Tucker MSS, IWM, 71/12/2.

23. Slim had relinquished command to go to Burma and head up Burma Corps (BURCORPS). The division was taken over by Major General T.W. Rees, who would later command the 19th Indian Division in Burma.

24. *Tiger Strikes,* 117; and WO 169/7529, May–July 1942, PRO.

25. The 11th Indian Brigade, 4th Indian Division, was part of the garrison. Some units continued to fight for 36 hours after the capitulation.

26. There are many reasons for British shortcomings in the North African campaign. Two very good books that focus on these issues are David French, *Raising Churchill's Army* (Oxford: Oxford University Press, 2000), and Niall Barr, *Pendulum of War: The Three Battles of El Alamein* (London: Jonathan Cape, 2004).

27. See Tucker MSS, IWM, 71/12/2.

28. See Marston, *Phoenix from the Ashes,* 41–47, as an example.

29. To understand the campaign at the strategic, operational and tactical levels, please see Moreman, *The Jungle, the Japanese and the British Commonwealth Armies;* Brian Farrell, *Defence and Fall of Singapore* (Stroud: Tempus Publishing, 2005); Tomoyuki Ishizu and Raymond Callahan, "The Rising Sun Strikes" and "Coping with Disaster," both in *Pacific War Companion* (Oxford: Osprey Publishing, 2005).

30. There were exceptions; the 2nd Argyll and Sutherland Highlanders and the 12th Indian Brigade carried numerous exercises without much direction from Malaya Command. See Moreman, *The Jungle, the Japanese and the British Commonwealth Armies,* 12–28.

31. Many books cover the war in Burma from the strategic, operational, and tactical levels. Useful titles include Raymond Callahan, *Burma, 1942–1945* (London: Davis-Pynter, 1978); Louis Allen, *Burma, the Longest War* (London: Dent, 1984); William Slim, *Defeat into Victory* (London: Cassell, 1956); Marston, *Phoenix from the Ashes;* Moreman, *The Jungle, the Japanese and the British Commonwealth Armies;* and Allen Jeffries, *British Army in the Far East* (Oxford: Osprey Publishing, 2005).

32. This term refers to when an army expands due to mobilization, and disperses "regulars" throughout many units to spread experienced officers and men around.

33. Interview with Brigadier John Randle, 7/10th Baluch Regiment, Apr. 10, 2000, UK.

34. Some Malaya veterans were able to escape from the debacle as well, but many more men and officers from the Burma campaign escaped to influence future reforms.

35. Among the excellent firsthand accounts of the campaign that have been written are John Randle, *Battle Tales form Burma* (Stroud: Leo Cooper, 2004); and James Lunt, *Hell of a Licking: The Retreat from Burma, 1941–1942* (London: Collins, 1986).

36. For a more detailed discussion of the First Burma Campaign, see Allen, *Burma, the Longest War;* Callahan, *Burma, 1942–1945;* Marston, *Phoenix from the Ashes;* and Moreman, *The Jungle, the Japanese and the British Commonwealth Armies.*

37. See Tucker MSS, IWM; and WO 169/7529, Aug.–Nov. 1942, PRO.

38. Personal Diary, Oct. 23, 1942, Holworthy MSS, IWM, 91/40/2.

39. Personal Diary, Oct. 23, 1942, Tucker MSS, IWM.

40. See *Tiger Kills,* 150–60; Chenevix-Trench, *The Indian Army and the King's Enemies,* 223; and Tucker MSS, IWM. He created a system of "Patrol Master," which continued in the division for the remainder of the war.

41. General Tucker recognized this fact and had ordered a training directive to deal with mountains as the division moved across Libya. See Tucker MSS, IWM.

42. *Fourth Indian Reflections,* 38.

43. Chevenix-Trench, *The Indian Army and the King's Enemies,* 229.

44. For an exhaustive discussion of this period, see Marston, *Phoenix from the Ashes,* 79–110, and Moreman, *The Jungle, the Japanese and the British Commonwealth Armies,* 46–76.

45. See the actions of the 2/1st Punjabis to understand the environment and the limitations of the army at the time. Marston, *Phoenix from the Ashes,* 86–91.

46. See Marston, *Phoenix from the Ashes,* 88.

47. See Moreman, *The Jungle, the Japanese and the British Commonwealth Armies,* Marston, *Phoenix from the Ashes,* and Jeffries, *British Army in the Far East,* for more information.

48. Ibid.

49. See WO 172/1960, 17 Ind Div., 1943, PRO, as well as Marston, *Phoenix from the Ashes.*

50. See WO 172/1936, 5 Ind. Div., and WO 172/1943, 7th Ind. Div., 1943, PRO. See also Lieutenant General Frank Messervy Papers, MSS (7 Ind. Div), and Major General Sir Douglas Gracey Papers, MSS (20th Indian Division), for more evidence of training and lessons work being done by the units. They are located at the Liddell Hart Centre for Military Archives, King's College, London. See also Marston, *Phoenix from the Ashes,* and Moreman, *The Jungle, the Japanese and the British Commonwealth Armies.*

51. No major comparative analysis has been done regarding the performance of Indian Army formations in the Italian campaign.

52. See *Tiger Triumphs* (HMSO, 1946), as well as WO 169/14766, 8th Indian Division GS, Mar.–Dec. 1943, PRO.

53. See Tucker MSS, IWM and WO 169/14735, June–Dec. 1943, PRO.

54. There are many books on the battles in and around Cassino. Three of the best are John Ellis, *Cassino: The Hollow Victory* (London: Andre Deutsch, 1994); E.D. Smith, *Battles for Cassino* (London: Scribner, 1975); and Fred Majdalany, *Cassino: Portrait of a Battle,* 3rd ed. (London: Orion, 1999).

55. See *Tiger Triumphs* as well as WO 204/7275, "Attack on Cassino: NZ Corps and 4th Indian Operation instructions," and WO 169/18776, Mar.–June 1944, PRO.

56. "23 March Situation of the 4th Ind. Div.." Major General J.K. Shepheard MSS, 99/69/1, IWM.

57. See *Tiger Triumphs* and WO 169/18797, May–June 1944, PRO.

58. See *Tiger Triumphs.*

59. Brigadier E.A. Ardene MSS, 97/7/1, IWM.

60. See Major General Denys Reid MSS, PP MCR 06 Reel 7, IWM. The general theme after each operation is a system of "General Tactical Lessons," all listed after narrative of an operation; as well as WO 169/18813, 1944, 10th Indian Division PRO, "Much information regarding combat experience has been gained in the Italian theatre of operations...all commanders must apply the lessons to training."

61. The 8th Indian Division carried out lessons and training exercises during this respite. "Record in convenient form knowledge acquired...attention will be called to incidents from which valuable lessons can be learnt." See WO 204/7570, "Training Instructions 2, 7, and 8," Aug.–Dec. 1944, and WO 169/18798, July–Sept. 1944, PRO.

62. Without General Tucker in command, the division carried on with lessons and training directives under the command of Major General A.W. Holworthy. See Holworthy MSS, 91/40/1, IWM and WO 169/18777 July–Sept. 1944, PRO.

63. See *Tiger Triumphs* for more details.

64. The division was complimented highly by senior officers for their efforts in Italy as well as North Africa. See Holworthy MSS, 91/40/1, IWM, letters of Sept. 9, Sept. 29, and Oct. 5, 1944.

65. See *Tiger Triumphs* and WO 169/22249, Mar.–Apr. 1944, 10th Indian Division.

66. See Marston, *Phoenix from the Ashes,* 133.

67. Due to space considerations, a detailed discussion of the fighting in Burma is not possible. Please consult the books listed above for more detail. They include many personal accounts, from the soldier's to the general's perspective.

68. Some units had become so adept at jungle warfare and patrolling that they were able to cause considerable damage to the Japanese advance. See 14/13th Frontier Force Rifles fighting in Marston, *Phoenix from the Ashes,* 142–45.

69. See Marston, *Phoenix from the Ashes,* 146.

70. Both the 5th and 7th Indian divisions were flown into the fighting in Kohima and Imphal to reinforce the garrisons.

71. See Marston, *Phoenix from the Ashes,* 170–79, and Moreman, *The Jungle, the Japanese and the British Commonwealth Armies,* 146–60, as well as the countless MTPs and AITM that are available at the British Library and National Army Museum and IWM.

72. The XV Corps, 25th and 26th Indian, 81st and 82nd West African divisions, continued its advance down the Arakan region of Burma and were successful in tying down Japanese forces in the area. Ramree Island was seized by February 1945.

73. Slim, *Defeat into Victory,* 327.

74. See Marston, *Phoenix from the Ashes,* 211; and interview with Major Coppen, Nov. 1, 1999, UK.

75. 9/13th Frontier Force Rifles, interviews with Major Lamond, Oct. 27, 1999, and Major Wright, Dec. 20, 1999, UK.

76. Lieutenant General Hanaya, "Story of the Japanese 33rd Division," General Evans Papers, IWM.

77. Auchinleck Papers, Apr. 23, 1945, University of Manchester.

78. See Marston, *Phoenix from the Ashes,* 47–49 and 222–33.

79. Ibid., 49–50 and 218–20.

80. John Masters, *The Road Past Mandalay: A Personal Narrative* (London: Michael Joseph Ltd., 1961); 312–13.

Chapter 8

1. Daniel P. Marston, Susan Sinkinson, David Smith, James Rice, and my father, Shri S. P. Sundaram, read and commented on an earlier draft of this chapter. I thank them all.

2. On the disaffection of Indian *jawans*in this period, see Chandar S. Sundaram, "Soldier Disaffection and the Creation of the Indian National Army", *Indo-British Review: A Journal of History* 18, no. 1 (1990). Further revelations of this are in Chandar S. Sundaram, "Seditious Letters and Steel Helmets: Disaffection among Indian Troops in Singapore and Hong Kong, 1940–1941, and the Creation of the Indian National Army", in *War and Society in Colonial India, 1807–1945,* ed. D. Ellinwood and K. Roy (Delhi: Oxford University Press, 2007).

3. These aspects have been thoroughly examined in: Joyce Lebra, *Jungle Alliance: Japan and the Indian National Army* (Singapore: Asia Pacific Press, 1971); and K.K. Ghosh, *The Indian National Army: The Second Front of the Indian Freedom Movement* (Meerut: Meenakshi Prakashan, 1969). For a fascinating firsthand account of IJA involvement in the INA's formation, see Fujiwara Iwaichi, *F. Kikan: Japanese Army Intelligence Operations in Southeast Asia during World War II,* trans. Akashi Yoji (Hong Kong: Heinemann Asia, 1983).

4. See Edward Drea, "The Imperial Japanese Army, 1868–1945: Origins, Evolution, Legacy," in *War in the Modern World since 1815,* ed. Jeremy Black (New York: Routledge, 2003), 111. However, the Japanese attitude was not as monolithic as it might seem. See Henry Frei, *The Guns of February: Ordinary Japanese Soldiers' Views of the Malayan Campaign and the Fall of Singapore, 1941–1942* (Singapore: National University of Singapore Press, 2004).

5.   Mohan Singh, *Soldiers' Contribution to India's Independence* (Delhi: Army Educational Stores, 1974); and Mohan Singh, interview by author, New Delhi, Aug. 5, 1984.

6.   Leonard A. Gordon, *Brothers Against the Raj: A Biography of Sarat and Subhas Chandra Bose* (Delhi: Viking/Penguin, 1990), is the best biography of Bose. For the Free India Legion, one should consult Milan Hauner, *India in Axis Strategy: Germany, Japan, and Indian Nationalists in the Second World War* (Stuttgart: Klett-Cotta, 1981).

7.   India Command Weekly Intelligence Summary 178, Apr. 1, 1945, part III, appendix B, in L/WS/1/1433, Oriental and India Office Collections, British Library (hereafter OIOC)); quoted in Chandar S. Sundaram, "A Paper Tiger: The Indian National Army in Battle, 1944–45," *War & Society* 13, no. 1 (May 1995): 38. The Rani of Jhansi Regiment did not participate in any fighting. Its main role was the traditional genderized one of nursing. See also Carol Hills and Daniel Silverman, "Nationalism and Feminism in Late Colonial India: The Rani of Jhansi Regiment, 1943–1945," *Modern Asian Studies* 27, no. 4 (1993).

8.   Fujiwara, *F. Kikan,* passim.; personal correspondence from Lt.-Gen. Fujiwara to author, Feb. 10, 1984, and May 23, 1985.

9.   See, for example: P. W. Fay, *The Forgotten Army: India's Armed Struggle for Independence, 1942–1945* (Delhi: Rupa, 1994); and T. R. Sareen, *Japan and the Indian National Army* (Delhi: Agam Prakashan, 1986). Of the two, the Sareen book is quite poor and overly hagiographical.

10.   Sundaram, "A Paper Tiger," 42–46.

11.   Ibid., 46–47. Sareen ludicrously argues that the Japanese considered the Chin Hills sector important, when even the feeblest knowledge of Japanese plans and the geography of the area would reveal that it was merely a backwater. See Sareen, *Japan and the Indian National Army,* 144.

12.   Sundaram, "A Paper Tiger," 43, 45; Prem Kumar Sahgal, interview by author, Kanpur, July 29, 1984. On the Indian Army's transformation, see Daniel P. Marston, *Phoenix from the Ashes: The Indian Army in the Burma Campaign* (Westport, CT, and London: Praeger, 2003). See Chapter 7 of this book for a summary of the changes.

13.   Sundaram, "A Paper Tiger," 49; Louis Allen, *Burma: The Longest War, 1941–1945* (London: J.M. Dent, 1984), 227.

14.   South East Asia Command and India Command, Weekly Security Intelligence Summary 142, July 21, 1944, sect. D, page 1, L/WS/1/1433, OIOC; quoted in Sundaram, "A Paper Tiger," 49.

15.   Sundaram, "A Paper Tiger," 50.

16.   Ibid., 50–52.

17.   Ibid., 52.

18.   Sundaram, "A Paper Tiger," 53; South East Asia Command and India Command Weekly Intelligence Summary 177, Mar. 23, 1945, para. 2, L/WS/1/1433, OIOC.

19.   See, for example, Marshall Getz, *Subhas Chandra Bose: A Biography* (Jefferson, NC: McFarland, 2002).

20.   "Mystery over Indian Freedom Hero," BBC News, published May 17, 2006. See http://news.bbc.co.uk/go/pr/fr/-/2/hi/south_asia/4989868.stm (accessed May 19, 2006).

21.   The best treatment of the INA trials and their impact still remains Ghosh, *The Indian National Army,* chap. 8. For a full transcript of the first INA trial, see Moti Ram, ed., *Two Historic Trials in the Red Fort* (Delhi: Rajkamal, 1946).

22.   This term was first popularized by the radical Hindu nationalist V. D. (Veer) Savarkar.

23.   Ghosh, *The Indian National Army,* 224–37.

24. C.A. Bayly and T. Harper, *Forgotten Armies: The Fall of British Asia, 1941–1945* (Cambridge, MA: Belknap, 2005), 29.

Chapter 9

1. Very little research has been done on this period. I have begun my current research project in an attempt to fill this gap in the history of the Indian Army. Much of the information in this chapter was researched and presented in a paper entitled "The Punjab Boundary Force: A Reappraisal?" at Oxford University in November 2005. This work is also intended to form the basis of a full-length monograph.

2. Various formations of the Indian Army were involved with occupation as well as counterinsurgency warfare in Southeast Asia after the Japanese capitulation. These included operations in French Indochina, when the 20th Indian Division occupied and fought elements of the Viet Minh from September 1945 to April 1946. The 5th and 23rd Indian divisions also fought against Indonesian nationalists in the Dutch East Indies between September 1945 and May 1946. The sad but true statistic is that many units suffered more killed and wounded in the Dutch East Indies than they had fighting the Japanese in India/Burma. The most recent scholarship dealing with this episode was a University of London Ph.D. dissertation completed in 2002 by Dr. Richard McMillan, "British Occupation of the Dutch East Indies, 1945–46."

3. Ibid.

4. Wavell to Lord Pethick-Lawrence, Nov. 2, 1945, L/WS/1/1577, Oriental and India Office Collections, British Library (hereafter OIOC).

5. General Auchinleck to Wavell, Nov. 24, 1945, Official Correspondence: India, 1945, Wavell Papers, OIOC.

6. John Connell, *Auchinleck* (London: Cassell, 1959), 798. Nehru intended to go one step further; intelligence reports indicated that he was going to allow former INA members to join the Congress volunteer movement. See Sept. 28, 1945, L/WS/1/1506, OIOC.

7. Captain Shah Nawaz (1/14th Punjab); Captain P.K. Seghal (2/10th Baluch); Lieutenant G.S. Dhillon (1/14th Punjab).

8. Morale Reports, Jan. 1946, L/WS/1/1636, OIOC.

9. India Command Fortnightly Intelligence Reports, Jan. 18, 1946, L/MIL/17/5/4276, OIOC.

10. Auchinleck to Wavell, Feb. 13, 1946, Official Correspondence 1946, Wavell Papers, OIOC.

11. Correspondence with Major G.E. Mitchell, RIASC.

12. A minor disturbance occurred when 25 soldiers from the 17th Battalion, Maharrata Light Infantry, refused to follow orders after they arrived in Bombay from service in Malaya; this has been linked to issues surrounding customs examination. See Intelligence Reports, No. 5, 1946, L/MIL/17/5/4276, OIOC.

13. Intelligence Reports, No. 5, 1946, L/MIL/17/5/4276, OIOC.

14. Morale Reports, Mar. 28, 1946, L/WS1/1636, OIOC.

15. Intelligence Reports, No. 17, Oct. 1, 1946, L/MIL/17/5/4276, OIOC.

16. General Sir Reginald Savory Papers, 7603/93–81, Aug. 28, 1946, National Army Museum (hereafter NAM).

17. Indian Conference in London, Dec. 4, 1946, L/P&J/10/111, OIOC.

18. Army Commanders Conference, Mar. 1947, L/WS/1/1524, OIOC.

19. OIOC, L/MIL/17/5/4276, Intelligence Reports, Mar. 1946.

20. The 14th Punjab Regimental Centre demobilized 750 soldiers a month and was ordered to process 1,000 per month if need be. Lieutenant Colonel Cotton, 8002–68, NAM.

21. See Political Intelligence, 1946, L/WS/1/1009, OIOC.

22. Army Commanders Conference, Mar. 1947, L/WS/1/1524, OIOC.

23. Meeting of Ministers on Indian Questions, Mar. 13, 1947, L/P&J/10/78, OIOC.

24. Chiefs of Staff Committee, Mar. 18, 1947, L/WS/1/1045, OIOC.

25. See Mr. Liaquat Ali Khan to Mountbatten, Apr. 7, 1947, L/P&J/10/79, OIOC.

26. The Indian Army experienced a shortage of officers during this period, for several reasons. Many officers from the Second World War returned to civilian life; also, in 1945, the decision was taken that no more British nationals would be offered Indian Army commissions, in order to ensure the army's nationalization. There was considerable debate about how long this process would, or should, take, and some senior officers thought it would take as long as 25 years for everything to work out smoothly. In the end, however, political pressures took precedence over all other considerations, and the timeline for independence left five years for India and Pakistan to nationalize and establish two new armies out of the single existing force. Teething problems were inevitable. See Post War Officering of the Indian Army, L/WS/1/924, OIOC.

27. Mountbatten Papers, Official Correspondence Files: Armed Forces, Apr. 25, 1947, OIOC.

28. Letter of June 28, 1947, General Savory Papers, NAM.

29. See Intelligence Reports, Mar. 3, 1947, L/MIL/17/5/4276, OIOC.

30. Also highlighted in an intelligence report to Auchinleck in May 1947: "it would appear that the police, particularly in those districts which have suffered in the previous disturbances will tend to become partisan." General Pete Rees Papers, 50 Auk GOC Personal Intelligence—Punjab, OIOC.

31. Official Correspondence, Political Situation in India, Mar. 22, 1947, Mountbatten Papers, OIOC.

32. Intelligence Reports, No. 23–25, Apr.–June 1947, L/MIL/17/5/4276, OIOC.

33. Rees Papers, 50 Auk GOC Personal Intelligence—Punjab, OIOC.

34. WO 268/458 2nd Rajput Regiment, Mar. 1947, Public Records Office (PRO).

35. WO 268/453, 4th 6th Rajputana Rifles, Apr. 1947, PRO.

36. Many of the battalions were understrength for both men and officers.

37. Sialkot, Gujranwala, Sheikhupura, Lyallpur, Montgomery, Lahore, Amritsar, Gurdaspur, Hoshiarpur, Jullundur, Ferozepore and Ludhihana. It was originally 11, and then Ludihana was added. See Mountbatten Papers, July 20, 1947, OIOC.

38. Rees Papers, 48 Report on Communal Violence, OIOC.

39. Rees Papers, 59 "Special Order of the day, 1st August 1947," OIOC.

40. Rees Papers, 48 Report on Communal Violence, OIOC.

41. Interview with Major Riches, May 3, 2005, UK.

42. Major P. H. James, "Transfer of Sovereignty," *Royal Engineers Journal* (Aug. 1997): 118.

43. Mountbatten Papers, Official correspondence: Punjab, Aug. 8, 1947, OIOC.

44. Rees Papers, 51 Misc. drafts and reports, Aug. 14, 1947, OIOC.

45. Rees Papers, 73 Misc., Aug. 17, 1947, OIOC.

46. Rees Papers, 61, Aug. 25, 1947, OIOC.

47. See article "Massacres in the Punjab—Muslims butchered by armed mobs of Sikhs," *Times* (London), Aug. 25, 1947.

48. See Major General Shahid Hamid, *Disastrous Twilight* (Leo Cooper, 1986), 239.

49. Fifty-nine Special orders of the day, Aug. 31, 1947, Rees Papers, OIOC.

50. See General Sir Francis Tuker's account of the actions of the Indian Army in Eastern India, *While Memory Serves* (London: Cassell, 1950).

Chapter 10

1. Sumit Ganguly, *Conflict Unending: India-Pakistan Tensions Since 1947* (New York: Columbia University Press, 2001), 23.

2. Subhash Kapila, "India's New 'Cold Start' War Doctrine Strategically Reviewed," South Asia Analysis Group Paper No. 991, May 4, 2004, available at http://www.saag.org/papers10/paper991.html; and Gurmeet Kanwal, "Strike Fast and Hard: Army Doctrine Undergoes Change in Nuclear Era," Observer Research Foundation, June 29, 2006, http://www.observer-india.com/analysis/A607.htm.

3. General V. P. Malik, *Kargil: From Surprise to Victory* (HarperCollins, 2006).

4. See the bibliography at the end of the chapter relating to Indian and Pakistani civil-military relations for further readings on the subject.

5. Interview with senior official in the Indian Government.

6. General K. V. Krishna Rao, *Prepare or Perish: A Study of National Security* (Lancer, 1991), is one work that covers all the wars that India has fought with Pakistan with detailed analysis of the military battles. The problem with most such works is that they recount the land battles and describe in passing the air and naval operations.

7. Major General Ashok Krishna, *India's Armed Forces; Fifty Years of War and Peace* (New Delhi: Lancer Publishers and Distributors, 1998), 15–17.

8. Ibid., 17.

9. Ibid., 18.

10. Pradeep Barua, *The State of War in South Asia* (Lincoln: University of Nebraska Press, 2005).

11. Nagendra Singh, *The Defence Mechanism of the Modern State* (Bombay: Asia Publishing House, 1964), 171–73.

12. Chandrashekhar Dasgupta, *War and Diplomacy in Kashmir, 1947–48* (New Delhi: Sage Publications, 2002), gives the best overview of the role of the Western powers, particularly the UK in the protracted discussions on Kashmir in the UN.

13. Ashok Krishna, *India's Armed Forces,* 55.

14. Ibid., 58.

15. P. C. Lal, *Some Problems of Defence* (New Delhi: United Services Institution of India, 1977), 74.

16. Brian Cloughley, *A History of the Pakistan Army: Wars and Insurrections,* 2nd ed. (Karachi: Oxford University Press, 2000), 68–70. Also see Ashok Krishna, *India's Armed Forces,* 65–69.

17. Ashok Krishna, *India's Armed Forces,* 63–64.

18. Bhashyam Kasturi, "Intelligence Services: Analysis, Organization and Function," Lancer Paper 6, Lancer Publishers and Distributors, New Delhi (1995), 40.

19. M. Asghar Khan, *The First Round: Indo-Pakistan War, 1965* (New Delhi: Vikas Publishing House, 1979), 21.

20. Ashok Krishna, *India's Armed Forces,* 79.

21. K. C. Praval, *Indian Army after Independence* (New Delhi: Lancer International, 1993), 304.

22. Ashok Krishna, *India's Armed Forces,* 75.

23. Krishna Rao, *Prepare or Perish,* 157.

24. Lt. Gen. J. F. R. Jacob, *Surrender at Dacca: Birth of a Nation* (New Delhi: Manohar Publishers and Distributors, 1997), 94.

25. Vice Admiral Mihir Roy, *War in the Indian Ocean* (New Delhi: Lancer Publishers and Distributors, 1995), 177–232, for the role played by the Indian Navy. Also see Ashok Krishna, 61–62.

26. Ashok Krishna, *India's Armed Forces,* 86.

27. Krishna Rao, *Prepare or Perish,* 195–96.

28. The 1971 Indo-Pak War, available at http://www.bharat-rakshak.com/LAND-FORCES/Army/Patton3.html.

29. Ashok Krishna, *India's Armed Forces,* 90.

30. Mihir Roy, *War in the Indian Ocean,* 172–232.

31. Major R. G. Kyle, "Indian-Pakistan War of 1971: A Modern War," abstract, Marine Corps Command and Staff College, USA, Mar. 14, 1984, available at http://www.global security.org/military/library/report/1984/KRG.htm. See Chapter 3 for the comments made.

32. Ashok Krishna, *India's Armed Forces,* 97–98.

33. Kyle, "Indian-Pakistan War of 1971."

34. Amitabh Mattoo, ed., *India's Nuclear Deterrent: Pokhran II and Beyond* (New Delhi: Har-Anand Publications Pvt. Ltd., 1999), 23–24.

35. Major General Afsir Karim, "Pakistan's Aggression in Kashmir: 1999," *Aakrosh: Asian Journal on Terrorism and Internal Conflicts* 2, no. 4 (July 1999): 4–5.

36. Cloughley, *A History of the Pakistan Army,* 376.

37. Vinod Anand, "Warfare in Transition and the Indian Subcontinent," *Strategic Analysis: A Monthly Journal of the IDSA* 23, no. 5 (Aug. 1999); http://www.ciaonet.org/olj/sa/sa_99anv04.html.

38. Gaurav C. Sawant, *Dateline Kargil* (Macmillan India Limited, 2000), 9, 284.

39. Ibid., 172–77.

40. Cloughley, *A History of the Pakistan Army,* 376.

41. Nawaz Sharif visited China on a week-long trip to gain Chinese support. See Harvey Stockwin, "China refuses to bite Sharif bait, Urges Talks," *Times Of India,* June 30, 1999, available at http://www.jammukashmir.com/archives/archives1999/99june30a.html.

42. Afsir Karim, "Pakistan's Aggression in Kashmir," 10–11.

Chapter 11

1. For an example of the first genre, see D. R. Mankekar, *The Guilty Men of 1962* (Bombay: Tulsi Shah Enterprises, 1968). The seminal and most comprehensive revisionist account is Neville Maxwell, *India's China War* (New York: Doubleday, 1972).

2. There is a substantial literature on the historical origins of the boundary dispute. The more important works are Alastair Lamb, *The China-India Border: The Origins of the Disputed Boundaries* (London: Oxford University Press, 1964); Lamb, *The McMahon Line,* 2 vols. (London: Routledge and Kegan Paul, 1966); Lamb, *The Sino-Indian Boundary in Ladakh* (Columbia: University of South Carolina Press, 1975); Lamb, *Tibet, China and India* (Hertfordshire: Roxford Books, 1989); Parshotam Mehra, *The McMahon Line and After* (New Delhi: Macmillan, 1974); Mehra, *The North-East Frontier,* 2 vols. (1979); and Mehra, *An "Agreed" Frontier: Ladakh and India's Northernmost Borders, 1846–1947* (New Delhi: Oxford University Press, 1992).

3. High Commission in India to Commonwealth Relations Office, Oct. 21, 1959, FO 371/141272, National Archives, London.

4. D.K. Palit, *War in High Himalaya: The Indian Army in Crisis, 1962* (London: Hurst, 1991),79–83.

5. Steven Hoffmann, *India and the China Crisis* (Berkeley: University of California Press, 1990), 95.

6. See, for instance, Maxwell, *China's "Aggression" of 1962* (Oxford: Court Place Books, 1999), 15.

7. Sarvepalli Gopal, *Jawaharlal Nehru: A Biography,* vol. 3 (Cambridge, MA: Harvard University Press, 1984), 213.

8. Palit, *War in High Himalaya,* 246.

9. Harbaksh Singh, "NEFA 1962: How a Foolproof Defense Plan Collapsed," *Indian Express,* Apr. 25, 1979.

10. Palit, *War in High Himalaya,* 259.

11. P.B. Sinha and A.A. Athale, *History of the Conflict with China* (India: History Division, Ministry of Defence, 1992), chap. 7.

12. B.N. Mullik, *The Chinese Betrayal* (New Delhi: Allied Publishers, 1971), 380.

13. Gopal, *Nehru,* vol. 3, 224.

14. T.T. Krishnamachari to Prime Minister Jawaharlal Nehru, Oct. 30, 1962, T.T. Krishnamachari Papers, Correspondence with Nehru (1962), Nehru Memorial Museum and Library, New Delhi.

15. Maxwell, *India's China War,* 394.

16. Sinha and Athale, *History of the Conflict with China,* 184.

17. B.M. Kaul, *The Untold Story* (New Delhi: Allied Publishers, 1967), 413.

18. Palit, *War in High Himalaya,* 316.

19. J.K. Galbraith, *Ambassador's Journal* (Boston: Houghton Mifflin, 1969), 487–90.

20. State Department to Embassy in India, Nov. 19, 1962, *Foreign Relations of the United States, 1961–1963,* vol. 19, 398–99. Also see Kennedy's message to Nehru in State Department to Embassy in India, Nov. 20, 1962, Ibid., 403–404.

Chapter 12

1. Many of these Tamils of Indian descent were repatriated to India in the 1940s and the 1950s. The remainder has been granted Sri Lankan citizenship. They have, by and large, remained aloof from the Tamil separatist campaign, even though there have been isolated incidents of unrest.

2. The Eastern Province also has a large number of Muslims who are predominantly Tamil speakers. Districts such as Trincomalee and Amparai also have large Sinhalese populations.

3. The attack destroyed eight military aircraft, three Sri Lankan Airlines planes, and one cargo plane. It sent the island's tourist industry plummeting and further weakened its long-suffering economy.

4. For instance, in May 1985 the Tigers launched a daring attack on the Buddhist sacred city of Anuradhapura in the North Central Province, killing 150 people and wounding many others. In April 1987 the Tigers killed 127 Sinhalese, including 31 off-duty policemen in the Eastern Province. In June that same year, 30 Buddhist priests were massacred at Arantalawa,

also in the Eastern Province. In August 1990 the Tigers killed 175 Muslim villagers praying in a mosque in Kattankudi, Battaicaloa District.

5. The Tigers began recruiting large numbers of children during their confrontation with the IPKF. The trend continued in the 1990s despite increasing pressure from the international community. At present, the LTTE has given a commitment to international agencies to stop child recruitment, but doubts about their sincerity remain.

6. The ambush, initiated by a land mine explosion and followed by attacks with firearms and grenades, cost the lives of 13 soldiers and left another two dangerously wounded. The incident sparked off widespread riots against Tamils in the capital Colombo and several major cities.

7. For instance, the Tigers captured two 122-mm howitzers and two 120-mm mortars from Mullaitivu in 1996, while the overrunning of the Elephant Pass yielded three 152-mm artillery pieces.

8. Some military sources put the figure as high as 50,000.

Chapter 13

1. Robert Jervis, *The Meaning of the Nuclear Revolution* (Ithaca, NY: Cornell University Press, 1989).

2. Ashok Kapur, *India's Nuclear Option: Atomic Diplomacy and Decision Making* (New York: Praeger, 1976), 194.

3. Scott Sagan, "Why Do States Build Nuclear Weapons? Three Models in Search of A Bomb," *International Security* 21, no. 3 (Winter 1996–97): 54–86.

4. K. Subrahmanyam, "Politics of Security: When Vajpayee Said 'No' to Going Nuclear," *Times of India,* Apr. 10, 2004, http:/timesofindia.indiatimes.com/articleshow/608713.cms.

5. For an overview of the various doctrines and a detailed study of India's, see Rajesh M. Basrur, *Minimum Deterrence and India's Nuclear Security* (Stanford, CA: Stanford University Press, 2006).

6. Rajesh Rajagopalan, *Second Strike: Arguments about Nuclear War in South Asia* (New Delhi: Viking, 2005), 89–106.

7. "The Cabinet Committee on Security Reviews Operationalization of India's Nuclear Doctrine," Press Release, Ministry of External Affairs, Government of India, Jan. 4, 2003.

8. "India Not to Engage in A Nuclear Arms Race: Jaswant" (Interview), *Hindu,* Nov. 29, 1999, 14.

9. Michael Krepon and Chris Gagné, eds., *The Stability-Instability Paradox: Nuclear Weapons and Brinkmanship in South Asia* (Washington, DC: Henry L. Stimson Center, June 2001). For an earlier formulation of the concept, see Glen Snyder, "The Balance of Power and the Balance of Terror," in *The Balance of Power,* ed. Paul Seabury (San Francisco: Chandler, 1965), 194–201.

10. Peter Chalk, "Pakistan's Role in the Kashmir Insurgency,"*Jane's Intelligence Review,* Sept. 1, 2001; reproduced on the RAND Corporation Web site, http:/www.rand.org/hot/op-eds/090101JIR.html.

11. T.V. Paul, "Chinese-Pakistani Missile Ties and the Balance of Power," *Nonproliferation Review* 10, no. 2 (Summer 2003): 1–9.

12. K.J. Holsti, *The State, War and the State of War* (Cambridge and New York: Cambridge University Press, 1996).

Index

About the Contributors

RAJESH M. BASRUR, who is Director, Centre for Global Studies, Mumbai, is the author of *Minimum Deterrence and India's Nuclear Security* (2006).

RAYMOND CALLAHAN, Emeritus Professor of History at the University of Delaware, has had a career-long interest in the East India Company's armies and their successor, the Indian Army of the Raj, and is the author of *The East India Company and Army Reform, 1783–1798* (1972).

BHASHYAM KASTURI is currently Associate Editor, The Jawaharlal Nehru Memorial Fund, and is the author of *Intelligence Services: Analysis, Organization, and Function* (1996).

DANIEL P. MARSTON is Senior Lecturer in the Department of War Studies at the Royal Military Academy, Sandhurst (UK). He has written *Phoenix from the Ashes: The Indian Army in the Burma Campaign* (Praeger, 2003) and is editor-in-chief for *The Pacific War Companion* (2005).

TIM MOREMAN is a Somerset-based freelance writer and academic, having lectured in the Department of War Studies at King's College, London. His writing includes a study of the Indian Army on the North-West Frontier, 1849–1947, and a book on the war in Burma and Malaya 1941–45. He is currently working on a new study of the First Arakan Campaign during the Second World War.

DAVID OMISSI is Senior Lecturer in Modern History at the University of Hull, UK, and is the author of *The Sepoy and the Raj: the Indian Army, 1860–1940* (1994).

DOUGLAS M. PEERS is professor of history at the University of Calgary and author of *Between Mars and Mammon: Colonial Armies and the Garrison State in India, 1819–1835* (1995), and the coeditor of *J. S. Mill's Encounter with India* (1999).

SRINATH RAGHAVAN is a doctoral candidate at the Department of War Studies, King's College, London, working on Sino-Indian relations.

KAUSHIK ROY is a lecturer of history at Presidency College, Kolkata, India.

CHANDAR S. SUNDARAM is an Associate Professor in the Humanities and Social Sciences Division, The United International College, Zhuhai, China. He has published articles on aspects of the colonial Indian Army and the Indian National

Army. He is presently researching the military culture of the late-colonial Indian Army.

CHANNA WICKREMESEKERA, who currently lives and works in Australia, has published *"Best Black Troops in the World": British Perceptions and the Making of the Sepoy, 1746–1805* (2002), as well as several other works on South Asian military history.

Lightning Source UK Ltd.
Milton Keynes UK
UKOW06f1156020217

293447UK00013B/63/P

COUNTRY WALKS AROUND HARROGATE

Volume 2 West

by

Douglas Cossar

for

The Ramblers' Association West Riding Area

(www.ramblersyorkshire.org)

ramblers
at the heart of walking

Other publications by the Ramblers' Association (West Riding Area)

Kiddiwalks (2005)
Douglas Cossar, *Ramblers' Leeds, vol. 1 East (1999)*
Douglas Cossar, *Ramblers' Leeds, vol. 2 West (2000)*
Douglas Cossar, *Ramblers' Bradford (1999)*
Douglas Cossar, *The Wakefield Way (2004)*
Douglas Cossar, *The Airedale Way (1996)*
Douglas Cossar & John Lieberg, *Country Walks in Mirfield, Emley, Thornhill and Denby Dale (2007)*
Douglas Cossar, *Country Walks around Harrogate, vol. 1 East (2007)*

ISBN 978-1-906494-03-2

Printed by Hart & Clough Ltd, Cleckheaton

Cover photograph. In the Washburn valley.
Photographs by Keith Wadd and Douglas Cossar.

Publishers' Note
At the time of publication all footpaths used in these walks were designated as public rights of way or permissive footpaths, but it should be borne in mind that diversion orders may be made from time to time. Although every care has been taken in the preparation of this guide, the publishers cannot accept responsibility for those who stray from the routes described.

Contents

Where the walks start

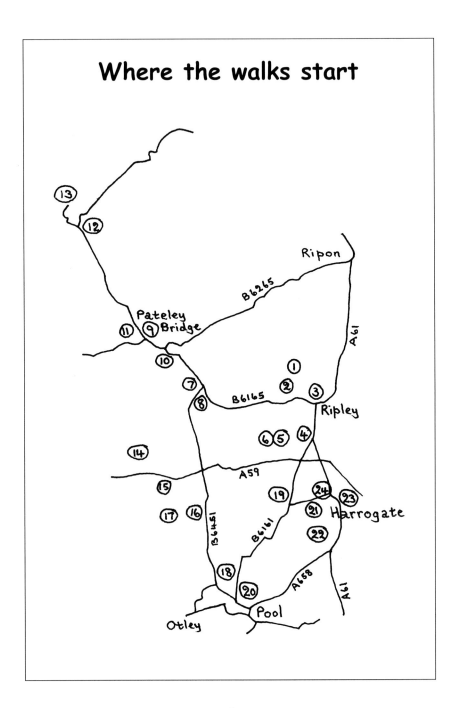

Introduction

This book describes twenty-four walks in the countryside to the west of Harrogate. Many of them are in the Nidderdale Area of Outstanding Natural Beauty. It is an upland countryside on the slopes of the Pennines, a landscape of pastures, heather moorland and steep-sided wooded valleys.

It is a splendid area to walk in. Even close to the built-up part of Harrogate, there is attractive countryside, and the walker will enjoy visiting the Pine Woods and Birk Crag and exploring the Upper Crimple valley, where it is hard to believe you are no more than two or three miles from the centre of town. A few miles further on is the beautiful valley of the River Washburn which runs down from the slopes of Greenhow Hill and Simon Seat to join the River Wharfe near Leathley. There is a rich network of paths throughout the valley, and the walker will not only appreciate the deservedly popular routes beside the reservoirs, but will follow many other enjoyable and less well-known paths that thread their way through the fields and woodland.

The dominant valley to the west of Harrogate is Nidderdale, the valley of the River Nidd which rises on Great Whernside (one of Yorkshire's highest hills), and winds eastwards down to the Vale of York. Nidderdale is explored by several of the walks in the book; the twists and turns of the valley provide different scenes, there are many riverside paths, and there are interesting and well-wooded tributary valleys. On the higher parts there are fine viewpoints from which on a clear day you can see across the Vale of York to the Yorkshire Wolds and to the fine escarpment that forms the western edge of the North York Moors.

Millstone grit is the main local stone, and it frequently comes to the surface, most spectacularly at Almscliff Crag near Huby, Guise Cliff near Pateley Bridge, and at the famous Brimham Rocks, where acres of exposed grit have been weathered into strange shapes. Millstone grit can also be seen in the older buildings of the area, and of course it is the building block of the dark stone walls that enclose the pastures. There is also some limestone - the River Nidd disappears into it a mile or two upstream from Lofthouse, and at nearby How Stean there is a fine limestone gorge.

The natural and apparently unspoiled beauty of the area cloaks the fact that it has a long industrial history. There was extensive lead-mining in the Ashfold Valley and on nearby Greenhow Hill, and there was also widespread quarrying. It may come as a surprise that coal was mined in several places (as it was over much of the Pennines). Linen manufacture was once an important industry in many parts of Nidderdale and the Washburn Valley. A fine monument to the former linen industry is the splendidly proportioned mill at Glasshouses. For those who, like me, enjoy small local museums, the museum at Pateley Bridge is one of the best, and a visit is highly recommended. It is particularly good on local industrial and farming history.

Walkers who appreciate wildlife will find it a rewarding area. Hares and roe deer will be chanced upon, and the rabbit is ubiquitous. On the upland pastures and moors, the cry of the curlew will delight the ear in spring and early summer. Gouthwaite Reservoir, a few miles up the valley from Pateley Bridge, is a noted place for a wide variety of birds.

The sketch maps accompanying the description of each walk are greatly simplified and are intended only as an overview of the route. They should not be relied on as an alternative to the route description, and it is strongly recommended that the appropriate Ordnance Survey maps be bought. All of the walks are to be found on Explorer 297 Lower Wharfedale & Washburn Valley, and Explorer 298 Nidderdale. These maps will not only help you to trace the walks described in this book, but will, it is hoped, suggest further walks for exploring the local countryside. The start of many of the walks can be reached by public transport, and the hourly Harrogate to Pateley Bridge bus service is particularly useful.

The walks average around six miles in length and are ideal for a half day's walk. In the summer, they can be done in trainers or a strong pair of shoes, but in the winter months soil turns to mud and boots are essential. Many people in any case will prefer to leave the walks till spring and summer, and there is a lot to be said for this. Whatever the time of year, bear in mind that some of the routes are on quite high ground, so it is advisable to carry an extra layer of clothing. Good waterproofs and a hat (to protect against the sun as well as the cold) are also recommended.

All the paths used in the walks are definitive rights of way or permissive routes, or footpaths to which the public has traditionally not been denied access. At the time of writing there were no obstructions, but a number of the stiles were in poor condition. At present there is a policy of replacing stiles by kissing-gates, and you may find that this has happened on some of the walks. If you encounter any obstructions (and this includes high crops across a path), nuisances, or other difficulties, please report them to the Rights of Way Officer, North Yorkshire County Council, County Hall, Northallerton, DL7 8AD.

This book has a companion volume, *Country Walks Around Harrogate, Volume 1 East,* in which a further twenty good walks close to Harrogate are described. Both books are overdue replacements of *Popular Walks Around Harrogate* (ed. J. Dickinson 1991, S. Barclay 1998) and its predecessor *Walks Around Harrogate* (ed. P. Goldsmith 1972, 1974) which are now out of print.

An immense amount of useful work is done by the Harrogate Group of the Ramblers' Association in protecting the local rights of way and in making them more accessible by waymarking them, by building stiles and footbridges, and by installing kissing gates. We hope that all who use this book will consider becoming members of the Association, further details of which can be found on the opposite page.

Keith Wadd
Chairman, Ramblers' Association West Riding Area, May 2008

The **Ramblers' Association**, a registered charity, is an organisation dedicated to the preservation and care of the countryside and its network of footpaths, and to helping people to appreciate and enjoy them.

Through its National Office the Ramblers' Association lobbies and campaigns for more effective legislation to achieve
- the preservation and improvement of the footpath network
- better access to the countryside
- the preservation and enhancement for the benefit of the public of the beauty of the countryside.

Since its formation in 1935 the Ramblers' Association has grown into a powerful campaigning organisation with a membership of more than 145,000.

The Association relies on many volunteers working at Area and Local Group level to help achieve these objectives.

The **West Riding Area** is one of the 51 Areas of the Ramblers' Association which cover England, Wales and Scotland. It includes the whole of West Yorkshire and parts of North Yorkshire around Selby, York, Harrogate, Ripon, Skipton and Settle, as well as the southern part of the Yorkshire Dales National Park. The Area has more than 4,500 members and is divided into 14 Local Groups.

The **Local Groups** carry out the work of the Ramblers' Association by keeping an eye on the state of footpaths in their area and monitoring proposed closures and diversions.
- They put pressure on their Local Authority to take action to remove obstructions and re-instate footpaths after ploughing.
- They do practical work of footpath clearance and waymarking, and can erect stiles and footbridges.
- Where the Local Authority has set up consultation procedures, e.g. Footpath and Access Forums, the Local Group will normally send a representative.
- Most Local Groups produce their own programme of walks.

Regular walks are a very important part of Ramblers' activities. As well as ensuring that local footpaths are used, they provide healthy recreation and the opportunity to make new friends. There are walks organised by the Harrogate Group every Saturday.

If you use and enjoy the footpath network, please help us to protect it, by joining the Ramblers' Association. For further information contact

The Ramblers' Association, 2nd Floor, Camelford House, 87-90 Albert Embankment, London SE1 7TW (Tel.: 020 7339 8500, Fax.: 020 7339 8501; e-mail: ramblers@ramblers.org.uk).

Or visit our websites: www.ramblers.org.uk   www.ramblersyorkshire.org.uk
www.willouby.demon.co.uk/ramblersassociation/harrogategroup.htm

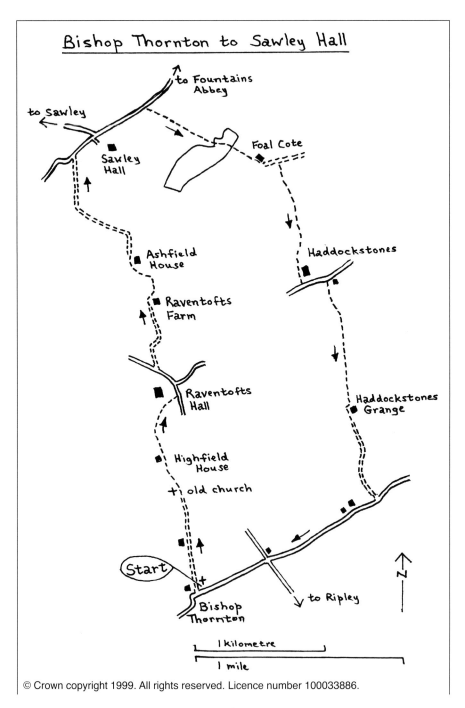

Bishop Thornton to Sawley Hall

to Fountains Abbey

to Sawley

Sawley Hall

Foal Cote

Ashfield House

Haddockstones

Raventofts Farm

Raventofts Hall

Haddockstones Grange

Highfield House

old church

N

Start

Bishop Thornton

to Ripley

1 kilometre

1 mile

1. BISHOP THORNTON to SAWLEY HALL

6¼ miles/10 km. Explorer 298 Nidderdale. Old tracks and field paths through attractive undulating pastoral countryside.

Parking in Bishop Thornton is difficult. People park on the kerb outside the parish church, and there is room for one or two cars in the lane beside the church, tucked well into the side. Buses from Harrogate are infrequent.

Take the lane beside the church. Ignore tracks to left and right and you will eventually be faced by two large gates: go through the right hand gate and continue by the wall on the left; go through another gate and keep on along the left hand edge of the next field. Pass through another gate to reach the old church and graveyard.

The church was built around 1460 by Sir John Walworth of Raventofts Hall, the Archbishop of York's forester, but by the 1880s it had become unsafe and the present parish church in the village was consecrated in 1889. The earliest gravestone here dates from 1690, and burials continued to be made until 1959. There's a fine view to the North York Moors.

Continue along the track along the left hand edge of the field. Go through another gate, cross straight over a cross track to continue along a good track. Pass to the right of Highfield House, but just before the bungalow turn sharp right for a yard or two, then sharp left with a fence on the right to a stile into a field. Cross straight over to a stile on the far side, which seems to be between two trees, but isn't, then continue with the hedge on the left. The next stile is by the corner of a high wall: cross and walk diagonally right across the field. Raventofts Hall is the house to the left. Go through a gateway and out onto a road. Turn left along it.

Ignore Watergate Road forking right, but take the next tarmac track forking right, signed to Raventofts Farm. *The large house in the far distance is the 18th century Sawley Hall.* Walk past the left hand side of Raventofts Farm and straight on to a gate which leads into a walled way. Bear left in front of two old stone gateposts, cross Hebden Beck by a substantial bridge, follow the path up to the left of Ashfield House, then continue along the farm access track. Reach the high wall enclosing Sawley Park and follow it to a road.

Turn right along the road. Ignore the entrance to Sawley Hall on the right and the road forking left to Sawley village. After you pass a large field on the right a bridleway sign points right through a gate. A track leads across the middle of the field, passing to the left of a copse. Having passed the copse, bear right towards a fence, then bear left and continue down the field parallel to the fence about 40 yards away on the right, to reach a large gate into Fish Pond Wood. The path bears left downhill, passes through a gateway in a broken down wall and drops to the bank of a large lake, a "Fish Pond" according to the map.

Bear left along the bank, cross the causeway and the bridge between two lakes, and back in the wood the path swings right, then approaching the top of the wood it swings left again, to reach a bridle gate at the top of the wood. Go through and bear slightly right to follow the fence on the right to Foal Cote Farm. Go through another bridle gate and walk straight through the farmyard. Follow the tarmac access road until just before a cattle-grid you go through a bridle gate on the right and follow the fence on the left down the field. At the bottom go through two bridle gates close together and continue along the left hand edge of the next field.

When you reach a marker post on the left, the bridleway actually bears slightly right over the middle of the field making for a bridle gate beside a large gate, but it may be easier to continue up the field edge, turning right in the field corner with the fence on the left, to go through the **second** bridle gate on the left (beside a large gate). Walk up the track to follow a fence on the left. Don't go through the gate into Haddockstones farmyard, but keep to the right of the fence/hedge/buildings/wall to a large gate out onto a road. Turn left along it.

Just before a left hand bend, with a bungalow ahead, take the track on the right, which leads to a gate, then continue with the wall on your right. When the wall turns right, keep straight forward to the corner of the wood and walk along with the wood on your left. At the end of the wood continue along the fence for a few yards, then go through a large gate in it and turn right along the track, now with the hedge on your right. Follow the track to Haddockstones Grange Farm. Immediately before the buildings take the track turning right, but in a few yards turn left again to pass through a gate and between two buildings. Continue forward along the track.

After a time the track drops between a wood on the right and a hedge on the left. At the bottom go through a gate, cross a beck and continue up the track, which leads to a road. Turn right along it. At the crossroads keep straight on to return to Bishop Thornton.

2. SHAW MILLS, GILL MOOR and WOODFIELD

5½ miles/9 km. Explorer 298 Nidderdale. A walk mainly on tracks through attractive undulating pastoral countryside and woodland. The return incorporates a section of the Nidderdale Way.

Shaw Mills developed as an industrial village in the early 19th century, but there was a corn mill there in the early 16th century, kept by a Robert Shaw, and there were Shaws who were millers there in 1672. John and George Metcalfe began spinning flax in 1812 at Low Mill, the old manorial corn mill of Bishop Thornton. Later silk yarn was produced.

There are infrequent buses from Harrogate to Shaw Mills. Cars can be parked on waste ground at the top of Town Street.

Near the top of Town Street turn up Grange Close. Between houses 4 and 6 on the right go up the enclosed footpath which leads up some steps into a field. Turn left and walk up the left hand edge of the field to a kissing-gate at the top onto Cut Throat Lane. Turn left past a large farm. After a bungalow the surface deteriorates, but there's a fine view. The track turns right and after a time left again. Pass a farm in the dip, cross a footbridge and continue straight up the other side, ignoring a track forking left. At the top go through a gate into a field and follow its right hand edge, to re-enter a walled track.

At the end walk straight across the next field to Hatton House Farm. Go through the gate and follow the track straight through the farm, after which the lane becomes tarmac. Soon it turns sharp right. A little way up ignore another lane forking left, and further up still the entrance on the left into a scrapyard, but at the next fork keep left, leaving the tarmac, and follow the track up to Gill Moor Farm *(in the 14th century a grange of the Archbishop of York)*. Walk straight through the yard and follow the farm access road to the next road junction.

Bear left along the road, but take the next farm access road on the left. Walk straight on at High Gill Moor Farm. The track goes through a gate and bends right – ignore a track forking back left here – and keep straight on to Low Farm. Immediately in front of the farmhouse ahead turn sharp left. Ignore tracks forking right and left and you will reach the start of a tarmac road. Turn left here through a double gate. Follow this track to Park House Farm. *(The Park in place names around here was Brimham Park – now known as Brimham Lodge -, a grange of Fountains Abbey, used by the abbot as a country residence and hunting lodge.)* Walk straight through the yard, passing to the left of the farmhouse, then bear right and then left into a fenced track.

When the fences end, keep forward to a gate, pass through, cross the beck and keep along the left hand edge of the wood. Go through the gate in the field corner, keep forward to the right of Woodfield Farm to another gate, then bear left to a fence corner with a footpath signpost. Here you join the Nidderdale Way, which is followed back to Shaw Mills. So turn left in the

Shaw Mills, Gill Moor and Woodfield

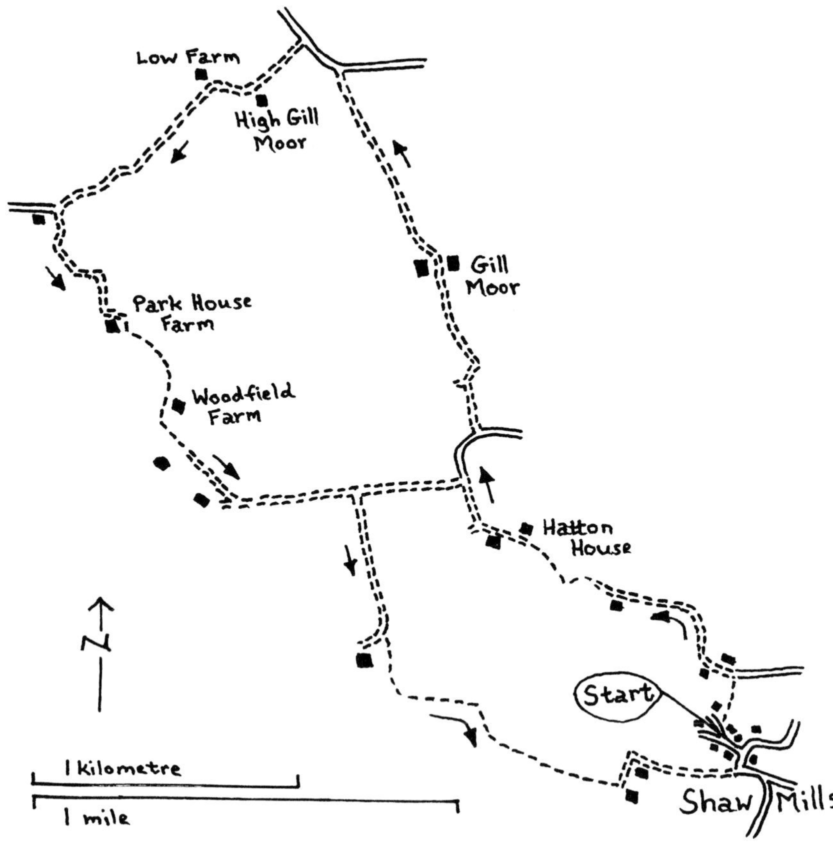

Low Farm

High Gill Moor

Gill Moor

Park House Farm

Woodfield Farm

Hatton House

N ↑

Start

1 kilometre

1 mile

Shaw Mills

direction of the signpost and cross the field to a gate. Cross the cattle-grid and keep forward along the track. Cross another cattle-grid and turn left at the junction on a track between fences.

You reach another track junction: keep left. Pass over another cattle-grid and join a tarmac surface. Follow the road until you pass through a gateway and reach a junction. Turn right down the tarmac access road to Beck House. When the road bends right to the house, fork left off it through a small metal gate and bear half right down the field, keeping well to the right of the telegraph pole, to two more small gates. Walk down to cross the footbridge over Thornton Beck and go through another small gate with a large footpath signpost beside it. Turn left with the Nidderdale Way to follow the wall on your left.

Go through the gate in the field corner (there is an old stone stile to the left of it) and bear slightly right over the next field, choosing paths which lead up to the top corner. There go through the large gate and follow the fence and wood on your right. Follow the fence along through several fields, until you reach a walled lane at a farm. Turn left down this past the farm, then follow its access road, which soon turns right and leads back to Shaw Mills. Turn left over the bridge for the village centre.

3.   RIPLEY and CAYTON GILL

5 miles/9 km. Explorer 298 Nidderdale. A walk through part of the Ripley Castle estate which then follows the Nidderdale Way to Low Kettle Spring before branching off to Bedlam and returning across the fields to the Park Wall.

No. 36 Harrogate-Ripon bus to Ripley. There is a large free car-park at the entrance to Ripley village off the A61 Harrogate-Ripon road.

Walk through the village, passing the cobbled square, stocks and Boar's Head on the left and the Hôtel de Ville on the right. Towards the end of the village fork left through a gateway with an old milestone on the right (Pateley Bridge 9½) along a stretch of disused road. At the main road to Pateley Bridge turn right for about 45 yards and go through a small metal gate on the left. Cross straight over the field, passing to the left of the end of a line of trees marking a former hedge, to reach a stile in a fence and continue in the same direction over the next field to a large notice by Newton Beck which points out that the next section of path is by permission of the Ripley Castle Estate.

Ripley market place

Cross the beck by the footbridge and turn left. Pass the corner of a wood, then follow the wood on your left, but when the wood bends left, keep straight on, slanting up the field to a stile in the top corner. Newton Hall is up to your right. Cross the stile and another in a few yards and keep forward along the tarmac access drive. Shortly after the road begins to descend, take the track forking left off it through a gate and drop to cross Newton Beck again. Follow the track up the other side, and at the top of the hill turn right along a track with a hedge on the left. Here you join the Nidderdale Way.

Pass through a gate at the corner of a wood and continue along the track with the wood on your right. The track reaches a fork: the left branch passes

14

through a gate, but you keep right, down to a couple of seats with a fine view to the Kilburn White Horse and the North York Moors. Now continue downhill on the track. At the foot go through the gate into the field and follow the track as it first bends left along the field edge, then just before the field corner turns right, crosses a beck and passes through a gate and follows the left hand edge of the next field up towards Cayton Gill Farm.

Old milestone at Ripley

Much new tree planting has taken place around here. Pass through the gateway out of the field and bear half left with a fence at first on the right and soon on both sides. The fenced path ends at a gateway: go through and walk straight downhill to a gate. Keep forward across the dip, then bear half left across a large field. The clear path soon leads along the bottom of a bank and eventually reaches a wood. Ignore the gate on the right and turn left parallel to the wood on your right. At the end of the field go through the kissing-gate on the right, turn left to cross the beck by a ford (there are stepping stones of sorts), walk forward to join a track and follow it uphill.

Near the top of the hill pass through a gate and follow the track to the B6165. Turn left, soon dropping down Scarah Bank, then take the farm access road on the right to Low Kettle Spring Farm. On approaching the farm a track forks right up to some buildings and opposite this there is a large gate on the left: go through (here leaving the Nidderdale Way) and bear half right down the middle of the field, but when you approach some trees on the left, bear left

Ripley Castle

15

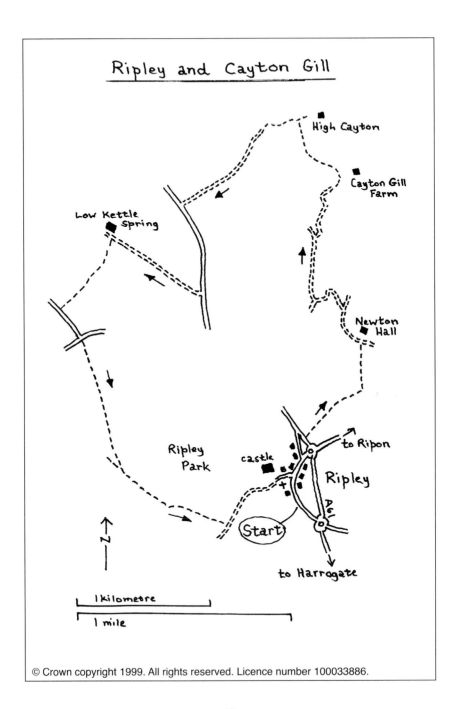

Ripley and Cayton Gill

down to them to find a footbridge concealed in them. Cross and turn right, and walk across the field to a gate on the far side.

Go through and walk uphill with a fence on your right. At the top cross the stile by the gate and bear slightly right up the next field to another gate with a stile beside it, and now follow the wall on the left up to a sort of stile to the left of a gate which gives access to a road. Turn left along it back to the B6165. Cross diagonally left and go through the small gate on the left of the large entrance gates to a house. Walk straight along by the wall on the left to cross the stile by the gate, then continue by the wall/hedge on the left through this field and the next one. Cross the fence in the next corner (no stile or gate) and walk straight across the next field, roughly parallel to the hedge on the left.

The field narrows, there is a small wood on the right, and you pass through a gate at the end. Now follow the fence on your right. It kinks right and left on the way up. At the top cross over left to pass through a kissing-gate beside the Ripley Park wall, which has been coming up from the left. Follow the wall as it soon bends left, and go through another kissing-gate in the next field corner. High Rails Farm is to your right. Now follow the Park Wall all the way back to Ripley. *A short way along notice a plaque on the wall about the "Monks' Cross", dating back to the time of Fountains Abbey, which can be seen a short distance into the wood.*

Rambling around Ripon

The Ripon Group of the Ramblers' Association has published Rambles around Ripon*, a collection of 15 local walks ranging in length from 1½ to 9 miles, and a guide to the* Ripon Rowel Walk*, a 50-mile circular walk starting in Ripon and extending as far north as Masham and as far south as South Stainley, with 12 small circular walks en route.*

A leaflet is available from the Ripon TIC describing the Sanctuary Way Walk*, a 10-mile walk (with shorter possibilities). In 937 King Athelstan granted the right of Sanctuary as part of the Liberty of St. Wilfrid. The Sanctuary Boundary of the settlement in those days, within which anyone could be granted sanctuary overnight, was marked by eight Sanctuary markers. In 2005 local Rotary Clubs created and installed replica Sanctuary markers close to the original sites, and this walk links them. Interpretation boards have been set up along the route.*

4. KILLINGHALL AND HAMPSTHWAITE

5 miles/8 km. Explorer 297 Lower Wharfedale. This is a pleasant walk in the Nidd valley just to the north of Harrogate. The route is mainly on pasture land, and there is also some riverside walking. The views are not extensive, but always enjoyable. The village of Hampsthwaite has several features of interest.

The walk starts at Killinghall church on Otley Road, Killinghall (GR 284 583). Park on Crag Lane (off Otley Road beside the school) where there is an extensive verge. The No. 24 bus from Harrogate to Pateley Bridge (Mon-Sat hourly, Sun infrequent) stops outside Killinghall Church. Alternatively take the No. 36 Harrogate-Ripon bus (every 20 minutes), get off at the stop at the entrance to the village, walk forward for a short distance, cross the main road and pick up the walk at Crofters Green [*] below.

From the end of Crag Lane cross the main road by the school, turn left and walk along towards the village. If you don't have a dog with you, go through the metal gate **before** the church and follow the tarmac path through The Glebe, which has benches and a children's playground; pass through the gate at the far end and turn right along the track to the main road. Otherwise go along the broad footpath on the village side of Killinghall church, and this soon leads on to the main A61. Turn right for 100 yards, crossing at the island, and then turn left along Crofters Green [*].

Go through the gateway of Nidd House Farm, then in 20 yards go over a stile on the right and into a field. Keep by the hedge on the left, shortly crossing a stile, and at the end of the field go through a kissing gate, cross a track and continue by the hedge on the right. Go over a fence (or go through the large gate beside it) and continue by the hedge on the right to another kissing gate. Cross a track and continue straight ahead on the access road to Spruisty House. There are views of Bilton and Harrogate across to the right.

Turn left through a footpath gate immediately before the farm, and follow a high stone wall, then keep in the same direction across the field to a stile. Turn right when a lane is reached. Immediately before the farm (Spruisty Hall Farm), turn left through a footpath gate and follow the field edge round to the right, then go through a gate into the farmyard. Keep straight on between the farm buildings, then go through a green farm gate into a field. There are good views to the right towards the Nidd Gorge. Bear half right over the field towards Spruisty Grange Farm. Cross the stile to the left of the large wooden shed, bear left between the farm buildings then bend right to pass through a large gate.

Immediately go through a kissing gate on the left, then follow the left hand edge of the field. At the end of the field turn right along the track for 40 yards, then turn left over a footbridge and through a kissing-gate. Follow the hedge on the left, and cross a high stile into a paddock beside a red-roofed house. Cross another high stile out of the paddock, and keep in the same direction across a narrow field, cross a stile then veer right across the next field to a kissing-gate and a junction of tracks at the far corner. Take the track that goes straight ahead, and when it turns sharp right go straight ahead through a gateway into a large field and follow the high hedge on the left. Go over a stile in the bottom corner, and cross straight over a narrow field to a stile and a tarmac path.

Turn right along the path. When it becomes a tarmac road (the old A61) fork left at a footpath sign down a track and under the new and charmless A61 bridge across the River Nidd (the old bridge is to the right). Go through a kissing-gate and walk along the right hand edge of the field. Go through another kissing-gate and keep forward along the edge of the next large field, at the end of which the path turns left away from the river and climbs up the hillside beside a hedge. Turn right along the lane at the top (view across the valley to Ripley) and continue on it into the hamlet of Crag Hill. Go through the gate at the far end of Crag Hill, and continue along the tarmac road. *Soon there are good views up Nidderdale, and Hampsthwaite and Clint also come into view.*

Follow the lane until a track forks off on the right. Turn right into it, but immediately strike left down the field towards a hedge corner, and keep by the high hedge/fence on the right. When the fence turns sharp right, keep forward towards a gateway in the wall ahead, but don't go through: turn right to follow the wall on your left down towards the Nidd. Turn left over a stile and follow the right hand edge of the field. Continue through the next field, and when you reach a ditch marking an old field boundary, cross the stile on the right and follow the path through a belt of woodland. Cross the footbridge over the Cockhill Beck and turn left along a broad path with the beck on the left, and an extensive field on the right.

Follow this path until you reach a white footbridge on the left. The walk continues over it, but first keep along the path into the centre of Hampsthwaite, which you reach with the primary school on the left and a small ruined stone building (a former cobbler's) on the right. Cross the road to the village green.

Hampsthwaite's small village green is an attractive place. It has a beautifully presented information board pointing out places of interest in the village. Encircling the nearby tree is a convenient seat.

Now retrace your steps to the white footbridge. Cross it and bear left to follow the left hand edge of the field. You reach two gateways on the left close together: go through the second of these and keep on along the left hand edge of the next field. At the end of it go through the gateway just beyond the trough and walk forward a short distance to a stile. Cross and walk up the right hand edge of the next field. At the top of the field go through the gate and now leave the track by walking straight forward towards a wall corner. Past it bear left and head towards a large metal gate.

Go over the stile beside the gate and walk past the front of the house (Myers Green), then cross a narrow lane diagonally right to a stile Keep by the hedge/fence on the left to a stile in it, cross and turn right, now with the hedge on the right. Follow it through this field and the next one, but before you reach the end of the one after that go over a stile by a gate on the right, and walk straight across the field towards a redbrick house. Cross the stile by the gate and turn right along Crag Lane which soon leads to Otley Road by the school and close to the church. (Those who came by the No. 36 bus will now jump to the start of the walk description to return to the A61.)

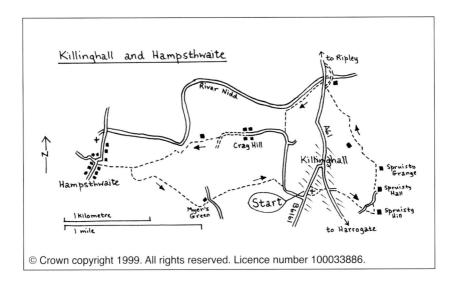

5.   From HAMPSTHWAITE by TANG BECK to KETTLESING BOTTOM

5¼ miles/8¾ km. Explorer 297 Lower Wharfedale. By field paths and quiet country roads in the undulating pastoral countryside west of Harrogate.

Park by the village green in Hampsthwaite. Alternatively drive along the Birstwith road and park in a large layby just before the narrow bridge. No. 24 Harrogate-Pateley Bridge bus to Hampsthwaite (Mon.-Sat. hourly, Sun. infrequent).

Fork left at the village green at the bottom of Main Street and walk along the road towards Birstwith. Cross the narrow road bridge and immediately cross the stile on the left, to bear half right over the field towards a hedge corner. The path now crosses three fields parallel to Tang Beck on the left. At the end of the third field go through the large gate on the left of the barn, with Hirst Grove Farm up to the right, continue parallel to the beck to pass to the right of a pumping station and cross a stile by the gate out onto a road.

Cross to the stile opposite and continue still parallel to the beck up the next field, climbing gently, to pass through a gated stile halfway up the wall at the end of the field. Continue the same line, bearing very slightly right up the next field, to a kissing-gate, then follow the hedge on the right along to a gate in the next corner. Keep straight on, through another gate – Birstwith Hall is to the left – and along the tarmac access drive. Pass a house on the right, keep left at the fork, and bear left along the road.

A short way along pass a road forking left to Hampsthwaite, then a partly thatched house on the right dating from 1754. At the next road junction keep straight on, but at the next one fork left into White Wall Lane. You are now in Tang. Cross Tang Beck. The road bends left. Pass Beck House, then just

The thatched house

before you reach the next houses on the left cross a stile on the right and follow the wall on the left to a stile in the next corner. Cross and turn sharp left, and in the next corner cross the stile ahead and continue with the wall on your left, but at the top of the field turn right with the field edge.

In the next corner cross the gated stile and keep on by the wall on the left to the next gated stile. Continue by the wall on the left the short distance to the next stile, then turn right, now with the wall on your right, in a short distance crossing an old stone step-stile. Follow the wall on the right to another stile,

21

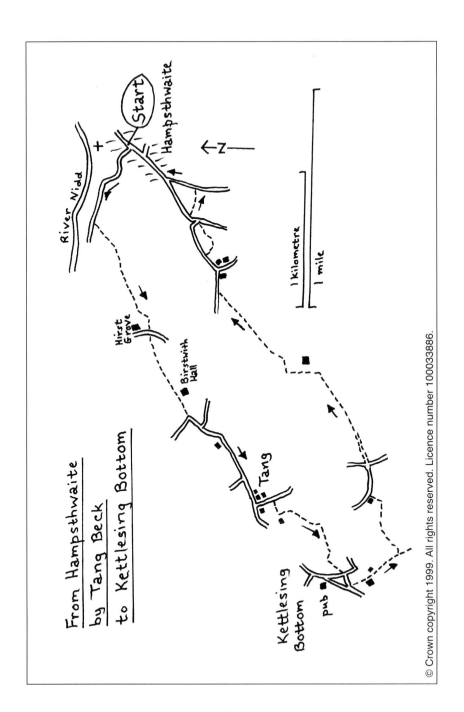

From Hampsthwaite
by Tang Beck
to Kettlesing Bottom

Start

Hampsthwaite

River Nidd

←N—

1 kilometre
1 mile

Hirst Grove

Birstwith Hall

Tang

Kettlesing Bottom

pub

22

then continue to a metal bridle-gate in the next corner. Go through and bear half right to a step-stile by some holly bushes, cross and follow the wall on the right. Pass through a gated stile and continue by the hedge on the right to another stile and the road in Kettlesing Bottom. *(Down the road to the right is the Queen's Head Inn.)*

Cross the road diagonally left to take the road signposted to Otley. A few yards before the next junction, and indeed before an access road on the left, cross the step-stile in the wall on the left and walk up the field to the corner of a garden wall. Keep on up with this wall on your right to the next stile in the top corner. Cross a tarmac drive and keep forward up another one ahead. Pass a house on the left and immediately bear left to a stile into a field. Walk up the field with the hedge on your left. Cross a stile on the left in the top corner and immediately turn right over another stile and walk up the right hand edge of the next field.

About 60 yards up you will come to the remains of a step-stile in the wall on the right. Turn sharp left here and walk across the middle of the field to a double stile on the far side. Cross it, and looking over the field to the far side you will see two trees close together; to the left of them there is a length of fence in the hedge, and in this fence there is a stile. Cross, and walk straight forward over the next field. On the far side cross a track and go through the wide gated gap, to continue forward with the hedge on the right. Cross a stile and bear slightly left to a small gate, go through, then diagonally left down the next field to a large gate leading into a drive which leads down between houses to a road.

Turn right along the road. When you reach a T-junction, ignore both roads and keep straight on along a walled path. This ends at a bridle gate into a field. Follow the hedge on your right, but when you reach a wooden gate straight ahead, where the line of the hedge is broken, go through, and now the hedge/fence is on your left. Go through the gateway in the next corner and continue by the hedge on the left. When the hedge is replaced by a wall, kink left through gates and continue in the same direction, now with the wall on the right. Walk down to the bottom corner of the field, go through the small gate and continue along the right hand edge of the next field.

Go through the gate in the fence at the end and turn left, to follow the fence on your left down. Go through the gate at the bottom of the field, immediately through another gate on the right, then turn left to walk down the field with the fence on the left to a stile by a large tree. Cross and turn sharp right to follow the fence on the right, but in the next corner don't go through the gate, but turn left and walk down the right hand edge of the field. Towards the bottom bear right alongside a wall, go through a gate and walk up the right hand edge of the next field. Go through the gate in the top corner and continue by the hedge/fence on the left.

There is a pleasant view to the left. You will come into a yard or two of walled lane with a stile at the end. Cross and now the hedge is on your right. The hedge reaches a gate and shortly afterwards is replaced by a wall. Here bear slightly left over the field to the far left hand corner. Go through the gate onto a road and turn right. When the road forks, keep left – *there is a fine view to Hampsthwaite Church and over Nidderdale.* At the foot of the slope a footpath sign points right over a stile. Walk down the field to a gated stile on the left in the bottom left hand corner.

Cross and follow the left hand edge of the next field. Keep forward to pass to the left of a house, cross another stile, keep straight forward over the lawn to another stile, then keep on to a gate and back out onto the road. Turn right to the junction, then left. Just after a red-brick house on the right cross a stile in the wall on the right and walk straight down the field, heading for a gap in the hedge at the bottom. Go through the gate and turn left along the beck, but the clear path soon bears right up to a stile in the hedge. Turn left down the broad verge by the road. At the road junction at the bottom turn right to return to the start.

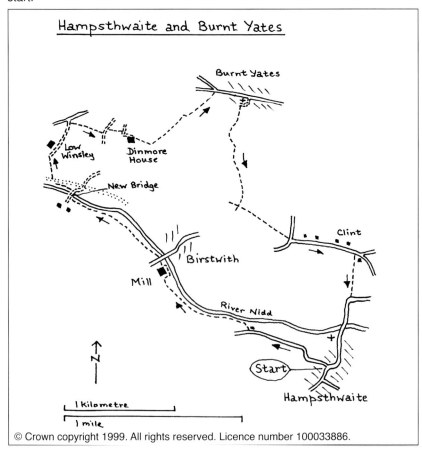

Hampsthwaite and Burnt Yates

Burnt Yates

Low Winsley

Dinmore House

New Bridge

Clint

Birstwith

Mill

River Nidd

Start

Hampsthwaite

N

1 Kilometre

1 mile

24

6.   HAMPSTHWAITE and BURNT YATES

5½ miles/9 km. Explorer 298 Nidderdale. Field and riverside paths through typical Lower Nidderdale countryside. Park by the village green in Hampsthwaite. No. 24 Harrogate-Pateley Bridge bus to Hampsthwaite (Mon.-Sat. hourly, Sun. infrequent).

Fork left at the village green at the bottom of Main Street and walk along the road towards Birstwith for just over half a mile to Fell Buildings, a stone barn on the right of the road some way past the narrow stone bridge. Pass through the gate (Nidderdale Way sign) and walk down the field, turning left along the bottom of the field with the River Nidd over the fence on the right. Shortly you go through a kissing-gate in this fence to follow the path along above the river. Several more kissing-gates keep you on the riverside path, until you enter a field and leave the river with a wall and a wood to your right.

On approaching the mill, go through a kissing-gate on the right (not the one straight ahead) leading into a fenced path. When the fence on the right ends, keep forward by the fence on the left. Turn sharp left along the river bank, passing the mill on your left. The path bends left away from the river and you cross a metal footbridge over the mill goit. Turn right, cross over the road and continue along the path parallel to the river although not always close beside it to a picturesque packhorse bridge (New Bridge).

New Bridge

Cross the bridge and turn left along the riverside path (here leaving the Nidderdale Way). Go through a gate and continue by the river until, just before a cross fence, you reach a stile in the fence on the right which leads across the disused railway to a gate at the other side. Cross the field to the wicket gate and make your way up through the pretty little wood to Low Winsley Farm. Join the drive leading up to the main Pateley Bridge road.

At the top of the drive, just before it reaches the road, turn sharp right into the wood along a broad track between walls. Cross the stile at the end of the wood and continue with the wall on your left to a stile at the other end of the field. Turn left and walk along the green lane for a short distance to a stile on the right by the end of a wall. Now follow the wall on your right until it turns away towards the bottom of the field, and then strike out straight across the middle of the field to the field gate ahead.

Turn right into the drive of Dinmore House, which passes between the buildings before ending in a gravelled courtyard. Bear slightly left across the gravel and pass through a gate into a small paddock at the rear of Stable Cottage. Walk straight through the paddock and leave it by a ladder-stile onto a green track. Cross the stile by the gate at the end of this and turn half left uphill towards a stone barn. Bear right before the barn to go through a gate. Turn left and follow the wall on your left through three fields to a gap-stile onto the B6165. Turn right along the footway into Burnt Yates.

Just past St. Andrew's church turn right along a rough lane. It bears right and at the end there is a stone stile on the left. Cross the stile and follow the track by the wall/hedge/fence through two fields. On entering the third field the track turns right, but you keep straight on down the left hand edge of the field, ignoring a gate on the left and passing a wood, to a gate in the bottom corner of the field. Continue down with the fence on your left to cross a stile. Here there are stiles both to right and left – cross the one on the left and follow the fence on your left. The fence joins a wall: follow this along to the gate ahead. Go through and walk across the field, passing to the right of the ruin of Clint Hall, to a gate leading onto a road at a junction.

Walk forward along Clint Bank Lane. Pass Clint Corpse-Cross and stocks on the left and continue down to the road fork. Here cross a stile on the right and walk down the field parallel to the wall on the left. At the bottom go through the gate out onto the road and keep forward along the road back to Hampsthwaite.

Clint Corpse-Cross and stocks

26

7. DACRE BANKS

4½ miles/7 km. Explorer 298 Nidderdale. A pleasant stroll, surprisingly tranquil and remote, giving a real sense of adventure; sometimes care is needed with route-finding, but large white painted arrows and waymarks are helpful. The car-park in Dacre Banks is on Oak Lane opposite the Royal Oak, and the No. 24 Harrogate-Pateley Bridge bus (Mon-Sat hourly, Sun less frequently) passes through the village. The walk starts at the telephone kiosk by the village green.

Cross the main road and turn right, passing the medical centre and public toilets. Take the first street on the left, Grange Road. Where this bends left, fork right off it up a ginnel, then keep straight forward up the tarmac lane. Walk straight through the farmyard, but when you reach a concrete track between walls, look up left to see a small gate into a field. Go through this gate and turn right, to walk up the right hand edge of the field. Pass through a gate and then a kissing-gate and walk forward a few yards to a cross track where you turn right across a bridge.

The track bends left and forks: keep right, i.e. straight on. The track bends right again in front of a bungalow and follows a wall on the left to a gate. Go through and bear left down the track towards a wood. Ford the beck and continue up the track, but thirty yards before you reach a gate fork left on another track up through the wood, roughly parallel to the beck on your left. When the track ends the path forks: keep right, i.e. straight on, and follow the path up to a step-stile at the top of the wood. Cross and bear half left up the field, passing well to the left of a tall, solitary tree. Eastwoods Farm is to your right. You are heading for a gate in what looks like the top left hand corner of the field. In fact the gate is on the other side of the access track to the farm.

Go through the gate and follow the wall on your right up the next field, ignoring a gateway in it. Reach another gate. Climb it, then walk straight over the next field to a step-stile on the far side. Turn right along the concrete access road to Northwoods Farm. At the farm do not follow the concrete track left into the yard but keep forward through a gate and along a gravel track, which soon becomes grass, with a wall to your right. Pass round another gate, cross a stile to the left of the left hand of two gates ahead and a little further on again go through the left hand of two gates which face you and keep the wall on your right until you pass through another gateway into a wood.

Follow the track straight through the wood, over the rise and through a gate, then continue by the wall on the left to a gap-stile in the next corner. Turn left to follow the wall on your left, but instead of going through the gateway in the corner turn right and follow the wall on your left downhill. Now comes the point where route-finding becomes trickier, but the white arrows and waymarks are very helpful! In front of the first holly bush you come to cross through the wall on the left and bear right down the next field, at the bottom crossing the wall in front where that wall meets a fence. Now follow the fence on your right, pass to the right of a large stone with a white waymark and drop to cross a beck.

Across the beck there is a wall, and in this wall tucked in behind another holly bush there is an old stile. Cross the stile and walk straight over the field to the next stile on the far side a few yards to the right of another holly bush, then bear slightly left across the next field to a large old stone step-stile (again by a holly bush) in the wall near the left hand end of the wood. Cross and bear half-right across the bottom of the next field to a gate, and through this walk straight forward over the next large field towards a wood in the distance. When you reach a wall, a few yards to the left of a gate in it there is a step-stile. Now your route-finding problems are over!

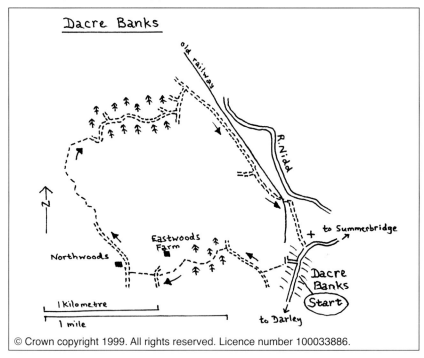

© Crown copyright 1999. All rights reserved. Licence number 100033886.

Before you cross the stile bear left along the wall to the field corner for a fine view up Nidderdale to Gouthwaite Reservoir. Over the stile walk down the sunken track with the wall to your right. Go through the gate in the very bottom corner and continue on the clear track downhill. Pass through another gate into woodland and keep on the track. At the end of a fence on the right ignore a minor track forking right, and a short distance further on after the track levels out and bears right ignore too a good track forking sharp left. When after a considerable distance you meet a T-junction by a corrugated iron hut go left, and ignoring a minor track forking left, leave the wood through

28

a gate. Keep forward the short distance to another T-junction and turn right through a gate.

You shortly have a fence to your left. The houses of Low Laithe are across the valley. Soon there is a beck to your left and the fence becomes a hedge. Pass through the gate at the corner of the wood and keep forward along the track. Pass to the right of a bungalow and some other buildings and continue along the good track, parallel to the line of the former railway to your left. Just before the track crosses a beck it is joined by another one from the right (from Harewell House), and after a time you cross a cattle-grid and the line of the old railway. Follow the track back to Dacre Banks. When you reach a T-junction in the village turn left to the main road, then right to return to the start.

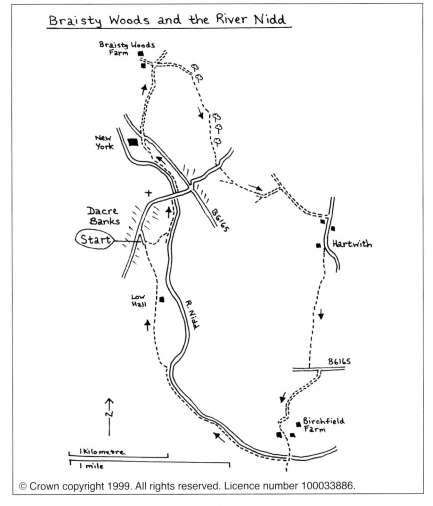

Braisty Woods and the River Nidd

8.   BRAISTY WOODS AND THE RIVER NIDD

6½ miles/10¼ km. Explorer 298 Nidderdale. Old tracks through glorious woods, fine views of Nidderdale and a beautiful stretch of riverside path.

The walk starts at the Royal Oak in Dacre Banks. The car-park in Dacre Banks is on Oak Lane opposite the Royal Oak, and the No. 24 Harrogate-Pateley Bridge bus (Mon-Sat hourly, Sun less frequently) passes through the village.

Walk along the track past the pub, away from the village centre, but after 30 yards turn left to pass between houses to a field. Bear right with the track, but when faced by a gate ("Private. No Entry") turn left, go through another large gate and walk down the right hand edge of the field to another large gate. Go through and bear slightly left over the next field to a stile in the fence which gives access to a path by the River Nidd (here you join, but very briefly, the Nidderdale Way).

Turn left. Pass the tennis courts and the bowling green and climb the steps to the road. Turn right over the bridge (here leaving the Nidderdale Way), then immediately cross the road and go down Riverside Lane. Follow the track until you reach a small car-park and a tarmac lane. Turn left (the tarmac soon ends) and follow the riverside path. After a time the path bears right away from the river. Ignore a track forking right uphill, keep with the clear footpath – *New York Mill is ahead* – the path becomes tarmac and leads to a T-junction. Turn right and walk up past the fire station to the main road.

Linens had replaced woollen cloth as the main product in Nidderdale in the 17th-century. It was in the late 18th-century, with the development of the power-driven spinning frame, that large scale production began. New York Mill was opened by Francis Thorpe in 1825 to spin yarn for linen cloth and sewing thread. It employed about 150 mill-workers and about 50 flax-dressers, bleachers and dyers. It was the first building in Nidderdale to be lit by electric light (1891). By the late 19th-century the production of linen had become uneconomic, and New York was producing rope and twine. In 1965 it changed to spinning artificial fibres for carpet and upholstery yarns.

Turn left along the footway for 45 yards, then cross the road into the bridleway opposite. When the surfacing ends at a house, keep forward on the stony track uphill. *As you climb higher, there is a fine view up Nidderdale and to Guise Cliff.* At Braisty Woods Farm you reach a T-junction: turn right for a few yards, then keep right at the fork. After a time you pass between houses and bear right along the track along the edge of Braisty Woods. Pass to the right of Woolwich Farm, through a large gate, along beside a pond, through another gate, then bear left round the large barn. Follow the track, ignoring a waymarked gate into the woods, and when you are faced by two gates side by side, go through the left hand one.

The path follows the bottom edge of the woods. Cross a stile in a wall, and the path is now deeper in the woods. You pass a panel giving you information about Old Spring Wood. When faced by a large gate into a garden, bear right – there is a large pond down on the right – to join an access track leading to the Summerbridge to Brimham Rocks road. Turning right down it would be a quick way back to Dacre Banks, but our walk turns left up the road for 50 yards then forks right on a track through a gate. The path follows the wall and the wood on the left. At the end of the field pass through a gap in the wall and keep forward to a bridle gate; just before this you are joined by a bridleway coming up from the right from Summerbridge.

Go through and climb to another gate, then continue by the wall on the left. The remains of causeying indicate that this was an old packhorse route. After a time you enter a walled lane, shortly passing an old watering trough on the left. The path climbs to reach a gate and a cross track. Turn right (signposted Hartwith) and follow this walled lane to the next road. *(There is a very extensive view ahead.)* Turn right along the road. When the road bends left at the Old Vicarage, Hartwith, go through the gate straight ahead and follow the hedge on your right. When the hedge turns right, keep straight down the field to a bridle gate in the wall at the bottom.

Go through and bear slightly right over the next field to the right hand edge, then follow the wall on your right along. *At the top of the hill if you look left you will see Harrogate*. Over the brow of the hill bear slightly left to a large gate to the right of farm buildings. Go through and follow the track forward through the yard, then continue down the farm access road. *Nidderdale opens up ahead.* When you reach the next road, turn left along it for 90 yards, then cross it to a bridleway sign. The path should go through the large gate, but you can pass round it, then walk straight down the field to join a farm access road and turn right down it (if the field is under a crop, you may prefer to continue along the road for a short way further, then turn down the farm access road on the right).

Follow the track down to a wood, where it forks: keep right (signposted White Oak) and follow the track down through the wood. Immediately after you emerge from the wood, go through a bridle gate on the left and bear half right across the paddock, aiming for a fence corner. Round the corner follow the fence on your right to another bridle gate, walk forward to yet another one and follow the wall on your left round to yet another one. Walk forward, then follow the hedge on your right. After a time the path bears right out of the field and drops towards the river; before it does, fork right and follow the wall on the right to a footbridge.

Cross the Nidd and turn right through a kissing gate along the riverbank, here re-joining the Nidderdale Way. The path crosses a stile, goes through a small gate, crosses a bridge over a side beck, passes some houses and crosses a double stile into a field (with a footpath coming down from the left between them). The embankment of the former railway is over to the left. Cross a footbridge over the quite wide Darley Beck and a stile. At the end of this field cross the stile straight ahead, ignoring the clearer path bearing left up to a gateway, onto a narrower riverside path which passes old stepping stones. Cross a stile. Some way along this field cross a stile in the fence, here leaving the river and the Nidderdale Way) and bear right up to a stile visible in the next wall, from which there is a fine view up Nidderdale to Summerbridge.

Cross the stile and turn left for a few yards to join a track coming through the gate on your left, along which you turn right. This is the trackbed of the former railway. Soon you are walking through woodland. Emerging from the wood you pass through the yard of Low Hall and continue along the old railway. *Look back for a view of the fine old hall, built in 1635.* Pass through a kissing gate, then another small kissing gate beside a large gate, and soon, when the old railway bends slightly left and becomes overgrown, keep to the right of the remains of the hedge to a fence corner, then bear half right down the field to a gap-stile in the next wall. Aim for a tall, three-storey building in the distance (this is the Royal Oak). Cross the stile and keep forward along the path, soon joining a track which leads back to the start of the walk.

Stepping stones over the Nidd

9.   PATELEY BRIDGE TO BRIMHAM ROCKS

8½ miles/13½ km (6¼ miles/10 km if you omit Brimham Rocks). Explorer 298 Nidderdale. Probably the finest walk in the book, a long stretch of riverside path, a beckside path through woodland, a gentle climb up to the rocks and a high level return route with excellent views. Park in one of the car-parks in Pateley Bridge. No. 24 Harrogate-Pateley Bridge bus (Mon-Sat hourly, Sun less frequently). Motorists may prefer to start the walk in the National Trust car park at Brimham Rocks, which means that the cafés and pubs of Pateley Bridge are available halfway round (start the walk description at [*] below).

Immediately before you cross Nidd Bridge from the town side, turn left along a public footpath. Follow this riverside path for a considerable distance. It widens to a track and you pass a weir, with a mill goit on the left which provided water to Glasshouses Mill. A little later you pass the large mill reservoir. At the road in Glasshouses turn left, but in a few yards go through a doorway in the wall on the right. Bear left, then right, to pass in front of the mill. At the far side, just past the smoke house, turn right down a track which soon bends left and you are back by the river.

The riverside path is clear. At one point you need to climb the bank to a stile in the wall at the top. Soon after that you need to cut across the corner of a field. Later you pass under the arch of a former railway bridge, immediately after which you climb the bank to follow a fence on the left along then drop to cross a beck by stepping stones. Further along ignore a footbridge over the river and keep forward by the river. When you are faced by a wide beck, the path leads you away from the river to cross this beck by a footbridge. Turn left, cross a stile into a field and walk straight up to reach the main road.

Cross to the lane opposite. When the tarmac surface ends, keep forward along the track and follow it to the next road. Turn left over the bridge, but a short way up the hill fork right on a footpath signposted to Pateley Bridge. You pass an attractive mill pond below you on the right, after which the beck is below you in a deep ravine. The route of the path is never in doubt as it follows the beck for quite a way, then crosses it by a footbridge. Bear right up the very stony track, but 30 yards before you reach a derelict brick building turn sharp left along a path through the birch wood, soon forking right along a narrower path.

Follow the clear path until you reach a fork. Here you can shorten the walk by omitting Brimham Rocks, by taking the left fork along a fenced path to a stile back into the woods, following the path to a footbridge, crossing it and jumping to [+] below.

The main walk keeps right at the fork. Go through a gate into the yard of a house, walk through the yard keeping to the right of the house and continue up the access track. Follow the track for a considerable distance, passing a

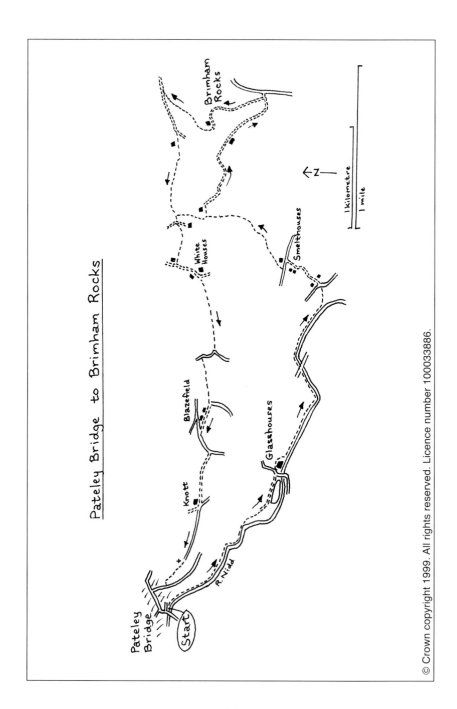

Pateley Bridge to Brimham Rocks

34

farm (ignoring a track forking right here), until you reach a junction with the National Trust Brimham Rocks access road. Turn left up it to the car-park.

[*]   Pass through the car-park and continue up the main access track, passing round the barrier. Follow it to the former shooting lodge, now the National Trust information centre and shop. When the tarmac track bends right up to the house, keep forward along an unsurfaced track, which in a few yards narrows to a footpath. Follow this path, ignoring minor paths to right and left, and passing a fine viewpoint on the top of some rocks, until, facing a sea of heather, you reach a junction of paths. Keep forward, bearing to the left, down a shallow valley, after which the path bears slightly left and keeps descending. Soon you have an old wall on your left. At what looks like the far end of this wall take a footpath forking left and dropping to a surfaced track a short distance below.

Brimham Rocks

Turn left along the track. It bears right towards a house. At the houses bear left along a track, but when it bends sharply right back to the houses, fork left off it on a clear path across the field to a ladder-stile. Cross and walk straight down the next field, bearing left at the bottom down to a stile. Cross and walk down the next field parallel to the fence on the right. Cross a stile by a gate and follow the track down, through another gate and down the next field. At the bottom cross a ladder-stile and the footbridge over the beck [+] and bear right up the track. At the junction take the track half left, which in a few yards crosses a cattle grid.

When the wall on the right turns right, fork half right off the track across the field to a gap in the wall ahead. Go through and turn right, to follow the wall on the right up to a gap-stile. Walk up the next field keeping close to the wall on the left. Cross a stile by a gate and walk up the edge of the next field to the houses at the top. Pass to the left of the houses along a walled path and turn left along the cross path at the top. After a time it widens to a track, which leads up to pass to the left of a house. At the junction cross straight over and take the right hand fork, which in a few yards leads to a gate. Go through and follow the wall on the left with gorse bushes on the right.

Go through a gateway and continue down the track by a fence on the right to join a farm access track. Keep forward along it. There's a fine view over Nidderdale to Guise Cliff. At the road turn right uphill. About 100 yards before you reach a junction with a major road a Nidderdale Way sign points left. Jump the beck and soon you are walking between walls. At the next road keep forward. About 30 yards after passing the entrance to Rock House on the right fork right off the road by a bench up a track. It leads along past the houses of Blazefield to another road. Turn left down it.

Walk down the hill, and where the road bends left, fork right off it along a track, which soon narrows between walls. At a fork keep left. When the path widens again to a track, keep forward up it. Join a tarmac lane and keep forward up it to Knott. At the fork keep left, i.e. straight on. You are now on the Panorama Walk from Pateley Bridge. Some distance after passing a bridle gate on the left, you reach another gate which gives access to The Rock, a fenced viewpoint with an information panel. When you reach a junction, keep forward past the entrance to Pateley Bridge Cemetery. Follow the path all the way down to the main road and turn right to return to the town centre.

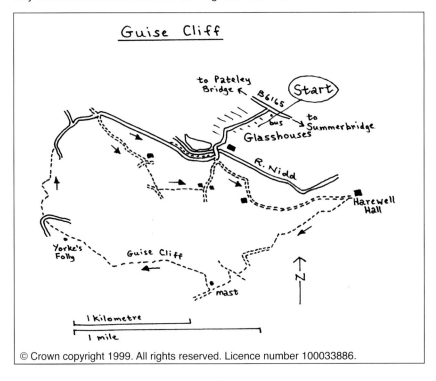

10. GUISE CLIFF

4¾ miles/7½ km. Explorer 298 Nidderdale. A fairly strenuous circuit, with a long, steep climb to Guise Cliff, and in summer there is fairly dense bracken to contend with, but the countryside is glorious and there are superb views. Caution is needed on Guise Cliff, as there are dangerous crevasses near the path.

The walk starts in Glasshouses. Bus 24 Harrogate-Pateley Bridge (Mon-Sat hourly, Sun infrequent) to Glasshouses Lane End (toilets by the bus stop) and walk down the road to Glasshouses Mill. Limited roadside parking in Glasshouses outside the Broadbelt Hall on the lower side of the green, outside the school (unlikely on schooldays), opposite the mill or on Harewell Close, a cul-de-sac on the left as you drive down. Yorkshire Country Wines in the mill has a tearoom.

Cross the bridge over the Nidd, and in a few yards go left when the road forks. *Note the fine proportions of the former Glasshouses Mill at the other side of the Nidd.* After a short distance ignore a track forking right at Low Fold and follow the road to Harewell Woods Farm. Here it forks. Keep left along the concrete road. When you reach the buildings of Harewell Hall,

Glasshouses Mill

don't cross the cattle-grid into the yard, but turn right up a track with a fence on the left. About 20 yards before the track reaches a gate, fork right on a descending track to another gate (there is a small pond to the left). Go through and bear left uphill, with the beck on your left. Aim for a small clump of trees.

Having passed he trees, head straight for the mast on the skyline and you will see a gate in the top left hand corner of the field. Go through and follow the clear path forward. It soon bends left to cross the shallow valley and starts to climb steeply. Ignore a path forking off right. Above you you will see a gate in the wall. When you reach it, you are joined by a path coming up from the right. Don't go through the gate, but keep forward uphill with the wall on your left. When you are faced by a fence, turn right along the path *(can you see Goûthwaite Reservoir?)*, go through a large gate, pass to the right of a large boulder, and a few yards further on turn sharp left uphill.

When you reach a wall on the left, the path forks: keep left and follow the wall up to a large grassy area, which is a fine place for a picnic. *There is an extensive view eastwards, which includes the white balls of Menwith, Harrogate, the North York Moors escarpment, and the Yorkshire Wolds.*

Go through the gate just to the left of the mast, and walk past the mast, then ignoring the stony track ahead, turn right on the narrow path along the fence. Turn right with the fence, then left with a wall on your right and continue along the edge of Guise Cliff. There is much bracken along here, and take care as there are treacherous crevasses very close to the path. *Soon there are fine views across to Pateley Bridge and Upper Nidderdale.*

When the wall ends, bear left and keep following the path. The path eventually reaches a redundant ladder-stile and goes alongside another wall *(some way along you can see straight ahead to Greenhow Hill)* and drops to a ladder stile and the two columns of Yorke's Folly *built around 1810 to provide work at a time of local unemployment. The workers were paid a shilling (now 5p) a day plus a loaf of bread. Yorke's Folly is another fine viewpoint for Upper Nidderdale.*

Continue along a rocky path that slants down to the road, and cross to the access point to Nought Moor (information board). Take the right hand of the three paths (signposted Bewerley). It leads gently down to a kissing-gate, where you enter Skrikes Wood. Continue on the clear path downhill, at first through heather, bracken and bilberries, but soon entering the trees. Note that this path was once cobbled, indicating some antiquity and importance. Cross the stile at the bottom and follow the clear path straight down the field.

Cross a stile onto a road and turn left down it. When the road forks at Turner Bridge, keep right. Now you

Yorkes Folly

have a choice of route back to Glasshouses. The easiest way is to keep along the road until you come to a footpath on the left, parallel to the road, which brings you back almost to Glasshouses Bridge. The footpath route involves a little more climbing and can be muddy after rain at Baylis Gap Farm. If you choose it, a few yards after the first entrance drive on the left go through a kissing-gate beside a large gate on the right and follow the grassy track.

Go through a gate with an ancient ladder-stile beside it and follow the hedge/fence on your right through two fields. Go through a gate and now the hedge/fence is on your left with a house beyond. Follow the track to another gate at Baylis Gap Farm. This is where it can be very muddy. Follow the track to the right of the farm, and where it turns left into the yard, keep straight ahead through a large gate up a concrete track, but when this soon bends right, go through another large gate and walk straight up the field towards a hedge corner. When you reach it, continue up with the hedge on your left. At the top go through a bridle gate onto a track and turn left for 5 yards then go through the large gate on the left and along a clear path which soon leads into a wood.

The path leads straight forward through the wood (don't be tempted down left). Usually the path is broad. After some time, when it looks as though the path is ending, bear slightly right and you will find that it continues down in your previous direction to the far end of the wood. Walk down the field close to the right hand edge to a large metal gate beside houses, go through and turn left along the track. When you reach a tarmac road turn left to return to Glasshouses.

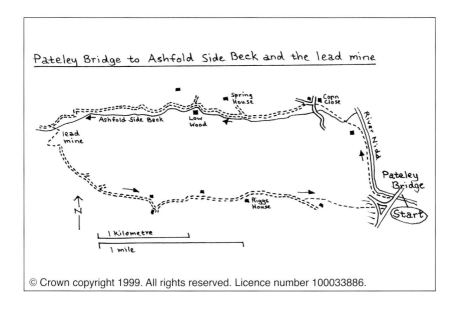

Pateley Bridge to Ashfold Side Beck and the lead mine

11. PATELEY BRIDGE TO ASHFOLD SIDE BECK AND THE LEAD MINE

5½ miles/9 km. Explorer 298 Nidderdale. Easy walking mainly on tracks leads up a side valley of the Nidd to a site of former industrial activity. Lovely countryside.

Park in Pateley Bridge. There are pay and display car-parks along Nidd Walk, the no through road on the town side of the bridge over the Nidd, and on the other side of the bridge on the left. No. 24 Harrogate-Pateley Bridge bus (Mon-Sat hourly, Sun less frequently).

From the town centre cross the Nidd bridge and immediately turn right *(there are toilets here)* to follow the tarmac path along the floodbank. After the tarmac ends, you pass a large caravan site. At the end of this pass through a kissing-gate, ignore the footbridge over the Nidd and go through the next kissing-gate straight ahead. Continue along the floodbank, now on an unsurfaced path. Pass through another kissing-gate and continue along the floodbank for a further 50 yards, then bear half left across the field on a clear path. Go through the kissing-gate in the far corner and follow the path with Foster Beck on your right, soon crossing it by a footbridge. Turn left and follow the beck on your left to another kissing-gate, then walk straight over the next field on a track to a kissing-gate beside a large gate.

Cross the road and take the minor road opposite signposted to Heathfield. After 100 yards keep left at the fork. Follow the road straight through Heathfield Caravan Park, and after crossing a cattle grid ignore the track forking right steeply up to Spring House. Now pass the much smaller Low Wood Caravan Site and follow the track up the valley. Cross two more cattle grids and pass through Westfield Caravan Park (ignore the concrete track forking right up to Westfield). The tarmac surface ends and the track rises high above the beck.

Eventually you will see across the beck the remains of a huge lead mine with large spoil heaps. Our route follows the path that leaves the high track (Nidderdale Way sign) and heads down to go through a gate and cross the beck by a footbridge. Immediately turn left and follow the beck for a short distance, past a ruined building, and begin to follow the path up the hillside, but in a few yards turn sharp right (Nidderdale Way sign) above the old buildings and follow the clear path up through the spoil heaps. Parts of this can be wet. At a broken down wall the path turns left, roughly following the wall, then when the wall peters out, keep forward to another wall and bear left, keeping this wall on your right. You are now walking round the top of the workings. When this wall shortly turns sharp right, keep forward, bearing left up to join a clear track and keep forward up this. The track soon bends right uphill.

Pass through a large gateway and continue along the track. At the first junction keep straight on (signposted Pateley Bridge and Toft Gate) and at the next fork keep right down to Brandstone Dub bridge across Brandstone Beck. Bear left with the track after the bridge, after a time entering a walled lane. At the second farm follow the track sharp left, now on tarmac.

Now follow this road, ignoring tracks left and right, to breast the hill and descend past Riggs House (on your right) to reach a tiny wood on the left and a larger wood on the right. Fork left off the road through the smaller wood, cross a stile and walk down the right hand edge of the field with the grounds of Eagle Hall on your right towards Pateley Bridge. Go through the kissing-gate in the bottom corner and continue down the enclosed path. Go through the gate at the bottom and walk down the track. On reaching the road, turn right for 25 yards, then take the ginnel on the left. At the next road turn left to return to the centre of the village.

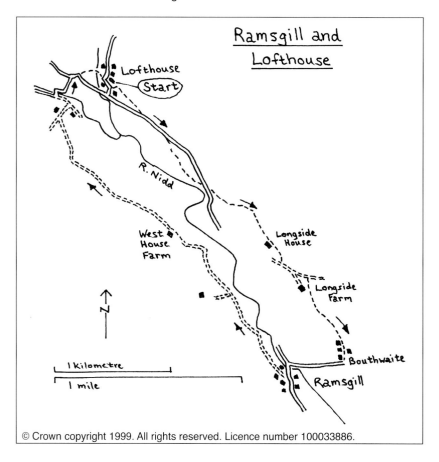

Ramsgill and Lofthouse

12. RAMSGILL AND LOFTHOUSE

5 miles/8 km. Explorer 298 Nidderdale. Easy walking, with fine views of Upper Nidderdale, partly on the Nidderdale Way. Park in the free car-park by the Lofthouse Memorial Institute (GR 102 734) (reached by taking the Masham road on entering the village).

Leave the car-park and turn left and left again to pass between the railings of the Institute on the left and the Crown Hotel car-park on the right. At the end of the pub car-park cross the gap-stile on the right and bear half-left across the field to another stile about half way along the wall on the left. Cross this and turn right along the wall on your right, passing through a gateway; this section can be muddy. Pass through a gap-stile in the next corner and bear very slightly right across the middle of the next field to a kissing-gate in the wooden fence on the right. Follow the path to the main road and turn left along the road.

Pass the access roads to the Old Vicarage and High Lofthouse Farm on the left and after another 40 yards go through the gap-stile on the right (Nidderdale Way sign) and bear half-left across to the wall ahead. Keep this wall on your right, but where it turns right keep forward, bearing slightly right across the field to the next gap-stile in the wall on the right about 30 yards before the far corner. Bear half-left across the corner of the next field, cross the stile and bear slightly right to the line of the old railway and bear left along this. Cross the stile in the facing fence and keep forward across the next field to a gate and footpath sign and the road again.

Cross the road to the gate and footpath sign opposite, turn right along the fence, but where this kinks right at a gate, keep straight forward over the field towards a large gate. A few yards to the left of the gate there is a step-stile: cross this and turn sharply left up with the wall to your left, soon however bearing right on a clear grassy track which leads up to a redundant gate. Now bear half-right up towards the wood to a gateway just to the right of a solitary tree (NOT the gateway in the top corner of the field). Now keep forward on the clear path parallel to but a short distance from the wall on your right, crossing a shallow ravine. In the top corner of the field at the edge of the wood you go through a kissing-gate and continue with the wood to your left. *There is a splendid view both up and down Nidderdale.* Follow the edge of the wood, passing through another gate, then keep along the edge of the wood to pass to the left of Longside House, formerly a youth hostel, and go through another gate.

Join a track coming out of the wood and follow it as it descends gently away from the wood. Join a clear cross track and turn left on it through a gate. Shortly the track forks and you keep left on the ascending branch. Go through a gate. Now you have a wall on the right. After about 30 yards go through a gate in it: Longside Farm is ahead but you bear half-left downhill (in the direction of Gouthwaite Reservoir) to a ladder-stile near the bottom of the wall on the left. Cross it and follow the wall/fence on your right, passing through an old gateway, then along an old line of hawthorn trees, across a beck coming from a concrete cistern, then on by the wall/fence on your right and downhill to a ladder-stile by a gate in the wall. Over this turn left down the edge of the field to cross a gap-stile in the facing wall. Now keep forward to bear left over a bridge over Lul Beck and follow the track to Bouthwaite. The track leads in front of a delightful old farmhouse and down to a T-junction (Nidderdale Way sign) where you turn right; ignore a tarmac lane towards the reservoir and keep forward on the minor road downhill. At the main road turn left over the bridge into Ramsgill.

Fork right off the main road in front of the village green and turn right again immediately after the first house on the right (Public Bridleway to Stean) to walk straight through the farmyard and out on the track at the far side. Keep on this good track until immediately after crossing a cattle grid it bends left uphill to Grindstone Hill House, where you keep straight forward with a wall/fence to your right and the track no longer clear on the ground. But having crossed the ladder-stile by the next gate the track is again clear. Cross the ladder-stile by the next gate and now the track descends a little before bearing left over another ladder-stile by a gate.

When you reach West House Farm cross the stile to the right of the gate into the farmyard and walk round the outside of the farm to rejoin the track at the far side. Bear right along the track with a wall to your left. Cross a stile by a gate then keep straight forward across the middle of the next large field to the next ladder-stile. Now you have a fence to your left and a lovely view right over Lofthouse and Middlesmoor. Ford a beck, pass to the right of a barn, cross another ladder-stile and keep along the fence on your left for about 50 yards before bearing slightly right down to the next gate and stile. Now head straight for a barn with trees beyond it. Pass to the left of the barn and follow the track steeply down to cross Blayshaw Gill by a stone bridge.

Follow the walled lane to the T-junction at Studfold Farm, turn right, steeply downhill in front of the farmhouse towards a caravan site, and bear left at the foot of the hill through a farmyard. The track bears left with How Stean Beck to the right (note the old limekiln on the other side). At the motor road keep ahead if you want to visit the spectacular How Stean Gorge, bear right over the bridge to continue the walk. At the next junction ignore the road left to Middlesmoor, but where the road to Lofthouse makes a sharp turn right keep straight ahead into the layby, pass through the kissing-gate by the large metal gate and bear right as directed by the signpost. Pass between a couple of stone buildings and the cricket pitch to reach another kissing-gate. Cross over the road to Scar House Reservoir to the stile to the left of the three garages, cross the Nidd by the bridge and bear right up to Lofthouse. At the village street keep right for a few yards to return to the car.

13. MIDDLESMOOR AND SCAR HOUSE

7¾ miles/12½ km. Explorer 298 Nidderdale. A delightful exploration of Upper Nidderdale, mainly on clear tracks and field paths; superb views. Some steep ups and downs. Much of the route is on the Nidderdale Way.

Park in Middlesmoor car-park at the head of Nidderdale; the car-park is near the top end of the hamlet, shortly before the tarmac ends, on the right (GR 092 743). Enjoy the view from the car-park before setting off, and do make time to explore Middlesmoor, a proud hilltop village of charm and character. (There are public toilets beside the Crown Hotel.)

Turn right out of the car-park, follow the tarmac to its end and continue up the stony track (In Moor Lane), ignoring a track forking right a short distance up. *Enjoy the views back down Nidderdale as you ascend. Opposite a small Yorkshire Water building on the right, notice an old milestone on the left, now illegible: this was once the road over to Coverdale.* After the walled lane ends, a clear track continues over the moor. Follow it all the way to Scar House Reservoir. *The view extends from Great Whernside over to the left, via Little Whernside to Dead Man's Hill ahead.*

Turn right along the tarmac road, but soon bear left over the reservoir dam; *a plaque tells you that the reservoir, which supplies water to Bradford, was opened in 1936.* At the far side of the dam bear half left up the stony track, in 100 yards turning sharp right onto a signposted bridleway (and Nidderdale Way). Cross a track coming up from the house down on the right and keep forward. The track passes through several gates, passes a small wood on the right and you are faced by a ravine. The track winds down, crosses a beck by a bridge, climbs steeply, fords another beck and continues to climb. About 200 yards before a flat-roofed shooting-house look out for a path forking right by a white topped marker post: follow this path, marked by a line of posts, down to pass through a gate in the wall on your right.

The track bears right downhill, soon turning sharp left parallel to a wall on the right. Pass through a gate in a fence – you are now dropping quite steeply - and another in a wall. Another track comes in from the right, and now you are following the wall on the left. Pass through another gate, losing the wall on the left, and at a fork keep left on the ascending track and pass under telegraph wires to a wall corner. Ignore the track descending sharp right and keep forward with the wall on your left. Go through a gate, bear right to ford a beck, climb to pass through another gate and follow the track as it passes behind New Houses Edge Farm.

Now follow this excellent track, which affords fine views over upper Nidderdale, past several farms. At Bracken Ridge Farm the track turns sharp right, then left again, to pass through a gate. Continue following it as it contours round the hillside and eventually ends at the large Thwaite House. Go through the gate and pass to the right of the house, turn left, then in a few yards right again, and in a short distance turn right again, through the right

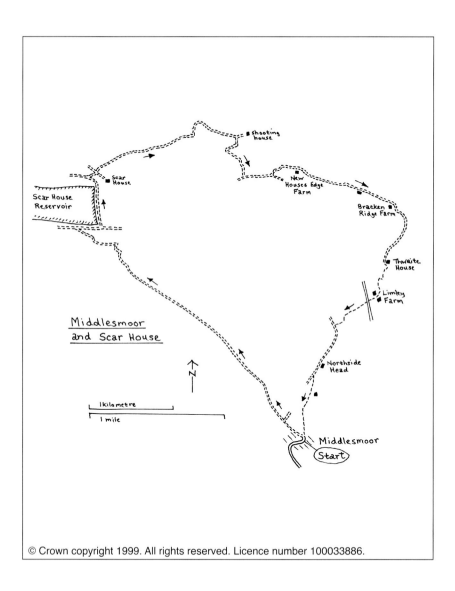

Middlesmoor and Scar House

N

1 kilometre

1 mile

Scar House Reservoir

Scar House

shooting house

New Houses Edge Farm

Bracken Ridge Farm

Thwaite House

Limley Farm

Northside Head

Middlesmoor
Start

45

hand of the two gates. The path drops, soon with a steep wood on the right. At a fork keep left, i.e. essentially straight on, but the path soon turns sharp right and descends by old steps. Part way down it turns sharp left again. At the foot ignore the old gateway in the wall and bear left, with a wall on your right, to a gate at Limley Farm.

Cross the dry bed of the Nidd and climb with a large barn on your right into the farm. Bear right through the farmyard, then turn left and continue through the farm (accompanied by the barking of many chained dogs!), until you reach a gap-stile in the wall on the right. Go through this and the gate a short way ahead, then cross over the middle of the field to another gap-stile onto a road.

Cross straight over to another gap-stile, straight up the next field to the next one, and now half left to the next one. Now bear right round the edge of the next field to a step-stile a few yards left of the corner, then slightly left to the next stile just to the left of a tree. Your next target is the left hand end of the wood up ahead, so first bear half-left, ford the beck and make your way steeply up to a stile by a gate in the top corner of the field.

Cross it and turn immediately left through another gate. *The view opens up left down Nidderdale to Gouthwaite Reservoir.* Follow the track past Northside Head House, then 40 yards before the wood on the right ends, cross a gap-stile in the wall on the left, bear half right to the next one, then straight ahead to the next one. The clear path continues forward, passing to the right of Smithfield Hall Farm and crossing the access track, to the next gap-stile in the wall ahead. Keep on towards the right hand end of the wood ahead, pass round it, through two more stiles, then on with the wall on your right to another stile. Walk straight forward across the next field passing two wall corners on the right (with your car behind) to a gate in front of the end of the building ahead. Turn right to the road and right to your car.

14. THRUSCROSS RESERVOIR

5 miles/8 km. Explorer 297 Lower Wharfedale. The walk is essentially round the reservoir, but it does have a section of easy moorland in Roundells Allotment.

By car to Thruscross car-park above the dam on the minor road down from the Stonehouse Inn on the Blubberhouses-Greenhow Hill road (GR 154 574). No public transport.

Thruscross was the last of the four reservoirs in the valley of the Washburn sanctioned by the Waterways Act of 1867 to be built, being completed only in 1966. The ancient village of West End with its 300 year old church now lies deep beneath this 142 acre reservoir.

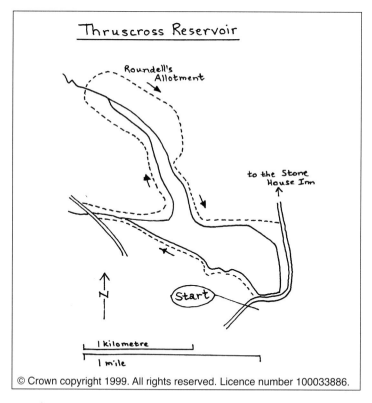

Return to the car-park entrance, cross the road to the barrier opposite and take the path descending through the woods, soon to walk along the bank of the reservoir. On the way you cross three footbridges and the ends of three ancient tracks, the last of which, Clogger Lane, formerly led down to Patrick Mills. Pass through a stile, turn right along the road, crossing Capelshaw

47

Beck, that once supplied power to West End High Mill, and in 20 yards go through a bridle gate on the right.

The path contours above the reservoir, largely in woodland. After a time you descend briefly almost to reservoir level and pass a large derelict house on the left. Shortly after this cross a stile on the left out of the wood and walk up with the wood on your right. At the end of this field cross a stile by a gate into rougher pasture and continue by the wood. The clear path moves a little way from the wood, but continues parallel to it. Cross a tall ladder-stile near a gate and bear slightly right to a seat with a fine view over the Washburn valley.

The path now descends steeply by steps beside the wood. Cross the Washburn by the bridge and ignoring the stile on the right into the wood, cross the stile ahead and climb the stepped path towards the outcrop of rocks. Pass between the rocks and bear right uphill to cross Roundells Allotment on the clear signposted path. Cross a ladder-stile beside a gate and keep forward up the slope. After a time the clear path bends right towards the reservoir and drops to a ladder-stile at the corner of a wood. Cross and walk down between the wood and the wall on the remains of old steps.

At the bottom turn left and cross the boardwalk, then continue along the path with the reservoir below on your right. After a time the path drops to reservoir level. When you reach a wood the path becomes surfaced. Cross over a tarmac road (the old road to West End) and continue on the surfaced path, which you follow until it joins a road through a gap in the fence. Turn right and follow the road over the dam and back to your starting point.

15. BLUBBERHOUSES AND BRANDRITH

5 miles/8 km. Explorer 297 Lower Wharfedale. A contrast between a sylvan riverside and high rough pasture. Fine views. One short, but steep climb, and parts of the route can be wet.

Blubberhouses Church stands where the unclassified road from Otley meets the A59 Harrogate to Skipton road (GR 167 553); adjacent to this junction is a Yorkshire Water car-park. Park here. Bus X59 Harrogate – Skipton (Mon-Sat roughly 2-hourly) to Blubberhouses Church.

From the middle of the car-park climb a few steps to the main road. Cross it (you will need to step over the crash barrier on both sides) and turn right for a few yards to find a set of steps descending on the left. This marks the start of a Yorkshire Water permissive path by the River Washburn. Follow the clear path through the tall conifers. Soon you are walking between the river and a cricket ground. Follow the riverside path for a considerable distance. After a time you have a broken wall on your right. The path passes through this and climbs slightly to run along an embankment with an old mill reservoir on the right.

Soon the path is back by the river. It broadens, and just before you reach a more open area the right of way bearing the Harrogate Dales Way link comes in from the right. The dam of Thruscross Reservoir is now visible ahead. Cross the river by a footbridge and turn right, joining a track which leads up to a good cross track. Turn left along this and follow it up to a tarmac lane. Turn right along this for 20 yards to find a step-stile on the left which leads to a path climbing steeply through the wood. Leave the wood over a stile at the top and bear right on the path which is still climbing steeply. Pass between gorse bushes, cross a little side beck and continue up to a stile in the wall at the top.

Turn left along the tarmac lane for 20 yards, then cross a stile on the right and follow the fenced path to a stone step-stile by Redshaw Hall. Cross and follow a short fenced path to a gate leading into a walled lane. *Brandrith Crags are visible on the moor over to your left.* Where the lane ends keep straight forward through an old gateway and on with the wall on your left (there are good views back), but soon the clear path bears right away from the wall to the top right hand corner of this field.

Cross the stile by the gate, walk forward for a few yards, then turn left to follow the wall on your left. At the end of the field go through another old gateway and continue forward now with the wall to your right. Follow this wall to a metalled road and turn left along it, here leaving the Dales Way Link, which turns right.

Where the road makes a sharp turn right, make a sharp turn left onto a track. *There is a fine view to Blubberhouses Church and Fewston Reservoir behind it.* In a short distance do not turn right with the track but keep straight ahead

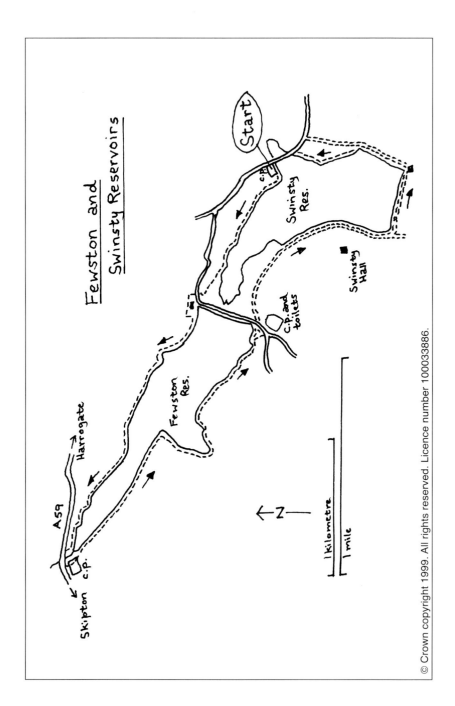

Fewston and Swinsty Reservoirs

Start

Swinsty Res.

Swinsty Hall

C.P. and toilets

Fewston Res.

Harrogate

A59

Skipton c.p.

← N —

1 kilometre
1 mile

through the gate along another track. Follow this track straight on until you reach the next tarmac road.

Here you could turn right and walk down the road to your starting point, but it is more pleasant to turn left and follow the road as far as the third gate on the right where there is a footpath sign. Walk down the edge of the field with the wall to your right. At the bottom turn right along a track and follow it all the way to a farm. Pass through the gate ahead (it can be muddy here) into the yard and bear right between the buildings to the road. Turn left down the road to the start of the walk.

Blubberhouses Hall

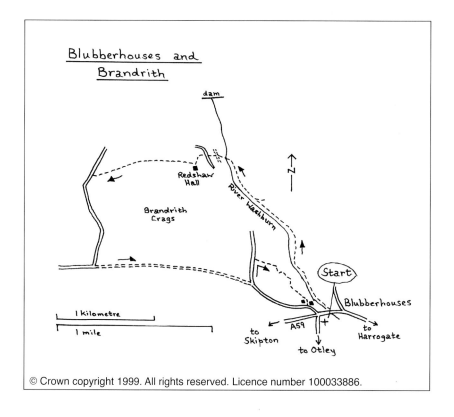

16. FEWSTON and SWINSTY RESERVOIRS

6 miles/9½ km. Explorer 297 Lower Wharfedale. Ramblers must be grateful to Yorkshire Water for laying out such attractive permissive paths round the reservoirs. This walk is a delight at any time of the year.

Access from Harrogate is via the Otley Road to Beckwithshaw, through the village, then take the right fork to Fewston. On reaching the T-junction at Bland Hill, turn right for a short distance, then left down to Swinsty Reservoir. Drive over Swinsty Lagoon dam and turn left into the Stack Point car-park. No public transport.

Swinsty Reservoir

Go through the gap in the wall and turn right along the path round the reservoir. Follow it to the end of the reservoir, and just where it begins to climb to the embankment, fork right off it onto a narrower path which very gently zigzags up to the road. Cross over to steps opposite and at the top turn left to follow the wall on the left. Pass above the Water Board house, and after a time the woodland path drops to the shore of Fewston Reservoir. Turn right along the path round this reservoir, and ignoring all paths forking right, follow it to the end of the reservoir and climb the steps to the A59. Turn left, cross the River Washburn and at the end of the bridge turn left again into the car-park and left again to walk to its end.

Pass through the gap to the left of the gate and follow the clear path. As you approach the dam at the end of the reservoir, you can either follow the main path as it bears right and climbs through the woods or keep forward on grass between the reservoir and the wood, bearing right at the end to climb through the wood. Both paths emerge at the road opposite Swinsty Moor car-park.

There are toilets in the car-park. As you face the car-park entrance from the road, the walk continues along the walled access road on the left. Pass the 16th-century Swinsty Hall and turn left over the reservoir dam. Continue along the access road, cross a bridge over a feeder beck and just before the gates fork left on a path through the trees. This leads round the reservoir and ends at a road. Turn left over the embankment and left again into the car-park from where you started.

17. TIMBLE AND THE RIVER WASHBURN

5½ miles/9 km. Explorer 297 Lower Wharfedale. Old tracks and field paths, glorious countryside, superb views of the Washburn valley.

Park in Timble village. The walk starts at the telephone kiosk. No public transport.

Take the lane opposite the Washburn Parish Council notice-board and the Ramblers' Association footpath map, leaving the telephone kiosk on your left. The track leads to a T-junction: turn left. Pass Highfield Farm and about 100 yards further on turn right into a narrow walled lane. *This is an old unclassified road, so you may – quite legally – encounter motor bikes on it! It can be muddy.*

In the bottom cross Timble Gill and climb the clear path opposite. In a few yards you cross another beck, bear left alongside it and soon re-cross it by a clapper bridge and continue forward with a wall to your left and the beck on your right. After a time you leave the beck and continue up a walled lane, which leads to a gate into a field. Keep forward with a broken wall on your right. When the wall ends, keep forward over the field. At the end of the field turn right through a gateway into another section of walled lane. It soon bends left and after a time ends: keep forward by the wall on your left. Go through a gate ahead, and the path now has trees on both sides. The walled lane leads to a farm track: keep forward up this and when you reach a tarmac road turn left along it.

Ignore a farm track on the left opposite a small wood on the right, but almost at the top of a rise take the next farm access road on the left, signposted to Carr Farm. Shortly before you reach the farm you pass a ladder-stile on the left, then a large barn on the right. Just after this, and before another ladder-stile on the left, turn right to follow a wall on the left along, over two stiles, and on to another ladder-stile in the corner of the field. Cross it and walk straight over the next large field: cross a beck in the far corner and a rather awkward stone step-stile. Walk straight across the next field, following the line of the power lines, go through a gateway, cross an old walled lane to a stile by a gate opposite, which leads into a wide walled lane.

Cross the stile by the large gate at the end, bear right then left over Snowden Beck and fork right, following the track up to the farm buildings. Walk straight through the yard to the stile opposite, ignoring the track on the right, and climb the hill ahead with the wall to your left. At the top of the field turn left over a stile in the corner and follow the fence on your right to another stile. Walk straight across the next large field to the corner of a wood, then keep about 20 yards to the right of the wood, pass to the right of a jumble of stones and gorse bushes and make for the gate in the wall ahead.

Timble and the River Washburn

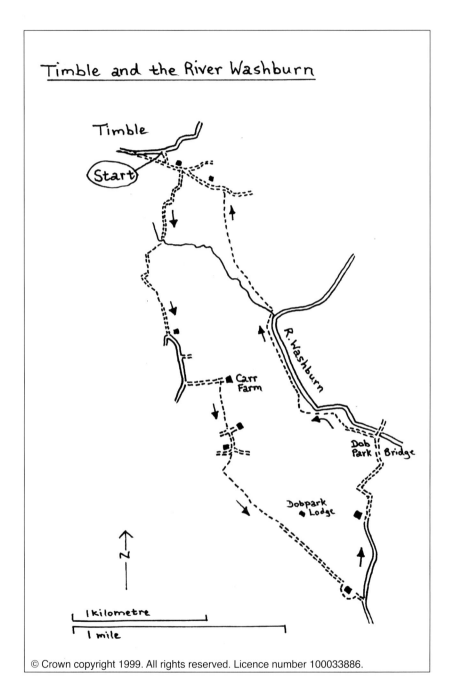

This leads into a wide walled lane. *The ruins of Dobpark Lodge are a field away on the left.* The lane leads to Dobpark House. 40 yards before this go through a gate and immediately cross the stile on your right and bear half-left round the outside of the garden fence to a stile, then half-left again across the corner of the field to another stile, then right along the access road. At the T-junction turn left downhill.

Follow this narrow metalled road down towards the river Washburn, ignoring forks left and right. Halfway down, just past Middle Farm on the left, the lane becomes a stony track. At the river you reach Dobpark Bridge with an ancient ford beside it. *The name Dobpark is derived from Dog Park and reminds us that this area was once part of the hunting-ground of the Forest of Knaresborough.*

Dobpark Bridge

Don't cross the bridge, but turn left immediately before it through a bridle gate and follow the track. Ignore a track forking left uphill and keep forward to cross a stile near a gate ahead. Walk straight through the long field to a stile at the far end, cross and follow the fence on the right to the stile by the gate ahead. Keep on by the fence on the right through the next field to the next bridle gate. Go through, cross the beck, and ignoring a stile beside a gate on the left, keep forward along a track. Go through another bridle gate, bear right down to cross another beck, then turn right through the wood, soon bearing left along a clear, partly cobbled path which leads to the river bank.

The path now follows the river along through several fields, until after climbing a bank you drop steeply to the confluence of the Timble Beck and the River Washburn. Cross the beck by the Adamson Memorial Bridge, erected by the Ramblers' Association in 1967, and turn left along by the beck. After a time you are led through the broken wall on the right. Bear left

uphill with the beck still below on your left. Go through a gateway and now climb steeply with a wood on your left. At the top of the slope bear right to cross a bank which marks an old field boundary, then bear half left, crossing through another old field boundary to reach the top of the bank, with the beck far below on the left.

The Adamson Memorial Bridge

Walk along the top of the bank up to a stile. Cross and continue up by the fence on the left. In the corner of the field ignore the gate and turn sharp right up the slope with a wall on your left. In the top corner cross the stile and walk forward the short distance to the next stile, cross and follow the wall on the right up. Cross the stile at the top and turn left along the track to return to Timble.

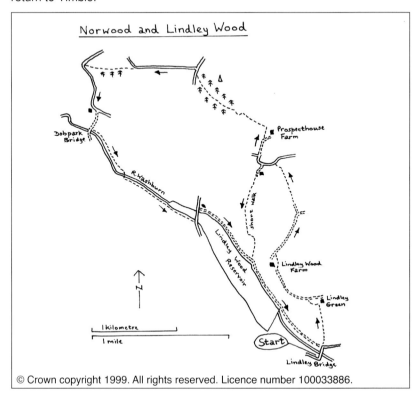

18. NORWOOD AND LINDLEY WOOD

6¾ miles/10¾ km or 3½ miles/5½ km alternative. Explorer 297 Lower Wharfedale. Glorious countryside; old tracks and field paths, woodland and riverside, very fine views. Both walks start with a steep climb, and the longer walk has one other short, but steepish climb.

Park in one of the laybys at Lindley Bridge (GR 224 483), which is reached by forking right off the B6161 Killinghall – Leathley road shortly after this makes a sharp left turn and following this narrow lane down to a T-junction, where you turn right. No public transport.

From the north side of the bridge follow the road uphill; pass the lodge and entrance gates to Lindley Wood Reservoir on the left and 35 yards further up take a track slanting back left. In a few yards at the gateway turn sharp right into an enclosed path which leads uphill with a wall on the right. Cross a stile and continue climbing on a clear path. At the top of the hill the path turns left and follows the wall on the right through a bridle gate *(fine views over Wharfedale and the Washburn valley)* and along to a stile and a track. Bear left down the track.

Emerging from the wood cross the cattle grid and walk forward on the track towards the house ahead. Ignore a track forking left to Lindley Wood Cottage, and just before the entrance to Lindley Wood Farm fork right and follow a tractor track through a large field. Soon this joins the old track which contours high above a wood. Leaving the old walled lane the track descends gently to cross a side valley (ignore a track forking right uphill on the way down). Go through a gate, cross the beck and walk up the other side, once more in an old walled lane.

Pass to the left of a ruined farm. The broken wall on your left leads you to another beck to be crossed, then walk forward up the facing slope with a gulley to your right. Bear left at the top of the slope to a step-stile in a short stretch of wall. Cross and walk forward a few yards to another stile, continuing then with the wall to your left. At the end of the field ignore the gateway in the corner, cross the broken wall to the right of it and follow the fence/wall on your left. The wall bears left into the next field, but at a large tree, beside which there is a gate in the wall, bear right down towards the beck and bear right, parallel to the wall on the left, to a road.

Turn left along the road. The shorter, alternative walk takes the next farm access road on the left (to Wood Top Farm) (jump to [*] below) but the longer walk continues to where the road turns sharply left: here keep straight ahead up the access road to Prospect House Farm. When the road turns right to the farm, and there is another track straight ahead, turn left along the wall for 30 yards and go through a gate in it. Walk straight across the next field towards two trees. Pass between them, go through the gate in the next facing wall and turn left to follow the wall on the left down to another gate in the field corner.

Go through and bear slightly right to reach a broken down wall, marking an old field boundary, and walk along with this wall on your right towards the wood. Where the wall turns right, bear half left to a stile into the wood. From the stile the path bears right, following the wall on the right, crosses a track coming through a gate on the right, and keeps straight ahead uphill. This is the second steep climb of the walk. Ignore all waymarks pointing left. The path becomes a track. You are joined by another track from the right. Keep forward along the track to the B6451. Turn right along it for 35 yards and take the minor road on the left.

Glorious views open up over Fewston and Swinsty Reservoirs and to Menwith Hill with Brimham Rocks beyond. Ignore all access roads to right and left. *Soon there are also splendid views to the left.* Follow the lane until it bends right and begins to descend. At this point cross the stile by the gate ahead and follow the wall on the left along. *Timble village is visible on the other side of the Washburn valley, with Simon's Seat beyond.* Follow the wall to a ladder stile, cross it and follow the path downhill through gorse and heather. Look out for where the path drops left into the dip, then walk down in the dip with a wall and the wood on your left. This lovely old path leads down to a stile and a narrow tarmac road. Turn left downhill.

Shortly after the road bends sharp left, it forks: keep right and walk down the tarmac lane towards the valley bottom. When the tarmac ends, keep on down the track. When you reach the river Washburn the walk continues over the stile on your left, although a detour right for a few yards to admire the fine old Dob Park bridge is recommended. Cross the stile and follow the path parallel to the river. Pass through a kissing gate and follow the left hand edge of the next field to a stile by a gate. Cross the bridge over the river and bear left.

When you reach the road turn left over the bridge. A short distance after it turn right along a track. Lindley Wood Reservoir is to your right. The track forks only once: here keep right on the track closer to the reservoir. Follow the track, which at times narrows to a footpath, all the way to the next road, where turn right for the car.

[*] SHORTER ALTERNATIVE. Follow the access road to Wood Top Farm, go through the gateway, pass to the right of the farm, but when the access road turns left, go through the gate straight ahead and follow the track along the left hand edge of the next two fields. At the end go through the left hand of the two gates and follow the fence, then the wall, on your right through two fields. The track drops, you pass through a gate, and now the wall is back on the left (there is a barn to your left). Where the wall turns left, follow it; cross the stile into the wood, and a clear path leads down through the it. At the cross track at the bottom turn left, here re-joining the longer walk. At a fork in the track keep right on the track closer to the reservoir. Follow the track, which at times narrows to a footpath, all the way to the next road and turn right to return to the car.

19. HAVERAH PARK, BEAVER DYKE and JOHN O' GAUNT'S RESERVOIRS

8 miles/13 km. Explorer 297 Lower Wharfedale. Tracks and field paths across open country and farmland, with two reservoirs and a ruined castle.

There are two sizeable laybys north of Beckwithshaw on the B6161 road to Killinghall. Park here. No public transport.

Haverah Park, within the Forest of Knaresborough, was probably created as a deer park towards the end of the 12th century, but by 1560 all the deer had disappeared and there was virtually no timber left. King Charles I sold the park in 1628 to the City of London, who subsequently re-sold the land to the Ingilbys of Ripley Castle in 1639.

In 1839 the Harrogate Water Company began the construction of a series of reservoirs, and access to the area was by permit only. However, largely due to the efforts of the Ramblers' Association's Corrie Gaunt, rights of way were secured in the 1960s.

Walk along the road back to Beckwithshaw and go through the gate on the right (signposted Springhill Farm) opposite the entrance to the cricket ground and walk along the track to the right of Moor Park Wall. Just before the track bends right away from the wall, ignore a track on the right to Keeper's Cottage. After a time you cross a cattle-grid and pass a Yorkshire Water sign saying *Haverah Park*. Springhill Farm is ahead across the valley. The track swings right, crosses the valley and climbs to the farm. Cross the cattle-grid into the farm and take the track swinging sharp left through a gate.

About 175 yards along the track forks: keep right through a gate into a field. Follow the track through several fields until you reach a track junction with a derelict barn over to the left. Ignore the track on the right and keep straight ahead. Pass through three gates, after which the track ends. Bear half right across the large field, parallel to the power lines – the route is reasonably clear on the ground – to a ladder-stile in the far corner. Walk down the path to a cross track and turn right along this.

Cross two bridges and then, ignoring the cattle-grid ahead, cross the stile by the gate on the right and walk up the hill, passing through two gates, to Long Liberty Farm. Turn left along the tarmac road, follow it through the farmyard, leave it through a gate and walk forward, ignoring the entrance to Reservoir House on the left, to a stile by another gate, then continue with a wood to your left. Cross a stile by another gate, and now you are just inside the wood, which is beautiful when the bluebells are in flower.

Leave the wood over a stile by a gate, Beaver Dyke Reservoir is below on the left, and turn left over the dam dividing it from John o' Gaunt's Reservoir. Go through the small gate on the right and follow the path uphill. Pass to the left of the farm buildings, where there is a gate, and walk across

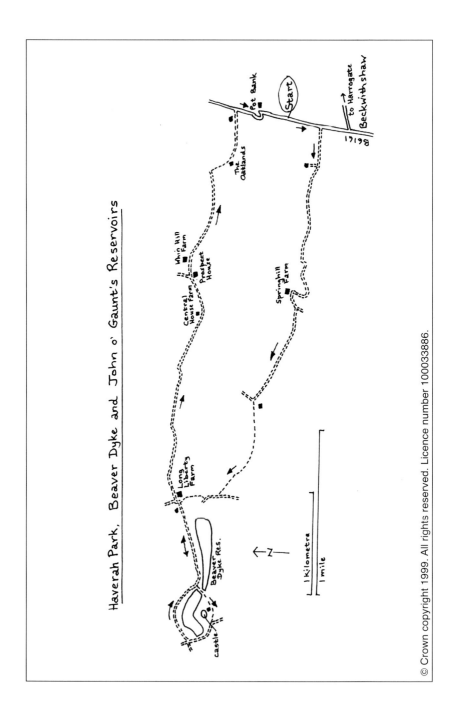

Haverah Park, Beaver Dyke and John o' Gaunt's Reservoirs

60

the field to the gap in the wall ahead. *Look right as you cross to see the fragmentary remains of John o' Gaunt's castle, a fortified hunting lodge which certainly existed before John of Gaunt became Lord of Knaresborough in 1372.*

Follow the path downhill with a fence and old wall on your left, ignoring a stile in it. Cross the causeway at the head of the reservoir, over a stile and walk uphill with the fence on your right. At the top go through the gap in the wall ahead, join a cross track and turn right down it, passing through a gateway. In 35 yards turn right through another gateway and follow the track downhill, over two becks, to a kissing-gate, then continue uphill with the old wall to your left. Pass to the right of the derelict farm, bear right and continue, still with the remains of a wall on your left.

Watch out for where the vestigial track bears right alongside the remains of a very old hedge and drops towards the reservoir. When you reach the dam you crossed earlier, retrace your steps up to the wood and through it back to Long Liberty Farm. Turn left along the road, but after 60 yards turn right through a gate along a track. Keeping field boundaries always on the left – the track is not always particularly clear – you will eventually pass along a short stretch of old walled lane, cross a stile by a gate, and now the field boundary is on your right, for the length of one field, when you join a much better track, which leads to Central House Farm.

Follow the track through the farm, then continue along the access road. Follow this through Prospect Farm, but where it turns left, keep straight forward to Whin Hill Farm. Pass this and keep on along the track. Go through a gate and continue with the wall on your left through several gates until you reach the end of a narrow wood. Turn right immediately past the wood and follow its boundary until you pass through a gate and reach another track by another Farm, The Oatlands. Turn left along the track past the farmhouse and follow it down and through Pot Bridge Farm and out onto the B6161. This is a busy road – take great care. Turn right and follow the road back to the start.

20. THE LEATHLEY LANES

6 miles/9½ km; old tracks and field paths, easy walking through pastoral scenery with fine views of Lower Wharfedale, the glorious Riffa Woods and an interesting church. One beck needs to be forded, which can be difficult after heavy rain.

Leathley Church and stocks

Park your car by the benches and telephone kiosk opposite the church at Leathley, on the B6161 Killinghall to Pool-in-Wharfedale road (GR 232 470). Notice the old stocks across the main road.

Bus 653 Harrogate – Bradford (Mon-Sat hourly) to the Riffa Business Park stop. Cross the road and turn left along the footway. The house on the hill to the right is Riffa Manor. Turn right into the access drive to Riffa Manor. Immediately before the entrance to the Manor turn left and pass to the left of houses. When the tarmac drive bends left, keep straight on up the grassy track to pass through a squeeze stile beside a gate and follow a broad track up into Riffa Wood. At a fork keep straight on, now on a narrower track. At another fork ignore a track dropping left further into the wood and stay fairly close to the upper edge of the wood. At the next fork keep right for a few yards to a stile out of the wood and turn left along the boundary fence. When the main walk comes up through a gate on the left, keep forward to another gate ahead in the field corner and jump to [*] below.

Take the road signposted Stainburn, in front of the old school and 18th-century almshouses, and almost immediately fork right onto the drive to Leathley Hall. Pass to the left of the Hall and where the lane forks keep left. Cross a stile by a gate into a grassy lane lined by some old trees. On reaching a fence ahead, bear left with the track to a stile and continue up the slope with the fence to your left. This is Leafield Lane.

Pass through a gate and go straight forward with a fence now on your right to walk between old hawthorn trees and through two gates close together with Riffa Farm down to your right. Continue along the lane to within a field-length of Riffa Wood, go through a gate and leaving the track bear half-left across the field to the far corner of the wood, where you ford a beck and go through a bridle gate into the wood.

Walk up the clear path, the age of which is shown by the remains of causey stones, passing a rock curiously carved as a head on the left. Enter a field

Leafield Lane

Approaching Stainburn

at the top of the wood. Those who came by bus will turn right here and follow their outward route back to the A658, but the walk continues by turning left and proceeding to a gate at the corner of the wood. [*] Go over the stile by the gate and across the field, bearing slightly left to a large gate.

Through the gate you follow the fence/hedge on your right, ignoring gates in it, and soon picking up a clear track which you follow all the way to the road in Stainburn; on the way you will bear slightly left to cross a beck and then closely follow the left hand edge of the fields, interrupted by a short stretch of walled lane.

Turn left along the road and at the second bend you will find a kissing-gate on the right; pass through and follow the wall/fence on your right up to another kissing-gate into the churchyard of Stainburn church. *Now cared for by the Churches Conservation Trust it is of Norman origin (notice the windows to the right of the porch) with an 800-year-old font* Post box in Stainburn *and lovely views from its porch to greet you as you emerge.*

On leaving the porch turn right and follow the path to the road. Turn right along it and walk through Braythorn as far as Gale Lane, a track on the left immediately before the former Methodist Chapel. The rather stony lane descends to cross West Beck by Green Bridge. Climb the other side and a good way up look out for a signpost on the left with some stone steps leading up to a stile. Cross and bear right over the corner of the field to the

Stainburn Church

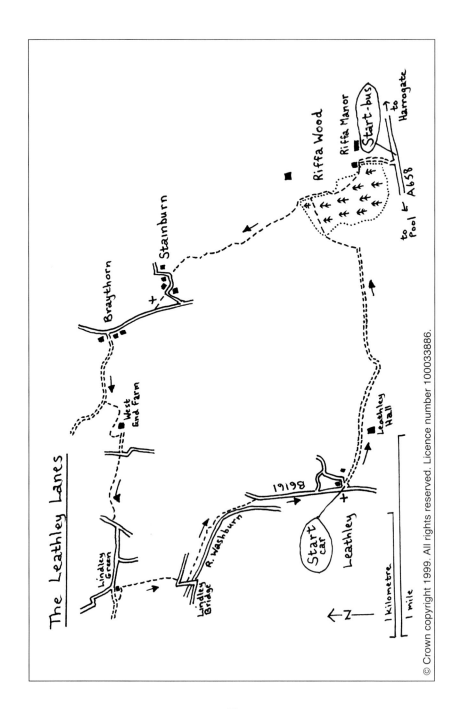

The Leathley Lanes

66

next stile, then follow the fence on the right to a stone step-stile. Cross and go through a bridle-gate on the right into a narrow belt of trees. Turn left, still in the trees, to another bridle-gate, then bear slightly right through the paddock to a stile in the far corner. Cross and then go through the large gate ahead – you are walking round the back of West End Farm – and continue forward for about 60 yards to a stile in the hedge on the left. Cross, walk forward to pass through a large gate and turn right along the farm access road.

Cross the Leathley - Killinghall road to the stile by the large gate opposite, and bear slightly right to a stile in the opposite fence, then straight across the next two fields to a step-stile on the far side. Care is needed here, because there is a substantial drop on the other side. The right of way now bears half right to the wall on the far side of the next field and then turns left along it, but you may find on the ground a clear path going straight ahead across the field instead to the field corner. Keep along the right hand edge of the next field to reach the road at a junction.

Cross straight over and follow the narrow road ahead to Lindley Green, ignoring a road forking left on the way. At the Lower Washburn Parish Council notice board, where the road bends right, keep straight ahead along the track. Where it begins to drop, and just before it bends right, cross a stile on the left and follow the wall on the left along. Go through a bridle gate and continue by the wall, turning right with it. Now make your way down on a clear path through Lindley Warren, Some way down, when the wall turns sharply left, keep forward and then bear right, ignoring a gate in the wall straight ahead. The broad grassy path is clear all the way down to a stile in the bottom corner of the field, then follows the wallside down to a gap-stile where you bear left to the road.

Turn right down the road to Lindley Bridge and the River Washburn. Just before the bridge pass through a stile on the left and drop down some steps to a path along a narrow goit. Follow this goit for a considerable distance until the path forks. Drop right here, then bear left to a stile near the river. The ground can be very wet along here. The River Washburn is now close by on the right. Follow the clear path which eventually turns left and passes the former mill house to reach the road. Turn right along the road to return to the car.

21. HARLOW HILL and BECKWITHSHAW

4¾ miles/7 km. Explorer 297 Lower Wharfedale. In spite of some road-walking this is a very fine round, with glorious woodland, field paths and distant views from the Pennines to the Hambleton Hills and the Vale of York.

The walk starts at the Harlow Inn on the B6162 Otley Road at Harlow Hill. Park in Wharfedale Avenue at the side of the pub. Local bus service to Harlow Hill.

Cross the Otley road from the Harlow Inn and turn left for a few yards then right along Nursery Lane ("Panorama Walk").

On a clear day there is a magnificent view over Harrogate, Knaresborough and the Vale of York. Harrogate buildings easily distinguished include (from left to right): the tower of St. John's at Bilton, the dome of the Majestic Hotel, the dominating spire of the former St. Luke's, the International Hotel and Conference Centre, the tower of St. Peter's, the War Memorial, the Station office block, the spires of the United Reformed and Baptist Churches in Victoria Avenue, Park Place flats in High Harrogate, the spire of Trinity Methodist Church, the Grammar School clock tower. The Kilburn White Horse is in the far distance (a little to the right of St. Luke's) and Knaresborough lies beyond Trinity Church.

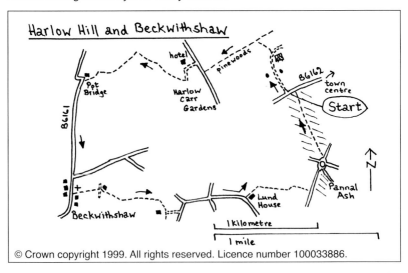

Harlow Hill and Beckwithshaw

Pass between the Observatory (1829) and the Water Tower to pass the Parks Department greenhouses, and when the tarmac road bends right downhill, keep straight ahead round a large gate along the track between rhododendrons that leads out to an open green. Cross straight over the grass to an information panel about the Pinewoods and turn left along the

68

tarmac path. It leads through the Pinewoods with more fine views right (see the Pinewoods Panorama information panel). When you reach Crag Lane, Harlow Carr Gardens are to the left, but you turn right. Turn left down the road signposted to the Harrogate Arms Hotel, pass in front of this and bear left to cross the beck and turn right along the path on the other side with the boundary fence of the gardens on your left, through glorious woodlands.

Just after crossing a wooden footbridge the path forks: keep straight ahead by the fence on the left, shortly joining the Harrogate Ringway footpath. A few yards further on there is another fork with a wooden fence between the branches: keep right of the fence, and a few yards after this, where the Ringway climbs some steps on the left, keep forward with a fence on the left (signposted to Pot Bank). Follow this fence, with the valley of Oak Beck below on the right, all the way to Pot Bank. Just before the house fork left up the permissive path and follow it to the road.

Turn left and walk uphill along the busy road to Beckwithshaw with views to the right over Haverah Park. Pass the cricket field. At the road junction take a look into the little wooded area on the left (The Copse) where there is a bench and an information board about the history of Beckwithshaw, then continue through the village. Immediately beyond the church go through the gap-stile on the left onto the footpath between church and house.

Go through two gates into a field and continue by the wall on the left past a solitary tree then straight down the field towards a house at the bottom. Cross the stile in the wall a few yards to the left of a gate. Cross the track diagonally left and pass through the gap-stile in the wall opposite into the tree-filled garden, where the path bears round to the right to a stile giving access to a field. Walk down the field close to a ditch to your right. Another path comes in from the right over a stone bridge: follow the fence on your right, it soon bends left, to reach a stile in the corner where wall and fence meet. Cross and continue beside the hedge on your right, cross over the next stile and follow the left hand edge of the field past farm buildings on your left, to the stile in the wall ahead.

Bear slightly left across the field to a stile near where the hedge meets the fence. Now turn right, to follow the fence on your right towards the bungalow. Near the bottom of the field bear left to a bridle gate, cross the drive and go through another gate into the field beyond. Follow the right hand edge of the field to the next gate and walk forward to join the Howe House Farm access road. Turn left along it, then left again at the next road, which you follow to the junction. Turn right along the next road and follow it to the crossroads at Beckwith Head. Here you cross the Harrogate Ringway.

Keep straight on at the crossroads, but on a right hand bend, just before a large house on the left (Lund House), turn left into a fenced path and follow it round to a farm track. Turn left, and when the gravel track ends, keep on along the fence on your right. At the end go through the kissing-gate and continue with the hedge on your right. Cross a stile, and the hedge is now to your left. At the end of the field go through the gate and cross the stile in the wall and follow a hedged path to Whinney Lane. Turn left and follow the footway to the roundabout. Cross over Beckwith Road and pick up an asphalt path on the left which will lead you back to Harlow Hill.

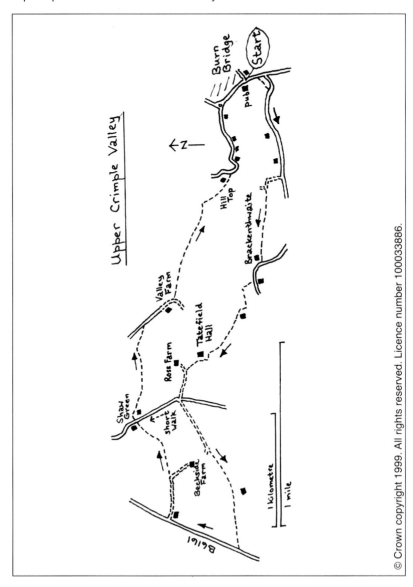

22. UPPER CRIMPLE VALLEY

6 miles/9½ km or 4 miles/7 km. Explorer 297 Lower Wharfedale. A walk by field paths on both sides of the valley with fine views over it.

Local bus to the Black Swan, Burn Bridge. Park in Malthouse Lane, beside the River Crimple in Burn Bridge, or in its continuation, Westminster Crescent.

Cross the road bridge over the Crimple near the Black Swan. Part way up the hill take the enclosed footpath on the right, signposted Great Alms Cliff. Follow it to the next road and turn right along it. Pass Maw Hill Farm and Brackenfoot Farm, both on the right and a post box on the left, and opposite the next house on the left turn right into a fenced bridleway. The path turns left and then right again. At this point fork left off it on a path up to a stile into a field. Follow the fence on the left up the slope, but near the top, when the fence bends slightly left, cross half right to a stile in another fence and head straight up the next large field to the left hand corner of the farmhouse at the top, where a stile in the fence gives access to an enclosed path which leads to the left of the farmhouse and out onto a road.

Turn right along the road and follow it to a stile on the right opposite Well Garth Cottage. Walk along by the hedge/wall on your right, pass a small stone building and go through a gateway, then turn sharp left to cross the narrow field to a stile in the fence. Walk straight across the next field, heading for a field gate on the left hand side of Bracken Farm. Don't go through, but turn right along the fence to a stile in it. Cross and turn half right to the next stile. Cross and continue the same line over the next field towards a small gate. Cross the stile beside it, bear very slightly right down the next field, parallel to the overhead wires *(fine view over the valley)*, but gradually getting closer to them to a stile in the fence just to the right of a telegraph pole.

Now bear right away from the wires to the bottom corner of the field in front of the farm below. Go through the gate and turn left, pass through a gateway into the farmyard, bear half right past a large tree and an old stone well and cross the stile by the left hand end of a barn with a weather vane on top. Cross and turn right past the barn and Tatefield Hall, which dates from 1671. Go through the small gate in the bottom corner of the field and bear slightly left over the next field to a stile in a wall a few yards to the left of a footbridge. Don't cross, but turn left along by the wall to join a concrete track coming from Ross Farm. Turn left along it to reach Shaw Lane by Newfield Farm.

For the shorter version of the walk, turn right, cross the beck and follow the road uphill to a stile in the wall on the right opposite Shaw Green, just beyond the first farm building on the right, and jump to [*] below.

71

Otherwise cross Shaw Lane diagonally left to the concrete drive opposite. When it swings right to the farm, bear slightly left across the grass, pass a solitary stone gatepost and walk across the field parallel to the beck below on the right but bearing slightly left away from it, to a stile at the left hand end of a hedge of trees ahead. Keep the same line over the next large field to a short stretch of fence bare of hedge. Cross the stile and keep the same line over the next field, keeping well to the right of the farm. Cross the stile at the left hand end of the wall and follow the hedge on your right along. Cross the stile in the fence at the end and continue by the wall on the left to a small gate in the next corner with a little bridge in front of it.

Bear slightly left towards the beck, cross it and go through a gate, then bear slightly left up the field and head for a solitary tree in the corner. Beside it is a stile. Cross and follow the fence/wall on your right to the next stile, then follow the hedge on the right to the B6161. *This road was part of the Dudley Hill to Killinghall turnpike created in 1753.* Turn right down the road, cross the infant Crimple and continue uphill past Crimple Grange at the top and take the access track on the right to Beckside Farm.

When the track swings right towards the farm, leave it and walk straight on across the field with a hedge on your left to a stile. Continue straight on down the next field to an old stone gatepost, then bear slightly left to the left hand corner of the field. Cross the stile and walk down the left hand edge of the next field to a gate where you can cross the beck. Bear slightly right up the slope and cross the field to the large house ahead. Cross the stile beside the large white gate, walk across the front of the house, bear left past its side and turn right down the drive to Shaw Lane.

Cross the road diagonally right to the stile opposite and [*] walk straight across the field to a stile in the next corner. Keep on near the right hand edge of the next field to the next stile. Go straight across the next field to the tall lone ash tree and continue by the hedge on the left. Cross the stile in the corner, walk straight across the next field to the next stile, cross and turn left down to a stile in the next corner, cross and continue by the hedge on the left down to a gate. Go through and bear half right across the field into a track running between the fence/hedge on the right and the beck far down below.

Just before the track passes through a gate fork left off it onto a narrower path. Follow this path over a stile and down to Quarry Lane. Keep forward along the lane, walk through Valley Farm and through the gate beyond, then fork left off the tarmac drive through a gate and walk across the field to the white footbridge. Walk straight over the next field to the stile in the corner. From here the path keeps to a fairly straight line across six fields to reach a footpath signpost. Follow the direction Hill Foot Lane, i.e. straight across the next field, cross the bridge and stile and turn half left up the next large field to a gate in the hedge/fence near a solitary tree on the far side.

Now keep forward parallel to the hedge on your left, through a field gate, then continue by the hedge/wall on your left – look left for a view of the fine Hill Top Hall – to follow round the garden wall of a modernised house to go through a small gate on the left in the corner into a walled path. Descend some steps and follow the path down to a stile onto Hill Top Lane. Walk straight downhill, round the left hand bend into Hill Foot Lane, pass Hill Foot Manor and then The Lodge on the right, *where a tablet in the garden wall records the site of the first Wesleyan chapel at Pannal in 1788.* At the mini-roundabout turn right to return to Burn Bridge.

LONGER WALKS AROUND HARROGATE

As you follow some of the routes described in this book, you will come across signposts indicating that you are on the Harrogate Ringway. Both it and the Knaresborough Round are attractive, varied 21-mile circular walks, around Harrogate in the one case and Knaresborough in the other. The route of the Harrogate Ringway is well provided with public transport, so can easily be walked in sections, and the Knaresborough Round can be divided into two sections using the bus service that runs via Ferrensby. With the aid of the OS maps shorter circular walks based on these two longer walks can easily be devised.

For leaflets about these walks telephone 01423-525194.

23. HORNBEAM PARK STATION TO WEETON STATION VIA ALMSCLIFF CRAG

7 miles/11 km. Explorer 297 Lower Wharfedale. A linear walk, partly along a little ridge, with fine views over the Crimple valley and Lower Wharfedale.

At Hornbeam Park station the large car-park is likely to be full on weekdays, but parking is available in nearby Beechwood Grove or on Hookstone Road beside the recreation ground. Train from Harrogate to Hornbeam Park or bus 110 (Mon-Fri two-hourly) to Hornbeam/Oatlands.

From Hornbeam Park Station walk up Hookstone Road, passing Beechwood Grove on the left, and opposite the recreation ground, between houses 48 and 50, take the bridle-path signposted Leeds Road. Follow the path past allotments on the right and a school and recreation ground on the left, and keep forward through trees to meet a tarmac road. Bear right along it – *there's a good view of the Crimple Viaduct through the trees on the left* – and at the next road junction turn right and follow this road to the A61 Leeds Road.

Cross at the island on the right and walk straight forward along the enclosed path. Turn left at the next street and right at the next one (Stone Rings Lane). At the end of the houses keep straight on downhill, cross Stone Rings Beck by the bridge and climb steeply up the steps, ignoring a path through a gateway in the wall on the left part way up. When the path levels out, there's a nice view over the Crimple valley. Follow this path to a road and turn left downhill *(first view of Almscliff Crag)*. Pass a row of houses, and when the road begins to bend left, cross it (care!) and cross the stile into the field on the right. Bear left down the slope, over the dip and up the other side to a stile.

Turn right along the enclosed path and follow it to its end at a small gate just before a beck. Cross the road and turn right for a few yards, then cross the stile on the left into another enclosed path. Ignore a path coming in from the right, go through the gate ahead and descend gently towards a recreation area. Immediately before this turn right on a path along the bottom edge of the wood. Follow this woodland path, which soon climbs gently, then bears left and descends again. Near the bottom the path is edged by stones. You emerge from the wood at a road. Ignore the bridge over the Crimple straight ahead and turn right along the road.

Follow the road, soon with the Crimple close by on the left, to the junction at Westminster Crescent. Keep forward, still with the river to the left, to reach another road junction by the Black Swan. Turn left over the bridge over the Crimple, cross the road, and part way up the hill take the enclosed footpath on the right signposted Great Alms Cliff. Cross straight over the next road to the enclosed path opposite and follow it up to a stile into a field. Continue with the hedge on the right. Cross the stile by the gate into the next field, and now there is a fence on the left and soon a wood on the right.

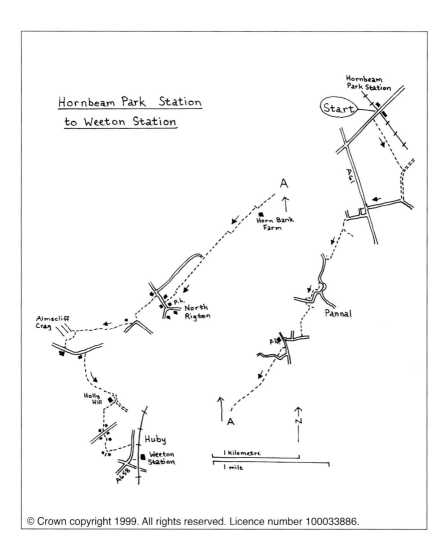

Hornbeam Park Station
to Weeton Station

Go through the gate ahead and leaving the wood behind keep straight up across the next field. Go through the kissing-gate where the wall joins the fence and continue with the wall on the right. When you reach Horn Bank Farm, go through the stile on the right in the field corner and follow the wall on the left along as far as the next gate. Beside it is a stile: cross and walk straight over the next field to a bridle gate. Go through and continue with the fence/hedge on the left. Go through another two bridle gates close together and turn right along the enclosed path. Go through another gate and the path turns left again.

Pass through another gate and continue by the wall on the left. After the next gate you pass a pond on the right. After the next one you are in a walled lane. When this turns right, cross the step-stile ahead and follow the right hand edge of the field. When the hedge turns right, keep straight on over the middle of the field to the next stile, then keep the same line over another three fields to reach a stile and a fork in the path. Keep left, and shortly the path bears right to another stile. Cross and keep forward. Go through a gate, bear slightly right to a stile in the fence and follow the house

drive down into North Rigton.

When you reach the road, the Square & Compass is 50 yards downhill on the left. *There you can also see the village stocks across the green.* The walk continues by turning right uphill. When you reach a small green on the left with a tree in the middle, turn left along the stony track. Go through the

North Rigton stocks

gateway to Hill Top Farm and fork left along a narrow footpath. Just before you reach a large gate at the end, cross the stile on the left and bear right with a fence on your left. Cross the stile at the far end and follow the path forward between hedges. The path soon bends left to a road on a bend: turn right along the road. *There is a fine view left over Wharfedale.*

About 75 yards along cross a stile on the right and walk diagonally left across the field to a kissing-gate. Cross the track and follow the wall on the right to a stile, then walk straight over the next field to the next one. Walk half right to pick up the wall on the right and follow it to the stile in the next corner. Now head up to the crag. This bit can be exceedingly muddy.

This rocky outcrop of millstone grit, also known as Great Almscliff, rises some 680 feet above sea level and commands fine views in all directions, while its precipitous western face is a favourite of rock climbers.

Almscliff Crag

To continue the walk, start back down the way you came up, but soon curve right round the foot of the crag to a stile in the wall. Now bear half left towards the large complex of farm buildings below. Pass through the barrier and walk down the enclosed path to reach the road by the farm (Cragg Farm). Turn left down the road. Pass several houses, at the end of which go through the small gate by the large one on the right, to the left of the entrance to Cliff House. Walk down the short concrete track, cross the stile and bear half left over the field to the next stile. Bear left down the next field, parallel to the hedge on the left to the stile in the corner.

Bear half right across the middle of the next field to a stile by a gate, and in the next field follow the hedge on the left down to a gate. Walk down the concrete track, through the gate and on down between the buildings of Holly Hill House. *(The following right of way is disputed at the time of writing and may be diverted.)* Immediately after passing a building on the right, go through the small metal gate on the right and walk along the steps on the front of the building, cross a stile where fence meets wall, walk straight across in front of this fine Jacobean house to a gap in the hedge ahead, to continue along the right hand edge of the next field to the next stile.

Walk on down the next field to the bottom, go through the kissing-gate and cross the beck by the footbridge and follow the path up the other side to a kissing-gate into the next field. Turn left, to follow the left hand edge of the field, go through another kissing-gate and on through the next field: leave it into a track which turns left down to a road. Cross the road and walk down the drive of Crossfield. Pass in front of the house into a hedged path. Cross a stile and follow the path to a high wall ahead. Turn left over the stile and walk straight across the field to the next stile. Bear slightly left over the next field, cross a little stone bridge in the middle and head for the bottom corner

of the wood. Go through the stile onto the main road and turn right along
the footway. Cross at the pedestrian crossing and go down the access road
to Weeton Station.

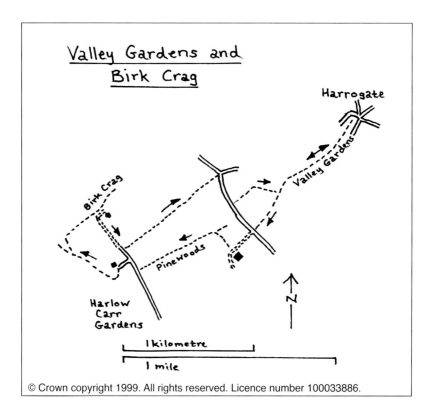

Valley Gardens and
Birk Crag

Harrogate

Birk Crag

Valley Gardens

Pinewoods

Harlow
Carr
Gardens

N

1 kilometre

1 mile

24. VALLEY GARDENS and BIRK CRAG

3¾ miles/6 km. Explorer 297 Lower Wharfedale. A stroll from the town centre, taking in fine gardens and woodland and excellent views, particularly from Birk Crag, high above the valley of Oak Beck.

Enter the valley gardens opposite the Pump Room Museum and immediately take the left fork to follow the landscaped stream on the left. Pass the refreshment kiosk and reach a circular area surrounding a garden sculpture. *This area was formerly known as Bogs Field, and a plaque records the existence of thirty-six of*

Entrance to the Valley Gardens

the eighty-eight different mineral springs for which Harrogate is renowned. You want to follow the broad path straight ahead beyond this circular area. Soon you are following on the right the boundary wall of the former Royal Baths Hospital.

At the top of the hill the main path bears slightly left. Ignore a minor path forking right by the War Memorial (your return route) and follow the main path into the woods. Cross straight over Harlow Moor Road and walk up the drive opposite, the access road to the Council Nurseries. Just before the road bends left at the nursery buildings, turn right past a gate on a path through rhododendrons. When you reach an open grassy area, cross straight over to an information board and turn left along the tarmac path through the Pinewoods. *Some way along a "Pinewoods Panorama" information board describes the fine view.*

When you reach Crag Lane, Harlow Carr Gardens are to the left, but you turn right along the lane and then left down the road leading to the Harrogate Arms Hotel. Pass the hotel and bear left down to a footpath on the right just before the large gateway. Follow the boundary fence of the gardens with the beck on the right below. A few yards after crossing a footbridge fork right down the slope (signpost); cross the footbridge at the bottom and follow the path along with the beck below on the left. Cross the boardwalk and climb the rocky path to reach a fence. Turn right uphill alongside the fence, then continue on the level now with a wall on the right.

After a time, with crags ahead, the path climbs through the wall at its end. Walk on past the rocks and climb the steps. Turn left at the top along to the summit of Birk Crag near Birk Crag House.

Birk Crag

Along the edge of the huge fold of rocks upon which Harrogate lies is a geological fault line through which the iron and sulphur springs emerge in Valley Gardens (Bogs Field) and the Pump Room. Straight out beyond the Crag in the distance lies Nidderdale with Great Whernside on the horizon. Ripon lies eight miles due north and over to the north east are the Vale of York, the Hambleton Hills and the Kilburn White Horse.

Walk back the way you have come, and when you reach the top of the steps, turn left onto the lane and bear right along it. When you reach a large aviary and rabbit hutches on the right, turn left along the footpath signposted to Cornwall Road. *Enjoy the extensive views for the last time.* When you reach the road cross, ignore Cornwall Road ahead and turn right, passing Irongate Bridge Reservoir and Claro House on the left and the Harrogate Spa Water bottling plant on the right.

Immediately after Claro House take the signposted footpath on the left into the woods, in a few yards forking right. The path bends right and you reach a better cross path: turn left along it. Ignoring minor paths to left and right, follow this path through the woods, until you emerge and reach a path junction. Turn left and follow your outward route back to the start.